Aspects of the Georgian Church

Aspects of the Georgian Church

Visitation Studies of the Diocese of York, 1761–1776

Judith Jago

Madison • Teaneck
Fairleigh Dickinson University Press
London: Associated University Presses

Associated University Presses
440 Forsgate Drive
Cranbury, NJ 08512

Associated University Presses
16 Barter Street
London WC1A 2AH, England

Associated University Presses
P.O. Box 338, Port Credit
Mississauga, Ontario
Canada L5G 4L8

The paper used in this publication meets the requirements of the American National Standard for Permanence of Paper for Printed Library Materials Z39.48–1984.

Library of Congress Cataloging-in-Publication Data

Jago, Judith, 1938–1995
Aspects of the Georgian church : visitation studies of the Diocese of York, 1761–1776 / Judith Jago.
p. cm.
Includes bibliographical references and index.
ISBN 0-8386-3692-6 (alk. paper)
1. Church of England. Diocese of York—History—18th century.
2. Church of England—England—Yorkshire—History—18th century.
3. Anglican Communion—England—Yorkshire—History—18th century.
4. Yorkshire (England)—Church history—18th century.
5. Visitations, Ecclesiastical—England—Yorkshire—History—18th century. 6. Drummond, Robert Hay, 1711–1776. I. Title.
BX5107.Y6J34 1997
283′.4281′09033—dc21 96-44601
CIP

PRINTED IN THE UNITED STATES OF AMERICA

Contents

Acknowledgments

I am grateful to Professor Stuart G. Hall, of King's College, London, who started me off in the eighteenth century as an area for study. Dr. John Walsh of Jesus College, Oxford, replied most helpfully to my questions about Henry Venn and John Wesley. Dr. W. M. Jacob of Lincoln Theological College encouraged me with reference to his study of the clergy in Norfolk.

Photographic reproduction is by kind permission of J. Arthur Dixon postcards and the Borthwick Institute of Historical Research, and I should like to record my thanks to Edna Meadows and Chris Webb of the Borthwick staff for their specialist help whenever I asked them, by letter, in person, and by telephone. Miss M. S. McCollom, Assistant Keeper in the Department of Palaeography and Diplomatic at the University of Durham, kindly provided me with details of Bothall, where Drummond began his career.

One memorable, wet June afternoon, Raymond Parkinson led the way through muddy undergrowth to the ruined church of Thorp St. Andrew to show me Drummond's burial place; he and his wife Margaret showed me their exhibition of archiepiscopal papers and memorabilia at Bishopthorpe, and Mrs. Habgood gave permission for me to look at Drummond's portraits in a private area of the palace.

Panics with computer and printer have been relatively few, but when they occurred I was rescued by Mr. Nick Frankum, and I record my gratitude to him.

My warmest thanks are to Dr. Edward Royle, Head of the Department of History at the University of York, whose friendly guidance came with outstanding patience. He generously brought his exemplary blend of critical encouragement to all the drafts that I have shown him and to every idea we have discussed.

Just when I needed special encouragement, the Warden and Trustees of St. Deiniol's Library in Hawarden awarded me some scholarship reading weeks—time and opportunity to reflect as well as to study.

It was with characteristic cheerfulness that my husband agreed to walk and drive with me around Yorkshire to recognize preaching places and parsonages, to stand in awe of gradients in moorland, and to envisage the clergy of the eighteenth century in that vast and rugged diocese.

Abbreviations

BIHR	Borthwick Institute of Historical Research
Br Lib	British Library
DNB	Dictionary of National Biography
ibid.	"ibidem," in the same place
MP	Member of Parliament
MS(S)	manuscript(s)
Q1, Q2, and on through Q12	Question 1, 2 (as used in the Paper of Queries)
sic	so, thus
SPG	Society for the Propagation of the Gospel
SPCK	Society for the Promotion of Christian Knowledge
VCH	Victoria County History

List of Abbreviations Used in the Tables

Bap	Baptist
Ind	Independents
Ing	Inghamites
Me	Methodists
Mor	Moravians
Pre	Presbyterians
Q	Quaker
RC	Roman Catholic

Aspects of the Georgian Church

Introduction

Robert Hay Drummond, who served the archdiocese of York from 1761 until 1776, has been neglected, buried below the altar of the parish church of St. Andrew, now ruined and open to the sky in waste ground near a boating jetty where visitors to Bishopthorpe Palace may arrive. Drummond's portraits in the palace are kept from public view. He has no biography apart from an outline survey completed by his son. His career provides information about the York diocese at a time when social, religious, political, and economic changes were gathering speed. He occupied the copremier position for fifteen years on the bench of mid-eighteenth-century bishops. Though under the powerful patronage of the duke of Newcastle, he managed to stand clear of that nobleman when necessary, and used his skillful eloquence to deliver some of Newcastle's other protégés from a political pit. As a builder and architectural patron, he gave the palace of Bishopthorpe its present grand entrance and west front. Aristocratic and authoritative, an Oxford doctor of divinity, Drummond was known by those of his own class as an amiable and welcoming host. While still vigorous and energetic, he made his primary visitation of the diocese and came face to face with over six hundred of his parish clergy.

Full documentation survives in manuscript for the 1764 visitation by Robert Drummond, a rare feature of eighteenth-century church history. The clergy returns for his 1770 visitation are not extant, but comparison can be made with those of Archbishop Herring in 1743. Drummond's returns of 1764 have not been published for the use of scholars, and this may be one of the reasons why this amiable archbishop has remained in some obscurity. Another reason is his own disregard for posterity; in this he was uncharacteristically out of line with eighteenth-century mores.

The usefulness of visitation returns for interpreting the performance of the church is limited by several well-known factors. The subjective inclinations of the returning writers is a major problem with visitation evidence. Some of the clergy—perhaps a majority—may have wanted to put themselves forward in the most flattering light so as to be recognized for doing their jobs well. Others, aggrieved by the unsatisfactory nature of their circumstances, may have deliberately stressed their parishioners' poor support for the church's ministry. These factors obviously restrict the usefulness to the historian of any or all of their answers. There are also apparent differences between those who gave much time and thought to their answers and those who hurriedly splashed their pens and ink in the briefest manner—one of the unquantifiable but nevertheless significant aspects of the evidence.

Apart from the possible theological and social bias of the Anglican clergy, another difficulty with the returns as a source is that the writers were not necessarily informed about the matters on which they reported. This affects particularly our reliance on the answers they gave about the extent and strength of Dissent and may affect topics such as education. A further difficulty comes from the social and religious gaps between many of the clergy and their archbishop; such gaps—and others, for example, from misunderstanding the question—caused differences which hinder the reader from getting a balanced overall picture. The study of the visitation returns, however, is enriched by the very detailed information provided by some clergy and by the attitudes they conveyed in their style of writing.

Despite such problems, the Drummond returns of 1764 are a rich store of information. Comparisons have been made with the returns of 1743 and with evidence from some Nonconformist sources. Modern studies of population changes assist these sources, and recent enquiry by some historians into diocesan evidence elsewhere adds to the debate about the eighteenth-century church.

The image of the Georgian church as a socially divided, unequal, and ill-organized body propped up by patronage and sapped by pluralism has been difficult for historians to remove because the truth in some of these criticisms hardened during the nineteenth century into received opinion. A "reformed" church set tougher standards of measurement than Drummond's generation would have understood, and the essence of an unreformed church is its faults. The difference which a study of Drummond's visitation returns makes to an understanding of the Georgian church is that, within the admitted restrictions, the returns provide in microcosm a look at so many aspects of church life across the diocese that the faults may be seen in the context of the ordinary, the good and the finest. What appeared to nineteenth-century and early twentieth-century critics as unmitigated evils now appear as faults awaiting correction in a structure that was sound enough to resist reform for more than forty years.

The eighteenth-century church had its own original enemies. Anticlericalism among the Hanoverian laity in general was fed by specific hostility to the established church among various groups of Dissent.[1] These enemies of the church yielded the stereotypes of worldly clerics in cartoons, satires, travel writings, and broadsheets. Arthur Young has been blamed for putting the English clergy in a bad light in comparison with their counterparts in France.[2] At times of political crisis during the eighteenth century, such as the Jacobite rebellion of 1745 and the affair of Wilkes in the 1760s, Tory and Whig opponents gathered anticlerical material if it advanced their causes. The second half of the eighteenth century saw struggles over subscription to the Thirty-nine Articles, in which dissenting political interests became enmeshed with Latitudinarian churchmen of the Feathers Tavern company; such struggles gave the church's critics plenty of targets. By the time that the Ecclesiastical Revenues Commission published its report in 1836, the immediately preceding years had been examined, and so had several decades before that, in a search for a convenient place to lay the blame; there seemed, however, no need to go as far back as the Reformation of the sixteenth century when the picture of the eighteenth century was readily available. The early nineteenth-century reformers and their successors repeated the faults of the eighteenth-century church and swelled the chorus. The Evangelicals, the Methodists, the Tractarians, members of the Oxford Movement, middle-class professionals, self-made industrialists, radical philosophers—all these contributed to the received opinion that the eighteenth-century church had been a disaster.

Literary stereotypes in fact and fiction, such as Laurence Sterne, the Vicar of Bray, and Parsons Adams and Woodforde, softened the edges of the harsher criticisms and became idealized for their heroic, though failed, efforts. But then the bad name turned sour. Local historians who wrote of their town, their chapel, their meeting, or their county heightened the so-called evils from which their own glories had struggled free.[3] A genre arose characterizing the eighteenth century as the age of inertia, and the eighteenth-century church was described with ever-increasing condemnation. From cosy, dormant, lax, somnolent, and quiescent, it became stagnant, inert, indifferent, sceptical, subversive, tainted, complacent, and slothful; and so on to degenerate, dissolute, a sham, defective, corrupt, a place of torpor and dead consciences, whose rubrics were a dead letter. Such a heavy weight of criticism was hard to move, but the nature of pendulums is to swing, and these opinions have been exposed to scrutiny. Pendulums themselves are museum pieces these days; quartz mechanisms and digital displays equip historians currently with some different tools for the portrayal of the times. Fashions in attitudes and schools of interpretation still divide opinions about the eighteenth-century church; it has not yet cleared its bad name, and the idea of the irreligious eighteenth century still persists,[4] though some of the criticism has acquired a much more balanced tone.[5] The reasons for the persistence warrant some enquiry.

The reformers maligned the eighteenth-century church mainly to justify their cause. In order to stress the need for the reforms, they portrayed the full extent of the downgraded situation before the reform. This emphasis was all the more urgent because of the church's reluctance to reform during the first thirty years of the nineteenth century. Sir William Scott argued in a parliamentary committee debate in 1802 on the Clergy Residence Bill that "the reformation of incumbents will be the persecution of curates"[6] and warned that enforced residence would mean clergy "carrying their resentments to their solitudes."[7] There was also some lighthearted reluctance. Sir Rowland Hill's Bunyanesque dream of an auction sale of curates[8] is charming to the modern ear with its Mr. Mean-Well, Mr. Good-Intent, Mr. Lead-head, Lord Ramble, Colonel Lofty, and the effeminate Mr. Giddy (who is so recognizable in the twentieth century):

> *Auctioneer* (to Mr Lead-head): Why, to be sure, it would seem as though you were not quite suited for your office; how came you to jump into it?
>
> *Lead-head*: Why, . . . it was all my father's fault, for he could never beat it into me to make me a good doctor. . . . I was fit for nothing but a parson; . . . my devotions were already made up for me in the common prayer, and as for making sermons, . . . there were . . . thousands which might be begged, borrowed, and copied . . . and so, Sir, he got Lord Ramble to give me the living, as he owed him a deal of money for his fees.
>
> *Auctioneer*: . . . where is Mr Giddy?
>
> *Giddy*: Coming, Sir.
>
> *Auctioneer*: Bless me! it sounds as if he would do charmingly as a waiter . . . they pick up many a bright shilling.
>
> *Mr Giddy gets up, and displays his white pocket handkerchief, takes*

out his smelling bottle, exhibits a spangling ring on his most delicately white hand. . . .[9]

The reformer's humorous dream soon hardened into historical reality. It was James Bean in 1809[10] who cast one of the first stones with the comment that "there was too great a disposition to consider the wickedness of the present times as exceeding that of a former period." He set the trend in motion, disclosing the preference for seeing the luster of the reformers' work shine more clearly against a darkened background. Defending the present could become a startling attack on the past, as when W. J. Conybeare[11] wrote, "The thermometer of the Church of England sank to its lowest point in the first thirty years of the reign of George III." Once the past was seen as more blameworthy than the present, it was not difficult to consign the whole of the eighteenth century to depravity. Gladstone advanced the view that the "administrative abuses [of the eighteenth-century church] had reached a most frightful height. . . . The clergy were, as a body, secular in their habits,"[12] and he recorded the wit of Sydney Smith with a patronizingly grudging appraisal.[13]

Other writers of the nineteenth century followed the trend. Social historians, local historians, general historians, ecclesiastical historians, and sectarian writers from the 1850s onwards continued to damn the eighteenth-century church with faint praise. Abbey and Overton acknowledged that it managed to retain its principles until a time for development should arrive,[14] but at the end of the nineteenth century, Mary Bateson's abhorrence of clerical subservience directed her criticism of the patronage system in the Georgian church.[15] Overton and Relton[16] drew a dismal scene. Ollard and Walker, studying the Herring returns in the 1920s,[17] thought that the eighteenth-century church lost ground in Yorkshire after 1743. Since the 1930s, some writers have looked more kindly at the eighteenth-century church and its clerics, recognizing a different set of expectations and not seeing all the faults so glaringly. Norman Sykes led the field to show that the eighteenth-century bishops had a daunting task and established that many bishops were not daunted as they tackled it.[18] But considerably after Sykes, both A. Tindal Hart[19] and L. E. Elliott Binns[20] kept the image of the eighteenth-century church as a broad and comfortable institution from which the Methodists emerged as the new light of the English world of worship. R. H. Tawney[21] described the prelates of Hanoverian England as the "servile appendages of a semi-pagan aristocracy" through nine editions of his work, from 1926 to 1948, and considered that the church did not give inspiration and guidance because it did not possess it, that its silence was due to "mere ignorance and inefficiency."[22] There is less reason for current writers to continue the exaggeration, but the comment "Nothing is so detrimental to real religion as the bad lives of the clergy"[23] expressed a common sentiment in 1803 and still serves as a lead-in to a particular field of nineteenth-century church history.

Regional studies such as those undertaken by John Walsh,[24] Arthur Warne,[25] William Jacob,[26] and Viviane Barrie-Curien[27] have provided fuller and more convincing historical details of the life of the eighteenth-century church at parish level than those available from the familiar writings of Laurence Sterne[28] and James Woodforde.[29] Sermons preached from Anglican pulpits have been scrutinized by James Downey[30] to show that the educated laity of the eighteenth century wanted to read sermons as well as to hear them. Rupert Davies, Gordon Rupp,[31] and then Henry Rack[32] looked again at the impact of Wesley and the Methodists on the theology of the Enlightenment. Walsh, in charting the development of the evangelical revival in the church, uncovered frequent Holy Communion and earnest parish visiting in many of the Yorkshire parishes quite apart from Wesley's influence.

The debate continues. F. C. Mather[33] has argued that Latitudinarianism is not sufficient as a descriptive title for eighteenth-century churchmanship. His studies of the continuance of high church practices such as frequent Holy Communion and weekday observance were based on evidence from various parts of the kingdom. His Yorkshire data, mainly from the Leeds and Pontefract deaneries, revealed the differences between north and south; he states that "in the intractable north the clergy did their best to make the system work." His use of the 1764 visitation returns uncovered the persistence of Caroline traditions in the old corporate towns, "where civic pride and conservative feeling reinforced traditional practice."[34] He saw the common ground between the high church traditionalists and the evangelicals in promoting frequent Holy Communion[35] and noted a revival of weekday observance among the Hutchinsonians.[36]

J. C. D. Clark[37] has reminded us that Whitefield and Venn were set on their paths respectively by the writings of William Law and the high church manual, *The Whole Duty of Man.* So we may read Walsh and Mather and the visitation returns and see that high church practices and evangelical traditions were both separately and together the inheritance of many parochial clergy. Clark also recognizes the importance of the coronation sermon preached for

George III by Drummond, judging that "few sovereigns have begun their reigns with such a sense of mission so clearly articulated for them."[38] Peter Virgin,[39] however, who has looked in detail at clergy incomes and social class in his study of the problem of church reform, portrays a church whose English clergy were divided north/south in their acquisition of social respectability. He casts doubt on some of Sykes's estimates of curates' pay, but his allegations of diminished efficiency of elderly eighteenth-century clergy have been countered by Frances Knight,[40] who also challenges him for reflecting more of a nineteenth-century picture than an eighteenth-century one. Jeremy Gregory has looked so favorably at the eighteenth-century church that he refers to the "eighteenth-century Reformation,"[41] and his studies of Archbishop Secker's Speculum incline him to reinstate the verdict of "omnia bene,"[42] with the proviso that the absence of a policy of retirement left several elderly clergymen literally deaf to the pleas for revival.

John Walsh, Colin Haydon, and Stephen Taylor all show regret that the criticisms of the eighteenth-century church have continued after the 1930s, and they combine to demonstrate the conscientious efforts of eighteenth-century clergy and churchgoers. They name Drummond as being among the pastoral and active bishops of the eighteenth century.[43] They agree that the church failed "to reform what it recognised as an evil," namely pluralism and nonresidence, but argue that the impact on standards of pastoral care "should not be exaggerated."[44] They conclude that the double strands of cautious optimism and cautious pessimism bind the history of the eighteenth-century church.[45]

Two substantial collections of evidence are used in this study. One is the set of clergy returns to the visitation of the York diocese conducted by Archbishop Drummond in 1764. The other is his own papers: a selection from his public and personal correspondence, his sermons, and his work of preparation for the visitation. Although the visitation returns of 1764 have been consulted for some histories of the Georgian church, they have not been used systematically as a collection. There is a gap of twenty-one years between them and the earlier survey conducted by Archbishop Herring in 1743, which has been well known in published form since the 1920s. This study couples the career of Robert Drummond with the information from his visitation returns of 1764 and a comparative look at the scene since 1743 to gain a fresh understanding of the Georgian church in Yorkshire.

Armed with the recognition of the limitations of the visitation returns outlined earlier, it is necessary to define the criteria for assessing their value. One approach rests on the expectations implied by the visitation questions. For example, in the archbishop's questions, he regarded two services each Sunday as the best achievement, so this criterion is used in cataloguing the clergy's answers on that point. Another approach is to take into account how well the clergy of the York diocese might be expected to deal with their situation, noting the difference between the few rich and grand incumbents and the many poorly paid curates and assistants. A further criterion is to consider what a reasonable answer might be in the circumstances of the eighteenth century. This leaves room for an evaluation of whether the church should have been complacent about those circumstances.

A study of the York diocese in 1764 reveals a church on the brink of great changes, at a time when most of those in secular and ecclesiastical authority preferred no changes at all. The growth of population, particularly in the north, could still be ignored by the church hierarchy in 1764, but the evidence is that the parish clergy in those growing northern towns were sufficiently aware of their task to address it with energy. The 1764 visitation returns, as a collection of individually written statements, show that the Georgian church was as strong in its reliance on the individual responsibility of its clergy as it was weak in its wish to alter the structure. The authority of the incumbent in his parish rested on the safety of parson's freehold however low the financial value was of that freehold. The key to the debate about the state of the Georgian church is that in 1764 the real problem was yet to appear. There was revival, but its full force had not gathered. There was population change, but its full impact on society came later. The signs are discernible in the visitation returns of 1764, but it is only with hindsight that a line may be seen from the repeated journeyings of Wesley and the existence of small meetings in private houses to the circuits of flourishing Methodist churches all over Yorkshire by the 1830s. What the church was not doing by the early nineteenth century, and what it has been criticized so severely for, was to minister efficiently to the large numbers of people in the densely populated industrial towns. This omission was covered by the Nonconformists, but in 1764 it cannot be seen as the moral failure of the conscientious body of clergy who were, within the constraints of their system, doing what was generally their best, providing curates, employing paid lecturers, organizing weekly catechism throughout the towns and traveling among the villages. Their best, and the efforts of their successors, proved not to be good enough, but it was their system that restrained them. Those who operated and led the system—kings, politicians and bishops—were not gifted with the visionary reforming ardor of their nineteenth-century inheritors.

In sum, the visitation returns and other evidence for the Church in Yorkshire in the time of Archbishop Drummond suggest that the familiar criticisms were made with what has been called the "reform perspective."[46] In 1764 the church was by no means a failure. The early nineteenth-century problems of a greatly increased population, poorly housed in an expanded industrial society, and of oversized parishes with insufficient manpower to bring the church's ministry to its people were not foreseen by the archbishop of York in 1764, and Wesley's mission was as much to the rural poor as to the urban poor of the eighteenth century. A survey in the 1790s (if such had survived—and the 1770 one did not) might have provoked a different response and a different estimate. By 1804 war, revolution, and revival were training a small reforming section of society to look at itself critically, and historians by 1884 had perfected that art.

Clergymen in 1764 who sensed the possibility of problems reacted variously. Henry Venn decided to assist the Independents by providing for their worship in a new chapel. Young evangelical curates sought wealthy evangelical patrons. Edward Rishton, the elderly traditional incumbent at Almondbury, sensed that "omnia bene" was no longer the case in his parish and neighborhood and wrote to say so to the archbishop. Wesley doggedly resisted separation from the Church of England and attempted through auxiliary societies to supply ministry where he saw it was lacking. Archbishop Secker's mind was occupied more with his wish to extend Anglican episcopal government in America, though he kept his image as a popular preacher and a conscientious, scholarly prelate.[47] Some of these reactions are well known to historians, but a gap exists in that Secker's partner at the top of the church, Robert Drummond, has been largely overlooked.

Robert Drummond's episcopal career began in Wales in 1748. This was ten years after John Wesley's heart had been strangely warmed in Aldersgate Street in London. Drummond spent his thirteen years as bishop of St. Asaph steadily acquiring a fund of experience that was to bring him to the duke of Newcastle's eye as the right man to become archbishop of York. By the time of Drummond's translation to York in 1761, Wesley had been riding and preaching in Yorkshire for over twenty years. But there were only six Methodist chapels to show for it since most of the preaching was still done in the open air and most of the meetings were in private rooms (sometimes licensed). Drummond was likely in the early years of his archiepiscopate to have been worried as much by the social upheaval created by disbanded militiamen after the Peace of 1763 as by disturbances from revivalist preachers, and Wesley was just one among many Enthusiasts. When Drummond made the survey of his diocese in 1764, there were significant differences in the official attitudes of church and state. Political freedom had been restrained so much by longer parliaments that an outburst against restrictions in the 1760s was felt keenly by many interested groups. Freedom to worship, by contrast, had been allowed for so long that when another sect arose in the eighteenth century—denying that it was a separate sect—no one was unduly perturbed.

The archiepiscopate of Robert Drummond opens two vistas on the Georgian church. The first is from a study of his character and abilities, and follows the path of his career. Here his papers throw light on the strong undercurrent of eighteenth-century patronage. Drummond's relationship with the duke of Newcastle underlay all his work. The second vista is from the life of the parishes shown in the visitation that he directed, with detailed information about his clergymen of the York diocese. The visitation returns are examined both separately and in comparison with the previous set of returns to Archbishop Herring.

Both vistas may be looked at from different angles. For example, the chronology of the archbishop's career shows the nature of his pastoral oversight and the way he regarded his duty. His correspondence and sermons reveal the extent of his deep concerns for his family and his work for the church. His regular attendance at the House of Lords underlines his commitment to monarchy and to party. Observation of the life of the parishes in this study is by the view from the vicarage as set out in the visitation returns.

Robert Drummond rose by the patronage system. With his aristocratic status, his generous hospitality, and his conformity to card-playing and horse-racing society, he does fit the image of the Georgian prelate before Sykes adjusted it. Schooled at Westminster, the most popular school for aristocrats, and at their most popular Oxford college, Christ Church, Drummond was a Whig aristocrat who in mid century proved that the church was a safe career. But we should ask whether the other usual assumptions follow.

Making a living as a clergyman, once duly ordained and inducted, was not straightforward for those who had no other income. Many eighteenth-century clerics were insufficiently paid. The solution available to some, that of acquiring more than one benefice, produced nonresidence and absenteeism. A few—sometimes well connected socially—were so adept at the practice of pluralism, especially as they gained experience as theologians and publicity as popular preachers, that they could draw income as a prebendary of a cathedral, warden of a college, and the incumbent of one or two or more parishes, all in different parts of the kingdom.[48] Drummond showed no inclination to criticize the system that allowed for a few rich clergy, as he himself came from a privileged class and remained there. His attention, with Thomas Secker, was directed at finding the right clergy to fill the parishes and at keeping out the unqualified and unfit. In dealing with these matters the church's procedures were stereotyped, and the loopholes made it easy for a determined interloper to maneuvre. Finding more money for some of the many poorly paid parish clergy, however, was a task that Drummond undertook in committee work with Queen Anne's Bounty. He let go his pluralist hold on his Northumberland cure when he received the see of Salisbury and is on record as having paid the slightly above-average salary of £34 per annum to his curate. His had been a much weaker hold on the living than that exercized by Samuel Horsley, one of Drummond's later successors as bishop of St. Asaph, who kept *his* first living of St. Mary, Newington Butts, fully thirty-three years after his induction.[49] In the matter of regular confirmations and visitations, Drummond was exemplary throughout his time in Wales and York.

Recognizing the limitations of the visitation returns as an exercise in self-appraisal outlined earlier, the archbishop's questions and answers may be used for the purpose for which they were intended—an audit of the diocese of York.

Supplementary to the visitation inquiry was that of the terriers, the lists that the clergy had to make of all the material assets of their parsonages and churches. It was in this matter that Archbishop Drummond broke new ground. He asked more detailed questions of the clergy than anyone had asked them before about their vicarage houses, and he asked them to write the answers in a grander and more systematic form, so that the terriers acquired an enhanced status. This accords with his interest in building, architecture and interior decor, and with his way of keeping the accounts for the work done. The terriers provide clarity and some completely new details of the domestic surroundings of hundreds of parsonages throughout Yorkshire, as well as specific lists of church silver, parish Bibles, and altar furnishings.

The Anglican members of the "unreformed" Church of England in the eighteenth century were not all domiciled in England. In

America, besides Quakers, Baptists, Roman Catholics, and others, there were nonparochial Anglicans who were under the commission of the bishop of London. How could such an arrangement cope with the many unconfirmed would-be members of the church and how could its ordinands receive their Orders? Episcopal government for the church in America was the one major structural reform which Drummond supported, and that was so progressive that he was unable to bring it to reality. He and Archbishop Secker worked together to provide what they saw as a very workable solution to a problem. They were opposed by powerful lobbies for Nonconformity in religion and by political pressures well beyond their grasp. Secker died in 1768 knowing that he had not achieved his aim but believing that he could influence events by the provisions in his will. Drummond outlived Secker until 1776, which was the year of American Independence. Drummond had long given up an unrealistic project. As with the visitation returns which he had gathered but apparently only begun to study, so he gave up theorizing and did what he was good at, touring the diocese for confirmations, as Sykes has given him credit.[50]

His tour of the diocese, however, did not lead him to understand the religious revival which had begun in some parishes before the specific impact of Wesley. What was the church to do? Some of the revivalists were within its own structure. Why did the new revivalist religion appeal so strongly to some people and repel others? What were the individual parishes doing about it, and what reply should the parson give when a Methodist itinerant preacher arrived and asked if he could preach in the parish church of Stokesley? Thomas Hudson, the curate in question, gave the wrong answer and took the rest of his life to get out of the difficulties that followed with the archbishop's ban. How should a nonresident clergyman react to his curate's favor towards the Methodists? Dr. Francis Wanley, rector of Stokesley, had already upset his parishioners by adding aloof behavior to his absenteeism. What did the incumbent do if a neighboring parson was drawing parishioners other than his own to services of an Enthusiastic nature? If he was elderly, like Edward Rishton of Almondbury, he could write to complain to the archbishop, but the answer he received was hardly sparkling and was directed at smoothing over the complaint rather than examining its details. How should a clergyman who sympathized wholeheartedly with the new evangelical ministry build up the religious life of his parish without losing favor in a church dominated by patronage? Henry Venn of Huddersfield published his sermons and distributed them to his parishioners and attempted a cool friendship with John Wesley, without seeking advice from the archbishop. Some of the revivalists were ordained Anglican clergymen whose newly ardent approach to religion led them outside the parochial framework. Others became committed followers of the revivalists and, as laymen and laywomen, were inspired to become leaders in their own areas. How did the church hierarchy treat them? John Nelson, a stonemason from the parish of Birstall, was to find that out at the hands of his own vicar, who thought he could get rid of the revivalist if he helped to press him for a soldier. Some people voluntarily left their own areas to become field preachers within the nascent organization of Methodism. Did the Roman Catholics appear to threaten the church in 1764 as much as some thought they did in 1743? Was the eighteenth-century church losing ground or dragging its feet in Yorkshire?

We arrive at the underlying question: What sort of leadership did Robert Drummond give to the church in Yorkshire during those times? With so many apparently divisive trends within the church, did he try to maintain its spiritual and physical fabric? What level of obedience did he command? Did he see the connection between population changes and the steady order being imposed on Methodist societies by Wesley as a challenge to the traditional ways of the Church of England? What difference did he make to the life of the church in Yorkshire? Did he assist the growth of education throughout his diocese? How he worked, how he was both helped and hindered by the system itself, how he acquired the respect of his contemporaries, and how he appeared to run out of some of his steam once his enquiry was complete, will be seen as the evidence is examined. He takes his place as the one at the center of the York diocese, traveling indefatigably to enroll thousands of people into church membership by confirmation, but settling eventually for the absorbing interest of rebuilding his palace. He was the utterly eighteenth-century aristocratic prelate who preferred to remain aside from the excesses of "canting," but in whose diocese the early evangelicals began their work of revival.

Chapter 1 introduces us to the Yorkshire awaiting the arrival of a new archbishop. It outlines the way in which national issues affected Yorkshire's political and religious life. The social and economic background of the northern province is given before a portrayal of the new archbishop's character.

Chapter 2 traces Drummond's career path—from a first appointment as parish priest in northern England to a royal chaplain and a prebendary of Westminster, then raised to the episcopal order in Wales, then serving briefly as bishop of Salisbury and then archbishop of York. Chapter 2 also sets out the way that social advantages and the patronage system made it possible for Drummond to get from parish priest to archbishop. His political intelligence led him to make a name for himself in the House of Lords. His sermons and his theology are considered. There follows a treatment of the reasons why he became archbishop of York but not of Canterbury.

Chapter 3 begins with Drummond's experience in visitations in Wales. It shows the church in the eighteenth century exercising its authority in detailed minutiae from Canterbury downwards and across the two Anglican provinces. The process of the visitation and the categories of the visited are examined. The chapter concludes with a look at Drummond's apparent disinclination to address the information collated (apart from a brief consideration of some of the York city churches), with the suggestion that personal griefs overtook him.

Chapters 4, 5, and 6 present Drummond's Yorkshire from the detailed analysis of all the answers to the visitation enquiries. Case studies, maps, and tables of data assist the text. The performance indicators of the church's liturgical and pastoral system are examined in the Yorkshire application of the church's calendar and the natural seasons. The parish terriers are appraised under Drummond's own restyling. Problems and opportunities are reviewed in Chapter 5, looking particularly at pluralism, the evangelicals, and clerical poverty. Chapter 6 considers the changes in population alongside the fortunes of the Church of England and the distribution of Dissent, dealing lastly with the questions how far and in what respects the church was losing and holding ground in Yorkshire in the mid eighteenth century, and why.

Chapter 7 looks at Drummond's contribution to the governance of the church by correspondence. As a recently translated archbishop, he solved old and new problems and coped with the increased amount of correspondence during the year of the visitation. His relationships with individual clergymen are outlined as well as the way in which he deferred to his patron. In particular, the correspondence with archdeacons is examined, and a last section presents the work of the two primates, Secker and Drummond, as they led the "unreformed" Church of England with characteristic eighteenth-century talents.

In conclusion, Chapter 8 reviews Drummond's career as a span of twenty-eight years and then examines his work during the year of visitation in an appraisal of his contribution to the Georgian church. Some perspectives are drawn for the lingering ill-repute of the Georgian church. The visitation returns of 1764 are assessed for their contribution to the Georgian church as a whole and also particularly for their insight into the history of the parishes of the diocese of York. Uniting these strands, Archbishop Drummond is regarded as the one who led the northern province of the Church of England in a manner which confirms some of the views on the shortcomings of his age but at a time when in some of the Yorkshire parishes the church was renewing the minds and hearts of its members in traditional as well as novel ways. Drummond's self-effacing nature has contributed to a comparative lack of attention to his visitation returns which reveal so much about what was strong and weak in the mid-Georgian church. Within the accepted terms of "safe churchmanship," he was competent and orderly, though no prophet, inside what was a faulty system. This study addresses both man and archive.

1

Yorkshire and Its Archbishop in the Mid–Eighteenth Century

The National Background in the 1760s—Political and Religious Change

In 1760 a new king, George III, began his reign and political changes were expected at the general election of 1761. Politicians who had exercised control in several English counties were hard at work to strengthen party interest. The duke of Newcastle, one of the individually most powerful ministers of the crown in the previous king's reign, began to lose his influence, particularly with regard to ecclesiastical affairs. Another faction (though still within the Whig party) under the earl of Rockingham was gaining support. The difference, from 1760, in politics, has been considered by several historians at national and at local levels. Frank O'Gorman has summed this up in writing that "the newspapers [by the 1760s] were beginning to reflect, and thus encourage, a vigorous local political life."[1] He attributed the growth of this vigor particularly to the ensuing affair of Wilkes, whose activities as a tribune-style journalist and member of Parliament, drew charges of seditious libel which he defended against the highest odds.

The unreformed parliamentary system relied on the bishops in the House of Lords as part of the aristocratic rock that governed the property-based social and political order. This meant that parsons who expected to prosper in a church career were likely early on to court the prevailing political party. Reaching the very top was possible for few clergymen. Once they acquired positions of influence such as bishoprics, their allegiance to party politics and to their patron was usually firm, especially if they looked for further preferment. Robert Hay Drummond, whose patron, the duke of Newcastle, had been forced out of office in May 1762, recognized the affair of Wilkes as a seriously divisive political crisis and withdrew from London politics for a whole year to ponder its consequences. The duke was annoyed by this and also by Drummond's criticism that he lacked parliamentary wisdom.[2] It drew the bitter remark from Newcastle that he had "*singly* carried [him] from the duke of Leeds' house to be archbishop of York."[3] Drummond wrote a letter of warning to the duke in which he set out his views on the nature of political opposition for members of the episcopacy,[4] stressing that he disapproved of a "formed opposition," preferring to take each issue in its circumstances. Such independent action by one of the bishops introduces us to Drummond as a man of political integrity, but one who was safe enough since his appointment in 1761 as archbishop to criticize his fallen patron. Government changes continued throughout Drummond's time as archbishop of York. It has been estimated that there were fifteen changes of personnel in the department of foreign affairs during 1763 and 1775, and five in the premier position itself.[5] These were not simply replacements of personnel, though this did happen and affected many people. The changes reflected the different policies of the king and his new ministers towards peace and war and taxes. The king was eager to put his ideas into practice, and the issues in the case of John Wilkes marked the 1760s as a period of political uncertainty. Other aristocrats as well as Newcastle wanted to protect their personal power, and many people feared a loss of law and order. The unruly behaviour of Wilkes and his associates shows that it was not only the mob who were to be feared.

Political activity was acute at times of general elections, and there had been two within four years (1757 and 1761). O'Gorman extended his comments about increasing popular interest to refer also to elections. He considers that within the unreformed and oligarchic system there was, by the 1760s, a "strength of commitment to parliamentary and representative forms and processes that had assumed an almost hallowed ideological status."[6] Very large sums of money changed hands at election times, costing Wilkes almost as much as Lord Rockingham.[7]

Yorkshire in the 1760s

Changes in population as well as changes in government affected the life of the church. The number of families in the parishes was the starting point of a visitation enquiry. By 1761 the year of Drummond's translation to York, the population of Leeds had grown from two thousand to five thousand families since the days of Archbishop Herring. Sheffield had doubled its inhabitants, and Hull, on Humberside, had almost doubled. Whitby, on the northeast coast, had had a slower rate of growth, while neighboring Lythe had stayed the same. The movement of people was inwards, towards the cloth-producing towns. This shows in the visitation returns. The increase illustrates the conclusions drawn nationally by economic historians who recognize the years 1743 to 1764 as the first stage in that substantial economic and demographic growth rate that started in earnest from mid century.[8] There was some awareness of this population growth at the time when it was happening. Drummond himself showed more interest in the state of Roman Catholic numbers,[9] and applied the factor of five persons to one family when adding up the recusant returns. This computation method applied generally means that the five thousand families of Sheffield would have consisted of twenty-five thousand people. Population changes affected parish life not only in the number of seats taken or left empty in church on Sundays, but also in matters of benefaction, almshouses, charities, augmentations, catechism and schools, funds for the conveyance of vagrants, and places in houses of correction.

Industrial changes were felt by many families in the Yorkshire cloth-producing areas. The cloth industry continued to expand during the fifteen years of Drummond's archiepiscopate. Broadcloth and narrow cloth show steady increases in outputs during the years 1761 to 1767, with a great surge of production in both widths in 1764, and a proportional increase of broad over narrow by 1767.[10] The burden of pastoral care of these hardworking people traditionally rested on the clergymen, several of whom showed by their responses that they were offering the church's ministry conscientiously and to the best of their abilities, though some did not.

The archdiocese of York was extensive, consisting of more than 650 parishes. The two factors of urban growth and religious revival were not linked in origin, but their existence was so close together that they presented problems for the administrators of the church. Archbishop Drummond had an uneven task. Members of his flock were on the move and in some places they were growing rapidly in number. His diocese was too large for him to have a close and continuing knowledge of what his clergy and people were doing, though the visitation returns did provide him with a great bulk of answers to his particular questions. The unplanned revival from within was a more difficult problem. The archbishop could not know its extent or its strength because it was happening in the open air and in private homes—areas which the established church found unsuitable or inaccessible. Drummond's archdeacons were there to help him when he moved to the York diocese, but one of them, Francis Blackburne, proved to be unorthodox in belief.

The religious scene could have seemed unclear in pastoral and disciplinary matters to one such as Drummond who was arriving fresh to head its organization. For example, in Haworth, one of the chapelries of Bradford, William Grimshaw, the curate, exhausted himself in his encouragement of personal devotion and obedience to the Scriptures among his parishioners, but he could not be classified otherwise than as an Enthusiast. Two other clergymen, Benjamin Ingham and George Whitefield, were spasmodically active as unparochial and revivalist preachers in several parts of Yorkshire and had supporters from all ranks of society. John Nelson, the stonemason from Birstall who had been pressed for a soldier, encouraged his neighbors in ways of personal holiness even to the extent that some of them went with him from Birstall to York to support him during his military service. Alongside these efforts were those of Henry Venn, Christopher Atkinson, and Richard Conyers, the duly appointed and properly qualified vicars of Huddersfield, Thorp Arch and Helmsley. They were renewing the hearts and minds of their own church members. Meanwhile Wesley was "moulding and organising the original efforts of others of all sorts."[11] Specific problems for the established church grew in the 1760s, when Methodist lay preachers began to administer the sacraments[12] and when a dozen evangelical Anglican clergymen accepted Wesley's invitation to attend the Methodist Conference in 1764.[13] Lying as an undercurrent to these activities were the doubts in the mind of Francis Blackburne, doubts which were to grow into the Feathers Tavern petition of 1772, attacking the Thirty-nine Articles.

The Yorkshire scene which awaited the arrival of its new archbishop was one of uncertainty and imbalance. To illustrate the extremes that existed, politicians were willing to spend thousands of pounds in 1757 and 1761 for electioneering, while Francis Blackburne's archdeaconry officials were dealing in all seriousness with the nonpayment of sums of fourpence and eightpence by named laborers for petty crimes.[14]

The New Archbishop

Drummond had an advantage in knowing Yorkshire well.[15] He also knew London and had traveled in Europe, but his family home was in south Yorkshire. By the time he was translated to the see of York, he was neither old nor ill,[16] nor had he become lazy. If he needed quiet, his estates at Brodsworth, near Doncaster, provided the haven where he could work in his study or ride about his manors and fields. Drummond had more than one such place of safety: there were the estates at Brodsworth, the palace at Bishopthorpe, and—if the work of rebuilding there became too noisy—he had the leasehold of a house in Dartmouth Street, London. There was also that great bastion, the House of Lords, where the family life of the nation's aristocracy was protected along with its property.

The York city art gallery has a portrait of Drummond (not always on public view), painted by the artist Andrea Soldi. At Bishopthorpe the portrait of Drummond attributed to the artist Thomas Hudson, 1701–1779, is not given public prominence. It hangs on a darkish wall in a small service room leading into the private sitting room. It shows the archbishop seated on a grand carved chair—probably walnut with green velvet upholstery—and holding a large red book with fringed markers. He looks down, mouth closed but smiling from the eyes, a look of friendly regard. A mezzotint engraving by J. Watson of a portrait by Reynolds hangs in even darker obscurity, being tucked away in an alcove in the same small service room. For that, the archbishop wore the insignia of the office of Chancellor of the Order of the Garter, an office attached to the see of Salisbury.[17] Reynolds painted closer to his sitter than did Hudson. The archbishop's incipient smile is again warm in the eyes as well as in the mouth. These portraits introduce us to Drummond as a confident and authoritative prelate, whose conscience was not troubled. There was one occasion when he was approached ineptly for patronage and another when he was wrongly represented in a controversy, occasions that ruffled his aristocratic calm. His contemporaries agreed, however, about his usually genial, amiable, and hospitable character. Others appreciated his manner of speaking. One, Andrew Stone, had great cause to thank him for his informed defence of his conduct (see chapter 2). The Soldi portrait includes a formal languor that contrasts with the ordinariness of the hinted smile. These three portraits show Drummond holding a book, symbolizing the authority of the church he served and the Canon Law he understood. He looks well fed, his figure filled the canvases, and we know from the accounts of supplies sent to Bishopthorpe that he entertained substantially. He was well covered with face flesh, and the portraits confirm the idea of him as a man who preferred being at home with his family, who was effortlessly

Portrait of Archbishop Drummond by Thomas Hudson

in control, comfortable, assured, and fully aware of his aristocratic responsibilities.

At St. Deiniol's Library in Hawarden, North Wales, an afternoon's drive away from St. Asaph, there is a portrait of *Robert Drummond 1749–1761* by J. Smith and sons. It hangs at the top of the main staircase, the first portrait in a collection of three to be seen by the warden of the library as he leaves his study on the first floor. The portrait has the same green velvet chair as in the one painted by Thomas Hudson now at Bishopthorpe, though its background definition is not good. On a day with good light, it shows a younger, rather rosier Drummond. He wears billowing lawnsleeves and preaching bands and holds a large book with a mitered crest on its cover. His smile is characteristically firm, and there is the same direct eye contact.

It was Drummond who began the tradition at Bishopthorpe that each archbishop should leave his portrait there. The portraits of Drummond's predecessors were gathered retrospectively.[18] It is strange that his own portraits, the oil on canvas attributed to Hudson and the mezzotint from Reynolds, are both in an anteroom. There is a coincidence in that the artist Thomas Hudson has the same name as the untruthful clergyman of Stokesley, as well as more than half a dozen other namesakes (see Chapter 7). Drummond probably had a good rapport with Reynolds, sitting for two versions, and Hudson may have been allowed to see Reynolds's work to get inspiration for his own composition. Ingamells dates Reynolds's prominence to the end of the eighteenth century, citing the close friendship between Reynolds and Markham, Drummond's successor. It is likely that Reynolds was amiably encouraged in archiepiscopal portraiture as Drummond sat for him.

The contrast between these portrayals of Drummond—the Soldi, the Reynolds, the Smith, and the Hudson—with the portraits at Bishopthorpe of Archbishops Herring, Hutton, and Gilbert, favors Drummond. Herring looks away to his left, disregarding his public, with an expression of controlled preoccupation; he might really be studying the opposite wall. Hutton looks pale and too youthful to be authoritative. Gilbert looks weak and dark, and we know that he was indeed weak in the feet and ankles.[19] Drummond has eye contact with the viewers in all the portraits. He looks free from anxiety, personable, and with a conversational readiness, though we know that he had many private griefs. Two other eighteenth-century characteristics, which serve as title words to a recent study,[20] were being polite and being commercial. Drummond was a master of politeness in writing, a genre in which his colleague, George Legh, vicar of Halifax, also excelled. Being commercially acute, a quality not so widely spread among the aristocracy, was a talent which Drummond used to advise his relations about house purchase[21] and to advise the church about some of its official investments, especially those of Queen Anne's Bounty and the Society for the Propagation of the Gospel.

In practical matters Drummond's greatest opportunity came with his residence in the palace of Bishopthorpe. His first eight years were spent in designing and enlarging it, transforming it from a mainly brick construction to a mansion fit for a prince of the church. What he had seen on the Grand Tour could be bestowed on York. He began with the stables, and although only a quarter remains after some early twentieth-century dismantling, in its day it accomodated more than forty horses, with housing for grooms and space for carriages. The gateway was enlarged and its original clock informed passersby of the time. Drummond has had scant recognition for his grand extension to the palace itself. Designed by local architect Thomas Atkinson, it has much less of an impact than the house at Strawberry Hill, whose owner courted fame in a way that was alien to Robert Drummond. Dr. and Mrs. Drummond and their family could have stood at the three-canopied entrance to greet about twenty or thirty guests, who would have been able to admire the slim Gothic columns supporting the ogee arches as they walked over from the stables. As they came closer they would have noticed the shields with the archbishop's official and family details on them. The canopied entrance was not completed until 1769, and its building is likely to have been what Drummond turned his mind to when he was grieving for the deaths of his daughters. The interior accommodation was started in 1766 and provided the archbishop with a fine entrance hall, a drawing room and some service rooms, and a new door to the chapel. No work of much importance had been done at the palace for about a hundred years before Drummond arrived. We sense his disappointment in reading the catalogue of fraying drapes and dilapidated upholstery when we look at the inventories dating from the time of his translation. The items included "paper hangings eat with mice . . . an old knife tray . . . two mahogany dining tables one broke"[22] and contrast unfavourably with an inventory dating from 1724, which testified to better days with "the porter's staff with a silver head . . . a long table and two other tables . . . a set of fine tapistry[sic] hangings . . . two fine brass locks, two Dutch chairs," and much more.[23] These must have convinced him that something must be done; otherwise here was no suitable residence for a

The gatehouse at Bishopthorpe Palace, built for Archbishop Drummond in 1763–65 of stones from Cawood Castle.

Bishopthorpe Palace, aerial view

The new west front of Bishopthorpe Palace, built for Archbishop Drummond in 1766–69

prince of the church with a taste for comfort on a grand scale and family life to the full.

The Drummond family at home was less a scene of domestic harmony than that of life among the workmen. There were gangs of men with cartloads of materials—lifting, unloading, banging and mixing, sawing, fixing, carrying and laying, making a great deal of noise and dust. The bills spell out that Drummond was not only building new in stone, but also repairing the old, paying about £8 for over twelve thousand bricks, and nineteen shillings for six days' work to repair tiling and clean out the gutter. Ten cartloads of sand and leading cost him £1. He was also a conservationist, paying £20—a huge sum—for 5,100 "old broad tiles," and £3 12s 0d for "Old Harry tiles."[24] A minor entry throws light on his personal care for his domestic chaplain: the sum of 9d was itemised for putting "your Grace's own glass in Mr Marsden's room." John Marsden, Richard Mackley, and Richard Clapham were the three domestic chaplains who figure in the Bishopthorpe papers for the early part of Drummond's time as archbishop. As members of the household, they had close knowledge of the archbishop and his family. A letter from Clapham cheerfully mixes information about arrangements for ordinations, information about a Roman Catholic gentleman, alarm at the illness and "griping pains" of his child to whom the archbishop was godfather "at the christening yesterday," with wishes for a safe journey and "happy return."[25]

For the family, the household, and the workmen at Bishopthorpe, the new buildings at the palace must have been a marvel. In the words of Sir Nikolaus Pevsner, the work "belongs to the foremost displays of Gothic fantasy in mid eighteenth-century England."[26] Next to the palace, the same architect rebuilt the ancient parish church of St. Andrew in the same style.[27] It now stands in ruins, abandoned since 1898. Drummond was buried beneath the altar. A cross now stands there, open to the air, marking not the archbishop's tomb but the place where the altar once was. A strange anonymity surrounds this most resplendent of aristocratic archbishops, and there is irony in Drummond's son's reference to the palace: "exegit monumentum aere perennius Robertus Drummond."

The arrival of a new archbishop could mean a number of things to the ordinary clergy in the parsonages. The service of enthronement would have left them untouched. Not even Drummond himself felt the occasion to be of sufficient importance to attend in person. It was solemnized by proxy and attended by some of the Minster hierarchy who may have recalled that such an event was customarily followed by cakes and wine. Only a few of the hundreds of parochial clergy had a right as prebendaries to attend. A new archbishop would have arrived as many as four or five times in the career of an ordinary clergyman. Herring was succeeded after four years, Hutton had a decade, Gilbert four years. Before Herring, Archbishop Blackburne had been in office for nearly twenty years. Of the Yorkshire clergy in office in 1761, and whose ministry had always been in that diocese, about a third would have had Drummond as their fifth archbishop.

What might the clergy be expecting? A visitation was a possibility, if the archbishop had any regard for Canon Law, and the clergy were also accustomed to archdeacons' visitations. As the parochial clergy contemplated the arrival of a new archbishop at the end of 1761, so Drummond himself was planning the strategy for his work in the north. Within two years he was organizing his primary visitation of the diocese.

The new archbishop's palace was nearer to the racecourse than it was to the Minster in the center of York. Race week, with its "hurry" and "great deal of company"—particularly Lord Rockingham in the summer of 1765[28]—found Drummond attending the races with parties of his guests, other Whig aristocrats and ecclesiastical friends, acquaintances, and colleagues. Such men might have met also in the Rockingham club, where the membership included six Anglican clergymen, foremost of whom was John Fountayne, dean of York at the time of the 1761 general election. The correspondence shows that Drummond was on good, though rather formal, terms with John Fountayne. The dean and his chapter colleagues had provoked a satire in the form of *A Political Romance,* written in 1759 by the vicar of Sutton on the Forest, Laurence Sterne. The satire was sufficiently hurtful to be suppressed from publication until a later date. It must have found very tender sensitivities in an age when satire was frequently bitter, especially from the pen of a compulsive satirist such as Sterne. The dean and Dr. Topham, an ecclesiastical official, were two of the main targets of Sterne's attack. The story centered on church attitudes and religious procedures, not on political or social ambitions. York was a social and political magnet for clergy and laity when Robert Drummond arrived there in 1761 to begin a lively and authoritative career as archbishop.

2

The Making of an Archbishop

Family Life

Aristocratic parents gave Robert Hay an advantageous start in life. He was born in 1711 as the second son to the seventh earl of Kinnoull[1] and the Honourable Elizabeth Drummond. At the age of twenty-eight, as heir to the Perthshire estates left to him by Viscount Strathallan, his maternal grandfather, he took the name and arms of Drummond. Most of the evidence for his family life until 1761 is available in the *Memoirs* compiled by his son.[2] His love for family life and his care for his estates at Brodsworth in South Yorkshire show in his correspondence.[3] He put his family's safety before his parishioners' during the rebellion of 1745, explaining his priorities in a letter to his cousin, the duke of Leeds.[4] It was not that he shrank from the imagined horrors of war, but that he had recently seen desperate battles in Germany and wished at all costs to be with his family—at that time, his parents, sisters, and brothers. He wrote with open sadness to the duke of Newcastle, his patron, when his mother was dying,[5] and his grief at the death of his parents included a sympathy for his sisters in their grief.[6] Later, when he had a wife and children, he kept family days with them.[7]

Drummond was at ease in London society, as the aristocracy divided their time between the capital and their country estates, and it was in London that he met Henrietta Auriol, the daughter of a merchant. They married in 1749, and family life flourished in the bishop's palace at St. Asaph in Wales, to which see Drummond had been appointed the previous year. It was a happy marriage, but drawn closer by griefs at the loss of their three daughters, Henrietta, Abigail, and Charlotte,[8] and of their second son, Thomas. Their eldest daughter, Abigail, was sixteen when she died, and she was said to be both beautiful and accomplished.[9] When Henrietta herself died in 1773, Drummond mourned her deeply. Six of their sons grew to manhood, though John Auriol, the fourth son, died at sea while serving on the warship *Beaver* in 1780, four years after the archbishop had died, and George Drummond, the archbishop's youngest son and biographer, died subsequently in a shipwreck on a voyage from Cornwall to Scotland.

The family's life was described by George Drummond, who also became a clergyman, as intimate and self-sufficient. Drummond himself took charge of the education of the children. His knowledge of history was said to be accurate, extensive, and profound.[10] History was his favorite topic in his familiar hours of instruction with his children. He drew up tables of chronology for family use. Church teaching was in their curriculum:

> He availed himself of every opportunity to impress on our minds this important consideration that inspired prophecy is evidence of the truth of divine revelation with all the zeal and fervour of honest conviction, founded on critical research and deep investigation of the subject.[11]

The key to all his career is that he was related to his patron. His uncle Edward Harley had married the only daughter and heiress of the first duke of Newcastle. That duke's sister married Thomas Pelham Holles; their son became the duke's adopted heir and in turn became the second duke of Newcastle. Drummond's dealings with the powerfully rich yet persnickety statesman tied him with family loyalties and national and church politics.

Early Career

Schooling at Westminster began when Drummond was six years old. He applied himself successfully and went up to Christ Church, Oxford, where he gained his B.A. in 1731 at the age of nineteen. The Grand Tour of Europe with his cousin, the duke of Leeds, continued his education in the wider sense. In 1735 he returned to Christ Church to study divinity. Earlier thoughts about a career in the army had evaporated. His decision to enter the church led to his ordination as deacon and priest on 26 and 27 June 1736 by the bishop of Oxford. He gained his B.D. and D.D. in 1745. Study must have appealed to him. He could have begun a career in the church without a second degree, but he clearly had ability. He may have decided that he wanted to aim high, and he may have enjoyed the student's way of life. His later correspondence bears witness to his grasp of Canon Law and to his ability to relate it to particular cases. He applied himself to the education of his children.

The combination of noble birth, sound education, worldly experience, and a discernible amiability gave Drummond a fine start to his career, and because his patron was the powerful duke of Newcastle he acquired a living, Bothall in Northumberland, just one month after his ordination.[12] He kept the usual custom of leaving the cure of souls there to established curates.[13] At the visitations of the time the curates appeared and Drummond was excused. The inference is that he was nonresident throughout.

This early parish history of one who became archbishop of York in the mid eighteenth century is an undisguised display of the customary attitude to absenteeism. That is, there was deemed to be no absenteeism while a curate was present. The salary paid to the curate was honorably suitable according to current rates. The value of the living was estimated by Drummond in 1740 to have been £280. A statement in a [c.1750s] diocese book (Auckland Castle Episcopal Records) has Charles Ward, M.A., in receipt of £34, 10s per annum. No relevant clergy visitation returns or churchwardens' presentments survive for Bothall or Hebburn for the 1740s and 1750s.[14] Drummond retained the livings of Bothall and Hebburn throughout his time at St. Asaph until his translation to Salisbury in May 1761. There is no hint of a bad conscience about the workings of such pluralism. It was acceptable among the church hierarchy according to the standards of the age.

Being in London kept Drummond in the eye of his patron, and he had friends at court. While he was dividing his time between London and the university, the queen marked him out as one suitable, from 1737, as royal chaplain. She had first noticed him much earlier, when he was at Westminster as a schoolboy.[15] The appointment as royal chaplain gave the young aristocratic clergyman a very special opportunity, for the king was about to travel abroad to fight his enemies.

Being on sovereign's duty on a foreign battlefield was like a second chance for a clergyman who had thought earlier of a career in the army. It was one to be relished as not many of the royal chaplains actually served abroad.[16] A royal chaplain had the obvious advantage of advancing in the church more quickly because of his unique closeness to the king.[17] Being close to the king and away from the rest of the court was both a responsibility and an opportunity. When the king returned from campaigning in Hanover, Drummond was made a prebendary of Westminster Abbey.

The German campaign lasted for five months, from May to October 1743. The evidence of Drummond's letters from every stopping point attests to the deep impression that the events made on him.

He was aware of his unique opportunities to observe as a noncombatant, and he proved to be a capable assessor of military and personnel matters. His letters during that five-month campaign are different from all subsequent correspondence and assisted his career enormously, though apparently ingenuously. His patron, the duke of Newcastle, had the idea of recruiting the able chaplain as his own war correspondent. Although there were official observers, news from his *protege* was a bonus. Drummond enjoyed the work, admitting that he wrote as one who saw only the outward appearances of things, knowing that the duke had other reports from people who knew the "secret springs,"[18] but along with the diffidence came thanks,[19] and a special type of secret information, namely the health of the king.[20]

The military action at Dettingen moved Drummond to great sympathy for the wounded and the dying,[21] and he even drew strength from personal discomforts.[22] Such self-knowledge enabled him in the next decades to tackle ordination, confirmation, and visitation with confidence, duties which some bishops admitted disliking. He may also have drawn satisfaction from knowing that he had coped with war. Rowdy crowds at confirmations in some dioceses,[23] held no terror for Robert Drummond, who had praised the "cool" behavior of soldiers in battle duress for their "most exact discipline, . . . continual silence and the most determined regulation yt cd appear in men. I hope to see it again so."[24] He saw it again in the different circumstances of a confirmation tour in 1768, reporting to Newcastle[25] that "the numbers were greater than five years ago" and that "the order and regularity were increased."

The making of an archbishop does not have to include foreign war experience, yet the campaign did prepare Drummond. He learned in early manhood how to survive away from home on arduous travels.[26] Sykes has written memorably about "the parallel problems of territorial extent and arduous itineraries . . . in . . . [the diocese of] York," and cites evidence for Drummond's efficient confirmation tours.[27] The size of the York diocese could be a deterrent to efficiency, and Archbishop Gilbert (1757–1761) had had to give up on confirmations.

Bishop of St. Asaph

Three visitations, loyalty in politics, and a buoyant correspondence during thirteen years in Wales provided Newcastle with enough evidence that his *protege* was suitable material for further promotion. These years when Drummond was enjoying family life and bringing new organization to the diocese show the bishop of St. Asaph as busy and productive.[28] It was wise behaviour, for although he and his patron were related, the bishop of St. Asaph was just one among dozens of other clergymen who depended on the duke of Newcastle as ecclesiastical minister.[29] The see of St. Asaph has been valued at £839 in 1735 and £1,400 by 1762. This was far better than the £280 per annum (less curates' salaries) derived from Bothall, which, as noted earlier, he continued to hold during his Welsh episcopacy, but there was another side to being a bishop. As a genial and aristocratic family man, Drummond fits the image of stewardly bishops who were great consumers and great employers,[30] instanced in the diocese of St. Asaph through the careful manorial control of mills and farms. Records of a water corn mill and lands in Nannerch and Abergele between 1750 and 1765 show the Drummond family as responsible church landlords. For example, the rent of the water corn mill for the lives of ten-year-old Robert Auriol and seven-year-old Thomas Auriol was ten shillings, one fat wether (turkey), and four capons in 1761, and four years later it was released for £121.[31]

Since Drummond was a landlord as well as a bishop, the question of his residence is significant. The matter has been obscured by a nineteenth-century criticism[32] that the eighteenth-century church in Wales was "the darkest and most hurtful period of the Church's history."[33] In the same volume, however, he uses the reports from rural deans to indicate a very high level of ministry:

> In 1749 the services were performed with regularity, not only on Sundays and holy days, but also on Wednesdays and Fridays in Lent, and in Denbigh, Oswestry and Wrexham daily; catechising was frequent, and the Holy Communion administered monthly, the numbers returned as communicating at Easter being very large.

This was a healthy state, despite Thomas's critical overview, and it refers to the first year of Drummond's episcopate and bears the marks of Drummond's efficient diocesan control (see chapter 3). The issue of Drummond's residence is clearer against the background that an annual stay of two, three, or four months was a very good record by eighteenth-century standards, and the achievement of three diocesan visitations was exemplary. His annual residence at St. Asaph for thirteen years gave scope to his interest in building; the only remaining feature is the stone garden wall of the bishop's house just below the cathedral.[34] He may also have been the anonymous provider in 1751 of "a copper fane [weather-cock] gilt with gold for the Tower" [of the cathedral] and in 1752 of a "parapet . . . on the north wall of the nave roof, to prevent falling slates cutting the lead on the roof of the aisle."[35] The best proof of his summer occupation of the episcopal residence in St. Asaph is of course in the letters he wrote to his patron from there in the months of June, July, August, and September throughout those years when he was bishop.

Drummond's letter to a new rural dean soon after his own appointment to St. Asaph shows us his eye for detail. He knew that the use of the Welsh language mattered,[36] even though he was not among Rupp's three Welsh linguists.[37] The letter might look like beginner's enthusiasm, but his subsequent visitations (see Chapter 3) prove otherwise. He was starting his episcopal career as a bureaucrat with a natural flair for organization and order. He asked the rural dean to visit every church and chapel in person to investigate domestic and church buildings, registers, and personnel. This work was normally done elsewhere by archdeacons, but because there was only one archdeaconry in the diocese of St. Asaph, held in commendam by the bishop,[38] Drummond was making provision. He stressed that all the registers of baptisms, marriages, and burials had to be on parchment or vellum. They had to be bound in book form, and not "only on paper, or perhaps on loose notes." They had to be "fairly transcribed, . . . and signed every page by ye Minister." The reference to "loose notes" is one which echoes a note of human frailty that he well understood. The Borthwick Institute has many of Drummond's "loose notes" of spontaneous jottings from his time as archbishop, when he had the benefit of help from a domestic chaplain and secretary.

One further testimony to his organization of diocesan affairs while at St. Asaph is his early direction to the parish clergy for the compilation of the parish terriers, the lists of material assets of the vicarage and church.[39] The survival of this evidence for St. Asaph assist our understanding of Drummond's subsequent directions to the York clergy in the matter of terriers, spelling out exactly what information was required and how it should be recorded (see Chapter 4).

Member of the House of Lords

For thirteen years while Drummond was bishop of St. Asaph he attended regularly at the House of Lords. He grew accustomed to the ways of the House and became a familiar and trusted member. Much of the business was routine, but there was an enjoyable, social side to politics, and Drummond did not regard the Lords as a dreary place.

A study of his attendance at the House of Lords from 1748 to 1760 shows that Drummond was different from some of the Welsh bishops who were frequently at the House and hardly ever in their sees, and similar in seasonally consistent attendance to some of the bishops of two important northern dioceses. The elderliness and sickliness of Edward Chandler and Samuel Peploe, bishops of Durham and Chester during the first part of the thirteen years studied, were replaced with the regular attendances of Joseph Butler, Richard Trevor, and Edmund Keene. Drummond's record, matching that of the conscientious holders of senior northern bishoprics, was one of reliable commitment during periods of varying political interest. It was a time when he had health, strength, and expectations. A man of his class and education, with the patronage of the duke of Newcastle—and he was a man of his times—would have expected to achieve more than the bishopric of St. Asaph.

He served on committees for enclosures and road development schemes. Amid the routine there were some clear peaks: he was there at important moments during the Seven Years' War, he was present at the accession speech of George III, he witnessed the murder trial of Earl Ferrers, and was at hand when beer went up by twopence a pint.

Two propositions occur. The first is that from routine grew recognition. The second is that the recognition sharpened into his being known as a Yorkshire man, although he was a Welsh bishop. His familiarity with the north and his regular attendances were put to use in the transport business of the House of Lords. During the 1750-51 session he served on a committee supporting a bill for conveying coals by machine, for repairing the road between Stamford and Grantham, and for improving the St. Albans Road and the Darlington Road. By the end of his first decade in the House of Lords, he had also dealt with the Oadby Common Bill and the Netherbridge Road Bill and presented the report for the Barnsley Common Road Bill. In 1760 he was on the committees for the Woodhall Moor and Sowerby enclosures and reported on the bills for enclosures at Owston Common and Adwicke in the Street. In January and February 1761, that is, well before the translation to Salisbury and York, he was on the committee for the Patrington Road Bill, the Norham Moor Bill and the Heslington Enclosure Bill.

Was Drummond using his association with Yorkshire and northern affairs deliberately as part of a wish to become archbishop of York, or was his conduct in the Lords a natural consequence of his being a Yorkshire landowner? Perhaps it is to be expected that an aristocratic bishop whose country home was in Yorkshire should aspire to that see. As an Oxford doctor of divinity trained in royal chaplaincy under the patronage of the duke of Newcastle, his upward path looked easy, but thirteen years in a Welsh see was a long time to serve. Serving on Yorkshire road committees, however, does not amount to serious striving. He had absorbing interests in the worlds of law, diplomacy, and finance, like his elder brother Thomas, Viscount Dupplin, who represented the British government in Portugal. He showed no dissatisfaction with the supposed low income for a Welsh see, presumably because the income from his Yorkshire estates and his wife's inheritance was sufficient. It would be wrong to regard his thirteen years as bishop of St. Asaph as the work of one in "transit."[40] His association with Yorkshire was a natural development, and his regularity in attending at the House of Lords was a willingness to get on with appropriate business. It would have been, at the same time, natural for him to think that his patron had further plans for him.

Theology, Speeches, and Sermons

Drummond was a long way clear of the Enthusiasts. His distancing from the revivalists' ecstasies in the Holy Spirit was part of the mainstream fear of "this horrid thing," and he disliked what he called "canting"—the preaching that sometimes led to ecstasies. Enthusiastic preaching had become part of the Anglican scene in the pulpits of some of the evangelical clergy such as Venn, Atkinson, Conyers, and Furly, and Drummond was to hear one such sermon from Richard Conyers during his visitation (see Chapter 4). The moderate Calvinism of the early evangelicals, believing in justification by faith and final perseverance, though repudiating predestined reprobation, seemed to Drummond and the majority of his contemporaries to be a "compound of gloom and absurdity," as Walsh has explained.[41] The evangelicals were disliked also for their precision and Antinomianism and for their attachment to "perceptible inspiration," but Drummond was at one with them in abhorring Wesley's irregularity. He would have agreed with their condemnation of Wesley's doctrines of entire sanctification and perfectionism.

Drummond upheld the Bible as the authority for church governance, and we know from what he wrote himself in a *Letter on Theological Study,* published along with the *Memoirs,* that he thought the Bible "its own best expositor." The *Letter* was not intended for publication but was written as to the son of a friend who was about to take holy orders.

It is a simple guide, suggesting the most suitable edition—a quarto of 1715 with marginal references—and the need to read it attentively. He advised against using a commonplace book, "I should think to *digest* good materials is better than to *compile* many," and went on to give advice about preaching, "I need not tell you what effect a clear, sensible elocution has, for I hear you have that talent."

That talent of speaking well was one that Drummond used in politics and in pulpits, and he won a reputation as a preacher laureate under George II in 1743, after the battle of Dettingen, that was to lift him to the height of coronation preacher for George III in 1761. But it was politics that earned him royal admiration. He defended Andrew Stone, tutor to George, Prince of Wales, in a deposition to the Cabinet Council on 22 February 1753, on a charge of Jacobitism. Stone was Newcastle's protege, but Drummond was the friend who helped him. Stone read out his own denial of drinking the health of the Pretender, and the bishop of St. Asaph was called in:

> He has known Mr Stone intimately ever since 1728, before Mr Stone had any view of a publick employment, and at a time of life when he was most likely to be unguarded in his conversation. . . . He never heard at any time any words said . . . nor of any action done which had the least tincture of Jacobitism . . . During twenty five years acquaintance he is confident he has sound notions of the constitution of this country and the support of it under the present Royal Family than ever to have entertained a disaffected thought. he knows Mr Stone to be a man of great virtue and probity. . . . He believes the king has not a more faithful subject, and upon principle.[42]

He delivered this splendid defence with such energy and "warm feeling,"[43] that the king exclaimed, "That is indeed a man to make a friend of!" After this, at the time of the debates on the Jew Bill in 1753, Horace Walpole gave him credit[44] (and Walpole was the one who had invented the charge and fanned the case against Stone, though not admitting to that until later on in his memoirs).[45]

The text for the victory sermon on 7 July at Hanau in 1743 was Psalm 8, verse 5, "For thou hast made him a little lower than the angels, and hast crowned him with glory and honour." Aligning the king of England in Hanover with our Lord sounds daring. The choice would have been seen at the time as a loyal stroke, possibly but not necessarily bold. It came within the traditional view of the sovereign as the Lord's anointed. Sermons since the Restoration had presented King David as the antetype of Charles II. The royal and priestly union of the nature of sovereignty was a theme closely linked with the messianic attributes of Christ. It was clever rather than bold, political as much as patriotic. The patriotism was limited also by the fact that it was not preached in an English cathedral or abbey, but to the king of England and his soldiers in Hanover.

The message and delivery must have been acceptable—only the scripture text has survived—for Drummond was chosen subsequently to preach three parliamentary sermons. These were at St. Margaret's, Westminster, on 30 January 1747-48 (King Charles the Martyr); at Westminster Abbey, before the House of Lords, on 25 April 1749 (a general thanksgiving for peace); and again before the Lords a decade later on 16 February 1759 (a solemn fast). The Society for the Promotion of Christian Knowledge (SPCK) chose him as their preacher for the charity schools sermon on 26 April 1753, and on 15 February 1754 he preached at the anniversary meeting of the Society for the Propagation of the Gospel (SPG). Being the preacher on these occasions was another way in which he gained recognition as something more than the bishop of St. Asaph. He was Dr. Drummond, the House of Lords preacher. He was Bishop Drummond, who gave hearty encouragement on a bleak fast. He was the aristocratic bishop who won contributions when he preached for orphaned children.

Untouched by the evangelical urge to expound on a Gospel text or the crucicentric teachings of St. Paul, Drummond took Old Testament texts for all his six published sermons. Upholding the word of God as the supreme authority was a different matter from the salvationist preaching of the revivalists. Drummond's view of "the glad tidings of salvation,"[46] remained traditional, founded on the eighteenth-century church's unmiracular and unmystical experience. His own preaching would not have appealed to evangelicals such as Samuel Furly or George Burnett who were to work for him in the Yorkshire parishes in the next two decades, but they were working within an established church resistant to change. The sermon for the Westminster school children was unexceptional for the age. Though he gave a critical commentary on the inclination to luxury among his own class, there were no radical ideas in his propositions. He argued for the implicit continuation of the poor as a class, saying that their labor was vital to the existence of society. His main plea was that since their parents had been unable or unwilling to provide for these poor orphans in what he saw as an increasingly brutal society, it was the duty of capable Christians to provide for and educate them. The organizers of the charity schools must have been delighted with their choice of the bishop of St. Asaph as their preacher. Within the first minute of the sermon he made a reference to the work of the SPCK. He concluded by declaring that it was the duty of those present—to God and their country—to contribute their part "to cultivate virtue and truth, and industry among them [the children], and to promote their happiness here and hereafter."

Only in the SPG sermon was there a hint of controversy. Drummond gave much stronger fiber to his hearers on that occasion. He conveyed a message that was passionate and hearty for the missionaries in America: God depends on man for action. He set out three sections as Objects, Difficulties, and Resolutions. He asked a few rhetorical questions to make the members squirm a little. Then he allowed them a brief relaxation. The information he presented about the work of missionaries and the need of the colonial people was geared to strengthening the Anglican cause against that of other Christian endeavors especially of Roman Catholics. He upheld the word of God as the supreme authority. It was an outgoing sermon, direct and plain: "Can anyone, who believes the Gospel, doubt of his Duty to communicate the glad tidings of salvation to all his fellow-creatures?" Drummond shared the attitudes of those who felt a strong link with the Americans. He was aware of the fast pace at which the Americans were commercially prospering. He explained in the sermon that it was "absolutely necessary" for spiritual matters to keep pace with temporal ones. He was also alarmed by the amount of work not properly organized in church affairs for the people of the American colonies. He told his hearers that "much, very much remains to be done."

There was a lobby in opposition to the line that Drummond favored. Although he had spoken of the absence of parish structure in America and was realistic enough to see that the bishop of London's commission required further development, the idea never prospered (see chapter 7). In looking at America, Drummond half saw, writ large, a problem which was to develop in Yorkshire but which he yet did not see there:

> Many of our own people in the outward settlements who have not a Minister within 100 miles; men of 50 years old . . . have never seen an

> instructor . . . or any place of religious worship . . . [where no parishes have been established, no churches erected.]

He and his immediate successors were unable to apply to England what he unsuccessfully wished for in America—the building of an appropriate institutional structure for the Church of England to meet the needs of the people and the challenge of freelance missionaries and revivalists to the church's authority. Similarly with regard to black slaves in America he was a man of his time. He showed a compassion about "this strange traffick" and referred to Africa as having been dispeopled by Europeans' cruelty, but his conscience seems to have belonged to that easier age before ardor against the slave trade was stirred up by Wilberforce.

By the time that George III succeeded George II in 1760, Drummond was still bishop of St. Asaph. By the autumn of 1761, he was archbishop of York designate, the ideal choice to deliver the coronation sermon. Archbishop Secker has left a "very particular account" of the coronation[47] and Drummond's sermon identified for George III that monarchy implied duty and service.[48] All that Secker wrote about it was, "The sermon lasted about a quarter of an hour." The text was from I Kings X. 9: "Because the Lord loved Israel for ever, therefore made he thee King, to do judgment and justice."

The obedience of those ruled was upheld as obedience given by free men. He gave the new king plenty of advice, setting Solomon as the pattern of kingly justice, summoning loyalty from all ranks and urging the new king to be ever mindful of his coronation oath, "an obligation which George III never could, and never wished to escape."[49] At the age of fifty, Drummond had *gravitas* appropriate to solemnity without the doddering of an ancient or infirm prelate. He was insurance to the new reign as it inherited a foreign war which did not seem to be nearing its end. (He was fortunate not to have fallen foul of some of Secker's mismanagements of the service, such as the muddles about the reading and the weight of the Bible itself, the accident to the Dove, and the scrum for seating at the subsequent dinner.)

Just as the king was beginning his new reign, so Robert Drummond was ready to begin the most important period of his working life. His patron had it planned, but there were several difficulties to negotiate on the path to York during the year 1761, while Drummond was drafting that quarter-of-an-hour sermon.

Archbishop of York

Newcastle had made ecclesiastical affairs a special interest[50] during the time that Robert Drummond's career was advancing, deriving pleasure from the "game of preferment."[51] Making Drummond into the archbishop of York became the *articulis stantis aut cadentis*[52] of the church,[53] because his enemies had increased their influence so that he lost the game though Drummond won the prize. Drummond wrote his thanks to the duke on 20 April 1761 for his translation from the Welsh see to Salisbury. The idea of going to York from Salisbury was a pattern in Newcastle's plan. It had been what Archbishop Gilbert did. How to achieve it again for Drummond at a time of crisis was the problem. He launched the complicated scheme that Drummond should go from Sarum to London en route to York, and this annoyed Lord Bute as well as the king.[54]

Drummond was one among many who were poised for preferment during the summer of 1761, but his behaviour contrasts favourably with theirs. Samuel Squire, another of Newcastle's proteges, gained the bishopric of St. David's in 1761 through what his contemporaries despised as "the result of his great talent for self advancement." Drummond was direct but by no means desperate. As early as February 1761 he called on Lord Bute. He received an indirect answer, reporting to Newcastle that Bute "was very desirous to promote everything in his [Drummond's] favour and he would talk to his Grace about it." A rival candidate for York was Dr. Thomas Newton, who wrote to the duke on 7 August 1761: "The Archbishop of York lies a dying. . . . I beg, I hope, I trust your Grace's kindness will be shown to me who has long solicited your favour."[55] Sir William Ashburnham, then dean of Chichester, wrote a week later with a nearer grasp of affairs: ". . . the death of the bishops of York and London will probably occasion a vacancy at Salisbury by the promotion . . . of Dr. Drummond."[56]

However, Ashburnham did not get Salisbury. It was no good just hinting at one's wish for preferment if one was not really close to the patron. Samuel Squire's methods of self-advancement had to be used if one was neither well born nor part of Newcastle's highest schemes. Drummond did open his heart to the duke near the end of June, admitting that he wanted York most of all. This is the closest we get to seeing the inside of Drummond's hopes:

> This being the case, I must leave it to my best friends to act for me, as they judge the properest. I shall go to Lord Bute tomorrow to take

> my leave of him, and probably nothing will occur, which will give me an occasion to hint anything towards York; if there is, it will be delicate for me to speak about it, considering the great favour I have so lately received. At the same time, I must own fairly and if I did not own it, your Grace knows this to be my great point in life. I must refer myself to your judgement and friendship in the mode and success of the affair.[57]

As well as being so open to the duke in these hopes for the "great point in life," Drummond was preoccupied in August of that critical year by the tragic death of his cousin's son, so that the family concern took first place. He spent time with them at their home to try to comfort them in their loss, and used even more time describing their grief in several letters to Newcastle. The link between the fall of Newcastle and the appointment of the new archbishop of York at the end of the summer of 1761 occasioned more trouble for Newcastle and his opponents than it did for Drummond, who contained his ambition with patience.

Newcastle was obliged to resign in May 1762. The relationship between Newcastle and Drummond went in two phases after Drummond's appointment as archbishop of York. The first showed a detachment from 1762 to 1764. The second, from 1764 until the death of the duke in 1768, was a time when Drummond was the dominant figure, when Newcastle pleaded for news, visits, opinions about elections, and when Drummond responded to his grumbling and self-pity by indulging him. By that time the archbishop did not need a patron. He could and did stand alone.

Two of Drummond's predecessors in the mid eighteenth century went on from York to become archbishop of Canterbury. We may ask why a talented administrator such as Drummond remained at York when a vacancy arose at the death of Thomas Secker in 1768. The answer is partly connected with the fall of Newcastle, and it connects with another question about his not being preferred to Secker at the earlier vacancy of 1758, when Newcastle was at the height of his power. There is little doubt of Drummond's candidature for Canterbury in 1758, though scant attention has been paid to it. It was in 1753, as noted earlier, that Walpole had approved of Drummond's able eloquence in the House of Lords. He wrote subsequently,

> March 20th [1758] died Dr Hutton, Archbishop of Canterbury, after short possession of his see. The Duke of Newcastle had great inclination to give it to Dr Hay-Drummond, bishop of St Asaph, a gentleman,

> a man of parts, and of the world; but Lord Hardwicke's influence carried it for Secker, who certainly did not want parts or worldliness.[58]

The significance here is not the sour testimony of Walpole against Secker, for there are many such lines in his memoirs, but his reporting of Drummond as a possibility then for Canterbury. If Walpole knew Newcastle's mind in 1758, and this was hardly another of his inventions, then Drummond may have regarded himself as a serious candidate, but would also have recognized Secker as a much more experienced candidate. Drummond's one appointment was as bishop at St. Asaph. Secker had been bishop of Bristol and bishop of Oxford, important sees with special tasks. In addition to a more varied experience of appointment, Secker was a popular preacher. This reputation had begun when he was at St. James's, Piccadilly, and continued while he was dean of St. Paul's. His sermons were not only well attended, but also bought once published. Drummond did not seek to achieve that kind of reputation at all, and certainly had not acquired it by 1758. Ten years later, when the vacancy occurred again at Canterbury, the duke of Newcastle could only weave fantasies about it. He wrote on 4 August to Drummond, asking him to accept the position of archbishop of Canterbury, "putting aside all private considerations of comfort, ease, &c."[59] A week later, however, Newcastle wrote to the bishop of Lichfield, complimenting him on his promotion to Canterbury[60] and saying that he much approved the measure. He did not regard his letter to Drummond as a blunder. He was not in a position to offer him the primacy but had advised him to accept it if it were offered. Drummond must have known that Newcastle was deluded. From the evidence we have of Drummond's ambition in 1761 being admitted only to the duke,[61] it might not have mattered to him to read, "Your Grace is the only person who can fully supply the vacancy, . . . in that High and most material Station." Perhaps it was even a pleasure to know that that was what the duke was thinking then. To do the duke justice he did add, "If your Grace will not accept the Archbishopric, I wish the Duke of Grafton will give it to his friend, the Bishop of Lichfield. I dread a Fool there; pardon the expression." As patron, he had the last word in being more than a mite patronizing, "PS We beg our compliments and best wishes to Mrs Drummond, and all the promising young gentlemen, *Peter &c.*"[62]

As ecclesiastical protege made into prelate, their roles were reversed so that Drummond became the spiritual director and Newcastle the disciple. He recommended what the duke might like to read. The duke reported back what he had been reading.[63] The archbishop of York had no further need of a patron. He had been primate in the north for seven years and had progressed from St. Asaph to Salisbury to York in the space of one year of parliamentary records.

3

The Making of a Visitation

Canon Law and the Purpose of a Visitation

A visitation by a bishop of his diocese was, and still is, a formal matter. This did not make it a formality, for it required much effort. Letters of intent had to be sent to all the clergy of the diocese. The Articles of Enquiry had to have handwritten headings to the addressees, as did the cover letters. Besides the paper work, there was arduous traveling for many. A visitation disclosed the legal status of the clergy who were visited as well as the diligence of the bishop who conducted it. Drummond conducted three visitations during his time as bishop of St. Asaph, all of which were useful experiences which he drew on when he went to York. Full records for 1749 and 1753 survive[1] but the visitation returns for 1758 have not.

Bishops were required by Canon 60 of Canon Law to make a visitation in person every three years.[2] Keeping to Canon Law had practical advantages and a well-prepared visitation enabled a bishop to know his diocese; it gave him the satisfaction of keeping his clergy alert. It has the current advantage to us of showing Drummond as a working bishop. His visitation of 1764 was the last diocesan visitation of the clergy of York during the eighteenth century for which there are complete records. By the mid eighteenth century (as now) confirmations could not be done other than by a bishop. Visitations, however, could be done by archdeacons. If there was not a visitation by a bishop, then confirmation candidates would have to wait. Drummond was exemplary by eighteenth-century standards for continuing throughout his career to visit, to ordain, and to confirm.

Experience from St. Asaph

All Drummond's work at St. Asaph, where, as we have noted, he was his own archdeacon, prepared him for his subsequent holding of the important office of archbishop of York. His visitations of the diocese of St. Asaph in 1749, 1753, and 1758 did not comply with the canonical three-year rule, but were close to its spirit. The first visitation took place over three weeks at the end of the summer of 1749, and in April 1753 he again sent out letters purposing, "if it please God," to visit his diocese in the summer. The visitation that time centered on Trinity Sunday. The visitation of 1758 was at the Michaelmas season, planned in May, and undertaken in the first three weeks of September. Orderly organization became Drummond's hallmark, getting to know his clergy and keeping to earlier church custom, as in Burn's explanation,[3] by his choice of autumn for two out of the three visitations.

Patterns of Ordination and Confirmation at the Three Visitations

Before the visitation of 1749, Drummond held an ordination at the cathedral church of St. Asaph on Sunday, 13 August. An ordination service, according to the Book of Common Prayer, takes longer than most other liturgical services. This was a tough start to the schedule of visitation, but Drummond, being resident, had time on Monday to gather his energy for the visitation beginning on Tuesday in the deanery of Rhos. Some of the newly ordained deacons and priests might not have been required at the visitation and could have set off again for their homes. More confirmations were written into these three weeks than the process of visitation itself. Different places for the visitation were used in 1753. The ordinations on Trinity Sunday were at the center of the program. Confirmations were done at the visitation places.

The same triple pattern of confirmations and ordinations figured in the visitation of 1758. Three months were allowed to the clergy from the date of the bishop's letter announcing the visitation to his arrival to meet them at Pool on 3 September. Ordinations were held at the end of the schedule this time. Two days' recuperation for the bishop were written into the program at the end of the visitation before the ordinations. The route was different again on this third tour.

Energy and stamina were Drummond's natural assets. The variations in route and timing of the threefold tours offered him a fresh view of the same liturgical services. If Drummond himself were not the preacher at the services of confirmations and ordinations, he would have had to organize in advance who was to preach when and where. Acknowledgments of requests and agreements to preach would have been required. Drummond had to allow for all that in his timing. All these details of organization were valuable experience, recurring later as he masterminded the York visitation of 1764. The collect for Trinity Sunday, at the heart of the St. Asaph visitation, might have given him encouragement. It reads, "We beseech thee, that thou wouldest keep us stedfast in this faith, and evermore defend us." The pattern of varied routes is also explained by Burn in his *Ecclesiastical Law.* Instead of the first idea of bishops visiting parish clergy once a year, there "grew the custom of citing clergy and people to attend . . . at particular places."[4] Drummond was showing his careful attention to the requirements of the job.

Documentary Preparation: Layout and Appearance

Drummond studied and used other bishops' printed material. This is clear from a comparison of his collection of it in the Bishopthorpe papers, where his annotations and alterations show the lines of his thought.[5] William Fleetwood [St. Asaph, 1708–1714] and Anthony Ellis [St. David's, 1752–1761] gave him ideas on presentation. The three Welsh visitations increased what we would call today his communication skills, and their purpose was to find out how well the clergy were doing their jobs. Making the print size larger was one of his improvements on William Fleetwood's draft. Spacing out his own name—R O B E R T—in capitals and placing it centrally on the page was another way of making his impact. The phrase *Ordinary Visitation* was given a central place in different style type in the 1753 Articles of Visitation and Enquiry. The document was larger than the one sent by Bishop Fleetwood. If all this was not Drummond's own idea, then he had a printing adviser with a *nous* for personal presentation.

Studying others' papers for their printing styles was not necessarily an everyday skill of eighteenth-century churchmen. Once one has seen a draft, it is easy to make improvements. It is even easier if one has an eye for readability. Bishops were among those in eighteenth-century society who were the most frequent readers as well as writers. The educated lay clientele at coffee houses discussed what they read in journals available there but would not have much sustained writing to do apart from sending letters to the *Gentleman's Magazine* and would not have to draft intricate material for printing. The owners of great libraries—aristocrats and gentlemen—who actually read the books in them, as well as relaxed in there after a day's fishing, included the richer and higher clergy. Being accustomed day by day to reading was a fairly restricted activity in the mid eighteenth century, even allowing for the growth of basic literacy.[6] The clergy were high on the list of the reading members of society. Academic study, as different from merely occasional reading and writing, was one of the disciplines by which a clergyman could advance in a church career in Georgian England. Scrutiny of the detailed appearance of printed matter appealed to Drummond as well as study of the subject matter of his text. The existence of several drafts for the visitation papers used by Drummond points to the theory of his willingness to spend time on such detail. The notes are in his own handwriting.

Documentary Preparation: Subject Matter

Getting the message to his clergy was Drummond's task. He tackled this in two main ways: by directing his rural deans in the way he intended them to work; and by continuing his study of other bishops' visitation papers. Before he began to plan the official Articles of Enquiry, he wrote a letter to Dr. Worthington and other rural deans in his diocese of St. Asaph. The letter is dated 17 January 1748.[7] We have already noted his eye for detail in this matter as he required them "to be watchful and . . . from time to time" to tell him of any other things of "ecclesiastical cognisance." He expected an acknowledgement and a reply.

As with the layout, so with the content, Drummond studied the work done by other bishops who had sent out papers of enquiries before visitations. The questions to the parish clergy covered different ground from the topics given to the rural deans, and show that he had studied the differences in detail. Overlapping occurred only in the ordination dates and the questions about residence or nonresidence. Asking a brother bishop for his drafts was a purposeful act, requiring more effort than simply inheriting the papers of one's predecessors, so we may infer that Drummond made a special point of acquiring Fleetwood's inquiry text. But it was not difficult for bishops to collaborate. This is an example of their pastoral role in church governance. At the House of Lords they were seated together and voted together. The size of the episcopate made them a working group who knew each other. Allowing for those who were too elderly or too ill or too preoccupied to be always at the House of Lords, it was clearly a meeting point for many bishops to exchange policies. Theological and temperamental differences may have kept some apart, but Drummond contributed to solidarity in church governance by keeping a continuity in his Articles of Enquiry.

Early experience at York

Three years before his translation to York, Drummond undertook a confirmation tour in the York diocese for Archbishop Gilbert, just one month before his own last visitation of St. Asaph. It was not unusual for bishops of large dioceses to get help from colleagues, especially if they were too elderly or infirm to set out on difficult journeys. Sykes referred to help for bishops at ordinations[8] but not specifically to confirmation assistance, but his treatment of the threefold work of bishops implies outside help throughout. Jacob has written about the help that the bishops of the large dioceses of Lincoln and Norwich, as well as York, received in the task of confirming, although for Norwich there were no confirmation lists.[9] The letter that Archbishop Gilbert wrote to Drummond[10] from Bishopthorpe on 2 August 1758, suggests that Drummond had volunteered to help. There is evidence that Drummond made sound capital out of the experience, for he kept meticulous records of the confirmation tour that August in 1758. Just over a fortnight after he had received Archbishop Gilbert's letter, Drummond reported from Brodsworth that the work had been accomplished. He added speed to efficiency:

> I have the satisfaction of informing your Grace that I finished the Confirmation last Monday so early as to get home in the evening from Sheffield. Everything passed with great ease and order at all the places.

He was pleased to tell Gilbert the figures,

> The numbers, so far as we could count them, were these . . .

at Doncaster abt	2000
Wakefield	5000
Leeds	5000
Sheffield	3000
	15000

> I don't believe there was a hundred difference more or less. I have some lists, but in the populous towns it was impossible to receive them. The persons concerned in the different towns kept great order. The Constables and Churchwardens all attended and everything was well conducted. Your Grace will give me leave to hint to you that you would make it still safer to yourself and others, if you could confirm at more places. As for example:
> Hatfield as well as Doncaster,
> Sheffield: Rotherham and Barnsley

Wakefield and Pontefract
Leeds and Wetherby.
Fewer numbers in a place, and frequent confirmations will bring only the proper persons before you: and bring all into a juster sense of this reasonable institution.

Yrs R Asaph.

The lists are with the letter[11] in order in the Borthwick papers, and the fact that Drummond had made them, and kept hold of them, not sending them on with his letter to Archbishop Gilbert, suggests that a confirmation tour may have been a good way of getting to look at a piece of possible preferment. The lists have marks and clergy names added. There is a pretty little stitched printed booklet with a decorative page heading pattern, entitled

INSTRUCTIONS
concerning
CONFIRMATION[12]

It measures 16 by 10cm, has twelve pages, and is next to two in handwriting[13]—one certainly Drummond's hand—with a few crisper alterations to the printed booklet. The eye for detail covered more lists of confirmations and stayed briefly to note that "James Kilner not in priest's Orders nor licenced." The lists are on pocket or sleeve-sized papers, folded into slips measuring 20 by 8cm, characteristic of the busy administrator.

Gilbert's letter of thanks was prompt (19 August) but pitiful:

> I continue very weak and lame; and I confess my Spirits are not proof against continual Alarms of Gravel . . . such numerous assemblies of people. . . . The noise and hurry is commonly the most disagreeable part which your Lordship's method is certainly extremely well calculated to prevent. . . . It would contribute also very much to the same end if the people in general were so well informed of the nature of the ceremony itself as to be serious and in earnest about it, which of course would give their minds another turn and make them not barely quiet and peaceable, but attentive . . . whenever I have the pleasure of meeting your Lordship, anything you may have by you prepared for this purpose.[14]

It contrasts strongly with the organized and hearty approach of Drummond. If one were not sure that Drummond was a straightforward clergyman, it might read as out of order that he should tell the archbishop of York how to plan a confirmation more economically. Suggesting improvements in the method of doing the business is an example of the amiability that characterized Robert Drummond's approach to people and life. Gilbert had his own labor-saving idea for the laying on of hands, dealing with candidates at the altar in batches,[15] and he accepted Drummond's advice without taking offense.

There is another prop for the thought that Drummond was making a career reconnaissance, in that it sounds as if Gilbert and Drummond were not closely acquainted in person. Helping out a senior colleague who was a personal friend would be a kind gesture. Helping out a senior colleague whom he scarcely knew would be to put duty at a fairly exalted level if he were not going to find it personally advantageous. It may be argued that the Drummond estates at Brodsworth made it easy for him to cover the bareness of ambition, and also that some neighborly acquaintance was likely. It may alternatively be argued that Drummond genuinely wished to be helpful. Some bishops then did not even travel to their own dioceses for years after consecration, let alone undertake tours of confirmation in the diocese of a superior, be he never so pitifully decrepit. Even if Drummond was not doing positive career planning in the modern sense, his work in August 1758 for Archbishop Gilbert subsequently served him very well, and it illustrates his capacity for doing a job thoroughly. He was a man whose mind was never far away from his work, even while playing cards.[16] He kept the lists[17] with his notes and he earned Gilbert's thanks. He added to his knowledge of some of the most populous towns of the York parishes, and he and Archbishop Gilbert had the satisfaction of complying with Canon Law.

Preparation for the York Visitation

Articles of Enquiry

Drummond's planning was thorough. A man who could do a double duty of visitation in two different dioceses in the heat of two summer months could undoubtedly put together a package for the visitation of a prestigious diocese in the space of two and a half years. Coupled with his correspondence and the new look for the terriers, the 1764 visitation emerges as the most significant of the century.

After Fleetwood's and Ellis's material, Drummond went on to look at Archbishop's Gilbert's papers to churchwardens, but his main new study was of Archbishop Herring's Articles of Enquiry. Tradition governed his decisions. Drummond's Articles of Enquiry are reproduced in full in an appendix. He mostly kept to the same format as Herring. An exception was to omit the question about the laity having to give in their names beforehand if they intended to communicate. This was an outdated requirement.[18] The forms of the questions were otherwise exactly the same from numbers one to six, but Drummond included at Q4 some details about augmentations. Drummond's eleventh question was about additional chapels and their state of repair and staffing and was in line with his growing interest in buildings and accommodation.

Archbishop Herring had allowed four and a half months, from early May until Michaelmas, for answers to his questions. Drummond allowed three months. Although allowing less time to the parish clergy, dealing briskly with them did not misfire. Perhaps his reputation and character could be relied upon to command their immediate attention. As an aristocrat with a European outlook and a Yorkshire home and family, he came among them as a former royal chaplain and coronation preacher; his attested amiability and full family life were the positive influences that led several of the clergy to write letters of welcome and 621 of them to send their returns to the visitation. Drummond was a different style of prelate from Herring, whose life had encompassed only Wisbech for schooling, less than two miles away from his father's rectory at Walsoken in Norfolk, and the short distance from there to Cambridge, where his studies from B.A. to M.A., from B.D. to D.D. had not been laced with any experience abroad.

Drummond was the fourth archbishop in the lifetime of some of the clergy to conduct a visitation. Many of the clergy who replied to Drummond had been in office when they had had Herring's questions twenty-one years earlier. Irritation as age hardened them, or casual ease as age had mellowed them, meant that they answered the questions accordingly, but they may have been softened by Drummond's more succinct cover letter when they realized that they had to do it all again. Drummond also wrote to the preachers for the places on the visitation route. Preaching to other clergy was not always agreeable to parsons in the eighteenth century. Although sermons were a vivid means of communication then at parish level,[19] a visitation was a different matter, as some who wished for advancement sought the limelight and others without confidence shunned it.

Newspaper Advertising

Drummond advertised services in the *York Courant*. This is a further example of his responsible regard for his diocesan duty. He was different from the bishops who found the crowds on confirmation days more wearisome than the travel itself.[20] He had advertising notices printed for the confirmation tours of 1763, and he did the work in three stages in May, June and August. His first tour covered Halifax, Bradford and Leeds; then he went to Malton, Scarborough, Thirsk and Stokesley; his third tour was to Weighton, Beverley and Hull. It was six years since he had confirmed in Leeds for Gilbert, so he recognised it as the most populous town in the diocese. His notice commanded the centre of the front page of the paper for the issue of 19 April 1763. There were also follow up notices. Ordinations were similarly advertised.

Filling in the Forms

Part of the business of the visitation was checking the validity of the clergy's titles. Drummond devoted time to considering how the titles themselves were granted. For this he had guidance from some of the provisions made by Thomas Herring when he was archbishop of Canterbury. Special use of words was needed for applying to be a deacon or priest, or be instituted to a benefice. Getting the right details in the right places on the right form was important as much in drafting the form as eventually in completing it. Drummond tackled the spacing and the wording in the forms for a **Title for Orders** and for a letter **Testimonial for Holy Orders.** One might find fault with the drafting in that it did not leave quite enough space for the entries to fit in between the printed text without being submerged. But as an example of official forms at a time when one could not just go to the post office and collect several forms from the shelf, it is of remarkable quality. Drummond devoted more care to the presentation of a letter of testimonial for a deacon than he did for a priest. Presumably it was better to guard against a mistake at the beginning of admitting a candidate for holy orders than later on. Drummond was aware of the importance of spelling out the requirements. Some of the details, for example, had to be adapted from the Herring originals. One very important form had in it the guarantee of pay for curates. The person employing the curate had to sign the form that said, ". . . [I] do promise to allow him the yearly sum of . . ." Getting the right information on to the forms included getting a signed statement upholding the doctrine of the Church of England.

Lecturers and schoolteachers had to have license forms.[21] A lecturer had to be in deacon's and priest's orders first. He had to be elected to a particular lectureship. He had to bring the certificate to prove his election to show to the bishop. In the presence of the bishop he had to read the Thirty-nine Articles. He was given three months after the award of the lectureship to make a declaration of conformity to the liturgy of the Church of England. It is not clear whether the declaration had to be in the substance of one of his lectures or whether it could be written and sent to the bishop or posted in the church where he lectured. The testimonial for a lecturer also had in it the guarantee against teaching anything contrary to the doctrine of the Church of England. This was especially ironic in Drummond's situation. While he was preparing the forms for use at his visitation, Francis Blackburne, archdeacon of Cleveland, was known to be seriously diverging from the church's orthodox doctrine.

Teaching the right doctrine to schoolchildren was strongly safeguarded in theory in the mid eighteenth century. The archbishop included the regulations *Concerning Schoolmasters* in his forms while preparing for the visitation. A schoolmaster had to read the Thirty-nine Articles in the bishop's presence and had to subscribe to the relevant clauses in the Articles and Canon Law. He had to swear the oaths of allegiance and supremacy and to declare conformity. At days of visitation he was required to attend and exhibit his license. The regulations related to a shrinking section of the reality, however. The growth of petty or private schools and the changes in some charity schools[22] meant that an area of unlicensed teaching was spreading. No provision was made for the licensing of a woman teacher, for although the form had the word *person* the provision was amplified with the pronoun *he*. The legal and social position of women ruled out the idea that anything significant could be taught or learned in schools organized by women. This attitude was characteristic of the age. The activities of women teachers of the eighteenth century remain mainly in obscurity. Drummond, as a man of his times, would not have given this idea any thought. He was preoccupied with fraudulent clergymen and unsuitable applicants.

The Formal Letter to the Bishops before the Visitation

Drummond succeeded in improving on the **Letter to the Bishops** that Archbishop Gilbert had sent in 1759. The improvements are considered on the basis of value judgments of communication skills. First, he complimented the recipients. He paid regard to the status of the bishops by giving much more prominence to them as recipients in his title page. He spaced out his reference to them as LORDS BISHOPS.

Second, he increased the message of his own authority. Instead of the fancy but anonymous pattern in printing that Archbishop Gilbert had used on the letter, Drummond had the crossed keys authority symbol of York printed in the lower center of the page. He had YORK spelled out below the crossed keys, in case anyone had missed the point. Third, he had already obtained their agreement to the measures contained in the letter; the printed letter was a formal reminder. Fourth, he put them under a little pressure by referring to doing his duty and obliging them to remember to do theirs. With all this improvement Drummond used the text of the formal letter that had been used before his time.

The Questions to Churchwardens

Drummond intended to make no changes to the process of old and new churchwardens swearing their oaths. He had the letter to churchwardens used by Archbishop Gilbert. A list of eight other items were in the letter. There seems to be no order of importance in the items either to the modern mind or to what might have been important to the eighteenth-century mind. Three topics relate especially to the character of the age. One was the behavior of the ecclesiastical officers who came to the parish. The churchwardens were asked whether these officers suppressed or delayed prosecutions, whether they accepted bribes, whether they delivered the Articles of Visitation properly, and whether any fee was taken for that delivery. This, to the modern reader is healthy stuff for an age of gaming, bribery, bravado, sporting brutality, and chance.

The second topic was the questions put to churchwardens about their own clergyman. These repeated some of the questions put to the clergyman himself. Was he resident? Did he preach one sermon at least every Sunday? Did he celebrate Holy Communion at least three times each year? Did he instruct the youth by catechism? Did he have a curate to help him? Was there a lecturer in the parish? The difference was that the churchwardens were given only enough space to write either yes or no. There were some other questions about the incumbent that did not occur on the Paper of Queries. The churchwardens were asked bluntly whether their rector or vicar was "pious and exemplary" and whether he read the proper prayer before the sermon, whether he visited the sick and buried the dead, and whether the parish registers were kept properly.[23]

The third topic in character with the age was about church repairs. The clergy of that time were generally horrified by the thought of having to organize church repairs. A recent study has argued that church repairs were a sort of litmus paper for people's generosity or meanness in the post Reformation centuries.[24] A contributor to the *Gentleman's Magazine* described churches as "kept like swine-flies; the floors broken up, the windows broken down. . . . Yet there are such things called visitations. . . . Let visitation duty be enforced."[25] If Drummond saw that issue of the magazine he must have felt reassured about doing his duty.

Legal Details: A Loophole and an Alteration

Pluralism was a commonplace feature of church life in the eighteenth century (see Chapter 5). Archbishop Drummond included the same loophole for it that Herring had left. A clergyman was forbidden "to serve more than one church in One Day, except that chapel be a member of the parish church or united thereunto; and unless the said church or chapel, where such Ministers shall serve them in Two Places, be not able in your judgement to maintain a Curate."

Clergy dress is not often mentioned in the Drummond papers. Thomas Herring had directed that the

> clergy . . . wear their proper habits agreeably to the Canons, and to that decency in apparel which is proper to distinguish the Ministers of Almighty God, and to preserve them to an outward Reverence and Estimation.

Archbishop Gilbert had not altered the rule in the *Directions* about clergy dress. Drummond deleted this rule in his draft and wrote instead, "The clergy are to be ready with their exhibits to deliver them in as they are called over before their archbishop." This distinguishes him as different from his predecessors, recognizing that the clergy by the mid eighteenth century had little wish to be seen as being different from other gentlemen. F. C. Mather confirms this idea of Drummond, identifying him as the aristocratic archbishop noticed by the high churchman William Cole as walking about without his gown and cassock, and "habited in every respect like a layman."[26]

The Process of the Visitation

Preliminaries

1764 was a busy year for the Anglicans of Yorkshire. The Exhibit Book[27] sets out the program of the three months of the archbishop's visitation, starting with the archdeaconry of Nottingham on 30 April, going on to Newark on 2 May, and to Retford on 4 May. Before the Nottingham archdeaconry was visited, however, there had been business to accomplish at the Chapel Royal in Whitehall,[28] where Drummond undertook ordinations on 8 and 15 April, in the course of which he declined to ordain the former slave trader, John Newton. Newton had been befriended by some Yorkshire evangelical Anglicans and also by John Wesley, and their advice about seeking ordination set him on a course that led to two refusals from the bishop of Chester, one from the archbishop of Canterbury, and two from two different archbishops of York. The bishops' unwillingness came from a mixture of their unadventurous attitude (and their secretaries') to an ordinand whose qualifications were different from usual, and of their rigid regard for the system they served. Drummond's withholding of ordination to Newton, passing him on finally to the bishop of Lincoln,[29] was in line with the uncompromising rules of procedural behavior between bishops and reveals the intractable face of the eighteenth-century church as it was governed by its traditions, particularly as these were interpreted by episcopal secretaries. The early part of the episode so enraged Wesley that he called it "a mere farce" and "so poor an evasion."[30] The encounter with Drummond in 1764 (or rather with his secretaries, who shielded the archbishop from the former slave trader), was a harsh disappointment for Newton after six years of seeking ordination, a setback lifted only by the intervention of the earl of Dartmouth.[31] Newton learned that rules and social protocol were stacked against the lowly man but that an aristocratic bishop deferred to an aristocratic earl.[32] Drummond's part in the episode was slight, a formality probably dismissed from mind directly, and although he withheld ordination because it was "his duty to demur—he could not do it with propriety," he wrote a reply directly, which Newton took back by hand to the earl, recommending that Newton should apply to the bishop of Lincoln[33] as the parish to which the earl intended to present Newton was in the diocese of Lincoln.

Drummond fitted in some business with commissions about land on 10 April, and his last attendance at the House of Lords was on

13 April. That left him about a fortnight to put everything together for the journey northwards to the York diocese.

The Visitation Routine

Reconstructing a day's business on a Drummond visitation reveals the value of his careful preparation. The time spent getting the print styles right, sending the letters out to the right people, altering small but important details would have let him sit back to listen to the sermon being preached before the day's work of ticking and checking. He was the man in charge who would have considered that if any hitch occurred, it could hardly have been prevented.

Apart from the sermons, there is little specific information about who sat or stood where, who called for whom and with whose assistance, who wrote, who ticked, who scrutinized and who approved. We have to guess at meetings of eye to eye between archbishop and curates. Did elderly clerics bend to kiss the metropolitan's ring? Would there have been a brotherly kiss to melt the ceremony or formality? Were there any handclasps and reminiscences between former university acquaintances? Was Drummond actually there in state throughout the procession of clergy summoned one by one to be presented to their visitor? It can hardly have been an inspection in the style of a guard of honor with a glazed survey by the one over the ranks of the others in an attentive line-up. The surest picture, as one builds upon the cross-referenced papers and what Drummond had required about the clergy being "called over" (see above under "Legal Details"), is of the archbishop seated in full view, a place for the chaplains and secretaries with their lists[34] for checking. The checking can be authenticated. It was done on three very large parchments, with seals and affixed statements. The parchment lists include the non-returning parishes and the names of the clergy who were excused, some of whom are known to us from their letters of apology.

The Itineraries of the Visitation

Map 1 shows the presumed itinerary. The program, which has the touch of Drummond's careful organization, was set out in the Court Book as follows:

> Monday 7 May 1764 at Doncaster 8 am–12 noon
> George Hatfield, V of Doncaster preached
> This was the beginning of the primary Visitation . . . and all and

singular Rectors, Vicars and so forth living and abiding within the Archdeaconry aforesaid . . . to appear on the days hours and at the places . . . specified . . . to undergo the Visitation.

Wednesday 9 May 1764 at Rotherham 8 am–12 noon
Rev Mr John Griffith of Treeton preached

Friday 11 May 1764 at Wakefield 8 am–12 noon
Rev Mr Thomas Hudson, Curate of Idle preached

Saturday 12 may 1764 at Leeds 8 am–12 noon
Rev Mr Godfrey Wolley, Vicar of Wistow preached

Monday 14 May 1764 at Skipton 8 am–12 noon
Rev Mr Henry Wilson, Rector of Slaidburne preached

Wednesday 16 May 1764 at Ripon 8 am–12 noon
Rev Dr John Fogg, preb. of Ripon preached

Friday 18 May 1764 at York 8 am–12 noon
Rev Mr Guy Fairfax, Curate of Bilbrough preached

Wednesday 20 June 1764 at Beverley 8 am–12 noon
Rev Mr Francis Best, Rector of S Dalton preached

Thursday 21 June 1764 at Hull 8 am–12 noon
Rev Mr Arthur Robinson, Vicar of Holy Trinity, Hull, preached

Saturday 23 June 1764 at Scarborough 8 am–12 noon
Rev Mr Henry Egerton, Rector of Settrington preached

Monday 25 June 1764 at Malton 8 am–12 noon
Rev Mr Conyers, Rector of Kirby Misperton preached

Wednesday 27 June 1764 at Thirsk 8 am–12 noon
Rev Mr Daniel Addison, Curate of Thirsk preached

Friday 29 June 1764 at Stokesley 8 am–12 noon
Rev Dr Francis Wanley preached.[35]

The only hitch to these events concerned the preacher at the final place. A note in the archbishop's hand has, "By mistake, Mr Deason, never had my notice and was not prepared: but Dr Wanley preached." The archbishop had the freedom to decide the times for departures but was at the mercy of other people's lateness or illness. There is a memo in the archbishop's hand,

> To write to Dr Sharp that I shall finish my Visitation at Stokesley Friday 29 June and from thence go to Durham from whence I can set out Monday July 2. I thought to confirm at Hexham Wed July 4. But I desire his advice how to shape my journey and fix my time for that and the Consecration of ye chapel at W[etherby?] . . . I shall not be

confined in time, having done all my business, but the times must be fixed as far as can be conveniently.[36]

This shows that he was prepared to make the fullest possible use of the journey, not sparing himself in the height of summer, but taking an interlude between the end of May and the middle of June. John Wesley, who was touring the county of Yorkshire on his sixteenth visit since 1742, also took a two-month break. A comparison of these two tours of the diocese and county by two great church leaders indicates their priorities for places to visit and stay, where these coincided, and where they differed. Wesley's likely itinerary is drawn on Map 2.

Wesley and Drummond had similar reasons for undertaking their tours in 1764. Each viewed the tour as a necessary duty. Each was carrying out an audit of work being done. Each expected to find old friends and known colleagues getting on with the work. Each was prepared to deal with any irregularity, though the archbishop could command long-established authoritative machinery to put right unsatisfactory situations. Their methods of touring were similar, too. Allowing for traveling times, one or two days at each stopping point were necessary for the archbishop to complete his visitation processes. Wesley sometimes managed two places in one day. He would arrive in the morning to preach, ride on in the afternoon to the next site, and after preaching a sermon, was ready the next morning to set off. (The last part of his journey, from Halifax to Huddersfield, must have been the most pleasant, for he recorded that he met Mr. Venn, who rode with him from Halifax to Huddersfield.)

The similarities in the choice of places to visit are set out in the following table:

Itineraries of Wesley and Drummond in Yorkshire in 1764

WESLEY		DRUMMOND	
28 March	Sheffield		
30 March	Rotherham		
31 March	Doncaster		
10 April	Hull		
11 April	Beverley		
12 April	Pocklington		
12 April	York		
16 April	Thirsk		
17 April	Helmsley		

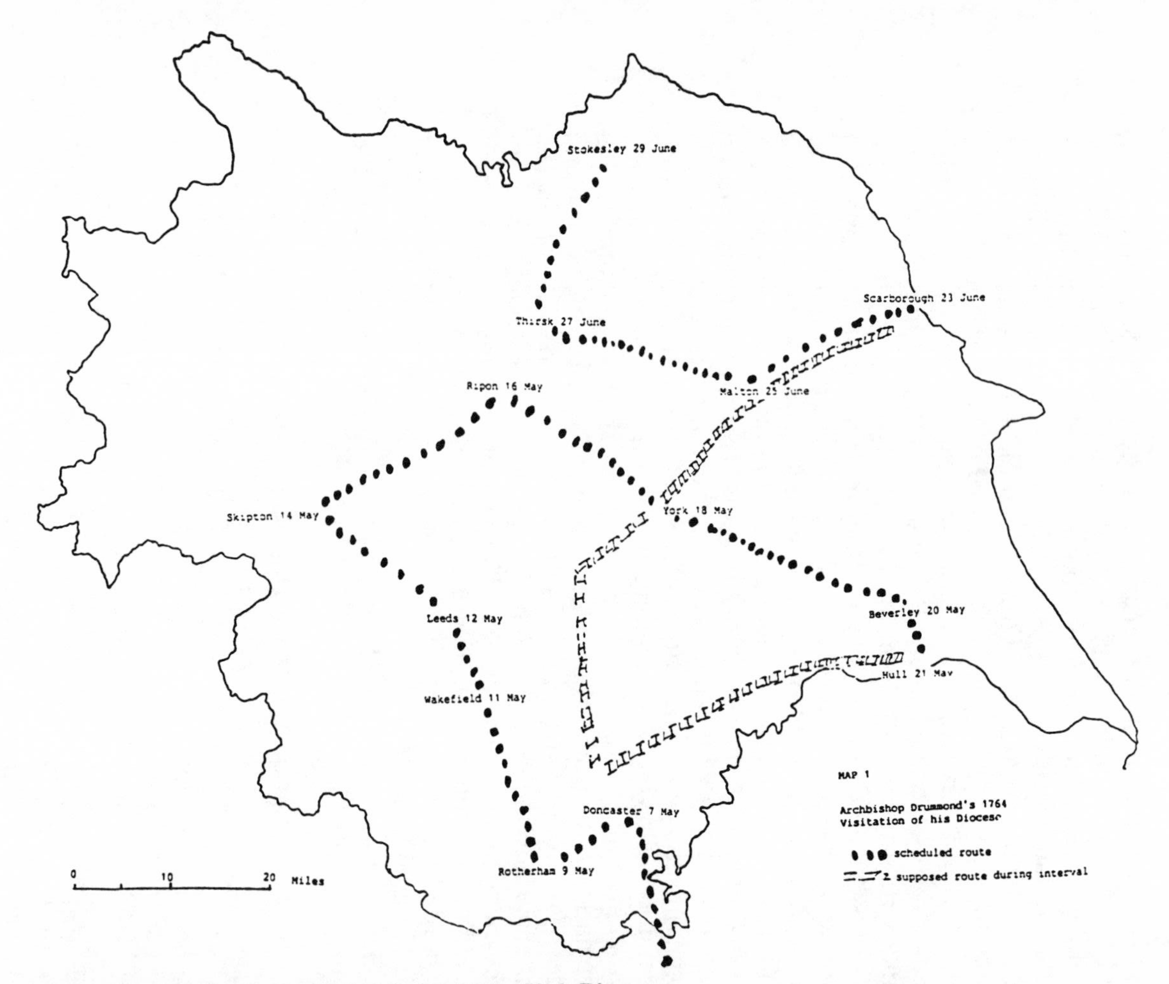

Archbishop Drummond's 1764 visitation of the York Diocese

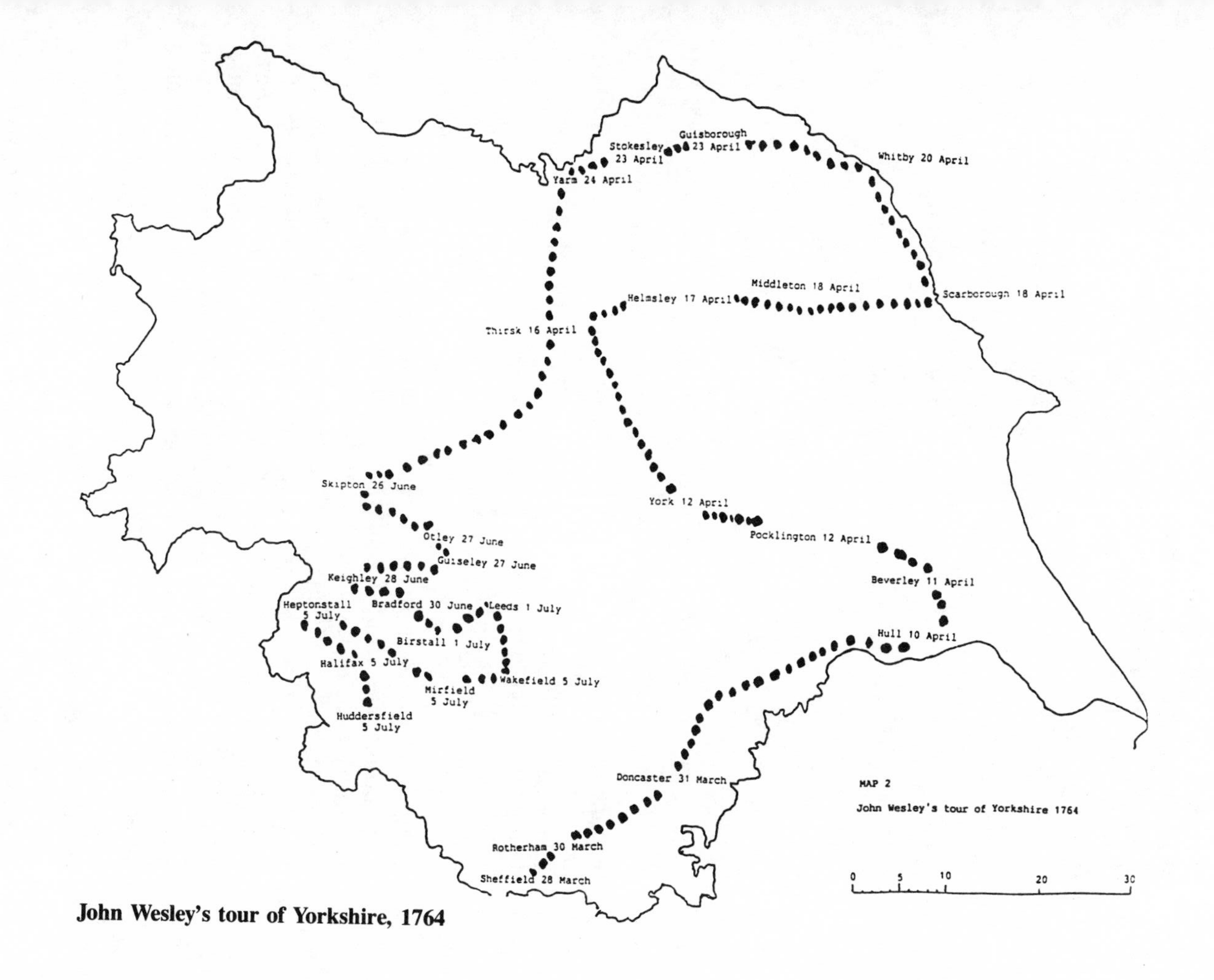

John Wesley's tour of Yorkshire, 1764

18 April	Middleton		
18 April	Scarborough		
20 April	Robin Hood's Bay		
23 April	Guiseborough		
23 April	Stokesley		
24 April	Yarm		
		[4 May	Retford]
		7 May	Doncaster
		9 May	Rotherham
		11 May	Wakefield
		12 May	Leeds
		14 May	Skipton
		16 May	Ripon
		18 May	York
		20 May	Beverley
		21 May	Hull
		23 June	Scarborough
		25 June	Malton
26 June	Skipton		
27 June	Otley & Guiseborough	27 June	Thirsk & Hexham
28 June	Keighley		
		29 June	Stokesley
30 June	Bradford		
1 July	Birstall		
1 July	Leeds		
5 July	Wakefield & Dewsbury		
5 July	Halifax & Huddersfield		

Omissions in the tour from what might have been expected of Drummond are Halifax and Huddersfield. Halifax was the largest parish by area in the diocese, and George Legh, the vicar, was of an appropriate scholarly and social standing to make a stop in Halifax acceptable, but we know that Drummond had already been to Halifax for confirmations in the previous year. Huddersfield was perhaps less accessible. Tradition may have determined the route, but we know from Drummond's advice to Archbishop Gilbert in 1758 that he was not so traditional that he could not alter a schedule.

Examining the Clergy

The main purpose of the visitation was to audit the health of the church by collecting what the clergy wrote about the parishes and chapelries, and by examining their credentials. Although the checking was a formal process, it was the opportunity for the archbishop to match faces to names and to be seen doing so. The church took responsibility for its appointments, and a visitation demonstrated its sincerity.

Verifying the Testimonials

The clergy who arrived at the visitation to exhibit their orders would already have established their suitability as clergymen. Names, address, a certificate of age, and a testimonial to be sent in twenty days beforehand were required from candidates for holy orders. Witness to the good character of applicants had to come from three signatories "who really do know the person," in the place where they lived if they were at a distance and had left the university for "any considerable time." The gravamen of the testimonial was underlined bitterly for those who found out too late that they had written too hastily or had been misled or deceived. Their letters of apology to bishops were often aggrieved and full of irritation. Rejection of a candidate on grounds of immorality had to be made within one month of application. Bishops wrote to each other to guard against the poor testimonial or the imperfect one or even the perjured or forged one. The possibility of an unsuitable man being ordained was not just an imagined worry. Of course, the good man duly appointed could then be led astray. That was an ordinary risk and did not involve retrospective criticism of bona fide signatories. An unsatisfactory curate was being warded away from the diocese of Lichfield during the final stage of Drummond's visitation of York. The archbishop had to write four letters in June 1764 about this man, who had fathered a child in Leeds. But if a man had been disciplined and even debarred from the ministry, there was still the threat that he might attempt reentry into an appointment in another diocese. The case of the notorious Henry Perfect, who lost his testimonials in circumstances so suspiciously careless that the two archbishops wondered how he had got them in the first place (see chapter 7), illustrates why Drummond took visitations so seriously. He knew that time spent in his visitation could minimize disaffection, promote respect, discover inefficiency, and strengthen the ties of Christian observance throughout each individual parish.

So the clergy were reminded that they had to get their licenses and testimonials out of their cupboards and be ready to exhibit them on the day.

Examining the Terriers

As well as sending in the returns to the Articles of Enquiry, the clergy also had to bring the parish terriers for scrutiny at the visitation. Although the articles included a question about charitable provision, the terriers contained detailed information about the parsonages, church furnishings, plate, bells, and other materials. Archbishop Drummond raised the status of the terriers as legal documents, by directing that they should be written on more substantial pieces of parchment, and by requesting even more detailed information on them. A study of their importance is included in the next chapter.

Following up Afterwards

The archbishop's correspondence shows how the archbishop followed up afterwards the issues that arose during the conversations he had. But his opportunities to discipline any erring clergy were limited, and his prevailing amiability took away much of the sting of criticism. The case of James Hampton,[37] absentee incumbent of Moor Monckton, illustrates that the process of law for one who failed to appear in person did not necessarily bring fierce censure. Hampton was charged with his failure to appear at the visitation and compounded this by carping about the fees claimed by court officials; he also complained about the behavior of one of the officials who dealt with him about his terrier. Drummond was mild in his reply, "I am no friend to fees, but they must attend office and business must be done by Office." He went on to make a different point:

> I wish you would reside, for it would be agreeable to all that would be near you. If you do not, let me advise you not to make the Indulgence given to you an inlet for bickerings which are really beneath you and there would be none of these sort of slips to common business.

It was a clever tone to take, and it was this very mildness that drew an apology from Hampton: "I am sorry to think . . . [that I was] in the least degree offensive. . . . If I had been resident [I could have] obeyed any orders," although he explained that the "irregular and unjustifiable" conduct of the officers "hurried me perhaps into a greater warmth of temper than was consistent with . . . maintaining quietness and order."

As to the matter of residence, he said that he would "return into Yorks . . . soon after Christmas," but not for long because,

> . . . the situation of the parish, cold and aguish and covered with water during a great part of the winter, and the condition of the Parsonage house. . . . such that no expense can render it a decent habitation . . . [I could] never make it a place of continual residence.

So Hampton had got away with absence from the visitation, persistent absenteeism in the living that he was appointed to serve, and suffered only a mild rebuke from the archbishop. Drummond had shown some concern for regulation and good order but saw no need for reformation.

A personal encounter during the visitation process puzzled one clergyman, who may have been overawed by the archbishop at the moment of their meeting, so he wrote soon after when he realized what the archbishop had meant. This was William Preston of Crathorne, who had been questioned about Roman Catholics, a topic in which Drummond was always interested. Preston's letter[38] of 21 September, admitted that he "gave no satisfactory answer, not then recollecting, or perhaps not well understanding the nature and drift of it." Drummond appears to have thought that Roman Catholicism might have been spreading among servants employed in Roman Catholic households in a neighboring parish who were then sent to Crathorne as a sort of hiding place, "as to an Assylum, to be screened from notice." When he questioned Preston about this, Preston remembered that a Protestant maidservant had gone to Yarm previously and had "come back a Papist" but explained that "no body ever persuaded her . . . [she] had been a convert near half a year before. . . . If this, my Lord, was what you alluded to . . . [I am] heartily sorry."

He went on to ask a favor, whether he could have leave to live six miles away from Crathorne to be near a physician, assuring the archbishop that he would not be inattentive and had a resident curate. So what Drummond tried to learn by asking an obscure question led to yet another absentee incumbent. He may have had in mind the Roman Catholic presence at Rudby, where they were listed at twenty-three Roman Catholic families in 1743—but that figure has been subsequently seen as referring to persons and not families. Yarm and Rudby were also significant as places where Methodist societies had been formed, but the archbishop was not then so concerned about that.

The Visited

The Clergy: Long-Standing Incumbents

There were forty-eight parishes where clergymen were still in office at the 1764 visitation who had been there for the 1743 visitation. Of these forty-eight, there were twelve who had been inducted before 1720 and thirty-six whose inductions were between 1720 and 1743. Some of the most elderly were among those who sent in apologies for nonattendance on Archbishop Drummond. The oldest clergyman of all was Nicholas Gyrling of Newton Kyme, who had been ordained deacon and priest in 1702 and 1703. He sent excuses and sent his exhibits. Some of these elderly incumbents had curates to attend for them, but they all had to complete the Paper of Queries before the visitation and deliver it beforehand if they did not attend on the day.

The Clergy: The Absentees

Poor health was the main reason. Living at a distance was another reason, usually because of plural holdings. Some of the letters had thin excuses. Robert Fisher, from Bolton upon Dearne, had had "rheumatism last week." Pierrepoint Cromp and John Jones lived as far away from Yorkshire as Kent and Sussex respectively. Cromp had no intention of altering his absentee way of life, which centered on his wife being the only daughter of a JP in Kent. Jones lived 220 miles away from his parish of Darrington, but promised the archbishop that, "very shortly, God willing and without fail," he would be "down in Yorkshire." He added that there were "not above 60 houses or families, 40 of which, if not more, are only cottages, and the Inhabitants but thin and few."

This statement naturally provoked the archbishop to find out more about the cure of souls in Darrington. It was characteristic of him that he showed no irritation with Jones but was furious with the curate who had been left to look after the impoverished parishioners there. A note in his own hand reads,

> Mr Dade [the curate] was not at the Visitation -non Lic^{d}—does not reside—knows nothing of Jones and is idle. He . . . .^{d} me [the text is not clear] and I privately admonished him to mend his conduct. . . . . . . till Mr Jones comes who corresponded from Lewes.

So Dade had the blame for unsatisfactory ministry in Jones's absence, and Jones had won credit simply by his correspondence.

Six excuses in one letter came from John Carne, for not attending at the Nottinghamshire part of the visitation. He was too late, his father had died, he did not know what the appointed time was, he had a large family and two parishes to look after, and the former curate and churchwardens were to blame for not delivering his answers on the Paper of Queries. Carne had been advised by the archdeacon that he ought to have a curate who was resident. The archbishop made no comment on this letter.

The Clergy: The Conscientious

Getting to know his clergy as individuals was made easier for Drummond when some took the initiative and wrote to him. He had been archbishop for just one month when George Legh from Halifax wrote to him. It sounds as if Legh had already made a personal call on Drummond to pay his respects. This was socially the custom. They must have talked about Legh's large parish. The topic particularly was confirmations. When Legh checked his information once he was back home, he found that he had been relying on memory and that more details were necessary. Drummond had obviously asked him about the pattern of previous confirmations. Legh wrote,

> Halifax 22 Dec 1761
>
> [When I saw you] . . . at Brodsworth . . . ye account I gave of ye latest Confirmations at Halifax was such as requires to be rectified thus: After ye Diocesan's 20 years absence ye only Confirmations here in Abp Blackburne's time was
>
> AD 1737 Sept 10, 11, 12, 13.
>
> The only ones since his time were these three following:
>
> 1744 Herring — no. 4000
> 47 " — no. 3000
> 55 Bp Keene for Abp Hutton — no. 3500
>
> In ye first . . . in 1737 my then newly rebuilt Chapel at Rippenden, about 5 miles off was consecrated and afterwards several children were confirmed *there*.

Legh stressed the size of the parish of Halifax. This cannot have been new information to Drummond as a Yorkshireman, but Legh put his point strongly again in relation to the amount of work awaiting the new archbishop:

> Halifax Vicarage alone, having . . . 12 chapels . . . (and a thirteenth as yet unendowed and unconsecrated) containing about 40,000 people, on such occasions creates much work to ye Diocesan.

As the vicar of the largest parish in the diocese in terms of ground area, George Legh had huge responsibilities and directed a team of many curates. He was meticulously careful on paper, though he had reached a time of life when he indulged himself with several holidays. His follow-up letter to Drummond adds to the picture of him as a man of precise detail, and genuine warmth. Although it was a letter of statistics, he wrote, "Many happy new years to your Grace, to your Lady and to your whole family,—. . . not only a formal wish but a cordial one, . . ." In that greeting he had managed to turn a customary ending into an expression of the right amount of formality with a genuine hope for the future.

One month after sending out the letters announcing the visitation, Drummond received a reply from Septimius Plumptree. He wrote about a problem he had with catechizing. He went into detail about the fault being his, and said he had a plan to put it right, and this led to an interesting payoff for him. At the visitation he was presented because his curate was nonresident. Drummond, after making his acquaintance with Plumptree as a correspondent, decided in his favor, and ruled that the presentment was malicious and that there should be no process of law against Plumptree.

Lay People in the Parishes

The visitation by Drummond presented the opportunity to interview the clergy about the job they were doing. A majority of the questions in the paper of Queries, however, related to the laity—their church affiliation, the numbers within families, their attendance at church, their part in the administration of and benefit from charitable bequests, and even their moral behavior (in the question about penances). As individuals and as corporate congregations, the laity were the church's concern; they were its members, though ordinary parishioners were unlikely to know why their vicar had set off to a visitation center, especially as more than half the parishes had an absentee vicar anyway.

Readers of the *York Courant* would have known about the visitation because of the archbishop's notices for ordinations and confirmations. That other great traveler, John Wesley, would have been advertised only by word of mouth. How were these important visitors received? Both men would have caused some stir of novelty as they discharged their appointed tasks. People in the ten towns where both Drummond and Wesley visited amounted to 13,741 families. This count omits York, where, using the visitation returns, there were more than 2,500 families. It may have occurred to some out of the 13,000 or so families in the ten towns visited by both leaders that their town was doubly important that year. It is not possible to gauge the response of the dissenting communities of Presbyterians, Quakers, Independents, and Roman Catholics to the visitation by the archbishop of York, but John Wesley's visits had an appeal beyond his own congregations, just as Whitefield had in New England.[39] People were thrilled to hear a traveling preacher.

In the centers visited by both leaders, namely Doncaster, Rotherham, Wakefield, Leeds, Shipton, York, Beverley, Hull, Stokesley, Scarborough, and Thirsk, the impact of visitation fell mainly on the Anglican clergy. The strongest inference from the data for the ten towns and from Wesley's journal is that the Anglican visitation of the diocese and the Wesleyan tour of Yorkshire were separate from each other in most aspects. The timing of the visits did not clash. The routes were opposite. Although there were similarities of purpose and achievement in their two itineraries, there was a distance of mutual knowledge and concern so great that they might have been in different parts of the country at different times.

Confirmation candidates made up the largest section of lay people who had direct contact with the archbishop. He was preparing for them; similarly, they were preparing for him. They had to be apprised of the catechism and depended on their rectors, vicars, and curates for their instruction. Detailed analysis in chapter 4 shows the wide variety of methods for instructing candidates for confirmation from the clergy answers to Q4. Most candidates received their instruction during Lent. Some started especially to complete their course when a confirmation was due. The method of learning the catechism was by a prescribed form of question and answer. Explanations were not always given in a formal sense, and many clergy said in their written answers to the archbishop that they explained it as best they could.

The findings of the two visitors on their travels is evidence of devoted worship in the parishes and chapelries as well as in the sectarian societies. The coupling of the information allows us to see the work of the church in the year 1764 in a light that is brighter than was admitted by Mary Bateson[40] and W. E. Gladstone,[41] for example, in the nineteenth century, and a stronger light than has been discerned even by recent writers.[42] The encounters with ignorance which nineteenth-century writers condemned with horror may well have existed before the 1830s but were not rampant in the 1760s. The implications of Wesley's work were not yet apparent to the archbishop as he conducted his visitation in the summer of 1764.

The Results of the Visitation

Archbishop Drummond took a large volume measuring 36cm by 24.5cm in a grand brown leather binding,[43] rather like a giant wallet, with hand stitching and leather ties. It has sixty-four leaves (128 sides) of individually watermarked pages, but the first four leaves are the only ones containing any data. The entries, however, are crowded. The title page reads,

State

of the Diocese of York

1764

> collected from the Answers to my Queries received at my visitation and from other materials by me
>
> R Ebor,

and begins directly with the

Scheme of visitation 1764

and its lists of the appointments from 30 April to 29 June and the accompanying places from Nottingham and Newark round to Thirsk and Stokesley. Over the page, still in the archbishop's hand, we read the unsurprising statement that,

> The Diocese of York contains four Archdeaconries viz 1. York or Westriding 2. Cleveland or Northriding 3. Eastriding 4. Nottingham.
>
> The Archdeaconry of York contains the City and County . . . and all the Westriding south of the River Nid. What is north of the Nid in the Westriding is in the Archdeaconry of Richmond, Diocese of Chester, to which diocese this Archdeaconry was annexed in 1541 32.Hen.8 upon its new creation.
>
> The Archdeaconry of York contains 5 Districts or Deaneries,

and there follows a list that sets out for the archdeaconry of York, the rectories, vicarages, curacies, appendant chapels, peculiars, medieties, double cures or distinct cures, amounting in total to two hundred parishes or churches, of which twenty-five were peculiars. This occupies the whole of page 2. Page 3 is empty. One might expect similarly laid out lists of the other archdeaconries, but expectations are not always a satisfactory guide. Instead, other details are next: at the top of the next page the archbishop wrote, "pag. 1 /" and the double page spread is ruled in sections which he completed under the heading, "**Archdeaconry of York—City of York**" and entered in millimetric handwriting some of the information from four of the city churches:

St Trinity in Goodramgate
St Trinity in King's Court
St Crux in Fossgate, and
All Saints Pavement.

By that last one, he had turned overleaf and had written, "pag. 2." There were no more entries in the chart. All but the last four leaves are ruled up similarly. Blank end pages remain inside the inviting and substantial leather covers, and one is left with a sense of disappointment. Was the task too great to complete? Did the archbishop's heart sink at the prospect of continuing? Where was the secretary or the chaplain? Did the archbishop simply lose interest? Were the revelations from the first of the four entries so numbing that he abandoned the project on their account? Were there domestic preoccupations? Was there "a visitor from Porlock?" Was there more urgent work?

As we envisage Drummond at his desk with the large leatherbound volume, his mind stored with five months of busy encounters, there is the possibility that he was considering the revival of a plan to unite four York city churches, following the program initiated in 1547.[44] He made a chart as follows: **"Benefice, Value, Incumbent, Curate, Service, Charities, Miscellaneous Notes."** *Value* was not stated in the returns so he had to refer to another list in order to make his entries. A side section had space for the name of the patron (also absent from the returns), making yet another reference book necessary. Mention of the incumbent's house meant that he also had to refer to the newly written terriers.

Among the papers deposited at Bishopthorpe in 1586 was a deed, resting on an act of 1547, for uniting seventeen decayed parishes with twelve others.[45] His newly received visitation returns may have prompted him to continue the work begun earlier. At the top of page 5 Drummond refers to the two acts of Parliament relating to unions of churches and to the deed found among his papers. He wrote,

NB 1547 1 Edward 6. An Act pass'd in Parlt., empowering the Mayor Recorder and 6 Aldermen being Justices together with the Ordinary or his Deputy to unite the Churches in the City, to pull down the superfluous ones, to preserve the former rights of patronage by proportionate turns and to state the first fruits and tenths according to what all the churches were rated at, before they were united. -Nothing then was done, but St Ellen's Stonegate demolished, wch was rebuilt in Q Mary's time.

1585 28 Eliz. Abp Sandys with the Mayor &c did make several Unions: & reduced 40 or 41 churches to 23.

The question emerges: was Archbishop Drummond proposing to use his power as ordinary to continue the post-Reformation unions? Would the patronage rights have made it easy for him to have achieved this? Two were vested in the king, one was his own; the fourth was jointly between two gentlemen, one of Yorkshire and the other of Lincolnshire. All Saints Pavement had been a problem for some time: the northern and southern parts of its churchyard were removed in the seventeenth century for street widening.[46] St. Trinity in King's Court had its stained glass removed "between 1763 and 1770,"[47] suggesting that either St. Crux or St. Trinity Goodramgate would have been the survivor in Drummond's possible union plan.[48]

One inference would be that Drummond failed to make further use of the visitation returns, but this depends on the idea that making use of them consists only in writing out something else about them. He could have made use of them by having them brought with him, arranged perhaps by deaneries, when he went on his subsequent tours of confirmation, and when he held his services of ordinations. His own testimony about studying was that it was better to *digest* good materials than to *compile* many. In that frame of mind, his secretaries and chaplains could have been instructed to provide the details of incumbent, patron, parsonage, value, and charities, as well as the information about population, dissenters, and services on the occasions of the confirmations and ordinations, using all the books of reference along with the returns. In the absence of direct evidence, however, this remains speculation.

Looking at the reasons for his discontinuing the task of writing in his leatherbound book, we may remind ourselves that the archbishop did indeed have other things to do, several of them requiring him to be out and about instead of copying out minutiae in longhand on his chart. His apparent turning away from the material that could have led him to discern problems and opportunities marks him as the aristocratic prelate of an age that was satisfied with the status quo. His nature would have preferred table talk with his household. He might have relaxed with his port or cider or madeira while playing cards with guests, and yet discovering in conversation with them what was happening in their part of the diocese.[49] If he decided to stay at the desk before setting off again on his travels, it would have taken many hours to read through and ponder the visitation returns, and there was, as we have seen, always the correspondence, which would have taken precedence over the chart. Otherwise there were times for prayers in the chapel, instructions to give to the builders, moments for reading the newspapers, and hours for teaching the youngest children. Enough is known of his character and pattern of life to see him as mainly a man of action, decision, and hospitality, touring his diocese and making contacts, inviting guests and sharing his substance with people. He had learnt how to reduce desk work to an efficient minimum, making brief notes, and directing the secretary.

Domestic tragedy struck Drummond repeatedly. It was in June the year after the visitation that his daughter Henrietta Auriol died (see chapter 2). The favored Abigail died the following summer, and Charlotte died in 1769. These were not infant deaths and would have caused deep grief. Their illnesses are not specified, but some recurring hopeful and polite references to their uncertain health in the correspondence suggest that the Drummonds shared frequent anxieties about their daughters. In 1773 Mrs. Drummond herself died. One may of course expect to face the death of a marriage partner, and in that age of insufficient medical knowledge husbands were frequently saddened by the deaths of wives in childbirth. But the Drummonds together knew the bitter loss of four grown children. Abigail's death, recorded by the youngest son in the *Memoirs,*[50] occurred in an age when some parents showed their daughters more ambition than love. The cumulative impact of all these deaths may explain why the archbishop lost the urgency to extend the chart he began with the visitation returns. Family was his first priority, in a time before an English gentleman—let alone an aristocrat—had to have a stiff upper lip.[51]

Further losses followed. By the time that these family griefs had wounded the archbishop, the local vicar of Brodsworth, Matthew Buck, had died. He was buried in 1767 in Brodsworth graveyard. Drummond had also lost his patron and his ecclesiastical partner: the duke of Newcastle and Thomas Secker both died in 1768. Drummond's relationships with these two people had been absorbing during the first seven years of his archiepiscopate. He conducted one further visitation of the diocese in 1770, for which the extant documentation in the *Court Book* is a list of names of parishes, chapelries, clergy and, churchwardens and a record of the proceedings against those who were charged with various irregularities. The remaining years were ones where Drummond hardened his regard for posterity and convinced his youngest son that he wanted no memorial. He made his will early in 1776, with all the precision of which he was capable, providing for his own family.

4
The State of the Diocese

Introductory Summary to Performance Indicators

Effective drafting of the archbishop's visitation enquiries for 1764 produced answers suited to modern analysis for a picture of Yorkshire church life as presented by its parsons. Comparative analysis with the earlier returns of 1743 allows for critical assessments of the growth of church life and its governance in Yorkshire in the mid eighteenth century. Non-Anglican sources for some of the same areas supply a balance to the information from the visitation returns.

Sunday services and sacraments were obvious topics in the archbishop's lists. He did not use the term *preaching,* but he referred to the "sermon." Catechizing and education questions produced replies in such detail as to be key indicators of parish life and clergy performance. The administration of parish charities was another indicative topic, but one where the great variety of answers makes it less suited to analysis.

It is helpful to view the church against its seasonal background. The Book of Common Prayer was the church's calendar as the underlying and familiar basis of church life since the time of the Reformation. It had had to lie very low while the English kingdom of the world was turned upside down, but the bishops were able to hold to it very firmly again after the Restoration. The seasons of the year as observed in the *Book of Common Prayer,* were of far greater significance in the 1760s than they are now, and in the York diocese the seasons bit harshly into its exposed and less populated parishes. The church is about human life and death and eternal life. The seasons control life and death in nature, and in 1760 they exerted a momentous influence on human survival. So much in worship and ministry had been changed and has since changed that the church's calendar and the seasons remain as the only constants for an understanding of the Georgian church.

The Restoration church was an experimental institution, its members treading with care over upturned ground. Some Anglican clergymen were still wary of the dissenters in the first decades of the Georgian century. Some were to remain uneasy about the Roman Catholics. Yet there were quite a few eighteenth-century Anglican clergymen whose education had been received in the dissenting academies. This had an effect on the way that magistrates applied the laws granting licences to dissenters for their meetings, as clergy influenced local thinking and especially as some of them became magistrates.[1]

The calendar of the church's seasons and festivals—Advent, Christmas, Epiphany, Lent, Easter and so on—laid over the natural Yorkshire seasons accompanies this interpretation of the 1764 visitation returns. The Georgian church was accustomed to the comfortable pattern in which the themes of sermons were implicit. One would not expect a sermon about the story of Jacob and Esau, for example, on the feast of the Annunciation. Advent traditions let the clergy preach about Death, Judgment, Heaven, Hell, and the Second Coming. Over this pattern in the Yorkshire parishes there came the vigor of the revivalist preachers and the literary gifts of Laurence Sterne. Presiding over this scene, Archbishop Drummond transfers from being implicitly one of Rupp's "amiable nonentities"[2] to being recognized as an effective administrator, a place previously denied him because of his successful self-effacing qualities.

The summer season—May to August—was the time when most could be accomplished both at diocesan and at parish level. Easter was selected for a counting of communicants because more people would attend then. The incidence of Holy Communion throughout the Georgian church was generally three, four, or five times per year. This reflected both the special nature attached to it as a sacrament and also the backlog of unconfirmed adult church attenders, unconfirmed because some bishops had not conducted enough confirmations. Archbishop Drummond, however, continued his confirmation tours in Yorkshire throughout his archiepiscopate. The *Book of Common Prayer* services of Morning and Evening Prayer in the parish churches were those used for Sunday worship. Mattins could be as late as one thirty p.m. on a winter Sunday if a parson had had other services to fit in and if he and his parishioners wished to get back home before fogs made moorland travel impossible. Alternatively, Evening Prayer could be as early as one thirty p.m. for the same reasons.

The visitation returns of 1764 covered all areas of church life, allowing an assessment of the picture as a whole as well as parish by parish with other sources. So it emerges that even a conscientious clergyman could be ill-informed about remote and inaccessible parts of his parish. For example, the vicar of a parish of fifteen hundred families did not know that the Independent chapel in his parish was actually an Independent Baptist chapel, and it is not impossible that he had never been to the remote site of that chapel, high up and far away from sites of the Anglican chapels of ease within his parish and far away also from the main parish church. His record of observation—it was Henry Venn of Huddersfield—included the name of James Cartlidge as the "teacher" of the licensed Independent chapel. Baptist sources[3] name Henry Clayton as the Baptist pastor of a place known as Salendine Nook since the time of the Herring returns. Venn's information is well attested in other respects, but his preoccupation with ministering faithfully to his parishioners kept him within the township of Huddersfield itself, except when he went specifically to keep other appointments.[4] Seasonal considerations such as cold winds on exposed hillsides could have led him to prefer to get his information from his assistant clergy or from his parishioners and to pursue his writing of sermons.

Church Services

Every Sunday in the Christian year has its name in the church's calendar, whether it is Septuagesima or Rogation Sunday or the ninth before Christmas. The Georgian church had disentangled itself from some of the more obviously Romish connections, casting off the Assumption and Corpus Christi, honoring the English martyrs, and raising King Charles I to their ranks. It affirmed its distinctive character by having a special service on the anniversary of the accession of the monarch. The ordinary Sunday service, however, as the topic of Q7, touched the nerve of the clergy doing their duty to God and the parishioners, not asking about lay attendance. The replies open up a picture of busy and traveling Anglican clergy, some of them covering the miles between their plurally held livings to comply with the best provision of two services on Sunday. Some gave plain answers, and others wrote a rigmarole, most citing seasonal reasons and the custom of "time out of mind."

Frequency of Sunday Services

The worship of God in the Georgian church was to be conducted twice every Sunday. The form of the question (see Appendix) and the expectation by the archbishops in 1743 and in 1764 are so much the same as to make this the most significant question about parish worship on both visitation papers.

Analysis shows that across the Yorkshire parishes more churches held two services every Sunday in 1764 than any other pattern of provision. There were 224 parishes where Sunday services were held twice every Sunday both in 1743 and in 1764. The next best thing was to have one service every Sunday, and this also was the situation for about a third of the parishes in 1764. In 169 parishes there were services once every Sunday for both 1743 and 1764. This makes 393 parishes where an exact pattern of worship was maintained for the twenty-one years between the visitations. There is no reason to suppose that this altered during the archiepiscopate of Drummond, so the perception is that the Yorkshire parish clergy were providing their fluctuating populations with an unchanging and reliable measure of Sunday worship for over one third of the century.

In just under half of the 621 parishes, there were two services every Sunday in 1764. There are few surprises about their locations and many confirmations of expectation. The large places—large as to area and as to numbers of inhabitants—such as Almondbury, Birstall, Bradford, Dewsbury, Ecclesfield, Halifax, Huddersfield, Hull, Leeds, Pontefract, Rotherham, Wakefield, and Whitby all held two services on Sundays. Two services were held on Sundays also in many rural places where there were fewer than fifty families. In all there were 264 parishes (42.5 percent) where two services were being held each Sunday. Elsewhere, the pattern was mainly of one service on Sunday.

There were seventy-eight parishes (12.6 percent) where services were held only once a fortnight in 1764. Rarer patterns were restricted to a very small number. This was quite a satisfactory provision and included places with middling and large populations. Only two places (Kirby Misperton and Hunslet) had more than 440 families whose church had just one service on Sunday. The clergy in both these places were known evangelicals, Richard Conyers at Kirby Misperton and Henry Crooke at Hunslet. In this they are shown up for less than the best, except that Conyers conducted a morning service every day of the week in Helmsley as well as on Sunday, and Crooke held two services every Sunday and weekday services on Thursday and Saturday at Kippax, being locked in the pluralist trap.

Sunday Services in the York City Churches

The York city churches held only one service on Sundays. This practice was the result of long tradition, unrelated to the seasons. At St. Laurence and St. Margaret, Walmgate, there were Sunday services once every other Sunday, afternoons and mornings respectively. The only seasonal provision was at St. Maurice, where there was an anniversary sermon preached on 5 July, but where the Sunday service was held only once a month. St. Maurice's church was not falling short in its provision for its seventy-five families, as it had been annexed in 1586 to Holy Trinity, Goodramgate, along with St. John Delpike. Yet its extent was greater, meaning that its parishioners were more spread out and had farther to walk to get to church three Sundays out of four in the month. In sum, the distances concerned are small, and the city conditions made the seasons less important. John Bell, curate of St. Sampson's, York, put it most plainly when he wrote, "Morning or afternoon duty is all that is performed in any parish church in this city on the Lord's Day." He implied that anyone who wanted more than one service on a Sunday could attend a different parish church in the afternoon from the morning or of course go to the Minster. The Minster used the clergy from the York city parish churches. Richard Barnard, of Holy Trinity, Goodramgate, wrote that he attended or performed every day "at the Cathedral," and he also held the living of Heyworth, Nottinghamshire, where he resided some of the time. He did not explain exactly how he divided his time, but he did answer the last question on the paper, which many clergy simply omitted, writing, "I have met with no difficulties . . . no abuses . . . no corruptions in any Ecclesiastical officers. I have no advice to give nor proposition to make."

Surveillance of Sunday Services in the Cleveland Archdeaconry

The idea of surveillance of the clergy appealed to Francis Blackburne as a way of fulfilling his archdeacon's function. He conducted a detailed survey of "Sunday Duty" in his archdeaconry, its frequency and regularity, methodically sniffing out deteriorating situations. Although Blackburne held controversial views about the Church of England's official doctrinal position and held them with increasing impact from the 1750s, he was firm as the guardian of right practice by the parish clergy. He inherited a list begun for his predecessor in 1745, with intermediate checks in 1757 and 1761, using accounts given by churchwardens and chapelwardens. In July 1762 he sent his chart to the archbishop. The preamble spells out the rationale for making enquiries into this important area of priestly work. This was that those who had been criticized for default might have the chance to "rectify any mistake."

The Blackburne chart[5] of the Cleveland archdeaconry was undertaken because "some of the Gentlemen [that is, clergymen] insisted that the churchwardens had been mistaken." The third enquiry in 1761 allows the chart to show "at one view how the matter stood." Archdeacon Blackburne ended his preamble to the survey by saying that the chart needed "no farther reflection or remark of his own upon it," but he did add a grading scheme which makes the whole chart of considerable significance in relation to the 1743 visitation returns.[6]

He surveyed one hundred parishes and chapelries in the Cleveland and Bulmer deaneries and thirty-seven in Rydale. Three places in Cleveland won his marks for improvement: Craythorne, Danby, and Stainton. Stars of default went against Carlton, Middleton, and Marske. Five places put right their faults and thirty-nine were satisfactory. The best provision was for two Sunday services, but he let that pass if one had been traditionally held. His criticism was aroused if the observance fell from morning to afternoon or from fortnightly in the morning to every other Sunday in the afternoon, or to once every three weeks or less in winter. The Bulmer deanery had sixteen fault marks, only three places with spontaneous improvement, and six with improvement after inquiry. Rydale had eleven places marked as faulty, two with improvement, two with restored observance, and twenty-two without comment.

Blackburne's charts are evidence of some slackness. He was looking for gratuitous improvement as well as the correction of a fault. With regard to Sunday duty—which was the point of his enquiry—not much had changed between 1761 and 1764. By far the greatest consistency was in the clergy who manned the parishes.

From 1761 to 1764 in the Cleveland archdeaconry there were only a dozen new names of clergy among 137 churches and chapels. He noted the tendency for a clergyman who acquired a second or third living to reduce his services at the first benefice.

Three Examples of Default

At the rectory of Bransby the curate was Harker Crooke, later to be the notorious successor to Venn at Huddersfield. He had an ingratiating style of reply to the archbishop, saying that he did not live at Bransby, but resided at Terrington, but was "always at Bransby when any of the parishioners have need of the functions of my office," a phrase which lacks the ring of real devotion to duty. Harker Crooke wrote that the two curacies of Bransby and Terrington afforded him a very comfortable subsistence and enabled him to support his helpless mother, putting his own and his mother's interests naturally and unashamedly before those of the parishioners. The situation at Bransby was on a downward curve. Crooke did not conduct two services every Sunday as had been the case there when Blackburne's chart began in 1745. Instead, there was a service every other Sunday morning, and Crooke "read prayers for two families," presumably in the afternoon on those occasions. He wrote that the rest of the inhabitants lived at a distance, this having been occasioned by Mr. Cholmley, the lord of the manor, who had

> demolished the village of Bransby, and built convenient houses for his tenants in various parts of ye lordship, which is ye reason that people cannot be prevailed upon to come twice to church.

Archdeacon Blackburne accepted the observance at Bransby and marked it as a place where a default had been amended.

Birdforth Chapel was marked with the archdeacon's critical asterisk. In 1764 the service was held once a month. This had been so in 1761, in 1757, and often in 1743, although then it was written that sometimes the service was held once a fortnight. It was the smallest inhabited chapelry of the whole diocese, with only five families in residence in 1764. The fault remained and the reason excused it. John Nesfield had been the curate there since 1756, making the observance customary by 1764.

At Bulmer the fault was not corrected by 1764. The services had been held twice on Sundays in 1743, but since 1757 the observance had been halved. Talbot Leybourne had been vicar there since 1758. In 1764 the curate, Robert Atkinson, a new arrival since Lady Day 1762, though named in the archdeacon's list as curate in 1761, wrote that his rector did not reside in Bulmer because he had the archbishop's permission to live in Southwell. Robert Atkinson did not answer Q7 fully, and it is supposed that he was continuing the pattern of once-a-fortnight services for the ninety-eight families of Bulmer.

Three Examples of Improvement

At Dalby the same fault—holding services once every Sunday since 1757 compared with two in 1745—had persisted throughout the archdeacon's surveillance, but by the visitation of 1764 the rector, Thomas Lumley, wrote that he was conducting two services each Sunday.

At Fylingdales Richard Hauxwell had become the curate in the last year of Blackburne's survey but had not sent in a return for the chapelry. There had been no separate return for Fylingdales even in 1745, and the observance was given as the same as its mother church at East Harsley, that of once every Sunday morning. By 1764, when the population had increased to 320 families from 300 in 1743, Hauxwell was holding two services every Sunday and preaching two sermons.

At Feliskirk, from services twice every other Sunday in 1761, the vicar, Joseph Dowthwaite, was holding services in 1764 twice every Sunday.

The surveillance produced some of these alterations at the risk of wearying some of the clergymen of the Cleveland deanery. The thought that the archbishop was visiting and not the archdeacon may have inclined some of them to improve their output. Improvements subsequent to Blackburne's survey showed up at the 1764 visitation in fourteen parishes or chapelries across the three deaneries of Cleveland, Rydale, and Bulmer. But five of those improvements were spontaneous, that is, they were not among the places marked with a black star by Blackburne and may reflect an awareness that the archbishop was a much higher authority. Some clergy, however, took no notice at all. There were fourteen who carried on as before even though they had been black marked.

Some of the clergy may have known about their archdeacon's doctrinal difference with the *Book of Common Prayer* and may have thought that if he could get away with serious fundamental criticisms of the foundation of the faith of the Established Church, they too might get away with providing one service on Sunday morning and leaving the afternoon one to alternate Sundays, a pattern found in several of the Cleveland churches.

Blackburne had not hidden his ideas. He did not say that his sermon on 5 January 1753 "to a large congregation in the country"[7] was in the Cleveland area. But he did publish some remarks in 1758 after hearing a sermon in Cambridge, which may have reached the libraries of some Cleveland parsonages. Blackburne addressed himself to the theme of subscription to the Thirty-nine Articles, questioning the possibility of understanding their meaning.[8] His doctrinal position continued to put him on the edges of what was consistent with a dignitary of the established church, but the performance of his archdeacon's duties was exemplary and contributed to Archbishop Drummond's knowledge of the York diocese. Blackburne's two roles—as theological irritant and critical guardian—remind us that the Georgian church could do little to curb such characters. Drummond gave only slight indication of regarding Blackburne with anything as strong as distaste.[9] They might have agreed about Roman Catholicism, as Blackburne complained in 1765 that it was easier to import "popish books, rosaries, breviaries, missals, primers, manuals etc," than it was to get Wilkes's letter,[10] though Blackburne's views on episcopacy in England and America were outspokenly provocative.[11]

Case Studies of Sunday Services in the Rydale Deanery

The Rydale deanery was the area of the diocese with the wildest of the moorland countryside and also the distribution of some of the largest parishes with scattered populations and difficulty of access. If one were looking for a deanery where observance of the Church's ministry might be expected to fail because of the difficulties of its situation, Rydale would be that place. These case studies indicate the reverse, showing the commitment and industry of the parish clergy there.

Most of the parishes run from north to south, all of them inland and hilly parishes on the north Yorkshire moors. Pickering, for example, spans the length of the deanery from north to south. On the west of the deanery are the small parishes of Cold Kirby, Old Byland, Scawton, and Ampleforth; all these places had regular arrangements for Sunday services. In the mid south are the smaller parishes of Appleton (every other Sunday) and Barton le Street (twice on Sundays). The one center of closely grouped population contained the market town parishes of Malton and Old Malton. One clergyman, Geoffrey Walmsley, served all three churches: Old Malton and St. Leonard and St. Michael in New Malton, residing in the parsonage of St. Michael and ministering to the 550 families. At the center of the deanery is Sinnington, a place even today turned in on itself and in 1764 consisting of sixty-five families with a service every Sunday, conducted by its curate, Philip Dowker.

From Pickering (250 families and two Sunday services) there is the dramatic entry to Lockton and Levisham, two of the most inaccessible parishes even today. Isaac Whykes served Levisham and was also curate to George Dodsworth in nearby Ebberston and Allerston, and he somehow managed to get from Levisham to Ebberston and Allerston on alternate Sundays, holding a service every Sunday morning first at Levisham, a cul-de-sac whose modern escape route is the north Yorkshire moors railway. The gradients are so steep that a car in today's road conditions is safe only in dry and frost-free weather. A horse was not the answer, and walking would require great care in crossing the stream at the bottom of the valley. But Isaac Whykes was cautious. He spent ten years in Levisham as a deacon before he went for ordination as priest in 1762. Two years later he did get to Scarborough for the visitation. The distance from Levisham to Lockton is "750 metres as the crow flies, but 100 metres of ascent and descent at gradients of 1:2 in places," according to the two writers, not of a travel guide, but of an article about some excavations at the parish church.[12] Getting in and out of Levisham was more than a seasonal problem, and Lockton is literally an aside to the prevailing rural Rydale, still today shut-ended by St. Giles's rectory and patrolled by ducks.

Sunday Services and the Health of the Clergy

Poor health prevented some parsons from conducting services every Sunday. Obviously this was related to the seasons, in that ailments in the English climate are more difficult to overcome in winter and some ailments derive from winter conditions. The Yorkshire diocese, colder and windier than many of the southern, south western and south eastern dioceses, had surprisingly few clergy who said they went elsewhere specifically for health reasons, though some went to Bath and Bristol to take the waters. When clergy were suddenly ill and unable to make arrangements with a neighbor, then the church was just left without services. An attitude of realism prevailed about this. Clergy wrote their Sunday service answers with such phrases as "unless sickness prevents," "while health permits," and "while in health." As age increased, so did the tendency to ailments. Where the opposite was true, the parsons served their same parishes for life unless they were preferred for higher office in the church, there being no age of retirement.

Virgin estimates that there were 1,125 incapacitated clergy out of a national total of 7,500, but he sees that the "co-operative neighbouring incumbent syndrome" was used to overcome this. He cites this solution as an example of bishops ignoring a problem and clergy tackling a situation for themselves. The Yorkshire examples show that resident assistant curates were ministering where ill health was chronic.

Old age as well as ill health was noticeable among the Yorkshire clergy, but not all the elderly were ill and incapable.[13] Analysis shows that there were fifty-four parishes and chapelries where the incumbents had been ordained as deacons before 1720, when they were under twenty-five. By 1764 they would have been at least the same age as the century. The oldest clergyman of all was Nicholas Gyrling of Newton Kyme, deacon in 1702, priest in 1703, and resident rector still in 1764. His returns are brief and factual about his two services on Sundays. Some of these elderly men had curates to help them. For example, Owen Dinsdale, the curate at Wickersley, had taken over the ministry because the rector was "a very infirm old man and incapable of doing any duty," who could not be removed from Windsor where he lived, "without endangering his life." At Beverley St. Mary the vicar admitted to being in poor health and had a resident curate.

Robert Hewett, one of these elderly clergy (ordained deacon and priest in 1715 and 1718), served Allerthorpe, Fangfoss and Thornton juxta Pocklington all from as early as 1729. He must have been in reasonably good health by 1764, as the archbishop's records state that he attended in person at the visitation to show his orders. Seasonal worship at the chapel of Allerthorpe is stated on his return, where it is not entirely clear whether there was no service at all in winter, as he wrote at Q7, or "once every other Sunday in the afternoon except in winter." At Fangfoss he was similarly evasive, writing, "Once a fortnight in a general way in the afternoon except on sacrament day," when the service was in the morning. He resided at Thornton, a custom practiced by all his predecessors. He must have felt sufficiently conscientious about Fangfoss even though (or perhaps because) its population had declined from 19 families to 15 in 1764. Thornton had 104 families, showing an increase of 26 families during his time as vicar, and Allerthorpe had remained the same at 27 families. All three churches were rebuilt during the nineteenth century according to Pevsner's study, and Allerthorpe was alone in possessing an item of note: a silver cup made in York in 1570 by Roger Beckwith.[14] Robert Hewett had thus maintained a gentle control of the parishes and church buildings in his part of the Harthill deanery.

Weekday Services

The picture of the eighteenth-century church from the evidence of weekday services in the York diocese is of varied, if patchy, vitality. The following table summarizes the incidence of weekday services:

Weekday Services

Daily	Daily Ante Sacrmnt	Alt Days	Daily PW or Lent	Twice daily	Thrice daily	W&F	W&F Lent	Holy	Other
6	2	1*	9	2	1	50	104#	190	13

PW = Passion Week
* plus 1 place where 3 times per week
# including 1 place where daily in Advent also

Although the prevalence of pluralism did not foster the observance of regular weekday services, there were 190 clergymen (31 percent), including some pluralists (see next chapter), who still celebrated saints' days and kept fasts as part of the old high church tradition. Similarly, Wednesdays and Fridays during Lent were observed by 104 clerics (17 percent), and of these there were fifty (8 percent) who kept every Wednesday and Friday through all the seasons. These weekday services were to be found in varied situations—in large and small rural parishes, coastal towns, in remote places as well as those on main routes and in market towns. It was mainly in the most heavily populated towns that a *daily* service was held—Doncaster, Pontefract, Hull, and Wakefield—while at Leeds parish church there were *three* services every day, and at Hull St. Mary and Leeds St. John's there were two. Most of the known evangelicals departed from the tradition of keeping Wednesday and Friday for morning services, preferring to hold evening services at 6 A.M. or 7 P.M., when working folk might attend, usually once a week. Samuel Furly's and George Burnett's were on Wednesdays at 7 A.M., Henry Crooke's were on Thursdays and Saturdays at 6 P.M., and Venn's was at 7 P.M. on Thursdays. The exceptions to this pattern were Burnett, who held a Wednesday morning service in addition to his evening one, and Conyers, who held a service every weekday morning at Helmsley.

The solemn seasons of the church's year led some clergymen to hold more frequent weekday services. Two places had daily services throughout Lent, Thirkelby and Thornhill, and another seven held daily services during Passion Week. Two other places—All Saints, Pavement, York, and St. Michael, Ousebridge End, York—held daily services in the week before the celebration of the sacrament. At Kirkbymoorside the incumbent had a preparation for the sacrament on the immediately preceding day.

The York city churches had some features of weekday observance which did not arise elsewhere. At St. Dennis there was a daily service throughout Advent. At St. Helen's, Stonegate, there were weekday services three days a week on Monday, Tuesday, and Thursday. On 5 July there was a service at St. Maurice. None declared for holy days, while two observed twice weekly services in Lent, and one, St. Mary, Castlegate, held services every Wednesday of the year.

The stated reasons for not holding weekday services elsewhere in the diocese were mainly that the people were not accustomed to having anything other than Christmas Day and Good Friday, that there would not be a congregation because the parishioners were at work, and that the living was too small to support further endeavor. The bulk of the ordained clergy in the diocese had opted out of weekday services, but in the towns, where the bulk of the parishioners clustered, there was ample opportunity for weekday churchgoing. Although working people would not be free to attend in the mornings, they might know that parsons would be reading the state prayers. The return by Samuel Kirshaw of Leeds is worth reproducing in full at Q7:

> Divine Service is performed thrice every Day, with a sermon morning and afternoon on all Sundays in the year and every Friday evening whilst I am resident and on some one weekday about the end of every month upon ye subject of ye sacrament of ye Lord's Supper, or on ye Duty of observing the Holidays of ye Church of England.

Kirshaw, as noted elsewhere, was not an evangelical but allowed evangelical activity from some of his curates and obviously rated the effectiveness of the Friday evening service, which he took himself. His is an interesting case of keeping the strands of Anglicanism together before the Methodists and other revivalists separated from the church. At Scarborough, the curate, Scudamore Lazenby, was holding weekday services on Tuesdays, Wednesdays, and Fridays, and was aware of the competition that Nonconformity presented, having recorded the three licensed meetinghouses in the parish—one each for the Presbyterians, Quakers, and Methodists—the last having meetings oftener than twice on Sundays. Even the aloof Dr. Wanley of Stokesley,[15] where Methodism appeared to be growing, wrote on his return that there was a weekday service at Stokesley every alternate day throughout the year.

The keener edge of devotion that weekday services represent—about one sixth of the diocese—corrects the gloomy impressions of the nineteenth-century reformers and twentieth-century critics that the eighteenth-century church was moribund, and, because of the population distribution, most of Yorkshire's townsfolk would not have had to go far if they wanted a weekday service.

Audit

The York diocese consisted of hundreds of parish churches where services were regularly held on Sundays and weekdays, season by season, sometimes morning and evening, sometimes one or the other, and at hours known by custom to the incumbents and inhabitants. All the large parishes with growing populations had two services on Sundays. Archdeaconry surveillance in Cleveland was alert to this very issue, and the archbishop was kept informed; some reduction in Sunday services may be linked to a falling population in the north of the diocese. Incumbents in outlying areas of Rydale were faithful in conducting Sunday services. Allowing for poor health and old age amongst the clergy, some of whom were accustomed to make neighborly arrangements for such contingencies, Drummond's diocese of York was covered with parish churches open for services Sunday by Sunday. The parishioners of Yorkshire did not lack the opportunity for public worship in the established church on the Lord's Day, and it was only the Church of England that observed holy days. Town and country churches and evangelical and traditional clergy had their different reasons for holding regular weekday services.

Holy Communion

Customary Celebration

Most of the Yorkshire parishes followed the church's calendar in celebrating Holy Communion at the great festivals of Christmas, Easter, Whitsun, and Trinity. Some of the dependent chapelries had no Easter celebration because the people were expected to go to the main parish church. In other dependent chapelries the vicar of the main parish church might himself make the visit to collect his Easter dues. Marsden chapelry is of interest in this matter. In the southwest of the Pontefract deanery, Marsden straddled two main neighboring parishes, Huddersfield and Almondbury. The 1764 return for Marsden was completed by a curate who did not sign his name, who gave no dates for his ordination but is identifiable from clergy lists as having the same name as the chapelry, and who, according to the vicar of Almondbury, had held that office for twenty years. He was Mr. Marsden and he recorded the 146 families in the Almondbury sector and 63 in the Huddersfield sector. At Q10 he wrote that the sacrament was celebrated "by the vicars of Almondbury and Huddersfield when they come to receive their Easter dues." He also wrote that the vicar of Almondbury celebrated on 9 April (probably Maundy Thursday) and the vicar of Huddersfield celebrated on 12 April (Easter Day) in the visitation year.

There is just a hint that the curates begrudged the vicar the Easter dues in the Almondbury chapelries of Honley and Meltham when they both referred the archbishop to the vicar of Almondbury for the number of communicants in the chapelry and the Easter communicants in particular. This hint of begrudging is slight and the absence of figures might indicate simply that the curates themselves were not in attendance when the vicar came to celebrate. Edward Hasleham gave the impression that he was always at Honley, conducting divine service in

> no church besides my own, which I constantly have performed except sickness prevented me, on the Festivals and Fasts of the Church of England, Wednesdays and Fridays in Lent and every Lord's Day with a sermon morning and evening.

Mr. Sagar, the curate of Meltham wrote, "The real number of Communicants are best known by the vicar of Almondbury and he will no doubt answer this part of your Grace's query." He went on to say that the communicants were "generally about 60[16] at Eastertide, but particularly last Easter . . . ," and the entry is left blank. He cannot have been present. He might be excused for not knowing, in that the sacrament was celebrated only twice each year at Meltham chapel, and he might not necessarily be expected to know who was a communicant if Holy Communion was so rare, even though he had been curate there, according to the vicar, for thirty-five years. Hasleham, the curate of Honley for the previous two years, used a similar turn of phrase to that written by Sagar, "The number . . . your Grace will be informed of with the greater certainty by the vicar of Almondbury." No such detail was given, however, by the elderly Edward Rishton, who used plenty of words and no figures.

The Yorkshire Evangelicals and Holy Communion

Whereas the norm for the celebration of Holy Communion was three, four, or five times per year throughout the Georgian church, regular monthly celebrations have been seen both as the persistence of the old high church practice[17] and as a trend among the evangelicals.[18] Rack has warned, however, against seeing "simple indications of high or low views of the rite" from frequency of celebration or from attendance numbers.[19] According to the York visitation returns there were sixty places in 1743 where there were monthly celebrations and sixty-four by 1764; most of these were described as the "Sacrament of the Lord's Supper," terminology usually regarded as high church. The growth of a small group of evangelical clergy, described by Walsh as a force within the York diocese, also chose to include frequent holy communion in their pattern of worship. Walsh names nine clergymen as members of this group who were active in their parishes at the time of the 1764 visitation. By the end of Drummond's time, there were more. The members of the group who were in office in the Yorkshire parishes at the time of the 1764 visitation were as follows:

Thomas Bentham of Aberford
George Burnett of Ealand or Elland Chapel
Henry Crooke of Hunslet and Kippax
Richard Conyers of Helmsley and Kirby Misperton
Samuel Furly of Slaithwaite Chapel
Miles Atkinson, curate in the parish of Leeds
Jonas Eastwood of Cleckheaton
John Richardson of Haworth
Henry Venn of Huddersfield.

Walsh described their "awakened" ministries as being likely to appeal to the character of many Yorkshire people, whom he described as "simple, savage, peasant-like . . . and susceptible to strong revivalist preaching, and having strong feelings." As the archiepiscopate of Drummond continued, more clergy were known as part of the Yorkshire evangelical group. In addition to the nine named above, there were seven more identified subsequently:

Thomas Clarke who assisted Henry Crooke and followed Samuel Furly Joseph Milner who taught at Thorp Arch and knew the Atkinsons Matthew Powley who went to Slaithwaite and then Dewsbury William Richardson, brother of John, who went to Baildon John Riland who went to Huddersfield Walter Sellon who was ordained in 1760 and later went to Ledsham James Stillingfleet who went to Hotham.

Walsh traced the careers of most of these evangelical clergymen and established that they had experienced the same sort of convictions and sometimes conversions as had driven Ingham and Whitefield and Wesley. By 1764 the witness of Christopher Atkinson, one of the original Oxford Methodists, was wearing rather thin. He celebrated Holy Communion only three times per year at Walton, being an absentee curate, though he continued monthly celebrations at Thorp Arch. At Walton he had done nothing about the two augmentations awarded from Queen Anne's Bounty, leaving six hundred pounds in the hands of the Governors of the Fund, but his son, Miles, continued his evangelical tradition at Leeds. The awakened clergy of Yorkshire were leading their congregations into deeper spiritual channels within the framework of the Established Church.

Analysis shows that there were 131 parishes where the clergy celebrated Holy Communion more frequently than four or five times per year by 1764, and that the clergy involved consisted of known evangelicals and adherents of the old high church tradition. There were altogether thirty-seven parishes where holy communion was celebrated eighteen times in the year by 1764 and eight other parishes where there was a monthly celebration recorded in the 1764 visitation returns. In these eight parishes it is likely that there were in fact eighteen celebrations, given that it was proper to celebrate at the great festivals anyway. Whilst most incumbents who celebrated frequent communion were not evangelicals, such practice was common among most of those who were evangelicals.

One of those who did not celebrate frequent communion was Richard Conyers, one of the most ardent of the Yorkshire evangelicals in pastoral ministry. He copied out the questions on his return and wrote a supporting letter to describe his otherwise impeccable pastoral care of the large parish of Helmsley. The letter is a gloss on his answers, which were "according to the truth," and he added that there were "many other particulars which your Grace has a right to be acquainted with, and which I have long desired you should be." His first concern when he had arrived in Helmsley eight years before had been for the youth and children. His catechizing program was for those who needed a change from the "repetitions and plainness." He taught them in the evenings on Saturdays and Sundays, explaining "some part of the Old or New Testaments." This evening instruction was a seasonal extra to the catechizing within the services which he said was done "Once a week from Spring to the beginning of Winter, and on Fridays at 11 o'clock prayers." The villages of his parish were scattered, and almost all were more than two miles away from the parish church. He decided to undertake pastoral visiting, similar to the example set by Grimshaw in Haworth, so he set off once a week, sometimes once a fortnight, talking and praying with them, and he said that they welcomed him "readily and cheerfully." His other interest, in more frequent services of Holy Communion, had a practical purpose as well as a sacramental meaning. Conyers explained this to the archbishop in his supporting letter of 17 May 1764.

> There were very many poor children . . .
> I proposed a Sacrament every month and the Alms . . . to be laid out in the education of these poor innocents, and that the elder poor might have no reason of complaint, I proposed that the Alms at the 4 stated sacraments should be given among them as usual.
> One objection [was] . . . that these frequent sacraments w'd become burdensome to my flock . . . but the last year God [made it possible] . . . by putting it in my power to defray the Expense . . . myself . . .
> . . . and now the parish is not burdened and the poor have a blessing. There are about 450 communicants regularly on these occasions and near 40 poor children are taught. . . .
> I may be blamed by some as an Over-Doer in these matters, but God knows that it is only the desire of my heart to approve myself to Him.[20]

Financial help to provide monthly sacrament services had begun as early as 1731 at Wentworth, a chapelry in the parish of Wath upon Dearne. Lady Malton of Wentworth Woodhouse had settled fifty shillings per annum for the curate to celebrate Holy Communion there every month. This is an example of a small outgoing work of piety directed by a rich individual at a lower social class. She was Mary, wife of Thomas, Lord Malton, and Wentworth was the home of the Rockinghams; their son was to be prime minister from 1780 to 1782. By the time that some of the aristocracy were noticeably helping the church towards evangelicalism through patronage, such individual financial efforts were still acceptable, because the frequency of holy communion could otherwise be diminished for lack of money for wine.[21] Wentworth was one of the places where the Methodists had a licensed meeting house by 1764, and it was on John Wesley's main north-south route into Yorkshire. The practice at Wentworth, a small country chapelry, is a clear example that the evangelicals in Drummond's Yorkshire were not copying the Methodists, any more than they were in the large parish of Helmsley, for the establishment in 1731 of monthly sacrament services at Wentworth took place a decade before the northward journeys of John Wesley.

Audit

Frequent sacrament services were the practice of two different traditions within the Georgian church: the high church tradition and the "awakened" ministries of the evangelicals, with evidence of increase since 1743, but with most parishes still holding less than five celebrations per year. Nine known evangelical clergymen attracted other clergy and some aristocratic benefactors. Drummond's Yorkshire was mainly keeping to its earlier traditions, whether for frequent or infrequent sacrament services, but had a strong center of revival within.

Preaching

Sermons were preached more often than Holy Communion was celebrated, and they are reliable performance indicators because the information about them allows comparisons, is widely representative of different theologies, adds consistently to what is known already from published sources, and has plenty of detail to use selectively. Archbishop Drummond had preached at the coronation of the king, and most of his Yorkshire clergy would have known this. He was not famous as a "popular" preacher but had won added grandeur because of his association with the royal family. In fact, he was diffident about his own sermons, as his son explained in his introduction to the *Memoirs*.[22] Those that were published were done so by the authorities who invited him to preach. The Yorkshire clergy may have read his sermons if they subscribed to the societies for them. Drummond's reputation was that of a patriotic moralist, a defender of the constitution, a pleader for humanitarian justice and charity. He was above all a direct and plain preacher in the safe setting of ethical theology. As a man of his times, his example was as a stabilizer in the climate of the new views of the revival in the northern province. His contemporaries acknowledged him as "peculiarly virtuous as a statesman, attentive to his duties as a churchman, magnificent as an archbishop, and amiable as a man."[23]

Outdoor and Indoor Sermons

Field preaching by revivalists and sermons within walls were the two main types of sermons in England by the middle of the eighteenth century. Wesley and Whitefield and Ingham and Nelson and their followers had styles of open-air preaching that aimed for multiple response. Their sermons were constructed so that the unconverted would turn in repentance, gain salvation, and discover a living faith. The same sermons contained enough Bible teaching to sustain those who were already believers. Their indoor preaching was usually at meetings of their own supporters; only rarely did they get invitations to preach in parish churches. The revivalists were famed in America for drawing huge crowds in the open air (see chapter 3's note 40), and it was so in Yorkshire. By the sea at Robin Hood's Bay, for example, Wesley drew crowds repeatedly; and at Osmotherley a stone table was specially made for him to take his open-air stand.

Sermons within walls had more varied purposes: commemorative, seasonal, theological, moralist, fundraising, salvationist, penitential, and educative. Although sermons were a required part of the Sunday services, they deserve separate consideration, and the Georgian church in Yorkshire was served by preachers who knew how to uphold the traditional forms as well as to lead their congregations in different ways if they wished. It was the revivalists who won fame for their traveling as much as for their preaching, but it was the appointed parish priests who had the duty of the week by week presentation of biblical matter to their people. Parish preaching amounted to a massive weight of declaration in the lives of most of the Yorkshire parsons, many of whom stayed for thirty years or more in one living. If they preached once on Sunday for twenty years that made about one thousand sermons. If they preached twice on Sunday for ten years that made about the same number. Quite a lot can be gleaned from the visitation returns of 1764 about these parish sermons in Drummond's Yorkshire. Underlying them all was the knowledge that the archbishop expected the parish clergy to undertake this duty.

Parish Sermons

The responses to the archbishop's question about sermons reflect the style of the question and indicate the various ideas of the clergy about sermons and their purposes. The sermon question was a subsidiary to the incidence of Sunday services, leading the clergy to put their answers in a secondary category to that of Sunday duty. The question was put thus,

> Do you perform Divine Service in any church besides your own?
> On what days and at what times is Divine Service performed in your church?

If not twice every Lord's Day, with a sermon in the morning, for what reason?

The answers fall into a pattern. Some clergymen regarded the sermon so little that they did not mention it at all. Others included it in the sense exactly as conveyed by the archbishop, namely as part of the Sunday morning service. For example, John Hewthwaite, vicar of Cottingham, wrote, "I serve a small Curacy near Lincoln. Mr Wilson [his curate] performs Divine Service twice on Sundays with a sermon in the morning." A third type of response came from many clergy who preached twice every Sunday, and reported their practice, as did Henry Wickham, rector of Guiseley, who performed Divine Service twice every Sunday, with two sermons from Easter to Michaelmas and one from Michaelmas to Easter. At Hartshead chapel the residing curate was John Haigh, who was reported by his employing curate as performing Divine Service twice on Sundays, preaching twice, and not performing Divine Service at any other church.

The full picture, however, of the preaching of sermons in the Georgian church in Yorkshire in the mid eighteenth century, is not encompassed by these three types of reply. Far more than that may be discerned from those who preached twice. They might be preaching twice in their one church, particularly those who were known evangelicals, and there were many more who were not evangelicals who also preached twice on Sundays in their one church. They form part of the Yorkshire church scene where teaching the congregations went well beyond the call of duty. Such was Thomas Bowman, vicar of Hessle, where there were 100 families. Bowman reported that he preached twice on Sundays during the summer. William Mountjoy was curate for the absentee seventy-five-year-old vicar of Kirkburton. Mountjoy performed Divine Service twice on Sundays and "preached two sermons" to the congregation who came from 1,000 families in Kirkburton. Samuel Phipps, vicar of Penistone, held two services and preached two sermons for the 360 families. These styles of reporting allow a discerning reader to see two separate situations: preaching the same sermon twice to two different groups of people in the same church, and preaching two different sermons to the same group of people in the same church. Both situations indicate that parish clergy and laity were conscientious.

A further subgroup of Yorkshire clergy also preached twice on Sundays. These were the pluralists and nonresidents or near-residents who were carrying out their duties, taking two services every Sunday and preaching in each. Thomas Beevor, curate of Skelbrooke, wrote, "I preach at Skelbrooke one part of ye day and ye other at Boston." His turn of phrase in his answer stresses the preaching of the sermon rather than the performing of the service. William Hide of Guisborough put the stress differently: "I read prayers every day in the week in the Church, and preach and perform Divine Service twice every Sunday, except the second Sunday when I . . . do Duty at Upleatham, a Chapel of Ease."

His response was more precise than others who did not specifically mention the sermon or preaching because they were preoccupied by naming the places where they held services, and by the times and frequency of their Sunday duty. James Addison, rector of Cowsby, was changing his curates when he completed the visitation return. He wrote at Q7:

> Until August next, when Mr Hodgson will reside, I do Divine Service at Leke. Then Cowsby and Over Silton will be once every Sunday alternately morning and afternoon. In the meantime Cowsby has one service on Sundays morning and afternoon alternately with Sandhutton.

James Young, rector of Catwick, was similarly precise: "I perform Divine Service at this my rectory of Catwick and my Curacy of North Frodingham every Sunday at ye proper usual hours." The fact that these two clergymen omitted to mention the sermon as such does not mean that they did not preach. The omission may have another underlying meaning connected with preaching, but for most clergy in this category their main concern was with the financial value of the living. At Adwick on Dearne, where there were just twenty-four families, John Rowley was the curate. His answer to Q7 showed clearly that he was in difficulty:

> I read prayers and preach at the parish church of Wath every Sunday in the forenoon and do the same here every Sunday in the afternoon; the incomes arising from both being scarcely sufficient to support myself and family,

though he did not omit to answer the part of the question about the sermon. Cornelius Rickaby was curate at Bempton. He omitted to mention the sermon in his answer because he was preoccupied with both the ancient customs of the place and the low income (£13 6s per annum). He wrote,

> According to ancient custom [the service is on] one Sunday in the morning, the next in the afternoon, alternately, except ye first Sunday

> in each month according to custom time immemorial [when] no Duty is perform'd. The stipend is very small which I take to be ye reason.

Rickaby was also responsible for Grindall chapel and Flamborough and Bridlington, where the incomes were £5, £16, and £15 per annum respectively, giving him an income of under £50. With 550 families in Bridlington itself, it is not surprising that he was less concerned with reporting the preaching of sermons than with explaining the rigors of Sunday duty.

The sermon could be an arid or profitable liturgical exercise, spiritually uplifting for the preacher, morally demanding for the congregation, and subsequent material for a publisher. Such shades of difference, though apparently superficial and a part of the unquantifiable material of the returns, nevertheless pervade them utterly and may be discerned by a thorough acquaintance with them, so giving a more subtle insight to the parish sermons of Yorkshire in the mid-eighteenth century. The liturgical, or safe sermon, may be defined as one which was referred to plainly in their replies as "sermon" by the large majority of clergy who said that they met the archbishop's basic requirement of Sunday services with a sermon in the morning. No added flavor was given to that type of report.

A rather different type of sermon was likely from those who said that they preached twice on Sundays. Their own terms are the surest clue to their interest and commitment and to the kind of sermon they preached. Some of them probably preached the same sermon in the same church at their second service, but where they actually used the words "I preach two sermons" a face-value meaning is uppermost. Clergy who felt the impact of the revivalists would have learned to expect visible results from their preaching. Preaching was a demanding occupation, both physically and spiritually, and Wesley's writing attests to this. The early evangelicals had the same attitude, and they were prepared not only to have their sermons printed but also to distribute them to their parishioners. The evangelicals were a minority, though there were as many as seventy other parishes and chapelries not connected with the evangelicals where sermons were preached twice on Sundays. William Comber of Kirkbymoorside spelled it out in detail. He performed Divine Service twice every Sunday "with two sermons," and he looked after one other church and Gillimoor and Cockan chapels. Arthur Robinson of Holy Trinity, Hull, was bearing the full weight of a populous parish, preaching two sermons every Sunday and performing Divine Service twice every day in the week. Edward Hasleham at Honley chapel preached twice every Sunday (see earlier evidence for two services on Sundays), and Richard Hauxwell of Fylingdales Chapel had an additional incentive for his second sermon: he explained that the parishioners made a subscription for it. John Sarraude of Elvington was sensitive to the social customs of the employing and employed classes within his parish as he wrote about

> Divine Service in both my parish churches every Lord's Day alternately. Both the churches are situated at the extreme parts of either parish and when taken together are as nearly as may be in the middle of both by which servants and others that may not have an opportunity of attending Divine service in the morning may have an opportunity of [listening to] a sermon in the afternoon.

This reportage—which is unmistakable as the whole collection of the visitation returns is carefully studied—is a performance indicator of the Yorkshire clergy as active, busy, occupied, and at work for the church, ministering in this public way to congregations they could count as dutiful and responsive. It is, however, unlikely that jewels of exposition fell to congregations week after week.[24] A more sensible supposition is that the clergy whose characters emerge from the returns behaved accordingly in their pulpits. For example, John Dealtary at Acaster Malbis, Bishop Wilton, Skirpenbeck, and Bishopthorpe was one who underrated his own gifts, and his sermons, were probably like his letters—homely and moralistic. Similarly, James Deason of Danby, whose parishioners complained about his boisterous carousing, was incapable on some Sundays of stepping into the pulpit.

The Sermons of the Visitation

Whereas such an event as a visitation today would be highlighted by a solemn eucharist, the 1764 visitation days were characterized by that eighteenth-century feature, the sermon. Between 7 May and 29 June there were thirteen sermons preached in the course of the visitation at the centers chosen.[25] The preachers were not usually the incumbents of the parishes selected for the visitation, but were those who had acceded to the archbishop's particular request, with the exceptions of Daniel Addison, who preached in his own parish church of Thirsk on 27 June 1764, and Arthur Robinson, of Holy Trinity, Hull, who preached there on 21 June. At Ripon on 16 May, Dr. John Fogg, one of the prebendaries of Ripon, was the visitation preacher. The impression given in the Court Book[26] is of a formal occasion, specifically for the clergy concerned with the business of the visitation, and different, for example, from an event such as a confirmation. There is no suggestion of lay people being present in any substantial gathering for the visitation sermons.

Some clergymen of the eighteenth century preferred to avoid preaching to their brother clergy, but Dr. Wanley, rector of Stokesley, had climbed high enough up the ladder of preferment and education by 1764 not to mind having the clergy as his congregation and was willing to be a preacher at sudden notice on the last day of the visitation. As rector of Stokesley since 1750, with an income of £350 per annum, and prebendary of Weighton since 1750, with an income of £173 per annum, and doctor of divinity, as well as a personal friend of the archbishop, he was above anxieties.

Richard Conyers won a place of honor among his supporters for daring to preach an evangelical sermon as part of the visitation. As vicar of Helmsley and rector of Kirby Misperton from 1756 and 1763 respectively, Conyers was known as one of the Yorkshire evangelicals. "His preaching was aweful, earnest, and movingly pathetic, directing men to repentance, and pleading the mercies of God."[27] His ministry included having a large company of more than thirty people at his table on Sundays, allowing domestic prayers to widen into more public occasions. He was said to be nervous about preaching, yet he preached characteristically at Malton on 25 June 1764 and drew a snubbing rebuke from the archbishop.[28] The encounter illustrates one of the few situations when the archbishop could be outspoken against his clergy. But it was not "official" criticism, for the occasion appears to have been a very informal one, "in the street in conversation with several farmers." Drummond saw Conyers and took the opportunity there to speak to him: "Well, Conyers, you have given us a fine sermon!" Conyers chose to reply, "I am glad it meets the approbation of your Grace." "Approbation!" The sting followed sharply: "If you go on preaching such stuff you will drive all your parish mad. Were you to inculcate the morality of Socrates, it would do more good than canting about the new birth."

It is no wonder that Drummond felt irked by Conyers's style. There is even the possibility that Drummond deliberately chose him to reprimand, but there is no evidence for this. There is evidence, however, that others were equally interested in the sermon because the same source tells us that it was taken from Conyers's pocket during the dinner that followed. This gives us another insight into the sociable side of the days of visitation, suggesting a private dinner among friends, not an official one for all clergy, a time when they could enjoy company before setting off for home the next day. For Conyers, it was about half a day's ride back to Helmsley, but as he was also the incumbent of Kirby Misperton, the neighboring parish to Malton, he might have done some of his renowned parish visiting there on his way home. It is clear Conyers overcame his supposed nervousness about preaching (whether or not this was as a result of the archbishop's rebuke we do not know), for within a few years he joined two campaigns of preaching in Yorkshire. The first was with the countess of Huntingdon's work in 1767, and the next was in the autumn of that year separately with Whitefield.[29]

Henry Venn's Evangelical Sermons

Henry Venn's congregations in Huddersfield could expect more from sermons than in any other parish of the diocese in the mid eighteenth century both in style and content. Those who heard him season by season from 1759 until 1771 had the full benefit of his mature ministry with its "natural and affectionate"[30] manner. It must also have been strong, as his local affectionate nickname was "T'owd trumpet." His aim was to lead people to personal holiness within the Christian faith. Walsh records that there were nine hundred conversions in Huddersfield by 1762. It was unusual in the mid eighteenth century for preaching to be extempore, freely spoken from short notes; but this, according to Walsh, was Venn's style. Venn stressed in particular the importance of Sunday as the Lord's Day, and regarded sermons to be of great importance. He had them printed and distributed them among his parishioners once they had been preached. The idea of repeating the teaching in a sermon by letting the parishioners read it for themselves was itself grounded in a seasonal manner. Venn wrote,

> Tho' you have heard each of these points proved from the pulpit, I now send these proofs to you, my beloved Flock, in print also. I send them to you, in this manner, that you may more closely, and *more frequently,*[31] ponder on the important duty of keeping holy the Lord's Day."[32]

Audit

Archbishop Drummond expected the clergy of the York diocese to continue to preach from their parish pulpits, and his visitation returns show that they were keeping this part of their duty in varied and conscientious manner. Some of the most assiduous in preaching were the pluralists who went to their adjacent parishes. Equally faithful examples are found among those who served tiny congregations and those who were in large towns. Publication of sermons was current with the evangelicals. People were accustomed to sermons in church, and some Yorkshire situations were famed for repeated preaching visits by John Wesley. No clergyman would have written, "I do not preach a sermon," so the information here is necessarily positive, showing Drummond's Yorkshire as a diocese of busy preachers, with only the proud Dr. Wanley being criticized for his "wearying catechisms and the absence of a Lecture."[33]

Catechizing

The Season of Lent and the Discipline of Catechism

Lent coincided with the worst of the winter, so that catechizing in Lent is a performance indicator of clergy activity during the church's six weeks of stark withdrawal in preparation for Easter. There were no marriages in Lent. Farmers had to begin the difficulties of lambing in some of the worst conditions. The farmers who wove cloth when the weather was too bad for farming had bitter cold and dark to add to the harshness of machine work. But the early church, born in Mediterranean latitudes, had chosen Lent as the time for preparing catechumens who were to receive full membership at Easter. The Book of Common Prayer requires catechism to be undertaken every Sunday after the second lesson at evening prayer. By the 1760s catechumens were usually about sixteen years of age, but there was no tradition of an annual confirmation service. Confirmation had become so rare in some dioceses that a mythology had arisen. Some women of Bury St. Edmunds applied to be confirmed every time the bishop came to confirm, in the belief that "you cannot have too much of a good thing."[34] Archbishop Drummond has been singled out as one who assiduously managed confirmations on the grand total scale of over 40,000,[35] though this surely underestimates the reality.[36]

Catechizing could begin at a very early age. The practice was that children should repeat attendances year by year until a confirmation was planned and they were sufficiently ready or had reached the age of sixteen. Preparing children for confirmation was exactly and properly the task of the clergy, and a study of the attack that clergymen directed to this work leads to an understanding of its importance. Many of the 621 returns to the visitation of 1764 gave Lent as the catechizing time, but the difficulties of that hard season were such that several adjustments were made to the broad foundation.

The catechism in the *Book of Common Prayer* is a two-way exercise. Questions are posed. The clergy were required "to instruct and examine" so that the catechumens knew the answers to the questions. Learning was the need. Understanding was the underlying aim. The language of the questions and answers, however, is such that a child of any century is unlikely to grasp the meanings of the statements as they stand. A schooled child might be able to understand, if listening were the medium of schooling. But a country child of 1760, drilled in simple alphabet repetitions would be just as much adrift of the Book of Common Prayer catechism as a modern child who handles colored shapes, plays computer games, and sits in Wendy houses. In other words, the catechism as printed is unapproachable without explanation. Some clergymen of the eighteenth century undertook appropriate explanation. Some tried rote learning. Some used commentaries or expositions prepared by learned bishops. Some were unaware that such publications existed.

The timing of catechizing is important along with the method employed by the mid eighteenth-century clergy in Yorkshire. In spite of the difficulties of Lent as a season, many opted for a Sunday or Sundays in Lent as the best time to tackle catechism. According to the 1764 returns, they included it, as the Book of Common Prayer requires, in the service of evening prayer if there were two Sunday services. But because catechism was viewed as an exercise for children, some tacked it onto the service in order to avoid upsetting the adult members. This is where difficulties arose. The hardness of the season meant that staying afterwards used up the daylight. No one, clergy or children or parents, would choose to walk home in darkness, whether they were residents of Batley, Barwick in Elmet, or Kirkbymoorside.

So adjustments were made. The returns of 1764 show more variety in offering catechism to parishioners than in any other aspect of church life. Variations covered times as well as seasons, going from "Not frequently," and, "Soon," through to twice weekly specifically in Lent. All kinds of individual timetables were mentioned in the visitation returns. Instead of offering catechism only in Lent, several opted for the time from Easter to Whit, some during April and May, some during May alone, some throughout the summer, and some at Harvest. Some wrote that they catechized every Sunday throughout the year, some said twice weekly at the school, some said on Sundays and on weekdays at the school, some reserved it for Trinity Sunday, some used alternate Sundays, some said Sundays in summer only. Some catechized only before a confirmation. Only thirty-four parishes made a nil return on catechism. The dominance of the season of summer is clearly shown in the adjustments made away from Lent. More than eighty parishes chose Sundays in summer only in order to make best possible use of the daylight hours. There were eighty-eight parishes where catechetical instruction was given every Sunday throughout the year. These clergy must surely be regarded as especially conscientious and undaunted by the repetitive nature of this aspect of their work.

Thoroughness of approach characterized the clergy who tackled this task in the parishes with the largest populations. At Leeds the policy was to begin catechizing on the first Sunday in Lent and to continue "until we have quite gone through ye town." The Sheffield clergy catechized on Sundays from Easter to Whit but noted poor attendance except prior to a confirmation service. The unobtrusive returning style of Henry Venn of Huddersfield included the effective teaching method of repeating this week what was learned last week, "the exposition of which is wrote by their pastor." At Pontefract they even had a catechetical lectureship founded in 1754, and at the time of the 1764 visitation it was filled by no less a person than Francis Drake B.D., vicar of Womersley. The return from Drake at Womersley confirms this appointment and adds that the lectures were given every other Sunday. This was something of a drawback to the Sunday evening prayer at Womersley, which was held naturally every alternate Sunday. But, there being 35 families at Womersley and 987 in Pontefract, one may conclude that what Pontefract received in quantity, Womersley must have gained in quality.

The evidence is firm that clergy in smaller parishes and chapelries were similarly conscientious. The topic of catechism more than any other in the list of questions reveals a hardworking body of clergy faithfully coping with instruction in their parishes, whether they had many children or just a few. In the very large parish of Ecclesfield there were 534 families in the chapelry of Bradfield during the experienced incumbency of Christopher Butterfield (deacon 1727, inducted 1742). Butterfield's policy was to "call particular neighbourhoods each Sunday till ye whole be gone through." The phrase and the method are the same as those used by the vicar of Leeds.

The archbishop's Paper of Queries gave the clergy the opportunity to criticise their parishioners for neglect of duty in failing to send their children and servants to be catechized. Some clergy wished that their parishioners would recognize their duty more appropriately. Others covered up for them. It was easier to criticise when one was new to the parish, before one had made either friends or enemies. At Hinderwell, Nicholas Howlet had been in office for only a year before the visitation. He was outspokenly critical, "There is too great a backwardness (I hear) in attending this sort of instruction, and but few Expositions of the Church catechism at present in the parish." At Bradfield, as mentioned above, Christopher Butterfield had been with his parishioners since 1742 and he had no qualms about criticising them: "The parishioners are but too slack in sending their children and servants." A refreshingly clear return was sent by James Derbyshire, vicar of Sherburn in Elmet, who wrote, "It is the custom here to catechise every Sunday in Lent. No particular Exposition is used. I cannot justly accuse the parishioners of neglecting to send their children and servants."

Works of Reference

The clergy who named their authorities for exposition were in 197 parishes. Most of these referred to Wake's[37] or Beveridge's[38] or Lewis's[39] books. John Walker at Galmpton named "Bishop Williams,[40] Dr Stebbings,[41] Dr Clarke,[42] Dr Bray[43] &c &c." But the majority of clergy did not use expositions and some showed a very distant attitude to the use of reference books. James Borwick, curate of Whitby, where there were 1,699 families in 1764, wrote,

> The children of this parish are instructed publickly in their Church catechism every Wednesday and Friday in Lent as hath been usual. And at other times when their parents seem inclin'd to send them. I do not know that they learn any particular exposition of our plain Church catechism.

This distant attitude was matched by the rector of Routh, who wrote,

> I prepare myself to catechise six weeks in ye summer. I do not know whether or no my parishioners duly send their children to be instructed

and catechised nor do I know whether they learn any exposition of ye Church catechism as I cannot hear by my enquiries that they have any.

Another vague clergyman was William Thompson, rector of Addingham, who said that he catechized on some Sundays in Lent every year and that his parishioners were "pretty careful" in sending their children and servants, but in relation to exposition he wrote, "I have dispersed some of Lewis's Expositions amongst 'em," and added, "they may be read. I cannot tell."

Apart from these few vague instructors, the Georgian church in Yorkshire in the mid eighteenth century was staffed by several sensible clergymen who recognized the difference between the formal language of the Book of Common Prayer and the level of understanding of the young children sent to them. Thomas Newton, for example, of Carlton Husthwaite, wrote that he used a "plain and very familiar manner suitable to their capacities." At Horton in Ribblesdale, Joseph Hudson explained that "formerly they learnt to repeat Lewis's catechism, but finding that too much of a task for the greatest part, I have read Dr Clark's exposition to 'em and occasionally several of the small Tracts given about by the SPCK." Edmund Beeston of Burley Chapel bought "and gave away some of Synge's Tracts." Thomas Lewthwaite of Beverley St. John explained the catechism "from ye Scriptures themselves." Abraham Clarke of Hawnby gave his explanations "in as easy and familiar a manner as I possibly can," and Luke Thompson of Appleton catechized with the "assistance of those who seem to have wrote in the clearest manner upon the subject." The children sent to them were often very young. A sad form of sympathy may be evoked for the clergy who had worked out from their own studies what was to be explained, only to be faced by a group of under-fives whose needs were other than scriptural.

The visitation returns about catechism are particularly useful as performance indicators of the state of the church in Yorkshire because they represent almost all the parishes, and also because so very many of the clergy used their own words to describe how and when they did their catechizing. The evidence on this topic accords with findings in the Canterbury diocese for the eighteenth century, where there was regular catechizing even by 1806.[44] The overwhelming number of affirmative replies to the catechizing question is not related to residence or nonresidence. Catechizing took place in all parishes except thirty-four. The distribution of noncatechizing clergy is fairly evenly spread across residents and nonresidents, given that nonresidents were in the majority across the Yorkshire parishes. There were only three parishes where both the incumbent and the assistant were nonresident and where there was no catechizing: Full Sutton, Thorp Bassett, and Scorborough.

Reasons for not catechizing in those thirty-four parishes were often related to length of stay in a parish: so long that the clergyman was too elderly, or so short a time that he had not organised himself. Analysis shows only ten parishes where the clergyman was too elderly to bother with catechizing young children and only seven where the incumbent was recently arrived. One obscure reason for not catechizing was from William Pendlebury of Birdsall in the deanery of Buckrose. Pendlebury served the two neighboring parishes of Birdsall and Burythorpe, small parishes of thirty-seven and eighteen families respectively. He resided at Burythorpe because he said there was no house for him at Birdsall, and the parsonage house belonged to Lady Irwin and she had let it to a Quaker. He referred to the lady in subservient terms, allowing him £15 per annum, but in answer to catechizing he wrote, "I gave notice and desired them to send their children to be catechised and they said that they never were askt that question before and have sent none."

At Holy Trinity and St. John's in Leeds, where it has already been noted that catechizing was seriously undertaken, the two chapels gave a nil return to the specific question of catechizing because it was done from the main parish church. This reduces the number of noncatechizing parishes to thirty-two and underlines the main conclusion that catechizing was a continuingly thriving and seasonal activity throughout the Yorkshire parishes. The clergy had an additional spur to their catechizing programs as they recognized their archbishop's efficiency in confirmation, not leaving catechumens without that benefit.

The return for Hunslet chapel illustrates the interest in catechizing shown by the early evangelical clergy. The curate, Henry Crooke, had a written style as unique as his own fingerprints on the paper. He was his own worst critic, but he seemed not to realize it:

> When I first came . . . I catechised every Sunday . . . till I had only two children . . . then from Sunday afternoon to Saturday nights in Hopes of better success which at first was beyond my Expectations. It lasted only for a time. But twenty girls being lately sent from ye Foundling Hospital, I purpose to renew my catechising . . . I used no Exposition but endeavoured to speak as God was pleased to enable me.

Henry Crooke's individual manner came through also in his reply to the question about church services. He held two services on Sundays, and one on Thursdays and Saturdays, and added, "and all those days which a vain and deluding world sets apart for Sports and Diversions." Although his spiritual leadership was far ahead of his parishioners, he was firmly on course in knowing that the natural seasons governed their attendance. He wrote,

> Divine Service begins at 3pm or 7pm or 8pm and I endeavour through mercy to speak a Word according to ye Time and Season . . . and to paraphrase our most excellent Communion Service and thereby to show its beauty and Spirit.

Henry Crooke was vicar of Kippax as well as curate of Hunslet chapel, one of the "awakened" group of Anglican clergy, noted by Walsh, who referred to the clear vision they had of their parochial duties. They had decided to be at a distance from "connections beyond the framework of the Church," that is, Methodism, and "saw their duty primarily in their parish work."[45] Crooke added more of his attitude to his parish duties in his final comments on the visitation return, where he wrote,

> I have refused the Sacrament to John Walker, my Clark (sic), and to John Addison our Dog-Whipper—for Drunkenness in Both. I dare not say I have any great hopes of reformation in either of them especially in the Dog-Whipper.

Henry Crooke had been offering his brand of evangelical ministry in Hunslet since 1749 and in Kippax since 1758. It is appropriate to illustrate this section with Henry Crooke because although in the strict sense of the analysis of the returns his answer about catechising was a no, as one of the Yorkshire evangelicals he was among the keenest to promote the truths of the Gospel through the Church of England's ministry. His case also reminds us that the evangelicals were not a withdrawn or exclusive group in Drummond's Yorkshire. Henry Crooke's transparent answers show us that the distance between an "awakened" country clergyman and his traditionalist archbishop was not so great on the matter of catechism.

Audit

The Georgian church in Yorkshire upheld catechism as an aim and pursued it to its purpose of membership through confirmation.

Overwhelming evidence of catechizing activity throughout the diocese indicates that the clergy were performing their duty most carefully in this aspect of their ministry. If the practice did decrease gradually until it finally died out,[46] the decline did not begin either in Yorkshire during the time of Archbishop Drummond or in the Canterbury diocese in the time of Archbishop Secker.[47] Catechism drew together all kinds of clergy in this one activity—traditionalists, evangelicals, rural and urban incumbents, old and young, resident and nonresident. If one single test were applied to gauge the health of the Yorkshire clergy, catechism would be the most suitable, and its results would be positive. It is the one activity which presents the clergy transferring the church's doctrine to its young attenders prior to full membership, using published aids as well as their own initiative.

Schools

The Church's Responsibility for Education

Archbishop Drummond promoted the education of children. He successfully taught his own large family of sons and daughters, by their own testimony (see chapter 2), and sometimes preached for the charity school societies at their annual meetings. The diocese of York was rich in schools, and several were founded during Drummond's time, including one in 1766 at Cherry Cobb in the Holderness deanery especially for clergy orphans.[48] Schools are reliable performance indicators of church life, since most were controlled by clergy. The archbishop rolled through his questions about the names of the teachers, the subjects taught, whether the scholars were brought to church, the numbers of pupils, whether they were put out to trades, whether they were clothed and housed, and who administered their charitable status. The visitation returns are full of absorbing details in reply. The range of comment veers from the convictions of an individualist grammar school master preparing bright scholars for Oxford and Cambridge, to a curate struggling to teach a tiny class of children from simple families. One aloof priest wrote patronizingly of a woman in his parish struggling to describe the alphabet; one curate found that the schoolmaster's pay was never actually forthcoming, that the scholars had drifted away, and that there were perfectly satisfactory arrangements in the parish of which his was merely the chapelry, arrangements that superseded his efforts.[49]

Identifying the Types of Schools

The answers to the archbishop's questions have such varied patterns of reference that analysis requires additional comments throughout. In the Drummond returns there were 319 parishes with a school or schools, just over half the number of parishes studied. Three main types are described: public (that is, usually, free) grammar schools, charity schools with endowments, and private or petty schools. The usage was quite unstandardized among the reporting clergy, so that a mixture of terminology emerges from both sets of returns. Identifying a balanced pattern for the three types is not a straightforward task. The grammar schools underwent significant changes in the course of the eighteenth century, and it was a time when many villages and towns started schools for basic and practical education. A charity school is usually understood to mean one where a teacher drew an annual income to educate a given number of children from foundation investment, and this could also describe a grammar school. A charity school could also be continuingly supported by an annual charity sermon, the collections going to the school. This was so at St. Olave, York. Some changes occurred because of the practical difficulty of maintaining the founder's wishes against altered financial values, so that the status of a school might differ between 1743 and 1764. Where founders and benefactors determined the original guidelines according to their own whims, so whims and corresponding caprice might arise among their heirs and trustees. Sizes of school varied as much as curricular styles, boys as well as girls being taught in some schools, and schools for one sex only (more often for boys only than for girls only) sometimes in the same town as other foundations.

The variety of organization and teaching and payment and appraisal is nearly as great as the variety of styles of catechizing. Details of particular factors—both in 1743 and in 1764—emerge as unique to the town or village where the school was located. This is mainly because the clergy differed in the style of their reporting and in their estimation of the worth of the schools in their parishes and chapelries. The amount of information in both sets of returns offers scope for study and interpretation along with the accompanying details of population data and pastoral care for each parish.

Population Changes

Increases and decreases in the population affected the provision of schools in the parishes of Yorkshire during the mid eighteenth century. Several parishes showed increases and decreases of population with not much change in the schooling provided. A worse situation was where the population increased significantly and where the provision for schooling was less. This happened, for example, at Bishop Wilton, Ecclesfield, Hinderwell, and Pocklington. Improved situations are discernible where an increase in population was paralleled with more schools and more children in them, such as at Horton in Ribblesdale, Holy Trinity Hull, Kirkbymoorside, Leeds, and St. Michael in New Malton. A natural improvement was deemed where schools were mentioned in the 1764 returns but not in 1743, suggesting, but not without all doubt, that these were newly founded. Few abuses of funds and endowments are recorded; some schoolhouses without masters or pupils are mentioned. Some arrears of payments went missing.

Three Examples of Difficulties: Flockton, Thornhill, and Keighley

Flockton

The reference in the 1764 visitation returns by Samuel Brook of Flockton Chapel to a public school founded in 1699 for six poor boys to learn Latin is reason enough to think that the foundation was in use at the time of the Herring returns, when Brook himself had been there already for five years. It is less straightforward to move from the given details to say whether the education there was healthy or not by the time of the Drummond visitation, since the population had increased from seventy-five families in 1743 to ninety-eight families in 1764. The fact that the school had continued to operate would count this as a gain for the church; but there would have been increased competition among poor boys of Flockton for the six places, though the boys themselves might have preferred a practical life to the drill of Latin. Samuel Brook, the curate, gave the impression, however, that he regarded the school as an asset to the chapelry, mentioning that the school had been rebuilt since the foundation, that it included a small house for the master, John Hall, who was clerk of the chapel. It had gathered additional endowment with interest from one of the turnpike trusts near Wakefield. His later comments, however, uncover his own housing problems, and financial and teaching difficulties in the nearby parish of Almondbury. Brook wrote that,

> As there never was any house built at Flockton for the use of a curate, the Endowment was no more than £48 per annum and the occasional

> duty very small. I have been permitted hitherto to reside upon a small grammar school at Almondbury, to which I was licensed in 1732 endow'd only with £19.15s.8d and whereof £5 per annum to the school left by one Israel Wormall was obtained by a Decree in Chancery in 1753 but I never yet could obtain either the annual payment or the arrears due.

It sounds as if Samuel Brook had become so demoralized that he had given up on the pastoral ministry itself in Flockton and had settled for the schoolhouse in Almondbury, to make the best of an unsatisfactory provision. It should be added that Flockton was a chapelry within the large parish of Thornhill and was situated next to the even larger parish of Almondbury, where the rector, Edward Rishton, was the characterful and critical elderly clergyman, whose returns, noted earlier, showed how this situation had deteriorated, disclosing that poor Brook was so "disabled by gout and other infirmities that no children have been taught in it [the school] for several years."[50] It is more than likely that Rishton was making comparisons with the effective work done by John Murgatroyd in the free school in Slaithwaite, where Rishton would have known him during his forty-eight years as schoolmaster and curate from 1755 to 1767.[51]

Thornhill

Thornhill had its educational affairs apparently working much better in practice—though possibly superficially so—than was the case in Flockton. Sir George Savile, the MP, supported a school for all the poorer tenants of Thornhill parish who could send their children gratis. The master had £20 per annum. There is no mention of the pupils learning Latin, though they did have religious instruction. The superficiality is in the unendowed nature of Sir George's support: at his whim, the school could be discontinued, the master deprived of income, and the instruction cease, whereas the older charity foundation of 1699 for Flockton had loftier and more continuous aspirations. On the other hand, as Sir George grew older, it could have occurred to him to endow his school and give it a firm charitable status, although there is no evidence of this. Sir George served as MP for more than twenty years—when the population of Thornhill increased from 160 families to 436—and aligned himself in broad terms with the Church of England, referring to it as the "Church of Christ" in the 1772 Commons debate on the Bill for the Relief of Dissenters, so his role as a school benefactor was limited rather than grand.

Keighley

In Keighley, a large parish on the southern edge of the Craven deanery, the school had been founded by John Drake in 1713 and was described in the 1764 returns as a free school, the current master being John Leach. The rector of Keighley did not know how many scholars were in attendance, but knew that the children were not "cloathed, maintained or lodged," that English was taught, and that the master was obliged to teach Latin and Greek to "such as require it." The rector's lack of detail about the number of pupils sounds a little like a distance of communication between him and the school, as if he did not visit the school, leaving it entirely to the master. The population of his parish had grown to 700 families in 1764 from 450 at the time of the Herring returns. The number of pupils at Keighley School was put at thirty at the time of the Herring returns, when the reporting clergyman stated that the children were given appropriate religious instruction. Charles Knowlton had been the rector since 1753 and would have witnessed the past decade of population growth; moreover, he was resident, in contrast with the 1743 situation, where the item in the returns was left blank, but a resident curate was declared. His own residence as the rector in a growth parish may show his pastoral care as positive, but his detachment from the school suggests neither indifference nor actual support. The population growth since the foundation of the school might be seen as a deprivation for several children.

Three Examples of Improvement: Bishopthorpe, Bolton upon Dearne, and Leeds

Bishopthorpe

It is in character that the archbishop contributed to the improvement in schooling in the parish where his palace was sited. Two years after his arrival in York, he began annual payments of seven pounds to a new school in Bishopthorpe. The vicar, John Dealtary, was also a contributor; his annual sum was one pound. The schoolmaster drew an income of forty shillings and taught reading and writing and religious knowledge to twenty boys and girls. As a provision of schooling for a parish of only thirty families this was handsome. There was no school in Bishopthorpe until this 1763 foundation. It shows that in education Drummond was prepared to initiate and to contribute to the present and to the future, especially in a case where building was concerned.

Bolton upon Dearne

Three benefactions totalling 180 pounds in the parish of Bolton upon Dearne produced an annual income of 8 pounds for the Reverend Thomas Wilcock to teach the "three Rs" and religious knowledge to sixteen boys or girls. In addition to the sixteen children funded by the charity, Wilcock catechized another twenty every week. There was no mention of a school in the Herring return for Bolton upon Dearne. The total population by 1764 was ninety families. The educational provision in 1764 in this Doncaster parish was a clear improvement since 1743. The return is a straightforward performance indicator of two clergymen working in the parish, one as curate and the other as schoolmaster and catechizer, with weekly catechism for more children than were funded by the charity school.

Leeds

The Leeds clergy were well aware that the population of the city was growing. They were taking weekly action to include the new groups of people, whether transient or permanent, into the life of the church in the parish and the chapelries. Education was included in their priorities of action, as is clear from the style and content of Samuel Kirshaw's returns in 1764. The status of the schools improved in the opinion of the clergy since 1743, when the return mentioned two charity schools. The return for 1764 gives details of the free grammar school founded 1650 and the charity school supported by annual subscriptions. The omission in the 1743 returns of a reference to the style of the 1650 foundation being a grammar school sounds like a gap of understanding on an unfortunately large scale. The foundation consisted, according to the 1764 details, of a purchase of lands which brought in two hundred pounds per annum, to fund the master and the usher in teaching ninety boys Latin and Greek. The master and the usher were both clergymen in 1764 with M.A. degrees, and were both named by Samuel Kirshaw. Kirshaw was not an evangelical but showed some sympathy for them in appointing Miles Atkinson as his curate in 1766 and lecturer in 1770. Having a lecturer was not necessarily anything to do with education, in that a lecturer was an auxiliary reader of the church service. In the case of Leeds parish, generally the church was gaining ground because of the healthy state of the schools.

More Schools for More Children

A comparison of the Drummond returns with those of Herring shows that there were seventy-two more schools in existence in 1764 than in 1743, always remembering that this information comes from the incumbents. The gain of seventy-two schools consisted of new foundations of charity schools and represents the spontaneous growth of private schools supported by their parishes or chapelries. Where the subjects taught were specified in the 1764 returns for the seventy-two new schools, the provision was mainly for a basic education with religious instruction. Seven schools out of the seventy-two new schools taught classical as well as basic subjects, at Rawden, Burnsall, Hartwith, Slaidburne, Thornthwaite, Thornton in the Dale, and at Holy Trinity, Goodramgate, in York. Most of the seventy-two schools gave a positive answer to the question whether religious instruction was given. Most of the new foundations are listed as charity schools providing a basic education. Three out of the list as a whole are described as grammar schools—at Barnsley, Slaidburne and Thornton in the Dale, and the one at Thornton in the Dale was also mentioned in the Herring returns as a charity school then. Practical subjects, such as knitting and sewing were taught in four schools—Dishforth, St. Olave's, Barnsley, and Dewsbury. At two of these the school was responsible for getting apprenticeships for its pupils.

A list of the Yorkshire grammar schools was compiled at the end of the nineteenth century along with a summary of Yorkshire educational bequests.[52] These, with their picture of the guardianship of education exercised by the Cambridge colleges in their provision of scholarships for Yorkshire students, show the close links between the church and education. Some of the college fellowships were funded specifically for those in priest's orders. St. John's College had fourteen Yorkshire benefactions. In Beverley the city fathers were strengthening the ties between their cathedral city and education, providing scholarships and exhibitions for St. John's College students.

Some of these trends accord with the conclusions drawn by J. Lawson in his study of the endowed grammar schools of East Yorkshire.[53] He described the eighteenth century as a time when a drop in the demand for the classics was leading quite early on in poor rural areas to an increase in demand for private or petty schools.

The inferences here for the connection between clergy and village petty schools are that some educated clergymen found it difficult to identify wholeheartedly with the practices and curriculum of a school which taught reading and writing and accounts, when their own learning had comprised Latin and Greek; and that they saw a decline that distanced them from the activities of parish clerks or dames or dissenters, in contrast with masters and ushers. Lawson also cited the small fixed-rent charges of endowed schools as a reason for the decline in standards of teaching in grammar schools because the master had to apply himself to estate management instead of to teaching if he were to survive financially. A decline in episcopal licensing, possibly alongside the increase in dissenter schools, was another factor in Lawson's list of reasons for the increase of private schools.

Long before Lawson had reached his conclusions about the growth of petty or private schools in the eighteenth century, A. F. Leach had made some corresponding remarks about their clientele. Aside from his critical view of the "degrading" of grammar schools by alteration of the curriculum, he attributed the interchange of names for public and grammar schools as much to the late eighteenth century as to the nineteenth century. He considered that schooling was attracting a wider social range of families because of the changes in transport and income. His main comment was one which evoked the plain common sense of the Yorkshireman being applied across the rest of the country:

> The country gentlemen [of the eighteenth century] resorted to Chichester Prebendal School, or Sedbergh, or Warwick, or Stratford, just as much as to Harrow or Rugby. . . . The ordinary country gentleman sent his son to the nearest grammar school of repute as a matter of course."[54]

The debate about changes in status and style of schools during the eighteenth century has been carefully explored by R. S. Tompson and M. Sanderson.[55] Tompson described the development of the grammar schools' curriculum into more broadly popular subjects. Sanderson noted the growth of schools founded by private teachers; and both argued that grammar schools, instead of deteriorating as Leach had concluded, were upgraded by curriculum reform in response to client demand.

Tompson's statistics for grammar schools—whose curriculum was classics only—in the West Riding of Yorkshire show that none remained by 1799, and that seven schools (corresponding with the seven out of the seventy-two new schools mentioned earlier) taught classics and English. Of one other original grammar school Tompson was uncertain. He listed some of the other subjects taught in schools: penmanship, mathematics, bookkeeping, navigation, Hebrew, chronology, nature, but he gave no specific examples of these for Yorkshire. He also listed modern foreign languages, geography, correspondence, foreign exchange, and financial transactions,[56] as subjects that schools introduced in response to client demand for commercial knowledge.

The West Riding of Yorkshire was one of 14 English counties where Tompson studied information for 58 schools. The trend that he noticed—of spontaneous expansion of the curriculum in grammar schools during the eighteenth century—was underwritten at Penistone, in the Doncaster deanery, in 1785 where the parental influence was sufficiently strong to fund the repair of school buildings and the schoolmaster's house. Tompson concluded that the eighteenth-century grammar schools "were innovating, probably in response to public demands in education, and therefore their curriculum should not be viewed as stagnant or decadent."

Archbishop Drummond was drawn into a move for a curriculum change at Heath grammar school, Halifax. In 1769 the governors appealed to him as episcopal visitor because the schoolmaster, Thomas West, disagreed with their plan to introduce writing, accounts, geography, geometry, and natural philosophy. The lawyer in Drummond gave a cautious reply because the original charter founded the school "only for Latin and Greek." When Drummond heard soon after that a court-approved statute for instruction in writing in that school had been given in 1730, he allowed the suggested plan.[57]

Tompson's view that the middle of the eighteenth century was a time when changes in schools and curriculum were happening at a gathering pace assists the study of the visitation returns. It clarifies why the returning clergymen of 1743 and 1764 wrote with such a variety of reference to the schools in their parishes and chapelries. Some clergy stressed that the private or petty schools were not charity schools by using the phrase "not endowed," which made the situation clear. Others made no such comment. Confusion of classification remains for many schools, but there can be no doubt that the archbishop at the head of the diocese was keen to promote the education of children throughout the Yorkshire parishes, and did what he could, both in the small scene of the parish of Bishopthorpe and more widely through the exigencies of the visitation.

The main indication from the evidence of both sets of returns is that more private, petty, or charity schools existed for more children in 1764 than in 1743.

The redressing factor is that the increased number of schools and places for children in the schools may be offset by the increase in the number of inhabitants. In some cases a genuine improvement had taken place, providing more schools per population. The worsened situations included small parishes as well as largely populated towns, but this may show because the clergy in 1743 gave more information about numbers of children in the schools.

The York diocese in the mid eighteenth century was a place of unsystematic but changing education. This may be a comment on the educational provision for other dioceses, but it is one that cannot be omitted. No connection existed between the population numbers and the charity provisions. This is not surprising when the foundations of several schools had occurred well before the great alterations in industry and agriculture. What followed, however, was that there was no relation between the number of residents and their ability to organize their children's education. The wish to provide education for children of the parish could be as strong in places with under fifty families as in those with over two hundred families. Huge disproportions abounded alongside the charitable intentions of founders. In some parishes full instruction in English, reading, writing, accounts, and Latin and Greek if desired, along with practical subjects, were available to any who wished to send their children. Some places had no provision at all. Charitable endowments, local initiative, aristocratic provision at pleasure, ancient free grammar schools, and private teaching all found existence.

But besides the children funded by the charitable provisions and declared by the returning clergymen, there were also the children paid for by their parents. This is another whole sector of children in schools to emerge from a general study of the 1764 visitation returns. The point was stressed by several of the clergy in commenting on the schools. In addition to the funded children, whose number was entered in the returns, the custom in several parishes was for the schoolteacher to take extra paying pupils. This is a feature which is likely to have occurred even where the clergyman did not specifically say so. It alters the idea of the provision of education throughout the diocese, and the alteration is in favor of more children being taught than were recorded.

Audit

Although it is not possible to estimate how many more children were being educated in Drummond's Yorkshire than those numbered in the returns—space, incomes, and population being the variants—the feature itself is important as a norm for the 319 parishes of 1764. The overall verdict on the state of the diocese through education is of active schools in half the parishes. The activity was not confined to the achievement of teachers and pupils, for which there can be few accurate measurements, but consisted in changes of curriculum and changes in styles of school. The image of education suffering a decline in quality, deteriorating from classical studies, thinning from a grammar school standard to a veneer of literacy is partly true, just as the image of a church led by absentee vicars is partly true of the mid eighteenth century. But the fuller truth is that grammar schools were widening the range of their curriculum to include subjects now recognized as within the humanities, as well as those of practical use. The other performance indicator of the health of the church's role in education in Drummond's Yorkshire is that there were more schools in 1764 than there had been in 1743, and that more children were attending school. In keeping with the spirit of the age, however, educating children was unstandardized, each school an entity in its own parish, the only national aspect being the charity schools founded by the SPCK.

The Administration of Charities

Benefactions and Special Days in the Year

Manifold charities within the Georgian church are performance indicators across a wide range of disbursements in kind and in cash, in endowments and in housing. Benefactors liked to associate their generosity with their own birthdays or a favorite saint's day. This was one of the few ideas carried over successfully from before the Reformation, when founders and benefactors had established chantries for masses. Protesting against the doctrine of prayers for the dead, the eighteenth-century Anglican church maintained a lively memory of benefactors by distributing bread or coal or cash on the day chosen by the terms of the charity. Even if no particular day was selected, the seasons still dominated a charity with biennial dividends: Christmas and Lady Day were obvious occasions. Beneficiaries thus linked the church's calendar with the natural seasons once again.

The Extent of Charitable Support for the Poor

This was the first part of a question about parishioners as well as the incumbent. The range of answers to questions about benefactions, hospitals, almshouses, and augmentations draws a picture of an unevenly financed diocese, but of one where there was much inventive provision for the needs and comfort of the poor. Well over half of the parishes returning information to the archbishop had some form of charitable provision. This excludes schools, which have been treated separately.

Analysis shows that the charitable provision had no relation to the size of population then living in the parishes. Some of the larger towns such as Sheffield, Dewsbury, Halifax, Hull, Scarborough, Wakefield and Pontefract had almshouses, hospitals and benefactions, as would be expected. But some of the places with tiny populations had their own benefactors. Atwick, with thirty-three families, had almshouses and an income of three pounds per annum for the poor, provided by a Mr. Fenwick in 1689. At Halsham, with its thirty-two families, there was a hospital for eight men, each of whom had four pounds per annum and two women to wait on them, each woman having forty shillings per annum. The men and women, according to the rector, were paid punctually and regularly at Lady Day and Michaelmas.

The compassion of the benefactors was matched by their inventiveness in making endowments. Bread every week or money to buy it was one of the most usual charities, and only in one place—Whiston, in the Doncaster deanery—carried the stipulation that it was for those who attended church twice on Sunday. "Poor protestant people" were specified as recipients of one penny in bread at Helmsley, reminding us that bread could be charitably provided with only small amounts of beneficed money. The poor of Nunnington received cash payments from the interest on twenty pounds if they attended prayers on New Year's Day.

Clothing was also favored as a benefaction. "Rugg gowns" were provided at Hatfield for four poor men; a gown was provided for the minister. "By agreement with Mr Jenkins £1 10s is paid every third year in lieu of a gown." Six waistcoats for six poor widows were donated at Haltongill Chapel. At Haworth ten poor children, boys or girls, were "cloathed in blue" every year. Canvas cloth was given to the poor to the value of one pound every year at Heptonstall. At Ledsham five men and five women were each to have four pounds every year and clothes, and these were accommodated in a hospital handsomely endowed by Lady Elizabeth Hastings. At another hospital, in the parish of Loundsbrough, the benefactors were the first earl and countess of Burlington, and they provided six old bachelors or widowers and six widows with five pounds per year, paid monthly, and one pound every year to buy a greatcoat or gown. In addition to those comforts they also received one pound per year for fuel. This was in a parish where there were only twenty-seven families in 1764, representing a vivid hope for a high proportion of poor people. Silver is mentioned in only two places, and the silver cups noted in the visitation returns of 1764 at Riccall and Thwing are likely to be the ones surviving today and mentioned in Pevsner's survey.[58] The silver cup at Thwing had been presented by Archbishop Lamplugh who had been born there. Bibles were given every year in the small parish of Normanby.

At Patrington provision had been made for a livelier memory of the benefactor: the ringers received some cash and everyone enjoyed entertainment at the annual perambulation of the parish. The ringers were particularly well thought of at Patrington as the benefactor had also left money for the repair of old bell frames.

The seasons governed most of these and many similar bequests. Particular days such as Candlemas and Lammas were named. Certain dates were given, as twenty shillings to the poor at Kildale, half to be given out on 1 May, and half on 11 November. At Halifax the number of bequests was so great that the vicar, George Legh, wrote all that he could fit into the available space and then added, "On other articles I trouble not your Grace here, begging leave to refer to ye Terrier."

There was only a slight relationship between benefaction and the value of the living. Benefactors provided for 160 parishes where the living was worth forty pounds or more out of 334 altogether. The other 174 parishes, where the value of the living was less than forty pounds, had also bred their benefactors. Seventeen of the York city churches had a benefaction.

Charity Sermons

Some of the benefactions listed in answers to Q4 of the visitation returns paid for sermons to be preached. In some cases a different clergyman, perhaps with the title of lecturer, would preach the sermon, though it was usually the incumbent. Their use of the church's calendar assisted the clergy in teaching its members the right doctrine about the dead and giving them hope for eternal life. Favorite choices for preaching charity sermons were St. Thomas's Day, Christmas, Whitsun, Trinity, and New Year's Day.

The sums of money left for charity sermons varied greatly. Tickhill was least, with eight shillings to the preacher for a commemoration sermon on 1 August. It was ten shillings for the sermon at Himsworth on 19 December, the same at Garton on the Wolds for one in January; advancing to thirteen shillings at Pocklington for one on St. Thomas's Day (but the heir at law was refusing to pay that), and up to twenty shillings for one in April at Hutton Cranswick. The curate at Tong chapel earned forty shillings for a catechizing sermon. George Hicks Paul at Sledmere did rather better with £2.10s for a Christmas Day sermon, and at Hedon there was a charitable bequest of £3 per annum "to ye Minister for preaching a sermon every third day of August for ever payable the same day." Two congregations in evangelical parishes were beneficiaries under this heading: John Richardson, who succeeded William Grimshaw at Haworth, preached two sermons every Sunday, the afternoon ones being funded by an annual endowment of £10; and Richard Conyers at Kirby Misperton earned ten shillings for preaching a sermon every year on 17 September. We may conclude that people expected to hear sermons on particular days in the church's calendar and that the clergy regarded preaching as both a regular duty and a special duty.

Checking on Abuses

The archbishop's purposes did not have a seasonal basis, but they were to check abuses. This meant that the incumbents had to find out how the trustees were administering the charities. In several cases the clergy were themselves the trustees. Cases of abuse, though few, were mentioned in much detail. At Grindleton the curate, John Riley, reported that a Quaker had the discharge of letting the land that had been gifted to the parish, and that he (the curate) "suffered by it." Henry Crooke reported that a fifty shilling payment due from a charity had not been made since he came to the chapel of Hunslet. At Lastingham there were several small annual sums payable to the poor, one of which, according to the curate, had not been paid for the past eleven years. At Seamer the curate reported defaults in the payments due to him for preaching charity sermons and to the support of the children at the charity school (the founder's provision being for "hose and shoes and shirt and motley or blue cap"); some of the money was going to a dissenting minister two parishes away and some to the descendants of the founder. At Leven, Thomas Barker, the rector, reported that the son of "one Wilkinson of Hull (deceased)," was refusing to pay the twenty shillings his father had left to the poor. At Scawby the vicar had been able to put right an abuse where a house for two poor people had been in ruins and where rents from lands had not been used to pay for bread. The vicar had had the house rebuilt. At Scrayingham the rector had not only rescued the dwindled income from a benefaction to apprentice some poor children, but had invested it in 3 percent consolidated annuities at his own expense. He said that he was prepared to bear any fall in stocks, but hoped rather for a profit that he could donate for the education of children.

The visitation thus offered clergy the opportunity to make it known that they were informing the archbishop about frauds, abuses, and irregularities. This might have been sufficient to put right what had gone wrong in some cases. All this is in character with Archbishop Drummond, who worked effectively for a legally correct observance. The large number of places with a charitable provision of some type shows up the lack of such support in the other parishes. The style of answering in the negative in the returns without almshouses or benefactions ranges from the plain dash as a nil entry to the blunt "None," and the plaintive "We have nothing."

There is no evidence in the archbishop's correspondence to suggest that it was usual to approach rich people to make a bequest or a donation. In politics, by contrast, it was well understood that considerable sums of money were expended at times of general elections. Investing in the next generation by charity came from private individuals rather than from leaders of current political parties. Archbishop Drummond in his own will left nothing of this sort, providing as was the custom by primogeniture for his family in their as yet unborn generations.

Audit

The state of the diocese seen through its charities indicates that trustees were generally performing their duties capably and honestly. The image of the eighteenth-century "unreformed" church rests on the weakness of its unequal finances. It is not surprising that in a church where the majority of clergy survived on very low incomes with small hope of improvement, the charities consisted of tiny sums paid out once a year from quite small investment funds. The benefits in kind—the coal, the bread, the clothing—are in keeping with this unequal society, where rich men bought horses and houses and spent lavishly at election times, and then at moments of crisis thought of Queen Anne's Bounty or a hospital, or of bread for the poor at Christmas. Rich women were noticeable for their charitable provision in kind for the poor, the two outstanding benefactresses being Lady Elizabeth and Lady Margaret Hastings. Benefactors whose status must have been that of prosperous tradespeople could and did make provision in various ways for the poor of their hometowns and villages. The state of the diocese seen through its charities is one of faithfully keeping alive the names of founders of charities from earlier times, as many clergy included such details in their returns.

The Terriers: An Additional Audit to the Visitation Returns

Larger and More Detailed Terriers

The clergymen who referred the archbishop to the terriers instead of answering directly at Q4, as most did, had some understandable reasons for confusing the information required there with the information on the terriers. They may have thought that the information overlapped or even duplicated what they were required to set out more fully than ever before on their terriers. The new-style terriers are key indicators of the interest the archbishop took in the material provision of the church for its clergy. They were to be brought for scrutiny on the day of visitation. As well as taking much time and interest in the splendid additions to and refurbishing of his own palace at Bishopthorpe, the archbishop showed a corresponding interest in recording the condition of the parsonages and the items of furniture in the churches, in a way which has so far not been duly appreciated by historians. The terriers are a source of evidence which deserves attention. There was no way that Drummond could have done anything about the reported condition of the parsonages, for they were either the parson's freehold or the lay patron's property. His interest could only have evoked a continuing care for the buildings in good condition, warning against neglect of those in poor condition.

The parish terriers of the York diocese (in the Bishopthorpe papers in the Borthwick Institute) offer proof that Drummond gave a new direction to incumbents on how to describe the assets of their livings. It was a practice that he had begun at St. Asaph.[59] The terriers for the year 1764 have characteristics in common that point to the direct commands of the archbishop. Most show that they were responding to his specific questions (2 February 1764, Directions to the Reverend Clergy of the Diocese), as their layout, though far from standardized like the visitation returns, is generally in numbered or separated paragraphs on different topics, such as glebe, church furniture, clock bells, and wages of clerks and sextons.

All the terriers seen are on larger pieces of parchment than those of previous terriers. Almost all had far more detail than the previous terrier, whether those were as recent as 1760, or in 1749 or 1747. The additional details were noticeably about the housing of the incumbents and the furnishings of the church. The details given for the parsonages concerned the size of the houses, the materials used in their construction, the number of rooms and the style of their interior decor, and the type and construction of any outbuildings. The information about church furnishings referred to items necessary for church services, such as the books, the linen, the plate, and the communion table. Monuments were not described, nor were pews.

Most of the terriers of 1764 had a more efficient appearance, with lines drawn for the writing, with margins and titled headings. They were spaced out for easier reading, with a professional style of script. The difference is remarkable in this matter, in that the terriers of the very late seventeenth and early eighteenth centuries are almost all on small pieces of parchment, hardly more than scraps, with bare statements in unremarkable styles of writing. The difference is all the more noticeable when the same clergyman was completing the 1764 terrier as had written the recent one of 1760. He was responding obediently to the archbishop's particular specifications, if not for precise layout at least for enough space and for the order of writing the information. The archbishop may not have requested the references by names to benefactors and their bequests, but he may have given a charge to omit nothing. The size of parchment used was an obvious change because of the increased amount of information. These characteristic presentational features are a reminder of Drummond's eye for the print layout, which was noticed in his visitation preparations, discussed in chapter 3.

The larger size is significant because it gave a different status to the terrier, making it more impressive as a document, implying authority to which reference was made subsequently. Later terriers used the same format as that begun in 1764. Drummond's legal training led him to give guidance to the incumbents on how to present their information. It had significant results. His wish for more detail provides us with a fuller knowledge of the York parishes and their churches and parsonages, and shows how closely interested he was in recording the information about clergy housing. More than this, the formula required was adhered to for the next hundred years, as subsequent incumbents faithfully, but sometimes irrelevantly, copied the information they inherited.

To illustrate the changes, the terrier for Barton le Street in 1764 is a very large parchment, wide rather than long, spacious in layout, with margins proportional to the whole, and prepared as a professional job, with Sidney Swinney's signature as vicar at the foot. The earlier terrier was completed in 1760, written freely on a long, narrow parchment by Sidney Swinney himself, without margins and in bare terminology. The "dwelling house" of 1760 had become the "Parsonage house" by 1764. A similar modification occurred at Brompton in Pickering, where James Nelson was the vicar. "A house, a barn, a stable," of 1760 became in 1764, "A vicarage House built in stone and timber, covered with thatch, a kitchen, . . . a chamber above it" and several other rooms. "Adjoining to the west end of the house is a barn, and near the north east end is a stable built with stone and covered with thatch."

The request from the archbishop for itemized information is implicit in the style of reply from George Gowndril of Swine in the Holderness deanery. Gowndril set out his answers against fancy numbers in Roman lettering, thickly penned. He listed the information as if Archbishop Drummond had asked nine questions. There were indeed nine questions in the 1749 requests at St. Asaph.

To illustrate the way in which the 1764 style set the subsequent pattern, the curate at Bilsdale Chapel in the parish of Helmsley, William Deason, lodged a complaint against his vicar which was perpetuated. He wrote,

> the calf tythe which the curate always enjoy'd for serving the Cure, till now, that the present vicar of Helmsley lays claim to it, and exacts 5 pounds a year from the curate on that account who performs all the duty.

The complaint was current in 1764, but it was repeated exactly in the 1770 terrier, though the statement had been overtaken by the passage of time. It was as if the writer was frightened of altering anything that had acquired so firm a legal status.

The Parsonages

The point is not that by 1764 the clergy acquired much grander homes and outbuildings than four years or twenty years before, but that a full report of their accommodation was made available. Drummond was the one who elicited this information. The clergy replies show a willingness to supply full details and are in line with the eighteenth-century general interest in building and housing. They refer to building materials, location in relation to outbuildings, the number and styles of all the rooms including such facilities as wash houses, pantries, cowhouses, coalhouses, dairies, stables, and barn; they also describe the decor of the rooms, whether wainscotted, ceiled, or paneled. Members of the clergy were not asked about their parsonages' condition. The terrier evidence as a whole reminds us that the Anglican clergy—from bishop to priest—had a high regard for the parson's freehold and that some clergy thought their parsonages, whatever their condition, were worth having in an age of pluralism.

The reply from Henry Egerton, rector of Settrington in the Buckrose deanery, gave measurement details for his rectory. It was a fine place. Previous terriers had not listed such an amount of information. Egerton described the house as measuring

> 76′ in front from North to South, built with stone and covered with slate, containing the Hall, 16′10″×6′7″ floored with stone and ceiled with plaister. Drawing room 16′10″×16′10″ floored with deal and ceiled with plaister. Study 18′× 17′8″ wainscotted. Kitchen 20′2″×16′10″. Servants Hall 16′×13′. Brewhouse 19′×13′. Larder 9′×5′. Housekeeper's larder 6′×8′. Scullery 8′×7′. Butler's pantry 11′×7,′ all partitioned with stone walls except the housekeeper's larder.

He listed the seven chambers on the upper floor, giving their sizes as well, and the sizes of the two necessary houses, also built in stone and "covered with tyles."

Timothy Lee of Ackworth in the Pontefract deanery was so aware of the request for specific details that he set it out in the form of a chart. His terrier of 1764 was double the size of the one written in 1748, and the amount of detail was so much more that he presented the terrier in the form of a stitched, eight-sided booklet, an idea that he used again for the 1770 terrier. Lee's chart was as follows:

	floor	ceiling	length	breadth
One dwelling house built of stone and brick, front to North East			60′	15′
This dwelling house contains				
parlour	deals	paper	16′	15′
hall	flags	stucco	21′	19′
study	flags	paper	16′	15′
pantry	flags	limed hair	12′	
kitchen	brick	limed hair	23′ 12′	
servants' hall & passage	brick	limed hair	18′	17′

Over these are 6 chambers with deal floors, ceilings of 4 are paper, 1 stucco & 1 tapestry very old.

Over these are 4 garrets	plaister	limed hair		
One wash house built of stone & covered with tile instead of thatch by ye present Rector . .	brick	plain	26′	16′
One brewhouse			18′	18′
One corn barn, stone and brick by ye present Rector . . .			72′	18′
One other barn now a stable & coach or carthouse . . .	pebbles	plain	48′	18′
One stable, stone by present Rector			23′	14′
One outshut, cowhouse & fodderam by present Rector with 2 privies			48′	18′

Garden highway South, fold North, part for kitchen, part for flowers . . .

NB The grotto with 13 and a half yards were taken off the hemp yard and are the property of Dr Lee.

Dr. Lee was similarly scrupulous in recording the inscription on the church bells, one of which bore his own name and the other the warning, "All men who hear my mournful sound / Repent before you lie in ground." One of Drummond's regular correspondents was William Herring of Bolton Percy. His terrier describes a substantial house. He had two parlors, one of which was wainscotted, the other hung. Five bedchambers also had papered walls. He included the fact that he had insured the whole establishment, including the brewhouse, the barn, the laundry, the coach house, the dovehouse, carthouses and granary for one thousand pounds.

John Benson, vicar of Ledsham, also lived in some style, and may have owed some of this to Lady Elizabeth Hastings, who had made several benefactions to Ledsham church. Benson's vicarage was built of brick and stone, covered with slate, and the floor of

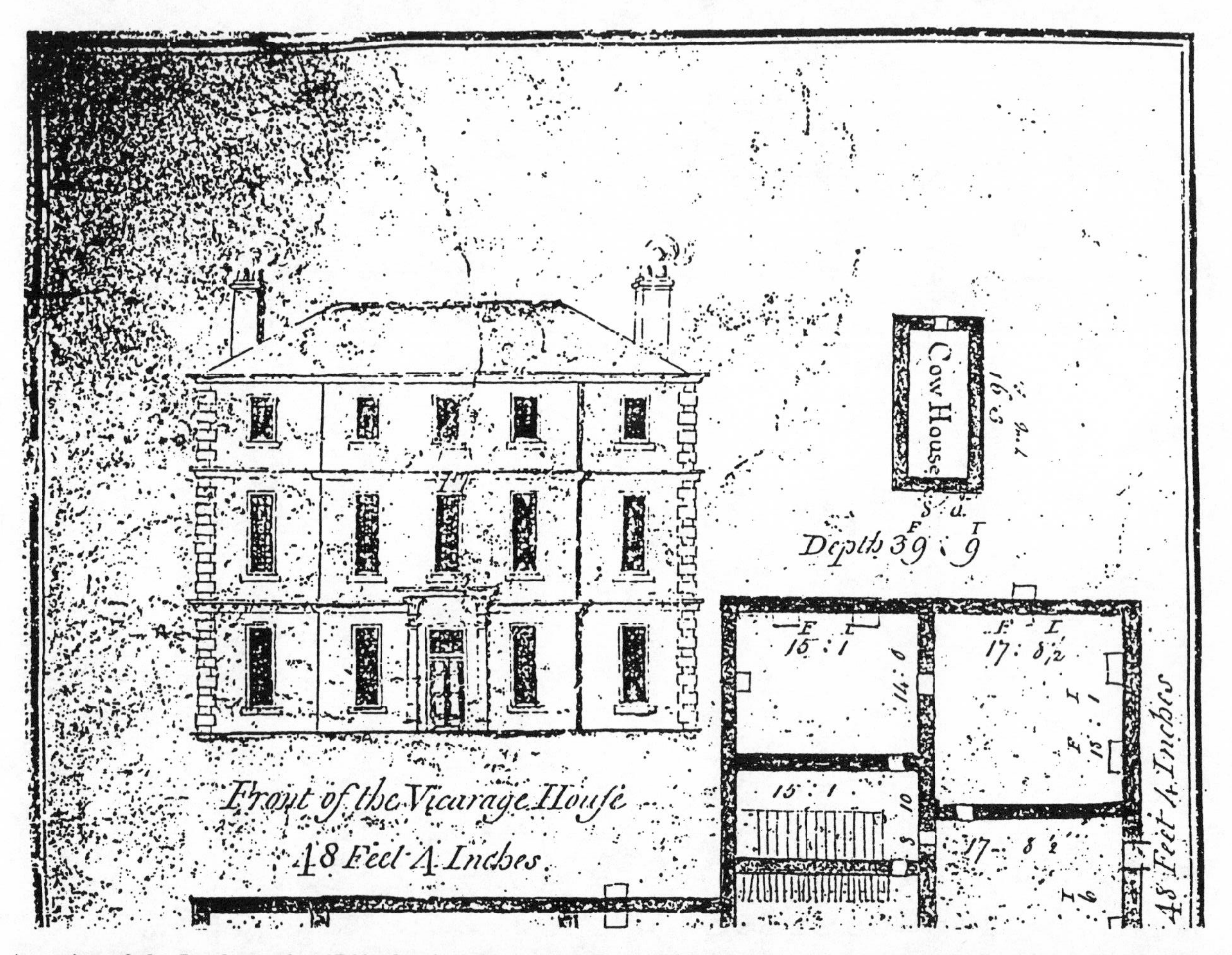

A section of the Leeds terrier 1764, showing the ground floor plan and the front elevation drawing of the elegant vicarage

an Award made about the Year One thousand Five Hundred and Ninety six by his Grace Matthew

Surplice Fees.

The Vicars of the Parish are intitled to and of right have and enjoy the Fees or Sums of Mon
six pence For the Churching of Women Eight pence each. For the Publication of the Banns of Ma
For the Reading of every Citation One Shilling. Mortuaries according to the Statute. Which Surpl
and performed at any of the Churches or Chapels of Ease in the said Parish save as to the Burials t

Furniture of the Chu

The Church is furnished with a Ring of Eight Bells besides the Tintinnabulum, a Sett of
Reading Desk ornamented with Gold Fringe a large Brass Candlestick with Thirty two Branch
last Supper of our Lord and other Designs, Moveable Seats and Matts and Cushions for the Comm
Particulars, weighing in the whole Six Hundred and Seventy five Ounces and two penny Weig

Flaggons.

No.	Weight Oz. Dw.	Inscribed
No. 1	67 . 0	The Gift of Edward Atkinson late Alderman of Leeds deceased for the Service of God's Holy Church there An: Dom 1676.
2	59 . 0	The Fleece engraved. Sumptibus Incolarum Parochiæ de Leeds. Anno 1764.
3	64 . 10	The Fleece Engraved. Sumptibus Incolarum Parochiæ de Leeds.
4	57 . 15	Dr. Thomas Pease Mercator Lagenam hanc Argenteam Ecclesiæ Parochiali de Leeds munifice d
5	60 . 10	In Usum Ecclesiæ de Leeds.
6	41 . 0	The same Inscription.
	349 . 15	

Cupps or Challices.

No.	Oz. Dw.	Inscribed
No. 1	20 . 0	For the Church of Leeds in Yorkshire.
2	19 . 10	For the Church of Leeds in Yorkshire. the Fleece engraved. Sumptibus Incolarum Parochiæ
3	18 . 17	The same Inscription ... D. ... D.
4	20 . 9	The same Inscription ... D. ... D.
5	19 . 0	Ex Dono Dnæ Annæ Crowle Xmo Augusti. MDCLXXVI.
6	18 . 15	Hanc Calicem Eucharistiæ Sacram. Maria Killingbeck, Vidua Rev. Johannis Killingbeck, h Vicarii Gratitudinis ergo. pie et munifice contulit Anno Dom. 1730.
7	18 . 9	The same Inscription.
	134 . 5	

Church and Church Yard

The Parishioners repair the Body of the Church and the Chancells except the High Quire
belonging to the Church Yard is repaired by the Parish save in such parts where the Walls of

The Parish Clerk and Saxton are appointed by the Vicar of the Parish for the Time be

Clerk's Dues or Wages.

There is due to the Clerk of this Parish from every Householder therein the yearly Sum of
Shilling, For the churching of every Woman four pence, for every Marriage by Banns One

Saxton's Dues or Wag

For every Marriage in the Parish Church Six pence. For every Passing Bell rung ther

Grafton Wicks
[illegible] Denison
John Thompson — Inhabitants.
Wm. Park
[illegible]

Details from the beautifully prepared Leeds terrier of 1764

the hall was laid with "plaister black and white." The parlor was wainscotted up "to chair height," and over the kitchen was a great bedchamber hung with tapestry and paper. The interior decor of Benson's other bedchambers was unusual, being hung, one with "yellow water stuff," another wainscotted to chair height, and the rest hung with "green water stuff," meaning watered silk. He paid tribute to Lady Elizabeth Hastings when he listed her benefactions: "To mention all the great and numerous charities of this excellent Lady so often spoke of would be too tedious and would require volumes."

The grandest of all the parsonages was that of Dr. Kirshaw, vicar of Leeds. The terrier of 1764 does handsome justice to this mansion, built in 1717, but not so grandly described in terriers before Drummond made his specific request for details. Samuel Kirshaw provided the archbishop with a parchment about eleven times the size of earlier terriers, a document so large that it has to be folded. In addition to listing the measurements, Kirshaw included a ground floorplan with a front elevation drawing of the elegant house, reproduced here by photocopy. The original sketch insert on the terrier measures 8 by 7.5 inches and occupies the top lefthand corner of the terrier. Kirshaw wrote that all the floors of the house were deals except for the kitchen, which was flagged, and all the rooms except one garret were ceiled or underdrawn.

The difference in the terriers is a performance indicator of Drummond's command of the diocese. He was the first to ask for this information, and he wanted it set out in a specified manner. Was he probing towards reasons for residence and nonresidence? His own Q5 had gone a little further than Herring's in 1743, asking whether clergy resided in the parsonage. The terrier went further still, its items clarifying the answers which churchwardens supplied about church property and giving context to the residence/nonresidence detail in the visitation inquiry.[60] But having secured this information, what then? He could not force a patron to provide a better house, or insist that a clergyman lived in an unrespectable residence. Perhaps he was making an aristocratic eighteenth-century assumption about the link between property, authority, stability, and status. He may have wanted to know in order to reassure himself that much was safe and well. He may have wished to hear about the dwellings of the clergy whom he knew personally.

Church Furnishings

The new style of terriers provided details of church dues, benefactions, surplice fees, clerk's wages, churchyards, and fence repairs in some cases as they had been listed previously but with much more detail about the furnishings of the churches. The amount of plate was not substantial for each church, but most had what was necessary to administer the sacrament of Holy Communion, that is, a chalice or two, a paten, a flagon, and possibly an almsdish. Some had inherited chalices from the sixteenth century and the late seventeenth century, escaping the depredations, but there is ample evidence for the donation of church plate throughout the eighteenth century itself. Some of the churches had vessels of pewter. A few mention basins of brass. A check through the commanding surveys undertaken by Sir Nikolaus Pevsner of the buildings of Yorkshire confirms the entries about silver made in the terriers and is a tribute to the safekeeping of such treasures. The vestry furnishings in St. John's, York, for example, included several oak chests of various sizes, a bachelor of divinity's [whose was not specified] hood, two surplices, and a book—Dr. Jewel's *Defence of ye Apology of the Church of England.* Most churches and chapels had copies of the *Book of Common Prayer,* a Bible, and a *Book of Homilies.* Some possessed altarcloths, some a pall for burials, and some even a Turkish carpet over the altar. In general, where the incumbent had a grand house, the church was also well furnished. Leeds parish church had so much furniture and sacramental plate that it was set out on the terrier in headed columns for "flaggons, chalices, dish and plates," with weights and inscriptions all itemized.

Even the supposedly poorer in the eastern deanery of Holderness, where absenteeism was sometimes pleaded on account of the climate, could boast some fine church furnishings. Robert Cotes, vicar of Hornsea, described his church furnishings thus:

> A large Bible and Common Prayer Book, a book of homilies, a carpet with a linen cloth for the communion table; two pewter flagons and pattens, also one silver chalice weighing 8 oz . . . another weighing 10 and a half oz [both with inscriptions] . . . a bell and a clock.

The parish of Hornsea had reached a good level of organization, judging from the detail on the terrier which referred to the ringing of the church bell "at six o'clock every night and morning during harvest." The clerk was paid in sheaves of corn for performing that service.

The clergy were aware that the archbishop's visitation was in the nature of an audit, that he was looking for high standards and might make improvements. James Borwick, the curate of Whitby, used the opportunity to make a complaint. He wrote on the reverse of the terrier and described a quaint and rather inappropriate custom of the parish clerk, presumably to earn extra payment at funerals:

> When the friends of the deceased are desirous to have a Psalm in the church and are willing to pay him a shilling extraordinary, he sings sixteen lines of some improper psalm. Which practice seems to have no countenance from the rubrick, is very troublesome to the Minister, and often absurd in it's [*sic*] self.

Borwick was apparently uneasy about the sexton as well as the clerk, for he added, "The wages of the Sexton (as well as the manner of appointment) seem uncertain."

Evidence from the Terriers about Absenteeism and Residence

It is well understood that the Georgian church in Yorkshire managed its work with more than half of its clergy absent from the livings they held. (The next chapter deals with this.) Some clergy were gross pluralists with disproportionately large incomes, yet some of these were worthy scholars and holders of canonries. The terriers of 1764 are important indicators of places with no parsonage house available, since some of the clergy who were nonresident did not volunteer the information on the returns that the church had not provided for them.

A further light is shed by the terriers on another group of incumbents who did have parsonage houses but who did not live in them. Without the terriers this information would be obscured. In these cases the clergy did not indicate in the visitation returns that there was no parsonage house; they merely declared nonresidence. Some gave as their reason that the parsonage house was not fit for a clergyman to live in, thus putting themselves in a social bracket above the individuals who were lowly enough to inhabit a poor parsonage. Putting the visitation returns with the terriers in these instances is to add to knowledge about absenteeism in Georgian Yorkshire. A study of the terriers has uncovered incumbents who did have parsonage houses but who did not live in them at Barton in the Street, Bossall, Bracewell, Todwick, Ulrome, Warmfield, Weaverthorpe, and Wharram in the Street.

Sidney Swinney D.D., rector of Barton in the Street, wrote on his visitation return that he was nonresident "on account of the badness and smallness of the parsonage house in which the tenant who farms the tythes does live." His terrier of 1764 described the house as built of stone and covered with thatch, containing three rooms on one floor. It had a barn, a stable, a coal house, two little orchards, and an acre and a half of land. Swinney was also rector of Thwing, but he did not live there either. On the return for Thwing he explained that he was nonresident "on account of the situation, but have taken a house at Scarborough in order to be at a moderate distance of it." Thwing was five parishes away to the south of Scarborough, and many miles away from Barton in the Street, which was halfway to York from Scarborough. This level of absenteeism was not frowned on by the archbishop, as has been observed before, provided that satisfactory curates were in residence, as they were in both these parishes. One such as Swinney would have considered three rooms under a thatched roof unsuitable for a gentleman, superior in social status from those others for whom three rooms and one-and-a-half acres were adequate and satisfactory accommodation. Swinney was a typical eighteenth-century absentee rector who was conscience-free in his declaration of Scarborough as his appropriate place of residence.

George Smith, curate at Wharram in the Street, wrote that "the house is a poor cottage not fit for any curate to live in." The terrier for Wharram in the Street describes the vicarage house as follows:

> Ten yards in length including the entry, and four and a half yards wide, with two rooms upon a ground floor only, floored with clay and covered with thatch as it has always been, to which is annexed a cowhouse 3 yards long and the same wideness. The glebe is one garth adjoining the house scarce half a rood.

It was probably the clay floor that ruled this out as a residence for any clergyman. Smith was also looking after Weighton, Wharram Percy, and North Grimston and had chosen to live at Grimston. In line with Sidney Swinney, who found three rooms insufficient, George Smith put himself, though a poor curate, in the ranks of the gentlemen for whom a mud floor was unacceptable.

Bossall was one of the cures held in 1764 by Spencer Madan. The brick-built parsonage house that he did not live in had what sounds to be adequate accommodation (kitchen, dairy, dining room, study, three lodging rooms, and two garrets), but may have been considered insufficient for one who became Bishop of Bristol (1792–94) and then Peterborough (1794–1813). The parsonage at Bracewell, unlived in by John Riley, the vicar, was of stone with thatch but no upstairs rooms, and the cowhouse adjoined, so that arrangement was probably not good enough. Hammond Turner, a fellow of St. John's, Cambridge, was the rector of Todwick, who explained that the parsonage was "not fit for me to live in. . . . It is little better than a cottage but serves for my tenant. . . . For such a purpose I keep it in good repair. The Todwick terrier describes a stone building, thatched, with three little rooms, one with a mud floor and an oven, three rooms, and a closet upstairs, this being "the habitable part of the house," and a "little old lumber room adjoining a hay loft." Ulrome and Weaverthorpe parsonages were "a mere cottage" and "in a ruinous condition in 1762," respectively, but at Weaverthorpe work was afoot to rebuild although the vicar, George Lawson, was in a poor state of health. At Warmfield John Garlick was newly inducted and found the vicarage house tenanted but a "poor mean place not fit for a clergyman to live in." The terrier describes it as "a very ancient edifice," with seven rooms downstairs, three upstairs, a building partly of stone and thatch and partly of mud and slate. Garlick wrote on his return, "If I cou'd meet with proper encouragement I wou'd contribute handsomely myself for the improvement of it" and added that he proposed to "spend some part of my time in it and, by your Grace's leave, some part at Stanley."

Sometimes the unhealthy situation as well as the unsatisfactory house led the incumbent to spurn the vicarage. This was the case for William Mosey, vicar of Lund and curate of Beswick, two parishes adjacent in the Harthill deanery. Mosey wrote on his return for Lund that he did not live in the vicarage because "the situation [was] so damp and disagreeable to my constitution that I was advised by friends and physician to leave it." He did not live at Beswick, and the terrier confirms that there was no parsonage there. Mosey had solved the problem by building himself a house not far from the church in Lund. Although Mosey was a pluralist, his situation at Beswick illustrates also the plight of singularists without accommodation.

Two of the York city incumbents had let their parsonages to tenants. Thomas Cautley of St. Helen's, Stonegate, had let a house in Swinegate given by Mrs. Margaret Prince. It had a kitchen, a back kitchen, and a parlor below the stairs, a dining room above the stairs, and three lodging rooms (bedrooms) with garrets over them. The rent was £8 2s 6d per year. St. Helen's also had a warehouse in Stonegate with a yard, both rented to Seth Agar at £2 12s 6d per year. Cautley was not a pluralist, but lived at Great Ouseborne, twelve miles from York. In his return he wrote that he proposed a Mr. Sowerby to be the residing curate for St. Helen's, but it was Thomas Moon who appeared on the day of visitations. St. Saviour's church, York, had "an ancient parsonage house inhabited by poor people in 1727," according to the 1764 terrier, and by that year it was rented "in 7 tenements," having had some extensions provided in 1764 by Richard Cordukes, the rector, as "a lumber room, a garret and two necessary houses." Cordukes was the incumbent also for All Saints, North Street, York, and St. Mary Bishophill the Elder. He did not live in any of those parishes but wrote on his returns that he lived in a house in York "at such an equal distance from my livings that I may readily perform all the duties which belong to them." He was conscientious both as a landlord and a clergyman.

The three parishes held by Laurence Sterne—a celebrated absentee—at the time of the 1764 visitation are disappointing for the literary glimpses they might be supposed to give of the author. The terriers for Stillington and Sutton on the Forest were written by Sterne's curate, Marmaduke Callis. James Kilner, his other curate, wrote the terrier for Coxwold. There were no books listed in the possession of the church of Sutton on the Forest, which was the living that Sterne had held longest, having been inducted there in 1738. However, at Stillington, which he had held since 1743, and where he must have preached many times, the church furniture does list "one pulpit, a reading pew and font for baptism in good and decent order," but again, no books. At Coxwold, the curate in 1764, James Kilner, gave a fuller description of the church furniture on the terrier, recording

> three bells, a clock, a large Bible, three folio Common Prayer Books, a book of Homilies, a parchment register for christenings and burials, a register of strong and durable paper for marriages, a cushion of crimson velvet for the pulpit.

The last direct connection with Sterne's writing in such matters was in 1760, when it was he who wrote the terrier. It is a very small piece, about A5 size in modern terms, and had only the following information: "I have no glebe land, parsonage house, orchard or garden belonging to the Curacy. The Rt Hon Earl Fauconberg pays the curate a stipend of £30 per annum." Tithes and surplice fees were added, and it was signed "Laurence Sterne." He had written the terriers himself in 1743, 1749, and 1760 for Sutton on the Forest. He had used no margins but had used the entire page, having ruled himself some closely made lines in 1760 and divided the page into two vertical columns in 1743, crowding the writing together. Although these pieces are disappointing in a literary sense, they provide valuable contrasts with the terrier of 1764 because they illustrate exactly what led the archbishop to authorize improved terriers. It may be thought that the physical appearance of the compared terriers is unimportant, but a clearer layout made it much easier for Drummond, and us, to know about the accommodation of the clergy and the provision made in the Yorkshire churches for the worship of God.

Of all the Yorkshire clergy who resided in their parishes and in the parsonage houses provided for them, one example will suffice. John Elam, B.A., vicar of Tickhill, a medium-sized parish on the Retford boundary of the Doncaster deanery, was a one-parish man whose visitation return is of average interest. His terrier for 1764 describes his ordinary vicarage as "built of stone and covered part with slates and part with tiles and part with thatch." He had a dining room with a floor made of firwood, a hall, a kitchen, a pantry, and a dairy, a cellar, and a closet paved with stone. The house also featured a study with four closets, and five bedchambers, two of which had "plaister floors and the other deal." None of the rooms was wainscotted or ceiled. The vicarage included a barn and a stable, and his garden was "a little croft, the sixth part of an acre." The terrier becomes more interesting when he describes the furniture of his church, and when we learn from this that there was a green cloth for the communion table, six bells, a clock, two silver cups, and two silver flagons with inscriptions recording their donors, who wished them to be for the perpetual use of the communicants, we recognize that here was a church well served by a conscientious parson. Elam received only £25 12s per annum for Tickhill but was content to minister to his 230 families and won from them a high level of attendance at church. There were only two dissenting families in the parish, according to the visitation return.

Audit

Archbishop Drummond broke new ground in requiring more detailed terriers, possibly because of a concern about residence and nonresidence for which the evidence is corroborative, possibly through a genuine interest in architecture, possibly for a wish for reassurance of "omnia bene."

Conclusion

Drummond's Yorkshire was a diocese with a mixture of robust and gentle activity, parochially busy with Sunday and weekday services, preaching, catechism, charities and schools, where the conviction and earnestness of the evangelicals were becoming noticed. The aristocratic and amiable archbishop was enquiring into the minutiae of parsonages and church furnishings as never before, so giving historians the chance to understand more particularly, for example, the personal circumstances of George Burnett in Elland chapelry, who wrote, "I reside in the town. The parsonage house is not finished."

The visitation of 1764 reveals measurable patterns of churchgoing, sacramental customs, preaching, residence and nonresidence, the observance of Lent, and catechism and educational practice since 1743 and to audit performance. The incidence of weekday services was proportionally small, but their patchy vitality indicates a church life that was animated and alert to traditions. Drummond was of course not conducting his visitation for posterity, but his conscientious approach to duty allows us to appraise what the clergy told him. What they told him shows us that the diocese was in a healthier state than some historians have thought about the eighteenth-century church in England. Since Yorkshire was such a significant part of the church as a whole, the returns for Drummond's primary visitation are a valuable source.

5

Drummond's Yorkshire—Some Problems and Opportunities

Pluralism

Pluralism, Nonresidence, and Absenteeism

Pluralism, or holding more than one living simultaneously, was normal for the majority of clergymen in the eighteenth century. One "living" in so many cases was not sufficient "to make a living." But pluralism is regarded as one of the unsatisfactory features of the eighteenth-century church—and sometimes as an evil—because it was part of a syndrome whose other features bred problems. The syndrome was pluralism, nonresidence, absenteeism, dispensations, and sinecures, with the effect that many parishioners had no clergyman living among them to minister to their needs. Well over half the York parishes in the 1764 returns had nonresident incumbents—346 parishes, leaving 275 with resident clergy. This pattern accords with that found in other dioceses, and while it is true that it led to abuses later on, pluralism as revealed in the 1764 York visitation returns was seen by some as the solution to their financial difficulties rather than as a problem in itself. There was much nearresidence, regular observance through resident assistant curates, and pluralist wealth could generate bequests, all of which are a long way from neglect and evil. Herein lay the trap. Being comfortable about pluralism, accepting its pressures as norms, meant that for a long time nothing was done to alter it.

Not until three quarters of a century later, did the Pluralities Act of 1838[1] reduce pluralism, with some exceptions, to the holding of two benefices. In this act the provision of curates was addressed with much detail. Would-be absentees were deterred by the more detailed information required for licenses which could be issued only by the bishops, whose powers were much increased. The act's 133 sections were more stringent than the Clergy Residences Act of

1803, which reduced nonresidence nationally by over one thousand cases.[2] The broad terms of the permission in the Pluralities Act for a cleric to hold two livings were that churches had to be within ten miles of each other, the combined population was to be no more than three thousand inhabitants, and the income was to be no more than one thousand pounds. By these standards, pluralism was not a major problem in the diocese in 1764. In Yorkshire in 1764 there were only two clergymen who held five livings, one who held six, fifteen who held four livings, and twenty-six who held three livings, making a total of forty-four (7 percent) who held more than two livings. Moreover, the visitation returns of 1764 frequently speak of two miles and three miles between plurally held parishes in most cases although the permitted distance at that date was forty-five statute miles. Only twenty of the Yorkshire clergy of 1764 (not all of whom were pluralists) lived a long way from their parishes, with residences declared in places such as Rotterdam, Lisbon, Bath, Bristol, Durham, Derby, Chester, Cambridge, and London. A further eighteen nonresidents did not declare their usual whereabouts. As regards the link between population and income, there were thirty-five Yorkshire nonresidents in 1764 with populations over one hundred families (or 500 people) whose incomes were less than thirty pounds per year in each benefice.

A corresponding group of just over fifty nonresident clergy were on incomes of less than twenty pounds per annum, ministering to less than fifty families (or 250 people). Twenty-four nonresidents drew benefits of over fifty pounds per annum for ministering to (or neglecting) parishes of less than fifty families. Seventeen nonresidents on incomes over fifty pounds held livings with over 150 families. So what the Pluralities Act was targeting—high incomes drawn for neglect of large populations—was only marginally relevant in 1764. Low pay was a more noticeable problem, and this was where the pluralist syndrome started.

The Ordinariness of Pluralism

The following two cases illustrate how ordinary pluralism could be. James Addison had been licensed as curate at Carlton Miniot in 1743, where there was also the dependent chapel of Sand Hutton. He accepted Over Silton in 1749 because he earned only £23.12s, so when he took Cowsby in 1757 (£31.10s), he was more comfortable. These places were small and close together, the numbers of families in each respectively were thirty-two, forty-five, thirteen, and thirty-three. By any standards such a ministry would admit conscientious performance, so Addison's "absence" from all four cures (he lived at Knayton, in the adjoining parish of Leake or Leke), was a technicality, as he explained, it being "more in the centre between my cures."

John Bradley had a comfortable life with less rugged winters in the four parishes of Gate Helmsley, Over Helmsley, Holtby, and Warthill just outside the York city deanery. His four churches were within a compass of two miles, but he did not conduct two services in each church every Sunday. His pluralism supplied Bradley with a combined income of just over £135 per annum. He had held three of the livings since his ordination in 1726, and the third, Holtby, he had acquired in 1753; that was a valuable addition, being worth £50 per annum, thus giving him a settled assurance from the age of about fifty. His returns in 1764 have the flavor of a gentleman's distance from his parishioners. He wrote exactly the same comment for each parish,

> There are four churches within ye compass of 2 miles. I perform Divine Service at two of 'em in yr turns. There are 62 small families in my four parishes and they can easily get to church where Divine Service is performed and to do 'em justice they most of 'em attend.

It was as if he were doing them a favor by his arrangements, regarding them all as "small" families. Bradley's level of ministry was not out of order, but it was limited. He catechized four times during Lent at each church and he celebrated Holy Communion four times every year in each church. With so few people in so close an area Bradley knew them all well. It appears that he had removed to Holtby when he acquired that parish in 1753 as he stated in the return for 1764 that he lived there in his parsonage house. He had in all respects a fair record of care for his livings. Two of them had been augmented by lot: Gate Helmsley in 1730 and Warthill in 1741. Bradley had stewarded these augmentations by purchasing freeholds in each case for £8 per annum. There was a benefaction from two closes (little ones, he called them) for the repair of the church at Holtby. A benefaction of £20 at Gate Helmsley provided £4 per year for the poor. From the point of view of the twenty-two families in the parish of Gate Helmsley the £4 per annum must have been a satisfactory compensation for having to walk to the churches in the other parishes on the Sundays when their minister was taking the service away from their home.

One gap in the acceptable cover supplied by John Bradley to his four comfortable livings was that he did not employ a curate. He could have afforded to do so. With a curate he could have provided two services each Sunday at each church. He obviously thought that this was not necessary in the terms as he explained them. His great defense must be that although he was an absentee clergyman in three parishes, he lived so near them that it was a better situation than that of an absentee clergyman in a much more extensive parish with more people. Traveling was not Bradley's custom. It is not surprising to find in the archbishop's Court Book that Bradley was excused attendance at the day of visitation in 1764. He sent his exhibits. He would not have had far to travel as his attendance would have been required at York on 18 May, when it would have been daylight until well into the evening. From Holtby through Osbaldwick was a short journey in relatively easy conditions. But, at the age of about sixty-five, John Bradley stayed at home.

Pluralism: The Flaws

The system that allowed more than one living to one parson within easy reach of three or four others also permitted an incumbent to be permanently away from five or six. The reason for having four and living within reach of them all, as in Addison's case, was subsistence. Other—less pastorally acceptable—reasons, as in the case of Dr. Hugh Thomas, were to retain ecclesiastically acquired wealth, and to recognize intellectual status. Hugh Thomas was rector of Etton (£160), rector of Wheldrake (£140), archdeacon of Nottinghamshire (£61), chancellor of York Minster (£580), and master of Christ's College, Cambridge, as well as being dean of Ely. Thomas paid his curates according to acceptable custom (£40 and £31.10s), and they were doing their work well. Archpluralism on this scale was curtailed by the 1838 act, but the individual case of Hugh Thomas did not amount to a major disaster for the Yorkshire church. It illustrates the difference between excessive and "normal" pluralism—the excessive pluralism of cathedral deans, college dignitaries, and diocesan officials who added wealth to riches from their livings, and the "normal" pluralism of parochial clergy whose poverty was not necessarily assuaged by adding a further benefice. The system was flawed in that it perpetuated differentiating awards and created opportunities for irresponsibility or stagnation. The original provision of parsons for churches during the historic spread of English Christianity is at the root of all this. Complex rights of patronage developed, and although the parish structure survived the Reformation, it did not keep pace with population changes. So the practice of pluralism, whether for survival or for aggrandizement, became a norm which Drummond and his contemporaries accepted. Its development into a serious problem came later with the great increases in population.[3]

Pluralism: An Open Door to Methodism

In rural parishes pluralism was an open door to Methodism if a nonresident incumbent lived a long distance away. For example, the vicar at Fenton lived in Chester, and the Methodists numbered seven families in 1764, though none in 1743. The archbishop's correspondence for 1763 contains a letter to a Mr. Otley in the Isle of Wight, urging him to reside or resign as vicar of Aughton; he must have resigned, for the 1764 returns show the incumbent as James Cookson, and it was his task to declare the eight Methodist families who had presumably found space during Mr. Otley's absence. The Methodists also found openings in places where the nonresident though near-resident clergyman was preoccupied or not particularly alert to change or challenge. The Methodists saw and used some of these rural openings as well as the obvious ones in the more populated towns. For example, William Burton was a nonresident in his parish of Barnoldswick because he taught at the grammar school in Coln, and by 1764 there were eighteen Methodist families in Barnoldswick, though there had been none in 1743. A near-resident in a small parish or chapelry might have been no more "absent" than a resident in a large parish, though either kind of "absence" could foster Methodism. Some rural parishes served by a nonresident incumbent opened the way for Methodism because they happened to be on Wesley's main route between larger towns. Hutton Rudby was one of four parishes held in near-residence by George Stainthorp, and a personal visit from Wesley, whose journal records his preaching there on 7 July 1758, was the start of a Methodist society which opened its own preaching house in the following year.[4] The journal also refers to a "huge congregation" at Hutton Rudby when Wesley preached there again on Easter Monday in 1764. Stainthorp did not regard Methodism as being in any way at odds with the church. He declared the Methodist meetinghouse but did not count Methodists in his list of dissenters and gave the number of Methodists as one hundred "joined in the Society," saying that they assembled three times a week. He gave the names of three who were their teachers. With such lack of tension, he and other pluralists of the eighteenth-century church allowed Methodism to grow, while at Haworth and Elland, for example, the style of the resident curates, Grimshaw (up to 1763) and Burnett were not exactly keeping Methodism at bay.

Traveling Pluralists

Where there was not enough money to pay curates, there had to be frequent traveling between the living where the clergyman resided and the others he served additionally. Thomas Leake of Bishop Burton expressed the financial background to this directly in his return, "My predecessors took on more to help them to live more comfortably than ye profits of this vicarage will allow a man to live." The returns describe a picture of the Yorkshire rectors and vicars and curates traveling about on Sundays from church to church and chapel. Sometimes they took two morning services and one afternoon one in three different places. This necessitous discharge of their duty was governed by the seasons, there being fewer prayers and more firesides in winter and more sermons on summer afternoons.

The financial provision was a key factor in determining the obligation of travel to take services. If the income was small, the amount of "duty" was less, and sometimes too small to warrant weekly duty. This was not always related to the number of inhabitants. Sutcliffe, for example, was paid only £16 per annum for ministering to 1,052 families in Heptonstall, and a further £10 for two hundred more families at Lightcliffe chapel. A similar difficulty faced Burton at Barnoldswick, where 273 families had to be served for only £5 per year. At the other extreme, Sidney Swinney drew £280 per year for a combined ministry to a total of 74 families. A "normal" situation was where clerics derived income of less than £20 per annum from three or four parishes or chapelries, demonstrating their dependence on pluralism. The direct financial connection of pastoral care given for the income received is not dressed up in any euphemism, but written most openly.

The same openness is discernible in the pluralists' accounts of their traveling. The distances they traveled were not great, and the pluralist clergy—who were the majority—insisted implicitly throughout the returns that they were managing their duty capably, using phrases such as, "two computed miles, three measured miles, within a mile and a half, two short miles." James Rudd of Kilham wrote that he had to travel to Wold Newton and although the journey was six miles "and the road exposed exceedingly to all bad weather . . . these reasons nor any other never have hindered me from performing Divine Service and preaching at least once every Sunday at Kilham above twice these twenty two years past." Nor did the writers of the returns give an impression of dashing, hurrying, or being exhausted by their journeys. They seem to have organized the timing of their two services in one place and one service in another, and alternate morning and afternoon services in a third in a way that enabled them to arrive at the appointed church without real difficulty. One of the factors was that many of the pluralists had their livings in adjacent parishes. The siting of the church buildings was sometimes more of assistance to the clergyman than to the inhabitants of scattered dwellinghouses, but it appears—as at Holtby and Warthill and two of the Helmsleys, as described above—that priest and people so disposed were able to make the journey easily on Sundays.

Where the clergy were capably conducting one, two, and three services on Sundays, there emerges a flavor of doing the job well, writing down all the times and places, and seasonal alterations to make the best of the daylight hours. This apparent satisfaction has to be set, however, against the fact that there were supposed to be two services in every place every Sunday; the openness of the returns indicates that this was not taken seriously, and that current practice had devalued the system to work according to clergy adaptations. William Mosey acknowledged this in his return for Kildwick: "The reason why it is not performed as the Act of Uniformity and the canons require, the living is so small." Thomas Dowbiggin was also aware that the system was not so satisfactory: "And to be plain and ingenuous I cannot pretend or rather afford to perform service twice a day, the income of the vicarage being so small as would not find my family with bread &c. I have been hitherto excused and hope I shall be." Although the travels of John Wesley are justly renowned for their extent as well as for their return-visit coverage, the Yorkshire folk must have grown accustomed to seeing about half of their ordained clergy as a mobile force week by week. In 1764 two services were not expected everywhere and it was accepted, for example, in the city of York that there were "morning" churches and "afternoon" churches.

Traveling the other way to church was not restricted to the clergy. Parishioners from Rawden, Overton, North Ottrington, Middleton on Leven, and Nunthorp, for example, also walked in the opposite direction to another church when their own vicars were off to preach at their other cures, or when the sacrament was celebrated at the mother church. The idea was attractive, however, to clergy whose reasons for not conducting two services were financial or inherited, or both. John Sarraude of Elvington and Sutton upon Derwent held one service on alternate Sundays in each church. He wrote,

> Both the churches are situated at the extreme parts of either parish and when taken together are as nearly as may be in the middle of both by which servants and others that may not have an opportunity of attending Divine Service in the morning may have an opportunity of . . . a sermon in the afternoon.

John Cook, of Foxholes and Rillington, had the same arrangement of alternate services, and mentioned another chapel at Butterwick as being "very near, where every well disposed person may attend." The practice became accepted, so that even in a nonpluralist parish, the parishioners were the travelers and the vicar conducted one service only. James Willoughby L.L.B., of Askham Richard, for example, where there were twenty-seven families, wrote, "the parishioners go to a neighbouring church in the afternoon." Viviane Barrie-Curien noticed this downward accommodation in the diocese of London.[5]

From the minister's point of view, Sunday was not the only day when traveling from parish to parish was necessary. Discounting pastoral visiting as such, because it was not widely practiced, families would have required the minister's presence in their homes to comfort the sick and dying and to baptize frail infants, but they in their turn would have had to get a messenger to the minister to ask him to call on them. Joseph Dowthwaite, Vicar of Feliskirk, wrote of his experiences throughout twenty-five years in this matter,

> I have been frequently called out of my bed at all hours in the night in cold frost and snow at the distance of 2 miles or more from my house to baptise weak children, visit the sick and administer the sacrament upon the least notice to the poorest man in my parish.

Dowthwaite was not a pluralist. His one parish in the Bulmer deanery bordered the western edge of Rydale. He looked after 180 families, and by 1764 was near seventy years of age. The situation of those who were pluralists would obviously have been more of a problem as age and populations increased.

The returns show that winter and financial constraint denied several villages the sight of their minister for three or four consecutive Sundays at the worst of times: Thropham, Drypool, Eskdaleside, Thornton in the Street, Newton upon Ouse, Brotton, Fraisthorp, Birdforth, Grindall, Hutton Bonville, and Marfleet.

Pluralists and Weekday Services

Pluralism was an obvious deterrent to regular weekday observance, even to the extent of cutting out holy days and fast days, but there were some who kept this practice, and some with only two parishes explained that they observed holy days alternately in both their churches. Grenside, Dodsworth, Driffield, Scott, Dealtary, Cotes, and Addison—these were some of the pluralists who celebrated holy days in one or other of their livings, whereas Buck, Coates, Rickaby, Knowsley, Hicks, Paul, and Deason were men for Sundays only. These, with the possible exception of Cornelius Rickaby, were not linked in any way with the evangelicals but were rather the inheritors of the older traditional ways of church worship. The view that saints' days in the eighteenth-century church were "all but ignored,"[6] cannot have been based on the Yorkshire situation in 1764, where 109 parishes out of 621 declared observance of holy days. Pluralism may obviously have contributed to its decline but had by no means eradicated it. The pluralists who kept the observance of holy days were from the whole range of locations across the diocese (see chapter 4), not just in towns. Some of the pluralists who celebrated holy days were also among the number—104 altogether—who held services on Wednesdays and Fridays in Lent—Scott, Sumner, Robinson, Cotes, and Rudd being among them.

Conclusion

Pluralism in 1764 was not the unmitigated affliction it appeared to later critics, so few attempts at the time were made to counter it. It was accepted as ordinary in a church whose clergy were mainly underpaid, a conclusion also of Viviane Barrie-Curien[7] from her studies of the Lincoln and London dioceses. Itinerant dissenting preachers could give attractive alternatives to parishioners, but the evidence is that traveling from one adjacent cure to the next was easy enough for the many clerics wishing to serve their parishioners satisfactorily. They took pride in telling their archbishop how they conducted their work, that the distances were within what was lawful for the services at the stated times, even though calls in the night to assist the dying were a trial of conscience. It is clear, too, that the worshipping congregations of Yorkshire in 1764 expected to walk a couple of extra miles to and from church, if it was the week when "their" vicar took a service in the next parish. Indeed, the parishes of Yorkshire were generally so large that churchgoers who did not live in the same township as the church would have had to walk there even if the vicar was a singularist and a resident. The visitation returns of 1764, however, reveal that although the Church of England was functioning capably, it owned some deep pockets of complacency. Fifty years later the exigencies of pluralism had damaged the church's work in places where clergy incomes and even the best intentions of ministry had not matched population growth, and where the Methodists had established their circuits effectively. With the exception of curates, whose situation is considered next, pluralism in the mid eighteenth-century church in Yorkshire allowed the majority of its beneficed clergy to make a living and do their duty. If the provisions of the Pluralities Act of 1838 regarding nonresidence had been discussed for legislation in 1764, there would have been little comprehension of the need.

The Need for Curates

Becoming a Curate

Petertide in the church's calendar has become the occasion for most services of ordination. In the mid-eighteenth century, however, ordinands had often to seek out a diocesan for themselves and ask for ordination, and the experiences of John Newton, the former slave trader,[8] expose the worst features of such a system. His unusual case, lacking the university degree and being outwardly roughened by a career at sea,[9] brought him in 1758 up against Archbishop Gilbert's secretaries and chaplain, officials who wielded the power of examining ordinands before they ever met the archbishop. The chaplain, a namesake, Dr. Thomas Newton, passed him on to a secretary who gave him "the softest answer imaginable" in a refusal explaining that his grace was "inflexible in supporting the rules and canons of the Church."[10] In the York diocese, once Drummond was in office, he put notices in the *York Courant*[11] to advertize the dates when he intended to hold ordination services. The archbishop was doing all that was usual for his part to ensure that curates should be properly ordained and appropriately licensed, though Newton's disappointment early in 1764 at the hands of Drummond's secretaries, the ordination service was a private one being held in London before Drummond set off for his primary visitation. Newton had made this (his second) journey to London not to apply to Drummond, but to Bishop Green, bishop of Lincoln, because the curacy he was being offered was in the parish of Olney in the diocese of Lincoln. Bishop Green, however, had not advertized any ordination service, and was in London because he preferred to be there for the court and the House of Lords rather than in his diocese.[12] Newton was apparently unaware of the bishops' need to make arrangements well in advance for such events as visitations and ordinations. Bishop Green was approached by the influential earl of Dartmouth, who was promoting Newton's cause. He opted out of holding an ordination service (one of the lengthiest in the *Book of Common Prayer*) specially for Newton, and advised Lord Dartmouth that Drummond was to hold a private ordination the next day (16 April) and that Newton should attend between nine and ten in the morning to be examined. It was noon before Newton got the information. His race against time was only one of the evasions which so enraged John Wesley (see Chapter 3). Finally, it was Bishop Green who ordained Newton on 29 April 1764. It was Newton's misfortune to be unaware of the protocol that allowed the archbishop of York to ordain a man even if Canterbury had refused him, but to demur to Lincoln, his inferior in his own province, if he chose.

Getting and Keeping a Curate

The visitation returns show that the pluralist syndrome led to a need for curates. This need became a problem in the eighteenth-century church. By the time that incumbents decided to employ an assistant, they were older and less likely to be alert to who was suitable. It was also financially worrying, as old clergymen tried to balance their budget to include a curate. Another benefice would be the financial answer, but this produced the further spiral of need for a curate to share the ministry. In seventy of the Yorkshire parishes, curates were working alone. In 180 parishes, curates were working alongside their incumbents, some of these being the places which were well served with chapels of ease with resident curates, such as Halifax, Sheffield, Wakefield, and Leeds (though in the large parish of Huddersfield the curates for the three chapels were near-resident rather than fully resident.) These are healthy conditions, and in the case of the seventy they made a reassuring counter weight to the absence of the benefice holder. In the case of the 180 it shows that the church was coping with its population by providing two clergymen, although curates were inadequately paid in several cases. Mather has referred to the work of Mme. Viviane Barrie-Curien,[13] showing the importance of curates in the diocese of London in the second half of the eighteenth century. Her conclusion, based on a sample from 1766 to 1770, where 88 percent of parishes had a resident clergyman or near-resident clergyman, is that the curates were serving as respected parish priests, doing duty as incumbents of nearby benefices.

Clergymen also advertized in the newspaper for curates.[14] Some of the clergy mentioned their worries about getting a curate in their returns to the archbishop. At Ledsham, John Benson, the vicar, wrote that he was

> in great distress for one. None but Litterati [sic] offer ymselves. Alas! Alas! Ye church formerly was supplied by ye sons of prophets but now University education is so expensive yt few can send their sons.

Benson was subsequently suited with Walter Sellon, one of the Yorkshire evangelicals, who had been ordained in 1760 and who was noted by Walsh as "a belligerent Arminian," whose relationship with John Wesley cooled. At Flamborough, Cornelius Rickaby lamented, "my late Curate having left me abruptly and as yet I have not had it in my powere to get another." Shortly thereafter the troublesome Thomas Hudson arrived in Bridlington to offer his tempting assistance to Rickaby before the archbishop's ban had been lifted.[15]

George Dodsworth, a triple pluralist, provides interesting details of the way he hoped to organize his absences from Cloughton, Allerston, and Ebberston. His return to the archbishop is kept in the form of "rough answers" which he sent to someone else (probably another clergyman friend) with a request to "put them into proper order" before the return went to Drummond. He completed the questions briefly ("So much for the Bp and his Queries"), and in the subsequent letter he asked, "Have you any young Gentleman that I could hire to preach two or three Sundays for me when I am absent? . . . He might come . . . on Saturdays . . . and return . . . Mondays. I shall be glad if you can." Dodsworth's problem in being absent was extended by the further duty he had taken on as curate to William Ward at Scawby, and by his wish to keep his requests for help from his neighbors—all of whom already did "double service" on Sundays—on an occasional basis (see below in "Neighbourly help").

Some clergymen had sons who followed them in the calling of priest and who helped serve the home benefice (the Robinsons at Egton, the Joseph Halls at Wortley and Bolsterstone, and the Gibsons at Fishlake and Sykehouse). John Cayley, Vicar of Bubwith, allowed his son to board in the town and to assist him in the parish, and this had been so for about ten months by the time of the visitation.

Keeping a curate was related closely to the monetary rewards available. One straightforward arrangement is referred to directly in the return for Wetwang, where Francis Best included his other living of Driffield in his reply, noting that, ". . . the two livings are worth near £90 pa., which my Curate and I divide equally." At Dewsbury, William Lamplugh felt the financial situation was biting into his benefice; he wrote that he paid £40 to John Horsfall "in hard money, over and above what the parishioners are pleased to give him." To make it sound better, some of the vicars and rectors referred to surplice fees as well as to the value of the living.

Reporting on the Curates

Assistant curates in Drummond's Yorkshire in the mid eighteenth century emerge as the most shadowy part of the visitation returns for 1764. Their names were not always given, and their salaries were often omitted. Their length of stay was not always stated and their place of residence was only occasionally supplied. This is one area where the reforms imposed by the Pluralities Act would have altered the situation had it applied in 1764. The request by the archbishop in the Paper of Queries included a direct enquiry about their canonical licensing and due qualification. This question was frequently glossed over in the returns. The vagueness about curates in the Drummond visitation returns contrasts with the benefice holders themselves, most of whose dates of induction and ordination as deacon and priest were dutifully recorded. Searches have to be made through the diocesan Act Books for curates' names and licensing dates, and some of the answers given by the returning clergy about how long the curates stayed do not match the information in the diocesan lists. It is as if the incumbents knew that if they could not remember the dates accurately, they would not be in trouble, because it mattered less.

The Conscientious Efforts of Curates

Shadowy the curates may seem, but some of them were more solidly acquainted season by season with parishioners, as the findings in the Lincoln diocese corroborate,[16] than many a nonresident incumbent. For example, Dr. Wanley, rector of Stokesley, was complained of in a letter to the archbishop because, being resident at

Ripon, he "has never administered the sacrament to or received it with his parishioners . . . and scarce condescends to speak to any of us."[17]

Length of stay in a parish by an assistant curate is one of the means of measuring how well they were known to the parishioners. In the 180 parishes where the curates were resident, there were twenty-nine who had served for longer than ten years, and of these eleven had been in the same parish for twenty years or more, the longest stays of all in this group being for thirty-four and thirty-seven years. Another nineteen parishes had had their curate for longer than six years. Most of these curates were singularists who do not appear elsewhere in the returns.

One of the connecting factors in the parishes with the longest serving curates is the relatively comfortable level of stipend paid by the incumbent to those curates, where such information is given. Of twenty-nine such parishes there is no information on curates' pay for six parishes, but in the others, the range is from £20 to £50 per year. Among the curates who were closely acquainted with their parishioners were those who added more services of Holy Communion to the standard seasonal four occasions. Just over half of the curates in this group held more than four sacrament services per year.

Holding catechism classes was a sure way of becoming acquainted with parishioners. Every curate in this group of twenty-nine parishes catechized the children. Attendance levels across the group combine to suggest that although the curates seem at first to be shadowy figures, church life in these parishes was enhanced by the curates' contributions to an established pattern of churchgoing.

One other observation about this group of twenty-nine parishes is that their geographical situations contained a variety which is representative of the diocese as a whole: nascent industrial towns, coastal resorts and industrial and fishing ports, York city environs, remote dales villages, and moorland and wolds settings.

Relations between Incumbents and Curates

The returns clearly indicate that some incumbents did not get to know their assistants very well. Often the curate was a new arrival. Sometimes he stayed only for a short season. When curates and their vicars did speak to each other face to face, it was likely to have involved a discussion about their shared responsibilities, and once decided was usually not followed up by further meetings. It was not only some incumbents who treated curates in a distant manner. The lay patron at Silsden, whose case is considered subsequently in chapter 7, had made trouble for Jonathan Jackson, the curate, for nearly forty years before Archbishop Drummond was called in to settle matters.

The example of Bugthorpe shows that vicar and curate could be quite distant from each other. Although the vicar, Edward Bracken, was assisted by a resident curate, he did not give his name, nor did he say how long the assistant had been with him, nor whether he was duly qualified. Bracken's reply, however, indicates that the parish was properly served, not just by the unnamed curate, but by a second unnamed assistant:

> When I got that Vicaridge I offered the old Curate to take the whole income and give me half which he refused; now have two Assistants, one at 10gns a year for the Sunday duty; and another residing a mile distance doing the weekly duty for the surpluss [sic] fees.

Edward Bracken resided in York and helped at St. Laurence once a fortnight. Quite close to Bugthorpe is the larger parish of Catton, where, for £35 per year, Laurence Eglin served as assistant to John Blake, the absentee rector who was master of the free grammar school in York, and about whose length of stay at Catton there is no reference in the returns. Piecing together what the parish life as organized by the curate might have been like at Catton, one may glimpse the real figure in front of its shadow. He conducted Sunday morning service once a week with a sermon. He drew about a quarter of the communicant population to the services of Holy Communion, with "still more" at Easter. He did the catechizing in Lent. Meanwhile,

> the Methodists assembled in private houses at uncertain times to the number of about 30 from this and other parishes. They have no certain teacher. There was a Meeting House for them at Stamford Bridge but it has been sometime closed.

Some may have inherited curates from their predecessors. Others may not have had direct contact with their assistants precisely because the whole point of having a curate was for him to do the work. Fathers and sons with shared ministries (see above in "Getting and Keeping a Curate") might have spent some of their time discussing their work, especially if they also shared the parsonage. For this period there is scant reference by the clergy to any need to meet and plan their work. There is a story[18] from a slightly later time, that when Thomas Wilson of Slaithwaite required the assistance of John Murgatroyd, curate in Almondbury until 1767 and schoolmaster there until 1786, he would ring a bell early on Sunday morning, "their houses being on opposite sides of the valley"—communication of a sort!

In the sixty-one parishes with the shortest stay assistant curates—from one month to two and a half years—information emerges about the frequency of Holy Communion. In twenty-eight of these parishes Holy Communion services were held more frequently than the standard four or five times per year, with twelve parishes recording their count as eighteen times, and Holy Trinity, Hull, celebrating the sacrament every week. Easter attendance figures provide a considerable variety of information. One reason why some incumbents did not answer the question about the annual salary might be that their curates were very new arrivals. There is a nil return on that point for fifteen parishes. Of those who gave figures, the levels of curates' pay range from five pounds to fifty-seven pounds per annum.

Canonical Qualifications of the Curates

Another patch of shadow obscures the matter of licensing. A straight affirmative answer to this question is a rarity. We read more that the incumbents believed their curates to be duly qualified and canonically licensed, rather than statements of such as fact. One explanation for this vagueness might be that the incumbents did not grow closely acquainted with their curates sufficiently to know these important details first hand. Laurence Sterne, who was frequently away, admitted the irregularity of Kilner, his curate at Coxwold for the previous two and a half years, "by some mistakes or other, either on his side or mine, something has ever prevented him obtaining his Priest's Orders.—He shall offer himself to your Grace the next Ordination."

Neighborly Help

For clergy who could not afford to employ a curate, and for those who could not find the right one even though they were looking, the idea of neighborly and mutual assistance was the answer. Whereas licensed assistant curates were costly or might stay for only a matter of months, ongoing mutual help between neighboring clergy was a safe and reliable course involving no expense. Illness, old age, infirmity, and the geographical impact of the seasons led many neighboring clergymen to make such permanent links with each other on an occasional basis, as George Dodsworth explained (see earlier section "Getting and Keeping a Curate"). The answers to Q7 [Do you perform Divine Service in any church besides your own?] in the visitation returns attest the occasional nature of this assistance, with phrases such as, "except when I'm either sick myself or assisting others yt are so" (Philip Bainbridge of Edston) and "sometimes to assist a sick brother, but not often on account of my bad health" (John Moore of Headingley) and "except occasionally upon the absence of a neighbouring clergyman" (Richard Waite of Kirkby Malhamdale). Richard Crockley, vicar of Cantley, expressed it quaintly, writing at Q6 [Have you a residing curate?], "No. I am my own Curate, and other people's too, occasionally, as you will find at your visitation."

Conclusion

Assistant curates bore the brunt of many parochial burdens, but it was often hard to find a suitable curate, so neighboring incumbents helped each other. Many incumbents did not have all the facts about their curates, and it was considered quite normal for a man to appoint a curate to a living from which he himself was almost permanently absent. A curate's length of stay varied enormously, from a few months to over thirty years. The evidence is that the Georgian church was ministering to its laity in a satisfactory manner via its short- and long-stay curates, most of whom were singularists. Catechism, regular Sunday services, maintenance of good attendance figures, and administration of the sacraments featured noticeably in parish life where curates covered for absentee incumbents. The incumbents who did not pay assistant curates but who made neighborly arrangements as each others' curates showed a similar attitude of conscientious attention to the needs of their parishioners and were open in explaining the details to their archbishop. The archbishop himself could be brought to intervene in a difficult situation, as at Silsden (see chapter 7), when it was recognized that his style of authority would solve the problem swiftly.

The Yorkshire Evangelicals

The influence of the evangelicals was resisted in parishes where a dislike for Enthusiasm was strong, and where an "awakened" church life was not welcome. Two main examples illustrate this, at Almondbury and Helmsley.

The life of the church in the parish of Almondbury in the mid eighteenth century was rasped by the rather crusty attitudes of its ageing vicar towards Enthusiasm. As the seasons passed and the church's calendar was observed, Edward Rishton had had more than one opportunity to discover his irritation with the neighboring evangelical parish of Huddersfield and the neighboring evangelical clergy in the persons of Henry Venn and Samuel Furly. The visitation enquiry gave Rishton the chance to complain to the archbishop. In writing his answers to the particular question about the Holy Communion services, he did not give the required figures, as noted earlier, but went on to say,

> I think it proper to acquaint your Grace that three towns in this parish constantly resort to Divine Service to the Chapel of Holmfirth in the parish of Kirk Burton and even prescribe and pay for seats there, and the same is done by two other towns in the Chapel of Slaithwaite in the parish of Huddersfield.

This agrees with the additional information he had written about Slaithwaite when he was answering Q2. He wrote,

> There are no licensed or other meeting houses in this parish if I am to except the Methodists. But of them there are Teachers without number. I am told, and believe it to be true, that the Curate of Slaithwaite holds what he calls Lectures but what I call Conventicles in two different towns in this parish.

It is clear that Rishton was suffering badly from the Enthusiasts, not only in his neighboring parishes but also from their influence in his own parish at a time of life—he must have been nearly eighty—when he could have expected to be peaceful. His parish was a large one for any clergyman to have, and he cannot have been au fait with all its details in 1764. Indeed, one of his neighbors, the curate at Holmfirth chapel, mentioned above, wrote on *his* return, "It is difficult to know the precise number of Communicants in my chapelry which I believe is 20 miles in circumference." Holmfirth was a chapelry in the neighboring parish of Kirk Burton and was about a quarter the size of Almondbury. Rishton had admitted that he could not keep up with what was happening in his parish in his answer to Q1,

> The Methodists I am told are pretty numerous in the remoter parts of this parish but they are such a vagrant sect that it is impossible to give

any account of them and besides they will not allow themselves to be called Dissenters.

He also referred to his "great age and infirmities," and it was as if he did not hold himself responsible for what happened beyond his normal reach, which was, by that time, his own parsonage, and as if pastoral visiting was not his duty if it involved difficult travel. At his age, this is defensible. He did have three chapels with curates in some of the remoter parts, and his own assistant curate was the schoolmaster in the neighboring chapelry of Slaithwaite, about five miles and two valleys distant, so *he* cannot have been fully absorbed with Rishton's work in the main parish of Almondbury except on Sundays, when Rishton depended on him. Among the Georgian clergy in Yorkshire, it was not regarded as a minister's usual task to visit frequently throughout his parish. Regular pastoral visiting was one of the characteristics of some of the evangelical clergy and was written of, for example in the cases of Grimshaw and Conyers, as requiring more than the normal ministerial effort to undertake and was surely linked to the seasons. It was as a result of the fame of Grimshaw's pastoral visiting that a revival reached Almondbury soon after the time of the visitation.[19] Opposition—perhaps fed by the vicar—came from one Joseph Kaye, constable and parish clerk. He inflamed a mob of "lewd fellows of the baser sort" to break into the preaching place and attack the Methodist preacher. It was precisely to avoid such riots as this one and its successor that the archbishop had counseled Edward Rishton "not to meet the evangelical movement with controversy and opposition," after Rishton had alleged that "sincere sober Christianity has received a deadly blow by the turbulent preaching and practices of these new Gospelers."[20]

Rishton of Almondbury may have had some understandable reasons for criticizing the enthusiastic efforts of his neighbors, and may have had a sense, at the end of a long life of ministry, that all was not quite right with the Church of England for it to have bred disturbers of "sober Christianity." The curate of Bilsdale, with a similar grievance, informed against his own vicar. In answer to Q2, William Deason of Bilsdale wrote, "Mr Conyers, Vicar of Helmsley, or his Curate takes the Liberty to preach once a fortnight in an old Barn whether licensed or no, I cannot tell." These occasions might have been the catechizing evenings that Conyers described in his letter to the archbishop.[21] He may have written that letter precisely because of William Deason's view of his ministry. But it is remarkable that Deason should have associated Conyers' Saturday evenings with the archbishop's question about dissenting meeting-houses. The evangelical clergy of Yorkshire had been close to Ingham and Whitefield at the outset, but they had made a formal break with the Methodists as early as 1741. The split was organizational and doctrinal and did not extend to personal disinclinations. The doctrinal difference was, as Walsh has explained, that the evangelicals abhorred Wesley's doctrines of entire sanctification, perfection and assurance. Walsh has outlined the phases of this development of the evangelicals' beliefs and has seen them as evolving in parallel with and not consequent on the growth of the Methodists. The parallel in understanding may be seen in a letter from Richard Conyers to John Wesley of 1763. Conyers wrote then, "As far as the doctrine you teach has come to my knowledge, I know not one part to which I could not subscribe, both with hand and heart." But their personal contact did not grow any closer. When Wesley called on Conyers in the following year, Conyers was not at home, and his housekeeper received Wesley with a rather fainthearted welcome. Nor did Conyers make any known reply to his copy of Wesley's subsequent letter to forty or fifty clergymen. Walsh's opinion is that by the last years of the eighteenth century the rapid growth of the Methodists frightened the evangelicals for the future of the established church. In Yorkshire this led them to band together to form the Elland Society, one of the "clerical clubs . . . like regional conclaves which took on the role of unofficial synods, in which something like a party line was hammered out on issues of faith and order."[22] One development from this was to spread the opposition within the Georgian church. Conyers left Yorkshire in 1775, his parishioners weeping, and he himself so upset that he could not go into his church to deliver his farewell sermon. He removed to Deptford, where, Walsh discovered, a lecturer contradicted him every Sunday evening for what he had said in the morning.[23]

The following table illustrates some of the activities of the Yorkshire Evangelicals, taken from the visitation returns:

Parish	Name of cleric	Types & Nos of Dissent	Nos. of Methodist Mtghouses/ mtgs p/wk	Sunday service	Holy Comm. per yr	Usual No at HC	Easter attendance 1764
Aberford	Bentham	10Ing 9Me 25RC	1–0	2	18	18	74
Elland	Burnet	Ind Me	2–0	2	18	—	90
Hunslet	Crooke	70Pre&Ind7Q3RC	1–3	1	4	170	169
Kippax	Crooke	4RC ?Me	2–3	1	18	80	102

Helmsley	Conyers	6RC 13Q	0–0	1	4	450	700
Kirby Misperton	. .	3Q	0–0	1	5	—	100
Slaithwaite	Furly	1Ind	0–0	2	12	65	80
Leeds	Kirshaw (& M Atkinson)	500	2–0	2	18	600	1700
Cleckheaton	Eastwood	32Mor21Ind3Q	0–0	2	4	100	150
Haworth	Richardson	40Bap	1–2	2	18	100	154
Huddersfield	Venn	100IndQMor	0–0	2	18	300	—
Ledsham	Benson	2RC	0–0	2	18	35	185
Thorp Arch	Atkinson	0	0–0	2	12	25	44
Walton	Atkinson	1RC	0–0	0	3	35	36

Please consult list of abbreviations for dissenter identification

Conclusion

At a time when some clergymen worked to serve more than one church for insufficient money, a band of ultraconscientious Anglican clerics could be nearly as irksome to the ordinary parish priest as revivalist activities organized by his own parishioners; and a traditional incumbent would be puzzled when some of his congregation met to sing hymns and pray in each others' homes on midweek evenings, but he could perhaps explain it as "dissenting" behavior. It became socially uncomfortable for some clergy to recognize that uneducated tradesmen and women of their congregations were leaders in such meetings. Disparaging the gifts of leadership among the uneducated laity prompted the vicar of Birstall to oppose his parishioner, John Nelson, before a magistrate. This was the background to the ready feeling of mistrust that greeted some of the Anglican clergy who experienced an "awakening" or spiritual revival during the mid eighteenth century, and it was a feeling shared by the archbishop. The evidence is, however, that Yorkshire parishes absorbed some of the ideas of the early evangelicals, and that where church life was receptive it was enriched accordingly. Frequent celebrations of Holy Communion, a devotion to pastoral visiting and a commitment to regular preaching were measurable throughout the York diocese in 1764, and fitted some of the existing thorough programs of catechism, patterns that were as much old "high church" and puritan as revivalist evangelical. The situation of Henry Venn's parish of Huddersfield, lying between the two other large parishes of Halifax and Almondbury, illustrates the problems and opportunities which he, as an evangelical, posed to his neighbors, neither of whom was evangelical. As a high churchman, Rishton of Almondbury had been celebrating Holy Communion monthly and at the festivals since his induction in 1726, and saw no place for evangelicals in his parish. Legh of Halifax, on the other hand, employed a dozen or so curates, including a known evangelical, to get on with the work of ministry in the chapelries, while he himself admitted that he needed plenty of time away.

In Drummond's Yorkshire, the Church allowed the evangelicals to nurture their fellowship, to develop their ideas, and to arrange their regular meetings so that, when the foundations were thoroughly laid, the Elland Society could make links with similar societies in London and burgeoned into the Church Missionary Society. It was also a time when the traditionalists and the hierarchy abhorred Enthusiasm, though Matthew Buck at Brodsworth hardly needed to tell the archbishop that there were no dissenters there, but added at Q11 "[no chapel] and thank God no Conventicle." Thomas Bright of Ecclesfield complained that the Methodists "swarmed in the next neighbouring parish . . . towards the south, namely Sheffield," and Richard Brinknell of North Ottrington thought it right to "observe to your lordship that Mrs. Heber is building a chapel at Thornton le Beans in my parish" (though there is no information on what type of chapel this was). Such informing, however, did not provoke Drummond into unwise action. His policy of noninterference was based on his knowledge of the legal limits of his powers and was in line with his wisdom in avoiding confrontation. He knew that the activities of the evangelicals were uncomfortable rather than illegal, and he had the example of what his predecessors, Hutton and then Gilbert, had found at Haworth, when Grimshaw was the subject of complaints.[24] Hutton found no fault with Grimshaw, and Gilbert's visit to Haworth led to a sermon from Grimshaw which reduced the whole congregation to tears. Grimshaw had died in 1763, but Drummond would not have courted a similar experience among other evangelicals, preferring to allow them space in the broad and comfortable church among its traditionalists.

Poverty: A Problem Partly Solved by Queen Anne's Bounty

The broad based pyramid of poorly paid clergy was much in evidence in the parishes of the York diocese at the time of the 1764 visitation returns. Some of those at the top were very well paid, but of the majority who were poor there were some who could scarcely manage and who supplemented their incomes with farming and schoolteaching. Queen Anne's Bounty went a little way towards solving the problem of poverty in the Georgian church, though this was as much by hope in and patience with the fund as by direct results for many poor clergy.

The features of the eighteenth-century church which have looked like wrongs or omissions to some critics—pluralism, nonresidence, and absenteeism—have as their explanation the unequal basis for the payment of the church's workforce at parish levels. While this may be admissible as modern comment, it has no foundation for being seen in that way by those who lived and worked under the inequalities of that financial provision. The situation then was generally accepted. This is not to say that there were no complaints. The visitation returns of 1764 contain some pathetic statements from clergy about their financial hardships. The instances of such pleas, however, were usually not made in the section which asked for comment about difficulties in the course of their work. In some cases, there seemed even to be a feeble acceptance by the poorest clergy of their situations, more especially among those who were elderly and who had suffered longest or who had experienced the lowering of the value of their incomes. Correspondingly, there is no direct evidence that the archbishop regarded the references to financial hardship as an area where he could intervene helpfully. The spirit of the age was not one where fundamental reform was regarded as possible, but Queen Anne's Bounty was one method of obtaining some assistance.

The historic but unstandardized organization of the Church of England stayed in the age of first fruits and tenths until 1704. First fruits were payments made to the crown (earlier to the Pope) of "the first year's revenues of spiritual benefices after these had been filled. . . . The charge was based upon the same assessment as that for tenths, which represented only the nominal, not the real value of the benefice."[25] In 1704 the Bounty Fund was established when the crown made over these monies back to the church to try to help poorly paid clergymen. The Bounty Fund allowed the possibility of augmenting the value of small livings both by benefaction and by lot. It meant that poorly paid clergymen had two hopes of attempting to improve their stipends. Under the auspices of the governors of Queen Anne's Bounty the sum of two hundred pounds, if granted by a benefactor, would be matched by the Fund. Every year the governors drew lots to see who would benefit from the fund without an additional benefactor. Some variations in the sums affected the fund's progress; by the time of the 1764 visitation, benefices worth less than forty-five pounds and twenty pounds[26] per year were eligible for augmentation in these ways. The capital sums were then available for the clergy to find suitable lands to buy as an investment, the interest from the purchase being their "augmentation." The augmentations were generally about seven pounds per year. While the favored clergy looked for land to buy, the governors of the fund held the capital in trust at an annual investment of 2 percent. According to G. F. A. Best, the fund conducted a "tolerably efficient routine of business." The correspondence between Secker and Drummond (see Chapter 7) uncovers some of their concerns about the routines, but Best's conclusion is fair: "It was not, indeed, faultless, and its mills ground rather slowly, but its work was good and solid, and for each man who had complaints about it there were a dozen to bless it."[27]

It might be thought that the church of the eighteenth century could go further in dealing with the problem of poverty. This would be to misread the temper of its clergy, both hierarchical and parochial. The bounty fund was small-scale royal initiative, and it had a slow and cautious start, administered by a corporation. Expecting more from a church which had lately emerged from strife might have forfeited the desired stability. It was not as if politics led the way. Reform was not to arrive until 1832 for the first of the parliamentary changes. The church was older and less likely to start changes. So the problem of poverty was addressed in a marginal way by Queen Anne's Bounty.

Virgin's criticisms of the bounty fund in its operation during the eighteenth century, as opposed to its shortcomings and mismatchings in the early nineteenth century, were that it was "cautious and conservative," that its innovative efforts were stifled by the Mortmain Act of 1736 which prohibited deathbed benefactions, that its grants towards parsonages were allowed to dwindle, and that instead of setting fifty pounds as the level below which private benefactions could be made, the figure was reduced to thirty-five pounds (and thirty pounds for receipt of augmentations by lot).[28] Despite these criticisms, he credited the bounty fund for its "consistent policy of opting for long-term good rather than more glamorous short-term gains."

The bounty disbursements drew their own contemporary critics. One featured in the press in March 1760:[29]

> There is said to be a large fund in hand . . . which is restrained from application for want of Lay Donations towards the augmentation of poor livings. . . . Such a restriction might have been wisely necessary at the first institution of this fund . . . it is a great pity a new Act of

Parliament is not obtained, for the entire investiture of the large sum said to be in hand, to the pious purposes it was granted for.

It is easy to see how speculation could occur about the operation of the fund, since the governors were likely to have large sums awaiting transfer while clergy looked about for land to buy.

An Assessment of Yorkshire Parishes to Benefit from the Bounty

By 1764 there were 192 parishes who had benefited from Queen Anne's Bounty. The heavy workload imposed on the incumbents by their large populations (around one thousand families) at Bingley, Birstall, Dewsbury, and Pontefract, shows that the bounty was making some contribution to the needs of the church. Guiseley and Raskelfe stand out more obviously, with respective values at £300 and £120[30]—surely not the deserving cases which the fund was supposed to be helping. A closer look at Guiseley shows that although the rector, Henry Wickham, was conforming to the letter of the enquiry by recording that Queen Anne's Bounty had been awarded to his parish, it was strictly to the two dependent chapels at Horsforth and Rawden that the augmentations had been made. A connection between Raskelfe and Thormanby, the latter a tiny parish with a value of £80 per annum but a population of only twenty-four families, clears up another apparent anomaly, in that John Nesfield, rector of Thormanby and curate of Raskelfe, was himself a benefactor to the chapelry of Raskelfe. The returns include the information for Raskelfe that the bounty was awarded by lot, and that £30 had been added to it by the present curate. Thormanby had received the bounty by benefaction as early as 1723.

Benefactions attracted further benefactions in Whitkirk, where the vicar, Peter Simon, recorded donations to the poor in 1573, 1631, 1635, 1677, and 1717. As well as receiving an augmentation from Queen Anne's Bounty, there was also a settlement of £10 per annum for a sermon on ten Sundays throughout each year at Whitkirk.

Investment of the Bounty

The clergy did not always write on their returns what the archbishop requested at Q4. He wanted to know if and when there had been an augmentation. He asked if there had been any purchase of lands, and if so, what they were, and what the annual income amounted to. He did not ask when the purchase had been made, but sometimes the clergy included it. Other sources provide it for some parishes. Investment of the bounty is a similarly elusive detail for some parishes. A benefaction just before the year of the visitation might have been difficult to invest if there were no appropriate lands for sale. Archbishop Secker explained the point about investment in a reply to *The Evening Post,*

> The money settled . . . ought to be laid out in land: and the Governors are not bound to pay any Interest for the royal Bounty in the mean time. They do, however, pay 2%. And before the Interest of the Fund was reduced to 3%, they paid more. The smallness of the Allowance was intended, partly to quicken the Incumbents in looking out for purchases, which Effect it hath had; partly to insure the payment of the principal money . . . And the Governors are always glad to accept purchases, when offered, provided the nature of the Estates be proper, the Income such as may reasonably be expected, and the Title clear."[31]

Although most incumbents with bounty money had bought land satisfactorily by the time of the visitation, there were forty-two who had not completed a purchase to augment their living. It was not always easy to secure the right piece of land.

Critics and Defenders of the Fund

Sensitivity about the bounty, aroused in 1760 when the *Evening Post* printed the gossip about funds, was inflamed again in 1762. Archbishop Secker drafted another reply. The draft began with a careful statement about the origin of the bounty and the procedure for augmentations:

> The money which arises from the Royal Bounty, or which Benefactors contribute, is paid to their Treasurer, who at present is Sir Jeffery Elwes.[32] And no more is allowed to lie in his hands, than appears to be necessary. The rest is placed out from time to time in South Sea Annuities . . . At the end of every year, so much of the clear produce of the First-fruits and tenths in that year, as hath not been appropriated, in conjunction with Benefactions, to Livings not exceeding the annual Income of £45, is appropriated to such as exceed not £20, by drawing Lots to determine, which of them shall be preferred. And no larger a part of the money, intrusted with the Governors, is left unappropriated, than will be requisite to answer just demands upon them; and to secure the payment of the appropriated sums, in case the annuities should continue below par.

The draft concluded with an invitation from the archbishop to anyone who required further satisfaction on any of the particulars to apply not to him, but to the bishop of his diocese. The other bishops clearly had some unquiet moments about such possible enquiries and managed to abort the publication of the archbishop's draft. The last paragraph on the page has the explanation:

> It was proposed at a meeting of the Governors in April 1760, that this should be published in the newspapers. But Bishop Hayter of Norwich having moved, that the Bishops should first take the ensuing summer to consider and inquire concerning the propriety of raising the Interest again to 2.5%, which he strongly recommended, the publication was postponed. It was proposed a second time April 13 1762; and postponed again, to avoid raising Discourse about a matter, which, it was said, might otherwise lie quiet.

The bishop of Norwich's preference for raising the interest from 2 percent to 2.5 percent irritated Thomas Secker. It prompted him to write another of his statements about the operation of the bounty, but not, in this case, with a view to publication in the newspapers; the note at the foot of the paper says that it was prepared for and the substance delivered at the meeting of the governors in 1760. The arguments about the payment of interest were fully rehearsed for the attention of that meeting:

> The first of the Rules . . . is . . . by . . . purchase, not of pension. I know not when we first paid interest to the incumbents, whether the Governors made any general Resolution to that purpose, or whether the practice prevailed gradually and silently . . . it is strange, if the possibility and probability of its lying long in the Funds was not considered. But if it was, accumulation seems to have been preferred to paying interest. If we have no Right to pay any, the less we pay the less we transgress. But supposing a Right, will it be prudent to return from the Allowance of 2% to that of 2.5%? It is said, that the Clergy are uneasy at the Diminution. The Bishop of Norwich saith his Clergy are. But he hath not said whether many of them have declared they are, or whether finding that some were, he hath presumed it of the rest. I dare say he hath not endeavoured to spread the uneasiness, else no wonder if it became general. Some clergymen elsewhere have been uneasy at the management of the Bounty in other respects: but few in this. And when any persons are uneasy, the first thing to be done, if it can, is to shew them that they have no cause. Now, if they have no right to any interest, they have none to complain, that only 2% is given them.

People continued to be disturbed by the thought of large sums of money lying in the hands of the governors and not being put out to the use for which it was intended. Five years after the matter was left to lie quiet, it arose again as a concern between the two archbishops in their exchanges of correspondence. The issue became so urgent that they were planning occasions to meet in order to settle the matter but were several times thwarted by the poor weather in the wintry days of January 1767 (see chapter 7).

An earlier view[33] of the operation of Queen Anne's Bounty was far less favorable than the comforting pronouncements of G. F. A. Best and made some realistic criticisms of the second half of the eighteenth century. Crosse picked out three features that hampered the working of the governors of the bounty and referred to a work by Hodgson, *Account of the Augmentations of Small Livings*, 1826. One was that the governors were too large a body: they were two hundred in number, with "all the bishops [except Sodor and Man], deans, lords lieutenant, privy councillors, serjeants at law, and the mayors of all the cities in England." The number was increased in 1713 to include all the queen's counsel. The second criticism was that the aim of efficient administration could not be achieved by selecting men who were already overworked. The main criticism leveled by Crosse was directed at the principles for awarding the augmentations, referring to them as "strange and unfortunate methods." Inequality was the crux of the charge against the ballot box method. Although this did initially attempt to deal with some of the very poorest livings by allowing no more grants to be made in one year to any cure exceeding ten pounds per year until all under that amount (of those drawn) had received benefit, the ballot permitted some livings "to have five or six grants in the course of a century, while others as deserving had no grant at all."

At the time of the York visitation of 1764, some of the outworking of these inequalities can be seen clearly. The poor parishes at that time were so much a worry to the governors of the bounty that they did try to improve the system. It was not until 1788, however, long after the visitation concerned in this study, that the upper limit of livings eligible for augmentation was altered. Abandonment of the ballot was not decided until much later than that. The ballot as an idea for doing business was a particularly eighteenth-century style, not condemned under the evil of gambling until the age of gaming had waned. It would have appealed to most people at the time as satisfactory.

The Yorkshire Clergy Attitude to the Bounty Fund

There are few direct remarks of thanks or gratitude for receipt of the augmentations from the bounty fund in the 1764 returns, but this means that clergy considered it was their right to win funds by lot. This attitude is simply the reflection of the eighteenth-century opinion that chance and gaming were appropriate ways to get results. The expressions of gratitude appear more towards the donor who contributed to augmentation by benefaction. Some of these attitudes were ones of natural subservience to a noted patron in a higher social class.

The more interesting cases involved those who tried to put pressure on the bounty fund and some who misunderstood the way it worked. Of all the details on this point in the returns, the liveliest is the direct request for the archbishop himself to supplement the amount subscribed by a local donor. Richard Crockley, writing from the parish of Cantley, next to Doncaster and within five miles of the Drummond family estates at Brodsworth, said he had no hospital, no almshouses, no benefactions to the poor, and referred to one bequest of 40 shillings to the vicar. He had received no augmentation from Queen Anne's Bounty, and he added,

> I don't care how soon your Grace procures it, it will admit of it, for it [the living] is but £32 per annum. [The sum of] £150 is already left to it (viz 40s per annum) [so] I imagine [that] will do the thing. Will your Grace draw your purse strings on the occasion?

Crockley's daring request is in character with his other terms of phrase. He declared himself a nonresident, but cheekily said that he was nearer to his church (living at Hall Gate in Doncaster) than if he resided on the parsonage. He is also the one, previously mentioned, who wrote wittily about being his own and other people's curate.

Matthew Metcalfe of Hartwith chapel described an offhand attitude he met in a landowner when he tried to buy land for investment. Metcalfe's living had had three augmentations by benefaction from the bounty since the chapel's consecration in 1751, but there had been no purchase. His explanation was,

> partly owing to Landseller's dislike to purchases of this sort on account of the nicety of tedious proceedings of the Governors and partly to the difficulty of meeting with an estate adequate to our principal.

Thomas Hudson of Old Byland complained that he had not had any augmentation from Queen Anne's Bounty, a situation, he wrote, which he feared was "owing to some omission in that affair as many other churches of superior value have obtain'd it in that way."

The curate of Pool chapel, John Alcock, stated that there had been a purchase following the augmentation but that he could not find the deeds. This is not surprising in that his return omits all sorts of other details. He gave no dates for his ordination, which from clergy lists was as early as 1717. He did not say in which year he had been licensed and wrote "nothing to answer" at Q6, whereas from clergy lists Dudley Rockett had been licensed as the assistant curate since 1753.

Leaving the augmentation uninvested for much too long was the situation at Skipsea. The vicar, a nonresident from Burton Agnes, also held the living of Burton Pidsea, the latter being at the further end of the Holderness deanery from Skipsea. Archbishop Hutton had given him the dispensation, and the augmentation had been bought by Archbishop Sharp. That situation goes right back to the time when the fund was first established (Sharp was archbishop from 1691 to 1714). This was a piece of poor stewarding by Thomas Bowness of Skipsea.

Conclusion

After an initial delay, the bounty fund won recognition, but by 1760 it had gathered some opponents for its policy of holding the capital before the appropriate purchases were made by beneficiaries. Later critics disliked its ballot-box method and its failure to bar beneficiaries from awards in subsequent years. The marginal effect of Queen Anne's Bounty on the problem of poverty was in accord with the pernickety conscience of Thomas Secker in addressing himself to the fund's accounts. But nearly one-third of the parishes in the York diocese drew benefit from the fund, and its application was taken seriously by most of its beneficiaries. Although ignorance among the clergy of its workings was not uncommon, the ballot method was generally acceptable to the eighteenth-century mind.

6

Population, Dissent, and the Church

Part 1: Population Changes and Dissenter Fluctuations in the Parishes

Introductory Analysis of Numbers and Organization

Finding out about the families of each parish was the archbishop's first priority. The incumbents generally knew how many people were in their care. Some gave an approximate number, but there were only eight blank entries. Q1 also asked about the number of dissenters and their different denominations within the parish.

Questions about Nonconformity had become more significant since the decline in evidence value of churchwardens' reports. By the 1760s churchwardens were reluctant to present people in court actions for nonattendance at church,[1] so there was less certainty about who was or might be Nonconformist, and "it was widely assumed that the Toleration Act had . . . made churchgoing voluntary."[2] Knowing who was a Papist was easier because the Catholic missions were not itinerant. Parsons were more familiar with Presbyterians than with Independents and Baptists, and Quakers were also identifiable. Sects such as Inghamites and Moravians were localized and less generally understood by the clergy. It was the Methodists who were the most difficult to categorize in the mid eighteenth century for reasons connected with their own growth and allegiance.

The parochial structure of the Church of England—the concept of the diocese divided into parishes—has remained a fundamental feature of the parson to person organization. The parish system was tested sorely by the exigencies of pluralism, nonresidence and absenteeism, and though these faults became abuses, the system had not failed its parishioners at the time of the 1764 visitation (see

Chapter 5). However, amid the rise and fall of different Nonconformist churches and Roman Catholic missions, the Anglican parish structure showed some signs by the mid eighteenth century of being unable to cope with other changes such as the population shifts and increases. Heavy burdens of ministry were being carried in matters of catechism, particularly in the more populous towns. The difficulties of redefining parish boundaries were not faced until the reforms of the late 1830s and 1840s, and in 1764 the imperfections in the parish system were scarcely noticed.[3] Where individuals had won their liberty, for example, to be Presbyterians, they nevertheless were Presbyterians in such and such a parish. The ground base stayed the same. Along with it, the responsibilities of the parish priest similarly remained constant, though in today's world the Anglican parsons in their parishes have many more thousands of parishioners—theoretically, by virtue of the established church—in their spiritual care than the early nineteenth-century reformers could have imagined, a reminder of the subjective nature of reforming standards.

The organization of other churches was of interest to the archbishops, who expected the parish priests to know how many meetinghouses there were, whether they were licensed, how many people gathered in them, and who their teachers were. Some of the answers might have been disquieting to Drummond, especially if he realized that 382 of the returning parishes had declared the existence of dissenters, even though there were 239 parishes apparently with none. Drummond was unlikely to have been able to take the enquiry further, as we can, to find that there were places where Methodist meetinghouses existed[4] where no dissenters were declared, but he could also read that there were places where the dissenters were so numerous that a full count could not be made. This was the case in Sheffield where, according to the vicar, there were many persons of the dissenters who "declare that they have no other reason for not going to church but the want of room." It was precisely this kind of sign, spelled out in simple terms, that should have alerted the archbishop to address a situation requiring change, but it was buried by all the other data and apparently went unheeded.

Gaining or losing members was the area in which the eighteenth-century churches did encounter variation. The rate of change, however, was slow, and in a comparison of population figures alongside dissenter types from the Herring and Drummond returns, an air of stability surrounded the gradual shifts.

In an overview of the dissenter statistics, the themes of stability and slow rate of change are emphasised from a study of the following particulars:

Parishes with dissenters both in 1743 and in 1764:	301
Parishes with no dissenters either in 1743 or 1764:	162
Parishes with some dissenters in 1743 but none in 1764:	68
Parishes with no dissenters in 1743 but some in 1764:	90
	Total 621

301 Parishes with Dissenters both in 1743 and 1764

The sameness of the figures in some cases gives a first impression of stability. Some places list exactly the same figures for 1743 and 1764, and the only doubt about the double information is whether the clergymen were the same ones at both dates, taking the easy way out. Guisborough reported 300 families on both dates. Lythe reported 423 both times. Owthorne twice reported 56 families. Hilston had recorded 7 families at both returns. At Guisborough, the incumbent had been in office since 1727 and might perhaps have been taking a short cut, but his entries for dissenter numbers suggest accuracy. At Lythe the elderly curate, ordained in 1714, had been licensed to the town as recently as 1760; the figures could only be doubted for 1764 if he had inherited the 1743 information from his predecessor and copied it. At Owthorne the vicar in 1764 was a man in the prime of his career, ordained in 1757, and inducted to his parish in 1763; he too, may have been able to call up vicarage records. The chances are just as much in favor of his doing an accurate count and arriving at the same number as before, precisely because there had been no change. At Hilston, where counting all 7 of the families was hardly an exercise, the incumbent was again a man in his early prime, ordained in 1750 and inducted in 1759.

Other examples underline the steadiness or gentle growth of population during the years between the returns to Herring and the returns to Drummond. Halsham grew from 28 to 32 families, keeping its dissenter count the same at 8 Roman Catholic families. Huntington had fifty-four families increasing to sixty by 1764 but lost one Quaker family. At Garton in Holderness the families were 22 and 24 for 1743 and 1764 respectively, and the 2 families of Roman Catholics featured in both returns, whereas the 3 Quaker families of 1743 had increased to 5 by 1764.

Distinguishing next between the different groups of dissenters during the twenty-one years between the Herring returns and the Drummond returns strengthens several of the views taken by scholars who have surveyed separate branches of the Christian faith more broadly and across a longer stretch of time.

Denominational Changes: (i) Roman Catholics

Two trends emerge here.[5] One is the steadiness remarked already as a feature of population in general. The other is an increase in Roman Catholic families when overall family numbers showed a decline.

At Ilkley, where the families increased from 130 to 150, the Roman Catholic families kept pace, with 16 in 1743 to 19 in 1764. At Hovingham, the Roman Catholic families were 11 in 1743 out of 160 families, and in 1764 they were 14 out of a depleted 148. Across the study of 301 parishes and chapelries, 37 locations show Roman Catholics holding their numbers steady, and 75 places show increased allegiance. In other words, in Drummond's Yorkshire there were increased opportunities for people to be open about their Roman Catholic faith or to convert to it.

The two archbishops of these eighteenth century York visitations, Archbishops Herring and Drummond, had differing attitudes to Roman Catholicism, derived from their different church careers and characters.

Thomas Herring had been closer to the Act of Toleration and was less accustomed to its impact, being ordained deacon and priest in 1716 and 1719. A royalist and a Cambridge doctor of divinity by the time of George II's succession, his archiepiscopal career saw him in York at the time of the Jacobite rebellion of 1745, so it is not surprising that he viewed Roman Catholics warily. He had been in several parishes in eastern England before he was dean of Rochester. As a royal chaplain he had been with the king on a limited royal visit to Cambridge; he had not been abroad with him and he had no acquaintance with the royal household in the capital. His attraction to the government was a financial one: he had stirred up the loyalties of "the Yorkshire folks" sufficiently for them to part with forty thousand pounds to overcome the Jacobite rebels[6] in 1745. He was persuasive as a political preacher, but is said to have been "colourless as a theologian."[7] The reward for his patriotism was the see of Canterbury in 1747. In comparison with Robert Drummond, he was much more anxious about the activities of Roman Catholics and guarded about their intentions. The strength of the Roman Catholic church in the York diocese may be followed in the recusant returns kept in the Borthwick Institute in the collection from 1705 to 1767. Ollard and Walker were aware of Herring's zeal towards the Roman Catholics. They noted that only two Roman Catholic chapels were declared and the names of forty Roman Catholic clergymen were supplied in the 1743 visitation returns. They estimated that the number of Roman Catholic priests was probably between fifty and sixty, considering that the Yorkshire clergy were deliberately reticent to declare information on those who were their neighbors.[8]

Robert Drummond had traveled more widely and did so as a clergyman in areas, particularly German cities, where Roman Catholicism had been part of the local fabric for many centuries. This gave him a greater breadth of understanding to cope with the mid eighteenth-century English background. His experience and disposition enabled him to approach the question of Roman Catholic observance in the York diocese with a greater degree of understanding and without the urgency that beset Thomas Herring. Nevertheless, Drummond, who had certainly experienced alarm at the time of the 1745 rebellion, had sufficient reason to be concerned about the strength of Roman Catholic missions in some of the York parishes, and the Bishopthorpe papers allow more than a glimpse into his private thinking about this issue.

There are two main shafts of light on this topic. One was provided for Drummond by Archdeacon Blackburne, who reported to him in detail about the Cleveland Roman Catholics. The other is a record of his own thought processes about the political impact of Roman Catholic observance five years into his time as archbishop.

Archdeacon Blackburne sent Drummond regular information about the numbers of Roman Catholics in the Cleveland area. He knew exactly how to add spice to his stock. On 6 August 1765 he ended with a report that there had been "rejoicings on the Pretender's Birthday at Catterick," and referred to "these daring and avowed enemies to religious and civil liberty." There was no great change in the Roman Catholic details from Cleveland.

Drummond made very careful use of the recusant returns, studying the whole situation of Roman Catholics. His interest was conscientious and his focus was microscopic. On 9 July 1767 he asked incumbents to give him "with all convenient speed" a "list of all the Papists or reputed Papists within your parish." The collated information was to go to the House of Lords and had to be categorized by parish, sex, age, occupations, and length of time of residence in the parish. Very few incumbents set out the information in chart form. Most used ordinary prose. Two exceptions were K. Baskett of Everingham and James Godmond of Holme on Spalding Moor, but William Wilkinson of Cottingham wrote, "I have enquired . . . . After ye strictest search I cannot find one."

Drummond's scrutiny of these replies consists of a collection[9] of awful scraps of detailed sums of Roman Catholic numbers, written in his own hand, tiny and unruled, squeezed and sometimes sloping, added up from all the deaneries and prepared for final dispatch to the House of Lords. His own interest led him to record their comparative numbers for the years 1706, 1735, 1743, and 1767. His conclusions were as follows:

> NB the numbers are increased greatly since 1706—if the lists *then* were authentic but they do *not* appear to be so
>
> 1767 ⅗ are female 3000
> 1000 are under 18
> 1000 are above 18 males 2000
> supposing the true number to be 5000.

He thought further about this, however, and wrote,

> The lists of 1706 and 1743 seem to be very imperfect, and those of 1767 perfect: so that the Increase is not so great as appears at first sight; probably not above one third in the last sixty years. NB when the Computation is by families, as in the Lists of 1743, a Family is computed at 5 Persons.[10]

On the reverse side of the 1767 numbers he wrote the parishes with the names of the priests and a list of numbers that might indicate their ages. The next list shows how many years the priest had been there, and the last list shows the names of "persons of distinction in ye parish." His consideration of males under and over eighteen related to the military threat. So Drummond was considering which notable English families might have divided loyalties and what the strength of their armed support might be. He gave this much thought as he went on to list the "resident persons of estate, Papists or reputed Papists and the reputed value of their estates in the diocese of York." He also made a list of the York parishes that had places of worship served by Popish priests or reputed priests, and he set out the name of the parish, the name of the priest, his age, and length of residence. The scrutiny continued more particularly under the heading, "N Riding," even though it reads more like diary notes and is written on a small scrap of paper, little more than 8 by 6 ins but is folded to make four sides and to be used one way and then another, ready for scribbling a memo in moments of inspiration.

The notes suggest that he summoned some of the gentry to call on him at Brodsworth to instruct them about their responsibilities as landowners and heard their accounts of the activities of the Roman Catholics in their parishes. Drummond was making this enquiry in the early summer of 1765. He wrote, "Sir Henry Lawson came to Brodsworth May 20 1765. Mr. Knatchbull a Jesuit his priest whom he promised to send away[.] not 20 converts in 25 years—no converts by him at Yarm." If Sir Henry lived in Yarm—a parish on the farthest northern edge of the diocese—it had meant a very long ride expected of him to explain himself to the archbishop in Brodsworth. A much shorter journey, but yet a difficult one encompassing the heights of Sutton Bank, was expected of Mr. Chomley of Bransby who "came here May 24 1765 and I spoke to him of the prudence necessary in Papism." Mr. Chomley must have been daunted by this warning tone used by Drummond, for he supplied the number of schools and their teachers and numbers, the places of worship, and "the property of residents and non-residents-y[nce] the Power."

The subject was by no means exhausted. Drummond pursued his thoughts and wrote, "Sent to Dr Kirshaw at Rothwell who [suggests] false returns for Mr Harper[.] Haddam—has 70 to 80 at Mass in a house of the D of Norfolk." This "house" could be Carlton Towers near Drax if it refers to the duke's own chapel rather than a mass house provided by him for others. Samuel Harper was named as the incumbent of Rothwell in the 1764 visitation return but was excused from attending on the day of visitation, and the curate, John Taylor, was the one who appeared and exhibited his orders. Harper had been inducted as recently as 1762. The number of Roman Catholics declared in 1764 was five families, whereas in 1743 Harper's predecessor, Ralph Eden, had counted twenty Roman Catholic families in Rothwell. Dr. Kirshaw was the respected vicar of Leeds, the next neighboring parish to Rothwell, and Drummond trusted him to know what might have been happening in the next parish. On the other side of Rothwell was Henry Crooke, vicar of Kippax, who wrote as his answer to Q2 of the 1764 visitation return, "1 Roman Catholic whom I am in great hopes of bringing over to the Church in a little time."

The Roman Catholics at Rothwell continued to be a source of anxiety to Drummond. Two years after the visits by Lawson and

Chomley, he received a complaint that Papists had been insolent to the curate at Drax, and after noting that this had been quieted, he repeated some of the details received earlier about Rothwell and then made the two following memos:

> Send to Bewlay [a housekeeper at Bishopthorpe] for all other papers abt Papists in lower drawer of desk in my closet.
>
> Send to Blackburne [the archdeacon] for list of those in the Yorkshire part of Chester diocese.

He then set out a paper headed "The progress of a process relating to a Papist" and made a list of acts of Parliament that dealt with the legal status of Nonconformists. His memo reads, "if a review of the law in general shd not be vid Test & Toleration Acts & gt an Occasional Conformity." He also made reference to papers written by the bishops of Chester and Norwich about the acts against Popery and then made a cryptic note, "Statutes ab^{t} Le[gislation for] Trimmers."

He further continued with notes about Roman Catholicism in Ireland and Scotland, noting that Lord Aston was the "only Scotch Lord Papist."

The special position of the Jesuits gave Drummond extra concern as he contemplated the English Roman Catholics. He reviewed the international scene since the assassination attempt on the life of the French king in 1757 and the subsequent anti-Jesuit wrath. He set out the dates when the Jesuits were banished from Portugal (1758-59), France (1761), and Spain (1767), observed that many Jesuits had gone to Canada, and posed a question: "Are they therefore our friends because they are cashiered by our enemies?" He was thinking of the relationship between the exiled foreign Jesuits and the English Roman Catholics when he listed the following:

> 1. The fact of the numbers [i.e. of English Roman Catholics]
> 2. The consequences which may be drawn from those facts
> 3. The means of bringing these consequences to a right issue.

These notes show Drummond as still very much the thoughtful politician, aware of his duty in the House of Lords as a guardian of the nation's safety. His notes on this paper ended with jottings that read like headings for further thought:

> Laws in being—how to be executed
> State of Foreign Min^{y} —reciprocity—if proper to tell the numbers of those ^{y}t can bear arms

Publication—Not a dispute of Religious Opinion but of Civil Safety
Intermarriage—Property if married
Those above 18 & under 50 fighting men.

This was written four years after the end of the Seven Years' War, showing that toleration and the safety of the realm were both fragile. Drummond's reasoning, however, suggests that he, no more than his clergy, was unwilling to admit that he was presiding over a resurgence of Roman Catholicism, persuading himself that the increase in recusancy was not so bad as the figures showed.

Denominational changes: *(ii) Quakers*

Quakers represent the most constant of the dissenters in this sample. The constancy is in the frequency of mention, but the mention is noticeably for loss. There were more places where Quaker families decreased than increased or held steady. An increase of Quaker family existence has been noted in 59 places, but this could be a difference in reportage rather than reality. For example, at Kildwick in 1743 there were none specified but by 1764 there were 26 Quaker families reported. The losses, however, were in 101 places and were by 1 or by 2 families, irrespective of whether the overall number of families changed. So, at Gargrave the population went down from 230 families to 189, and the Quaker families were reduced from 3 to 1. At Lythe the number of families remained at 423 but the Quakers were reduced from 3 to none at all. At Osmotherley the families grew from 150 to 230, but the 5 Quaker families did not feature at all in the 1764 return. The growth of 100 families at Kirkburton was accompanied by a drop of 10 in the Quaker families, from 30 in 1743 to 20 in 1764, but this might mean that the 10 Quaker families in the Holmfirth chapelry (which sent in no detailed return in 1743) were part of the overall 30 counted for Kirkburton in 1743. The clergy may not have known the true situation in some of these cases, but the marked trend is for a reduction in the number of Quaker families during the period 1743 to 1764.

The Quakers were the most thinly spread group of all Dissenters, making the losses of ones and twos correspondingly more stringent. To lose the one Quaker family in a parish, as at Birkin and Brafferton and Dunnington, was to remove the Quaker presence altogether in a community. To lose one Quaker family where there had been only two, as at Bardsey and Elloughton, was to place a heavier burden of Quaker practice on the one remaining Quaker family. In parishes which numbered seventy families, as at Dunnington, and sixty-seven at Bardsey, such gaps would have been noteworthy. Stability, on the other hand, must have been imperceptible at the time. No one would have remarked, in a parish of a steady twenty-six to twenty-seven in 1743 and 1764 respectively, that the one Quaker family was still there, other than to know them as the one Dissenting family in the community. Quaker growth, by similar acceptance, was unlikely to have been remarkable when it meant an increase from four to six Quaker families in Almondbury, whose population grew by five hundred families in twenty-one years. Some of the more serious reductions in Quaker observance were as follows:

	1743	1764
Halifax	60 Quaker families	9 Quaker families
Pickering	13	5
Pontefract	13	7
Rawcliffe	11	4
Scawby	7	1
Thirsk	16	7
Whitby	93	70

At Halifax, the meeting was in Brighouse in Rastrick township; George Burnett, curate of Elland, excluded Rastrick and Ripponden from his returns—unparochial chapels in his chapelry—so it might be that the bulk of the Halifax Quakers went unreported rather than that they had ceased to exist. At Pickering, the population fell by a half, so that probably accounts for the departure of its Quakers. Pontefract's population experienced considerable growth, while Rawcliffe and Scawby remained fairly stable.

Quaker historians cite a compound of deliberate withdrawal from the world's habits, exercised through excluding marriage rules, excessive quietism, and a growing number of "disownments" as the reasons for the decline in Quaker membership during the eighteenth century.[11] The process was gradual, so that children born to Quaker parents grew up as "birthright Quakers," and Punshon estimates that by 1750 80 percent of English Quakers were birthright members. Rowntree, writing in a mid-Victorian setting which was a long way from being permissive, had the sense to realize that children were put off by silent meetings, "sabbath after sabbath, for months on end." Emigration was not so large a factor in the numerical decline of English Quakers, most of which had occurred earlier.

Denominational changes: ***(iii) Presbyterians, Independents, Baptists and other Dissenters***

The English Presbyterians of the first half of the eighteenth century declined in numbers partly as a result of their disappointments in not remodeling the state church, and partly because of the loss of gentry support for dissent generally,[12] which in turn led to some "attrition of Dissent" in the countryside and to a concentration in towns, a feature clearly evident in the 1764 visitation returns. But by the same year that Drummond became archbishop of York, Joseph Priestley, though himself originally an Independent, emerged as the Presbyterians' leader and began to transform their theology. Whereas the Presbyterians had been the largest and most successful Nonconformist group throughout the Restoration period and even after the Glorious Revolution, their children were not continuing in Presbyterianism,[13] so the mid eighteenth century was a trough before a peak. A theological difference divided them gradually throughout the century into the minority of Trinitarians and the majority of Unitarians. Their combined fortunes changed in the last third of the century when they were fed from the Church of England by Francis Blackburne and then joined by Theophilus Lindsey and others who left the ranks of the Anglicans. The Yorkshire visitation returns of 1764 show a decrease in numbers of Presbyterian allegiance compared with 1743, though they were still in quite large concentrations of observance. In eight parishes or chapelries Presbyterians held their observance steady. In thirty-two places the count for Presbyterian families showed an increase. In sixty-six places there were losses to the Presbyterian numbers. In some of the parishes where there occurred a fluctuation in numbers of Presbyterian families, that change was extraordinary, as follows:

		no. of Presbyterian families	
	losses	1743	1764
Calverley		230	11
Coley Chapel		150	120
Idle Chapel		102	30
Luddenden		53	15
	gains	1743	1764
Bingley		21	154
Cottingham		122	150
Holy Trinity Hull		38	145

Kildwick	10	80
Whitby	39	63

At Holy Trinity, Hull, the great increase was part of the growth in population (679 families to 1,700), employment, and enterprise.[14] At Keighley a similar jump in population had led from 450 families to 700. At Idle, the loss accorded with the drop in population from 320 families to 294, and the figures tally with the Presbyterians' own records.[15] At Bingley, however, the figure could be lower than the reality.[16]

The main doctrinal difference between the Independents and the Presbyterians concerned the Trinity, which a majority of the Independents supported. Other differences were that they required new members to make a "statement of experience" as well as a profession of faith; in their rule by church meeting they "submerged the minister" whereas the Presbyterians saw theirs as their ruler.[17] The differences between Independents and Presbyterians sharpened during the campaign in the later eighteenth century for the repeal of the Test and Corporation Acts.[18] The Presbyterians still aspired, even in the later eighteenth century, to be part of a united (pre–1662) established church, as in fact they were in the chapelry of Morley (see below), a situation that attracted Blackburne and Lindsey. The Baptists and Independents drew closer to each other and to the evangelical Anglicans once Unitarianism held the Presbyterians, effectually destroying the Presbyterian cause for a united English church, though the Presbyterians themselves still nurtured their hopes until the 1830s. The Baptists and Independents also had links with George Whitefield and the countess of Huntingdon, who saw many of her societies develop into Independent churches.[19]

The Baptists, according to Rupp, had "simmered down" by the beginning of the eighteenth century,[20] and one of their own historians cites a source from 1740 as a time when their "churches were settled in peace and unity."[21] By the time of the visitation returns of 1764, the next period of Baptist growth may be discerned. In the eyes of some Anglican clergy, they were still "Anabaptists," and the York visitation returns of 1764 have more entries using that terminology than "Baptists." The Anglican parish clergy did not find it easy to distinguish between Independents, Presbyterians, and Baptists; this difficulty is not surprising, in view of these dissenters' interrelation on doctrine and reaction to political restraints throughout the eighteenth century. The Baptists themselves were divided doctrinally into General and Particular

Baptists, but this was not reflected in the visitation returns of 1764. The Baptist groupings in Yorkshire by 1764 were predominantly in the West Riding urban areas, including Leeds, Batley, Birstall, Wakefield, Bradford, and Halifax, with another sector over on the east coast including Bridlington and Hull.

One of the largest groups of Independents was reported by Sowerby chapel, Pontefract,—188 Independent families, (though recognized as Presbyterians until circa 1715). The same place also had 56 Baptists, and the total population had grown by about 120 families in the twenty-one years between the visitations.

Batley was a place for similar numbers of Independents and Baptists, the count being there for 52 and 66 respectively in 1764. The overall population there had grown from 622 families in 1743 to 819 families in 1764. Thomas Scott, the curate, was one of the most precise reporters of information regarding dissenters in the 1764 returns. He set out his information in the form of a chart for the four townships of his parish:

	The Church	Presbytns	Baptsts	Ind	Quakrs	Moravns	Methdists
Batley	224	—	1	51	1	—	49
Marley	72	129	4	1	—	6	47
Gildersome	65	6	60	—	11	1	23
Chirwell	40	22	1	—	1	—	4
	401	157	66	52	13	7	123

Scott was also the curate of the neighboring parish of Woodkirk and gave precise numbers of their dissenters too. At Woodkirk the Presbyterians had almost halved their strength in 1764 compared with 1743. The interesting case of Morley shows that the Presbyterian dream became a parish reality there. St. Mary's-in-the-Wood, the former parish church for Batley, became a chapel of ease when a parish church was built in Batley; it was returned to Anglicanism in 1660 but remained in the hands of Presbyterian trustees. The Church of England ceased to use the building in the 1690s and Presbyterian worship was resumed there. It never became Unitarian. Thomas Scott revealed only a part of this history when he wrote in his return that the meetinghouse was "taken from the Church in ye time of Oliver Cromwell." Scott was not the returning clergyman in 1743, but he had been in Batley since 1754 and Woodkirk since 1759 and had made it his business to know his parishioners.

Other dissenters such as Moravians, Inghamites, and Antinomians figured in the visitation returns without any obviously noticeable patterns of rise and fall, as individual Anglican clergy varied in their ability or willingness to include them.

Denominational changes: ***(iv) Identifying and Declaring the Methodists***

Archbishop Matthew Hutton took a look at the visitation returns that Thomas Herring, his predecessor, had requested and decided that nothing had materially changed except for the increase of Methodists,[22] shown by the fact that the greater number of references to Methodists came in the returns to the 1764 visitation enquiries. Mention of Methodists in 1743 was minimal compared with 1764. If Drummond knew that the Methodists were already concentrated in the manufacturing towns, he might yet have been surprised to read that at Wakefield they met on several evenings in the week in unlicensed houses, as well as an unknown number of times in the one licensed house. His vicar at Wakefield, Benjamin Wilson, also wrote the names of the joiner and shoemaker in whose unlicensed houses the church-attending Methodists met to sing hymns.

Exact categorizing remained a puzzle, however, for some reporting clergy as the vicar of Leeds had explained: in 1764 the Methodists were churchgoers as well as attenders at their own meetings in places where there was a church for them to attend. Thomas Colby of Birstall replied similarly, admitting that he did not know how to assess the number of dissenters because some of them brought their children to be christened at the church, adding that the Methodists had a meetinghouse that was not licensed. From the parish of Ecclesfield, William Steer had written in 1743, "We have abt. 560 Families in this parish . . . and one Papist and four or five of the Methodists—but those I suppose will not be of any long continuance." Steer did not have the gifts of mission and vision granted to the Wesleys, but it is to his credit that he was able not only to know and count those early Ecclesfield Methodists but also to identify them as such. His successor, Thomas Bright, wrote his own censure:

> families amounted to 756 amongst whom are 4 Popish, 2 Quakers, a few Dissenters, Enthusiastic or Methodist cannot ascertain the number. I believe there are not so many as I found upon my first coming hither tho' they swarm at present in the next neighbouring parish to me towards the south namely Sheffield.

It is precisely this attitude that allowed the Ecclesfield Methodists to increase: their supposed spiritual leader did not take the trouble to identify them, hinted that he was better at his job than his predecessor, and cast a slur on the ministry of his brother priests in Sheffield, whose efforts we know were of the highest order. The visitation returns of 1764 show us those clergy who viewed Methodist activities as outbursts of Enthusiasm in all its distastefulness. Comments of this type occur in sixteen of the returns.

But such attitudes were small-scale factors accounting for Methodist growth. Methodists grew in Drummond's Yorkshire where populations increased, in already large towns, and where John Wesley visited to preach. One of the largest groups of Methodists was at Batley, where Thomas Scott numbered them as 123 families.

It is less straightforward to uncover the areas where the incumbents were well disposed to the Methodists, and of course clergy attitudes were by no means constant. Henry Venn is an example of one who adjusted his views of Methodists and altered his "official" relationship with Wesley. Venn was guarded in his returns to the archbishop. The device was to keep silence. Declaring no Methodists was safe and strictly truthful, especially if there were no licensed meetinghouse: so long as the Methodists continued attending the parish church, their activities were not those of Dissent. Keeping silent about unlicensed meeting houses was safe too, for a blank space could not be faulted for untruthful statement. Venn sent an apology for nonattendance at the visitation day at Wakefield. He wrote to the archbishop on 22 April 1764 that "being called to London upon some business" he was "forced to ask permission to be absent." If he thus avoided a conversation with Drummond about the Methodists, his uncertainties were spared. Drummond's own attitude specifically to Methodists is not on record, but he may have known and been guided by Thomas Secker's opinion in 1761 that they were "well-meaning."[23]

Across the information as a whole, the Anglican clergy knew more about other dissenters than about the Methodists. This is what one would expect. Since the Act of Toleration, there was no need for dissenters to cloak their activities. But the rise of Methodism was having an effect both on the dissenting churches and on the Established Church, as the subsequent sections on geographic distribution show. The visitation was exactly the setting for information about all dissenters to be requested and set down. What has to be remembered at this point is that the clergy were not in possession of all the facts—partly because it was a time of changing allegiances—and that their information was less rather than more than the full truth. Accurate computation (as possibly different from knowledge of the truth) may be seen in the returns written by George Legh of Halifax, who applied the factor of five when changing numbers of families to numbers of individuals. He recorded 28 Baptist families or 140 Baptist "hearers" at the twice-weekly meetings in his parish; similarly, 9 Quaker families or 45 Quaker "hearers," continuing in the same way for all the named dissenter groups.

Denominational changes: ***(v) Continuity and Change***

Stability and a slow rate of change were noticed at the outset of this section comparing population and dissenter figures, and Guisborough was mentioned as a parish where the clergyman may have taken the easy way out in reporting "no change." Guisborough nevertheless represents both continuity and change in that the population was counted as three hundred families by the same clergyman in 1743 as in 1764, whereas he was particular in his reporting that the dissenters had undergone significant changes, as follows:

1743	1764
6 R Catholics 5 Quakers 1 Presb	3 Quakers 15 Methodists.

Some places were not available for consideration for any or some of the separate dissenting groups because of insufficient figures for comparison. This happened where the details were specified in 1743 but estimated in 1764 or where a composite number was placed on five or six of the dissenting groups in 1764, following either a gap in the 1743 return or actual numbers for two groups only.

Parishes with No Dissenters either in 1743 or in 1764

If the incumbents are to be believed, there were 162 parishes and chapelries with no dissenters either in 1743 or in 1764. The threads warrant unraveling and drawing out for separate examination.

The first and most convincing reason why these 162 places might have been untouched by Dissent is that the majority were sparsely populated. Anglican clergy could keep their direction over thinly spread parishioners. In 120 out of the 162, there were fewer than fifty families. Some, however, in these strongholds of Anglican loyalism had populations reaching 100, 150, 200, 250, and so on up to

436 in Thornhill. In sparsely populated places, the sameness of the way of life of the people in the care of their pastors was a very strong reason for there being no dissenters. Of these 162 places, the population was the same to within five families in seventy-seven places; in a further twenty-three places the population figures were increased by between only five and ten families, giving a total of one hundred places where a minimal change occurred.

The characteristics of the parish priest could have been a deterrent to Dissenters in these 162 cases. In the more heavily populated parishes in the no-dissent list, the parish priest was the same person for both the 1743 and the 1764 returns in eighteen out of forty-one cases. Analysis shows also that there were only 2 pluralists in those forty-one more heavily populated places: Robert Hewett held Barnby Moor and Thornton juxta Pocklington, and William Langstaff held Marske and Wilton Chapel. Hewett was in office in both livings by 1743. Langstaff was not. The archbishop himself might have been a deterrent at Brodsworth and Bishopthorpe. Would anyone dare to dissent from the Established Church under the nose of the archbishop? In 1743 one family in each place had so dared, but by 1764 there were no dissenters declared in either of these places.

What credence might be given to these declarations? In small parishes it was easy for resident clergy with the use of all their faculties to know what the Dissenter population was. Perhaps it is not unreasonable for one sixth of the diocese to have been unmarked by dissenting residents over a twenty-one year period. Nonresidents and pluralists without resident curates would have had a less accurate grip on the situation.

Another offsetting factor is that the clergyman may have been the one person in the parish from whom some Dissenters specifically withheld their dissenting activities. By 1764 there was really no need for this, but, for reasons connected with the licensing laws for meetinghouses, quiet may have been preferred and attendance at the parish church continued alongside other persuasions. Several clergy thanked God that they had no Dissenters to report to the archbishop. In the returns for large towns especially, some of the most scholarly and pastorally sensitive clergy, helped by their curates, provided numbers based on their week-by-week encounters with parishioners. In small parishes it would have been much harder to stay unnoticed as a Dissenter. The clergy had the opportunity there to know their people by name, and did name them if they thought there was a need to explain the existence of several one-person families.

The occasions when the returning clergy betrayed their distance from direct contacts with their parishioners are rare and noticeable for being rare. Thomas Bright of Ecclesfield wrote, "The person whom I sent round my parish, as mentioned in my letter to your Grace, reported to me that the no of families amounted to. . . ." and he trailed off! Bright also sent in a return for Hoyland, which has probably the most evasive terms of answering in the whole of the returns studied. Instead of declaring the number of inhabiting families in Hoyland, he wrote:

> Hoyland Chapel is a Chapel within the walls in the Chapelry of Wentworth. The dues are paid through the Chapelry of Wentworth to the Curate there, who has the Cure of all the Inhabitants and to whom belongs all parochial duties: to him therefore belongs the answer to this article of enquiry.

Bright continued to answer in similar and unhelpful vein for most of the succeeding questions.

68 Parishes with Dissenters in 1743 but None in 1764

68 parishes and chapelries recorded Dissent in 1743 but not in 1764. If we accept the 1764 clergy declarations of no dissenters in these 68 parishes as valid, this group is significant in marking the downward fortunes of Dissent. One explanation for the disappearance of Dissent accords with population fall. The trend in western Europe[24] during the second half of the eighteenth century was toward an increase in population, with a proportionally larger rise estimated for the population of England,[25] but some of the Yorkshire parishes went against this trend. In this group there are thirty places where a drop in population occurred. In some cases the drop was minimal, from 109 families to 105 families at Appleton le Street, from 114 to 110 at Wistow; but in others it was more substantial: from 80 to 59 at Barnby Dunne, from 80 to 36 at Maltby, and from 100 to 76 at Adlingfleet. These numbers have an even hollower ring when we remember Drummond's rule for computing the average size of family at 5 persons. Thus, 120 individuals (24 families) left their homes in Adlingfleet between 1743 and 1764, including one family of Quakers. At Coxwold there was a drop of 12 families. Could these include the 11 families of dissenters noted in 1743 but gone by 1764?

But as well as a drop in population in more than one third of the parishes in this group, there was another slice that experienced stability, or very small growth. At Muston the number remained at forty families at both counts. The degree of stability—using the population figures given by the incumbents in 1743 and 1764—is especially noticeable in twenty places (to within five families). For example, at Barmston there were thirty families in 1743 and thirty-two in 1764. At Hutton Pagnell there were seventy-two families in 1743 and seventy-three in 1764. Bishopthorpe and Brodsworth, residences of Archbishop Drummond, had stable populations. One Quaker family had gone from Brodsworth by 1764, and one family of Presbyterians had gone from Bishopthorpe by 1764.

There are other factors to consider alongside the coincidence of population fall with dissenter loss. All sixty-eight were already sparsely populated parishes, the largest being Pocklington with 235 families in 1743 and 200 in 1764. Many had fewer than 50 families.

Denominational losses were proportional. In twenty-two places the Presbyterians disappeared mainly in ones and twos. The most were seven families at Hessle and eight at Wickersley. The Quakers went mainly in ones. So did the Roman Catholics. The Baptists left in ones from eight parishes. The Roman Catholic figures provide a contrast to the rest of the kingdom. Whereas the trend was generally one of increased Roman Catholic observance, there were thirty-one places in this group from which Roman Catholic families had gone by 1764.

The disappearance of the dissenters in these parishes was a neighborhood feature. In eight of the deaneries with dissenter losses, the decreases took place in clustered parishes. There is no obvious physical geographical connection in that these were not less desirable places of habitation, such as Holderness, about which several of the clergy made complaints. Nor were they from places where there might be thought to have been less work available, as several were grouped on the north side of the city of York.

One link is with the incumbents. Twenty-six parishes shared twelve clergymen, and some of these pluralists lived near each other. Dissenters may simply have moved away during the twenty-one years between the two Yorkshire visitations. They may have decided not to worship God at all. They may have become Methodists and as such been excluded from special mention as dissenters. But they also may have stayed in their parishes and decided to begin attending the Established Church, possibly influenced by their parish priest and neighborhood custom. Whatever the explanation, this group of sixty-eight parishes represents an interesting light on the view of Ollard and Walker, who thought the church was losing ground between 1743 and 1764. In this case, viewed as the place of homecoming for a group of alternative Christians, the Church of England may be said to have gained ground.

Ninety Parishes with no Dissenters in 1743 and some in 1764

In 1764 ninety places declared the presence of dissenters who had not been listed at all in 1743. Here the population changes were substantial. This is not surprising. The ninety places include areas where fluctuating economic and social conditions affected working people most acutely. For example, at Barnsley, Dewsbury, Headingley, and Pudsey in the cloth producing areas, there were large numbers of people in 1764 in chapelries for which there had been no returns in 1743. In the market town of Masham the population went up by seventy families. Downturns feature in twelve places, most of these showing substantial drops. Increases of similar strength show in thirty-three places. Omissions in some of the returns for 1743 show us that these were the gaps that the dissenters filled.

The significance of this group of ninety places lies with the growth and nature of all types of Dissent. Here were the people who were using the freedoms which the law had permitted them since 1689. As a collection of ninety places where there had been no dissenters reported before, they were the dynamo of those who turned away from the established church.

The largest number of them, the Methodists, however, were not turning away from the church at all. Methodists in these ninety parishes featured in the returns of one third of the incumbents, and the figures, where they were given too, were of sizeable societies:

37 Methodist families at Brompton in Pickering,
25 at Catton,
50 at Kirkby upon Wharfe, (more than half the population)
20 at Bishop Wilton,
20 at Northallerton,
21 at Stockton Chapel,

Other groups of about half a dozen families were noted at Attercliffe, Eston, Headingley Chapel, Bilbrough, Settrington, Wilberfoss, and Acklam East. Given the special relationship of the Methodists to the Church of England, we should allow for more than the numbers stated even in these places where there had been no previous history of Dissent, for the opposing reasons of sympathy or of extreme distaste, as noted earlier.

Reliable information from Batley and Woodkirk (as noted with the Presbyterians), comes from Thomas Scott. In the township of Morley in Batley parish, Scott reported a Methodist meetinghouse "lately built and licensed." The Batley Methodists had had a strangely low impact on the worship in the parish church, as he explained,

> There are two sermons every Sunday. Prayers every holiday. And, at the request of some inclined to Methodism, my predecessor, Mr Rhodes, read prayers every Wednesday and Friday but not one of that sect have attended them of several years past.

Scott's predecessor had not recorded the Methodists in his list of dissenters in 1743, restricting himself to Presbyterians, Independents, Antinomians, or Baptists and Quakers. In Woodkirk in 1764 there was no licensed house for the Methodists, but Scott knew that they held meetings "at Nathaniel Harrison's house and Thomas Old's weekly." Trends of older dissenting behavior as noted in earlier groups of parishes, were of continuing importance for this group of ninety "no previous dissenters".

The Roman Catholics were reported in thirty-five places. This means thirty-five new places where previously there were no Roman Catholics at all, but the figures for the numbers of families are mainly of ones and twos. The highest was twelve at Aldbrough, Holderness, and seven and five at Husthwaite and Carlton Chapel, Cleveland, where the anti-Roman Archdeacon Francis Blackburne cannot have been pleased, especially as there had been an overall drop in the population of the Carlton chapelry from seventy to fifty-four families, a point which he might indeed have taken the trouble to find out.

Quaker strength in this group of "no previous Dissent" parishes and chapelries is in one respect as noticeable as among the Methodists and Roman Catholics, in that in thirty-four places there were Quakers in 1764 where there had been none at all in 1743. The previous pattern of Quaker observance being by ones and twos, however, is the same in this instance. The only place with a Quaker community was at Holmfirth chapel, where ten families inherited the Wooldale meeting founded in the seventeenth century, and these, as noted earlier, were possibly part of the Kirkburton total.

Presbyterians were not a growth sect in the mid eighteenth century. Professor Rupp concludes his chapter on the English Presbyterians by referring to their need for the "blood transfusion of an evangelical revival," but R. Tudor Jones saw the revival as "a mighty force" at work among the Congregational churches by 1750, enabling them to "leap over the confining wall of the Act of Toleration."[26] At Pudsey chapel Seth Pollard reported Presbyterians and Moravians in 1764 as being in the proportion of two to three to the Anglicans (that is, jointly two-fifths) out of 574 families. In the Herring returns the wording at Q1 is, "answered by ye vicar." The vicar of Calverley omitted to mention Pudsey chapel in 1743, but he did include Idle, reporting 230 families of Presbyterians for Calverley and Idle. We may guess at the fluctuations of the Pudsey Presbyterian congregation, as it had 250 individuals in 1716[27] and may have been affected in 1764 by the presence of the Fulneck Moravian community since its foundation twenty years earlier.

Other groups of "Old Dissent" in 1764 feature less remarkably in the data. In two cases only—Attercliffe and Cleckheaton—the 1764 figures for Independents at ten and twenty-one families respectively are not mentioned in the figures for 1743, but non-Anglican evidence corrects that omission.[28] The listing of Baptists in nine places in 1764, however, where none were noted in 1743, is a firm enough reminder of the legal freedom to be a dissenter. These figures show that such freedom was well appreciated in Drummond's Yorkshire in the mid eighteenth century, and the next period of growth for Baptists is also attested by the evidence from the dissenters' certificates[29] for licensing meetinghouses. In most cases where the records are kept for the granting of such certificates, the classification of type of dissenters is not given, but it is recorded for the Baptists at Hexham in 1758, at Hampsthwaite in 1762, at Guiseley in 1766, and at Scarborough in 1768. Other evidence of Baptist foundings comes from the Baptists' own records.[30] In the period of this study there were foundings in fifteen places between 1750 and 1777. These records include the case of James Hartley, 1752–1780, who left the Anglican church to become the Baptist pastor at Haworth for the following reasons: the established church depended on human laws, was of a national form, and was, in his view, unscriptural on certain matters.[31]

There is no evidence of a Jewish presence except for one family in Wakefield, possibly because the returning clergy thought that the question referred to Christian sects only.

Conclusion

Where parishes were small and where population growth was slight, there was least threat to the Church of England from Dissent, and it was in such places that the clergy declared that there were no dissenters at all. The parishes where a decline of dissenter numbers was found were sparsely populated and had population fall or minimal growth. By contrast, population change is most noticeable in the ninety places where dissenters were mentioned for the first time in 1764, and in these places the preponderance was for Roman Catholics, Methodists, and Quakers (but in ones and twos), with a few instances of growth among "Old Dissent."

The church appeared to be withstanding the incursions of multiple Dissent, and the old high church still had vitality with its numerous instances of weekday services and frequent Holy Communion. There were new stirrings with young evangelical curates, but the figures show that the position was precarious. The church was safest where the change was least. In large populous parishes where the incumbent had no curates, he could not possibly know all the dissenters, let alone the Anglican communicants. (Cornelius Rickaby of Bridlington admitted that he "could not come at the number [of communicants] as there are so many hamlets belonging." Benjamin Wilson of Wakefield did have a residing curate but wrote, "I do not truly know what number of communicants there are in this parish," and estimated above five hundred.)

The religious scene in Yorkshire in 1764 as reported to Drummond in his visitation returns was one where the Presbyterian theology was wavering into Socinianism and Unitarianism, and drawing one of his own archdeacons with it, but whose congregations were divided and their numbers falling in most places. Drummond was not to know that the Baptists and Independents were going to be revitalized by the witness of his Anglican evangelicals. What he did notice was the Catholic growth, and he tried to explain it away by looking at earlier faulty figures. The growth of Methodists was noticeable, but Drummond chose not to pay them any attention, possibly led by his clergy, many of whom were uncertain whether Methodists were actually dissenters. The visitation returns of 1764 are significant for their portrayal of the northern province in the last years of the old national church, before revival spoiled the chances of a single national church. The elderly Rishton of Almondbury may have recognized this when he wrote his details to Drummond. Drummond, with his calculations and memos on little slips of paper, was unaware of the significance of his own visitation.

Part 2: The Geography of Dissent

The geography of Dissent has some obvious patterns which show where the Established Church faced its competition. The concentrations of Presbyterians were in the Old and New Ainsties and in the northern half of the Pontefract deanery, matching a similar cluster in Harthill. More adjacent groups were in the northern part of Cleveland, and there were three distinct areas of them on the east coast. Some parishes, in a part circle round York, contained a few Presbyterian families, but inside the city their numbers were low. Clusters of Presbyterians lived together in all the populous areas of Bingley, Keighley, Halifax, Batley, Wakefield, and Leeds. Although their numbers dropped after the Herring visitation, their staying power in some places was assisted by large groups. In the relatively small area of Pudsey chapel, the Presbyterians along with the Moravians numbered two fifths of the total population. Pudsey's families were numbered at 570 by the curate, Seth Pollard, and the Pudsey Presbyterians may have been as many as 114 families (if the Moravians and Presbyterians were in equal numbers, but less than 100 when allowance is made for the likely strength of the Moravians who had a licensed meetinghouse at Fulneck). In Leeds there were 120 Presbyterian families. In Bradford there were 187. At Sowerby chapelry in Halifax there were reckoned to be 140, and in another Halifax chapelry at Coley there were 120. Bingley had 154. Batley (mainly Morley chapelry) had 157. Not quite such heavy numbers of Presbyterians lived in Hull and Beverley: 145 for Hull, and 83 in the two Beverleys. In Cottingham, between Beverley and Hull, there were 150 Presbyterian families. Fewer Presbyterians lived in the coastal towns. In Northallerton, only one family of Presbyterians was recorded.

Independents were sometimes identified with other dissenters by the Anglican clergy. Their historian, R. Tudor Jones, has suggested that their lack of profile was perhaps because their chapels and meetinghouses, following the freedoms begun by the Act of Toleration in 1689, were not being built until after 1750, so that they were recognized more once they started worshipping in a purpose built chapel. For example, their numbers at Hull and Whitby did not lead to chapel buildings until 1769 and 1770 respectively.[32] At Hull they were those trinitarians who had withdrawn from the Presbyterians. At Whitby, the chapel of 1770 was founded by an ex-Wesleyan who originally called it a Presbyterian chapel. Yorkshire had been predominantly Presbyterian rather than Independent or Baptist during the seventeenth century, and the growth of the latter came with the evangelical revival. In sum, the information in the 1764 returns about Presbyterian changes and the gathering forces of revival came just too early. Drummond could not have seen what was soon going to happen.

The Quakers were a people apart. In great contrast with the Presbyterians, the Quakers survived almost by default or by their individualism. They continued their observance in their ones and twos of families. Large areas of the Craven deanery had one or two Quaker families in their parishes, areas where no other dissenting sects lived, including the Roman Catholics. The Craven deanery was closest to Lonsdale, the historic home of Quakerism. The Holderness deanery, untouched by Methodism and devoid of Presbyterians, had greater numbers of Quakers than any other part of the York diocese. There were six Quaker families in Aldbrough, five in Garton, six in Hollym, four in Roos, and four in Sproatley. The uninviting natural features of the Craven and Holderness deaneries—frequently condemned by Anglican clergy who disliked the winters there—might have been bearable by the Quakers by virtue of their disciplined silences, their patience, their holding back from criticism, and their general stoicism.

The distribution of Roman Catholic families was less dramatic than the distribution of Presbyterian and Quaker habitation, for they had spread in more central parts of the diocese, with few in the northeastern and southwestern areas. As with the declaration of sympathy for the Methodists, however, the cautionary hand of under-declaration has been noticed in the writers of the returns, so that more Roman Catholic families might have lived in the given areas, but it is not likely that a significantly wider area than that given in the returns was thus inhabited. If Quakers were declared, for example, in the smallness of their ones and twos and threes, then there might have been more Roman Catholics than they were declared. According to the returns, there were concentrations as well as isolated families. In Egton, where a Roman Catholic mission had existed for some time, thirty-seven Roman Catholic families were declared. Neighboring Lythe and Whitby had twenty and ten Roman Catholic families respectively. Gilling and Hovingham had thirteen and fourteen. Across at Spofforth there were forty-three Roman Catholic families. What emerges from the geographic pattern is that there were no groups of Roman Catholics in the areas that harbored the Methodists. In Leeds, Sheffield, Dewsbury, Bradford, Halifax, and Huddersfield there were no mentions of Roman Catholics.

The Methodists grew throughout Yorkshire as Wesley preached and revisited in a long lifetime of traveling. His travels won him eventual acclaim, but the itinerancy of his preaching followers was criticized, mainly for social reasons. The upper classes disapproved of those who literally did not keep their places. Itinerant preachers were described unfavorably as "strollers" and "strangers." The same criticism was implied by James Wilkinson, vicar of Sheffield, who referred to the Methodists' teachers as being "many and those often changed," even though they were "said to be under the direction of Mr Wesley." Once the societies were organized, the circuits or "rounds" allocated and the connection acknowledged, the Methodist preachers continued their partnership with poverty, as the itinerancy put its pressure on their way of life.[33]

Wesley's deliberate approaches to the people of lower classes are well understood, even by writers who differ about his reasons. He has been described in Paul Langford's chapter on the eighteenth century as wanting to vanquish sin, not social deprivation.[34] Walsh put it more sympathetically, arguing that as the poor were closer to God it was a kind of sacramental act to serve them.[35] The parish clergy were in no doubt that Wesley's mission was to the poor. They referred to the Methodists as "a rabble," "discountenanced by the better sort of people," "entirely unknown to me and generally persons of a very low education," "the meanest sort of people," "disorderly," and "crazy visionaries."

The extent of Wesley's traveling and his unremitting return visits demanded a response from those clergy in the established areas of his regular route. He outlived and outworked several of the parochial clergy, but it was not until he was a truly old man that he was revered as a nonviolent, unthreatening, and almost customary figure, having been considered freakish for decades. Wesley himself named very few clergymen who were sympathetic to his cause. He respected Venn unreservedly, but their compact for restricted and permitted Methodist preaching broke down in 1765. Sympathy for Wesley's work was thinly spread throughout the returns. The general attitude was more socially critical than theologically condemning. One way of not giving him full recognition was to use the older spelling of his name, Westley, as if to identify him with a former understanding, casting out the innovative success of his itinerant ministry. At Beverley St. Mary, the vicar, Samuel Johnston, was so elderly himself (ordained deacon in 1710), that he referred to the opening of a Methodist meeting house in his parish by "Mr Wesley junr."

Part 3. How Far or in What Respects Did the Church Lose Ground Between 1743 and 1764?

Diocesan Control

From principality of Wales to princedom of the church in the northern province was the career move of both Herring and Drummond. Welsh experience served each well, especially as regards visitation practice. The purposeful nature of the 1764 visitation derived from Drummond's sense of duty, and he does not deserve to be included in the censure written of "typical" Georgian bishops by Peter Virgin:

> This, then, is a rough sketch of a typical Georgian prelate.
> (i) Promoted to the bench late in life, (ii) he lingered on in office until he reached the portals of death itself. (iii) If his see was poor, he tried to obtain a translation from it as quickly as possible; (iv) if it was large, he had no suffragan bishop to help him. (v) Most of his time was spent in London; he only visited his diocese in summer, occasionally touring the countryside. (vi) The episcopal visitations were not a pleasant part of his duties; travelling about was slow and tedious. (vii) Finally, it was almost certainly the case that he had not been promoted for such administrative capacities as he possessed. They are seven excellent reasons why the Georgian bishop faced an uphill task.[36]

Drummond did not have to wait until late in life for promotion. He achieved a translation from a Welsh see to the metropolitan office of York while he was in vigorous middle life. It is true that St. Asaph was a richer see, at £6,011, for example, than Bristol or Carlisle, at £2,161 and £2,592 respectively, but York, at £11,725, was half the value of Canterbury and half the value of Durham.[37] He displayed a noticeable contentment while he served in St. Asaph and at York. His strength was sufficient to deal with episcopal duties, nor is there any evidence that he found touring disagreeable, though he must have experienced the slow and tedious traveling conditions known to every eighteenth-century bishop. Drummond's administrative talents equipped him for the uphill task of his primary visitation and for the fifteen years of his term of office as archbishop. As successor to the ailing and ill-equipped Gilbert, Drummond recovered what ground the church may have lost since 1743, when he began clearing the desk work. An early nineteenth-century writer paid tribute to his attack.[38]

In the introduction to the published Herring returns,[39] Ollard and Walker agreed that "The Returns . . . of Archbishop Drummond show, speaking generally, that the Church lost ground between 1743 and 1764." This may be regarded as a bland opinion in the light of the particular evidence of the comparative analysis used throughout Chapters 4, 5, and 6 of this study. Despite 68 parishes having dissenters in 1743 but none in 1764, and 90 having none in 1743 but some in 1764, the Church of England did yet gain ground within those years in the numerical sense that in 301 other prevailingly typical parishes (48 percent) with dissenters at both dates there was a decline in families of Old Dissent. In an age when dissenter freedom could be tested in practice in any village or town, and when unorthodox doctrines inside and outside the establishment were available, the Church of England also held its ground in a theological sense, for "within the walls of its parish churches the greater part of the nation was baptised . . . and laid to rest."[40] This is not just a rose-colored view, for the same writer saw the frailties of the Church of England as a "machinery . . . maladjusted to its pastoral vocation."[41] In 1764 Archbishop Drummond did not find a deteriorating or deteriorated situation in Yorkshire like the one that Bishop Butler found in Hereford in 1789.[42] Drummond's Yorkshire, twenty-five years earlier than Butler's disappointment in Herefordshire, was a place where the Church of England was performing appropriately to its circumstances. In a sense this was a flattery to deceive because the system was not yet facing the widespread fundamental changes in society which required wholesale adaptation of the parochial system instead of administrative tinkering. Such a grudging assessment, however, discounts the significance for the history of the eighteenth-century church of a diocese still intact in the last stages of calm before the storm. In concentrating on the storm and its devastation, the calm beforehand has been overlooked partly because eighteenth-century church history has been underresearched.[43] Virgin, who has been criticized for concentrating on the early nineteenth century for a view of the eighteenth century,[44] deplores the "paucity of statistics to do with religious observance in the countryside" and claims particular value for "an admittedly small sample of seventy nine parishes, drawn from the diocese of Lincoln" for 1800.[45] So the returns for 621 parishes of the York diocese for 1764 have a fair claim to be recognized, within the limitations understood, as evidence for the church being in better array at mid century than supposed.

Introductory Statistical Survey to Parochial Audit

Analysis of the information from the 1764 visitation returns about the Church of England's performance has been put alongside dissenter statistics and subjective judgments of clergy capability. Methodist sources have been compared with some of the 391 parishes (63 percent) where Dissent was reported insufficiently. For example, at Baildon, Dewsbury, Mirfield, Sheffield, and Wakefield, where we know that Methodism was very firmly established, the incumbents sometimes declared no dissenters, and sometimes said that there were so many that they could enumerate the differences. Population figures for the 301 parishes (48 percent) where dissenters were declared both in 1743 and 1764 have been studied, and also for the ninety parishes (14 percent) where Dissent had grown since 1743. Identification of dissenter types revealed a close link with population changes. The population figures for 1743 and for 1764 in 162 parishes (26 percent) where no Dissent was reported at both dates provide a clear picture of stability of provision by the Church of England. The following table sets out data for twelve parishes (2 percent) where the performance of elderly clergy was open to question for what was an acceptable ministry and where the church could be seen to be losing some ground:

Twelve parishes with elderly clergy

Parish	Population in families		Annual celebrations of Holy Communion in		Easter attendance in		Sunday services in	
	1764	1743	1764	1743	1764	1743	1764	1743
Beverley St. Mary	580	480	18	18	194	200	2	2
Birstall	1700	1500	6	6	200	300	2	2
Bulmer	98	92	4	3	59	60	1	2
Catwick	15	18	4	4	0	30	1	1
Eastrington	145	137	4	4	58	50	1	2
Egton	199	144	5	5	175	150	0	1
Glaisdale Chapel	115	92	3	3	147	106	1	4
Hornby	69	67	18	12	144	180	2	2
Ledsham	92	78	18	15	185	185	2	2
Sykehouse	70	100	1	1	0	81	3	2
Wickersley	62	0	5	4	29	0	2	2
Frodingham	70	0	4	0	0	0	1	0

Key—Sunday services: 1 = once on Sunday

2 = twice on Sunday
3 = once a fortnight
4 = once a month
5 = less than monthly

Comment: Glaisdale chapel shows an improvement of observance in that since 1743 the population had grown, more people attended at Easter, and the incidence of Sunday services was increased.

Furthermore, in 34 parishes where the clergy were recently inducted, analysis disclosed 19 places where the church could be said to have gained ground, 5 places where it had lost ground, and the rest where standards of worship and ministry appeared to be unaffected. By contrast, there were 126 parishes and chapelries (20.3 percent) where members of the clergy were at the peak of their prime (taking their ages from the years of their ordination as priest between 1742 and 1748). Standards of ministry and worship in those 126 places showed the church to have gained ground in 28 places, lost ground in 12, and remained steady in the rest.

Parochial Clergy Audit

(i) Elderly Clergy

Clergy who were inducted to their parishes before 1720 and who were still in office in 1764 have been scrutinized to see whether the life of the church in their parishes showed signs of lost ground. Twelve parishes come within this scope. The above table shows that real loss of ground appears in only two out of the twelve. At Catwick and Sykehouse the incumbents failed to state the number who attended at Easter 1764—a factor which counts as a loss, especially as the populations had declined. At Ledsham the clergyman stood still rather than let ground get lost. Although there was an increase in the population there, John Benson, the vicar, gave identical answers at both visitations. Perhaps he was orderly rather than exact, having filed his papers with such care that he could turn in 1764 to what he had written in 1743. Lady Margaret Hastings of Ledsham Hall probably kept a closer eye on him than any archbishop, although her husband's followers, the Inghamites, may have detracted from his flock. (Walter Sellon, an evangelical, was appointed to Ledsham in 1770 after John Benson had completed what he called "ye decline of life.")

One parish, Frodingham, sent no return to the archbishop in 1743; the clergyman there in 1764 produced an ordinarily satisfactory set of answers which represent an improvement of behavior rather than loss of ground.

In the remaining eight parishes where these elderly clergy still attempted the cure of souls in 1764, and where five of them were resident, the population had grown since 1743, and the numbers attending church services were appropriately greater. Where Ollard and Walker may have glanced summarily and gained a general impression of deteriorating change between 1743 and 1764, a closer study reveals a more detailed picture. Elderly clergy such as Rishton of Almondbury, Legh of Halifax, and Gyrling of Newton Kyme had given their congregations an outstanding continuity of ministry. Such continuity could have its demerits as well as its benefits, as the evidence shows quite evenly. By 1764 they depended more and more on their curates, but it would be misleading to suggest that their long stay in office was in itself a loss to the church by 1764.

(ii) Change of Parson: Recently inducted and inexperienced clergy: those ordained after 1758 and inducted after 1759

A change of parson could affect people's habits of churchgoing either in favor of the Anglicans or in favor of the dissenters. For example, at Huddersfield when Venn subsequently left Yorkshire, he was followed by the antirevivalist Harker Crooke, but his was a special case because Venn had foreseen such a contingency and had provided separately with an Independent chapel for his congregation. Alternatively, a traditionalist could be replaced by an evangelical. The information in the returns for those parishes where the clergymen were new and inexperienced reveals their work as an important feature in the church's contribution to the later evangelical revival.

Prima facie judgments have been made about the level of church life for the parishes in this sample, using mainly the balance of numbers of communicants and numbers present at Easter 1764 but using also the answers for Sunday services and the frequency of Holy Communion. For example, Barnoldswick is seen as open to criticism because the Easter attendance was counted as only 22 out of a population of 273 families, and where only 37 communicants were known. Similarly at Pudsey chapel, where there were 574 families, it was a poor situation for there to be only 60 normally in attendance, where we know the dissenter activity to have been strong. But at Owthorne, it was commendable to number 140 communicants out of 56 families, and at Willerby to have 52 in attendance at Easter out of 27 families. In this group were Haworth, Elland, and Slaithwaite, places known for their connection with the evangelical revival. The patrons of many of these parishes were promoting the evangelical cause. Walsh has shown that a combination of aristocratic patrons and young curates brought evangelicals into Yorkshire parishes at a time when it was difficult for evangelicals to get preferment.[46] For example, the earl of Dartmouth, Lady Margaret Hastings, and the Countess of Huntingdon were vigilant for the evangelical cause, and a young curate such as Burnett in Halifax could work as an evangelical even though his vicar, George Legh, was not of the same mind. There were two results of this trend. Humbler patrons followed suit[47] and the evangelical clergy gained sufficient confidence to meet together in the Elland Society. What had started as a thin planting with aristocratic support grew into a network across the Yorkshire parishes, with the chapelries as the coordination point. So the church was husbanding its ground, though in 1764 this was just a small sector of the church scene in Yorkshire.

(iii) Middle Years of Ministry: Clergymen in Their Prime

Clergy within the ordination limits of 1742 and 1748 would have been aged between forty-one and forty-eight at the time of the Drummond visitation. There were seventy-nine of them, serving 126 parishes. A point to emerge first is that they were well-educated men. Fifty-nine of them had university degrees, mainly B.A.s and M.A.s, and eight had either of B.D.s, L.L.B.s or D.D.s.

As before, *prima facie* judgments have been made about the level of church life in their parishes. The church was losing ground in twelve of these parishes,[48] but the main picture is one of healthy competence. For example, Edward Bracken at All Saints, Pavement, Henry Goodricke of Aldborough, and Edward Moises of Masham with Kirby Malzeard all drew good congregations at Easter and were conscientious about the sacraments and Sunday services. To illustrate the loss situation, Joseph Hudson of Wibsey numbered 340 families with 950 communicants, but he counted only 25 at church at Easter 1764, and added that in 1763 there had been only 8. Some damage to the paper of his return cuts out information about the incidence of Sunday services, and the tearing of the page leaves partially decipherable words and phrases such as, "given so much disgust," "notorious," and, "a poor, ignorant. . . ." Joseph Hudson declared 40 Methodists and 13 Moravians

> and about seventy who never and other seventy, who, I believe . . . scarce ever go to any place of public worship. I am inclined to think that the Excess of preaching has almost extinguished Religion in this part, for, Those who were formerly the most zealous Dissenters given among the Methodists and Moravians are now become almost Infidels.

A combination of Methodist preoccupation and a possibly unattractive preaching style from Joseph Hudson in comparison with the fire in the belly of the Methodists may explain the poor attendance at Wibsey. It also illustrates what the established church was facing during the years of Methodism's growth.

(iv) Conclusion

The continued witness of the Anglican ministry throughout the changes in population and the increase in dissenter opportunity across the varied geography of the diocese, which the first two parts of this chapter has explored, puts Ollard and Walker's overall criticism in a rather simplistic light. Having considered the areas where the parochial clergy might be expected to have lost ground for the church, the amount of loss uncovered is slight. Some elderly clergy were found naturally to have outrun their earlier vigor. New and inexperienced clergy were found to have included some of the early evangelicals whose work brought renewed interest in church life. Looking at a group of clergy who were humanly at their best, analysis drew out a substantial group of midlife clerics with good educational qualifications. Loss of ground within this group showed as a minority feature alongside a series of commendable situations in parishes across the diocese. Although the material in the returns may be showing the best face of the clergy as they reported to their archbishop, the overall impression remains that these visitation returns amount to convincing evidence for the mid eighteenth-century church being well clear of dangerous loss, holding much of its ground since 1743, and, against the flow of estimators who have concentrated on later data, making numerical and theological gains in varied circumstances.

The Harsh and Sturdy Face of the Church of England

Harsh treatment of sinners can be read in the evidence of the Court Books of the York episcopal records of the eighteenth century. Its occurrence in the church may be one of the reasons why people preferred Nonconformity or nonattendance. Nonconformists could dismiss their members as a punishment, but the Church of England could require penance. It is not possible to say that those who were disciplined by the Anglicans joined the Nonconformists as a result, but there was a natural reluctance among individuals, rich and poor, to do public penance. Many preferred private penance or commutation. Penance was still an issue in the 1760s, so the archbishop continued to include a question about it in his visitation enquiry.

Records of archdeacon visitations in the East Riding from 1759 to 1773 show[49] that the courts sat three times per year at two centers during the months of May through October. The numbers of people presented at the court hearings varied from thirty-three to seventy-two. In a summary of presentments made from 1759 to 1773 in those sessions, fornication represented the largest number of cases.

Summary of Presentments 1759–1773, East Riding

Adultery	6
Baptism, refusal to bring child	1
Church, non attendance at	1
Churchyard fence not repairing	5
Church burying road, obstructing	1
Church burying road, obstructing	1
Church assessment, non-payment of	15
Chwdns neglect of duty not repairing church	1
Chwdns neglect of duty not answering articles	6
Clerk's wages, non-payment of	6
Clerical neglect of duty	1
Clerical neglect, not repairing glebe house	2
Clerical immorality/drunkenness	2
Drunkenness	3
Easter dues, non-payment of	6
Clerical neglect of duty	1
Clerical neglect, not repairing glebe house	2
Clerical immorality/drunkenness	2
Drunkenness	3
Easter dues, non-payment of	3
Fornication	152
Fornication, anticipated	15
Incest	2

Sacrament, not receiving HC	1
Sabbath breaking	2
Absolution under particular circs	2
Admonition to behave better	1
Articles	2
Assessments tendered	5
Certificate of frequenting church	1
Chwdns form of oath	1
Commutation of penance	10
Innocence, certificate of	1
Insanity, absolution on account of	1
Misnomer	2
Parsonage house, legal possession of denied	1
Penance lost, fresh one issued	1
Presentment, justification of, alleged	1
Proceedings stayed by the Court	4
Reference to law	6

It has been supposed that the moral work of the courts had become largely inoperative by mid century, but this evidence shows this to be not so in Yorkshire. Other charges, such as nonpayment of church assessment, adultery, churchwardens failing to answer certain articles, Sabbath breaking, and drunkenness represent very small numbers comparatively.

The courts also met to issue certificates of innocence once people had been cleared of charges against them. If people were not cleared, the church showed its harsh face. Penance was required. The penitent,

> in the presence of the whole congregation then assembled, being bareheaded, barefoot and bare-legged, having a white sheet wrapped about him from the shoulders to the feet, and a white wand in his hand,

had to say,

> Whereas I, good people, forgetting my duty to Almighty God, have committed the detestable sin of fornication with . . . have justly provoked the heavy wrath of God against me . . . I do earnestly repent.

There is evidence from the parish of Almondbury that penitents at the chapel of Honley had managed to do private penance. The vicar of Almondbury, Edward Rishton, complained about this in his return to the archbishop, and cast a slur on his curate for an imputed lack of authority to grant such indulgence and for possibly accepting money in the matter. At Almondbury in the 1760s, according to Rishton's answer at Q12, it was still usual to have public penances. He recorded twenty such instances, but we know him to have been old fashioned. He was also in dispute with a neighboring clergyman at the chapel of Honley because of private penances, but in his returns the curate, Edward Hasleham, referred to "several" public penances at Honley. The revivalist preachers and their readiness initially to weep with repentant sinners may well have been a preferable alternative to the church's disciplines.

The Court Books of the York diocese yield other information about the treatment of offenders in a way that is more sturdy than harsh. In addition to the overwhelming numbers who were presented for fornication, there are cases of people who were presented for altering the fabric of the church. Jane Lodge of St. Mary's, Castlegate, York, was presented in 1759 for having laid a stone with an inscription over her late husband's grave in the south aisle and body of the church of All Saints, Pavement. Robert Deighton of St. Crux was presented in 1759 for having built a two-story addition to his house over part of the chapel, using the chapel wall as a support. Henry Mason, a cabinetmaker of Beverley St. Mary, was presented in 1762 for raising the height of the pew in which he usually sat near the east end of the south aisle of the church. Seth Agar was presented in 1760 for building a house and sinking a soil hole and "taking up several dead persons' bones in the churchyard of St Helen's, Stonegate, York, and making doors and windows out of his warehouse into the churchyard, hindering the parishioners from going into it," and dirtying the church windows when he mixed his lime. However, the case against Seth Agar did not fill him with the sort of irretrievable anger to turn his allegiance to the dissenters, for he is named as a signatory to the terrier only four years after the presentment.

The continuing activity of the church courts in matters of morals, manners, and enterprise shows that the eighteenth-century church was well aware of some of the "signs of the times," yet not seeing others in its own house such as the strains on parish structure and the effects of pluralism. What the clergy of the eighteenth century did interpret as "signs of the times" were wars, rebellions, uprisings, and crises in politics and food supplies, and they saw them so clearly that a massive hoard of published sermons accumulated on these themes.[50] The business of the church courts swept up some of the behavior of those who had not heard or heeded the jeremiads and furnished more material for further sermons.

Those who found themselves before the courts may have been

in some confusion about the role of the clergy in society. Virgin draws attention to the "fundamentally incompatible" roles of a clerical JP and instances a cleric who might sentence a man to prison one day and be obliged the next to console the same man's family.[51] Clark sees the increase of "squarsons" as part of a sinister subtext, a bid by the clergy for "a monopoly of education, piety and political acceptability."[52] Anomalies abounded. For example, a dissenter wanting a meetinghouse licence and an innkeeper wanting an alehouse licence would both apply to the civil magistrate who might be the vicar of their parish church. If either had to settle a marriage or inheritance dispute, a church court would hear the case, where the notary might not necessarily be a clergyman. Servants who stole from their employers could be brought before the "squarson" of their village, who would send them to a house of correction; however a fornication charge and the bastardy of a woman's child (the usual proof) would come under the spiritual jurisdiction of the archdeacon, and she could be referred back to her vicar for penance in the parish church.

The issues which concerned the church courts—moral, social, and practical—and the robust manner in which the cases were conducted, recording them all in detail,[53] presents the Church of England during the 1760s as a business in traditional, but perhaps rather creaking, order. The business was conducted on a regional and seasonal basis—three times a year in two centers from May to October—in seasonal accord with other activities of the eighteenth-century church. The subject matter of its work was accepted at the time and for a long time thereafter. So the 1760s were not a time when the church courts had quite outrun their effectiveness though there existed by then other known escape routes in religion for an excommunicated person.

How Tolerant Was the Church towards Dissent?

Since the accession of George III, the established church felt comfortably safe from "the Stuart option,"[54] but this situation prevailed within the guarded framework of recusancy. It eased some of its restraint on Protestant dissenters, who were still officially and legally restricted by the Test and Corporation Acts. Relaxation of animosities went both ways in that some dissenters "returned" to the Church of England, notably Thomas Secker, who found his dissenting origins no hindrance to reaching the position of archbishop of Canterbury and who became especially ardent in defending the position of the established church against foreign and immigrant Nonconformists (see Chapter 7). An impressive toleration literature was available for study. Richard Burgess Barlow[55] has suggested that some clergy might have been familiar with the ideas expressed by Dr. Isaac Watts in his *Essay Against Uncharitableness.* It is not fanciful to think that some of the Yorkshire clergy may have been acquainted with such ideas as follow:

> How ridiculously unreasonable is it for a Man of brown Hair to shut his brother out from the Rank and Species of Men, and call him an Ox or a Lion because his Locks are black or yellow. I am persuaded there is a Breadth in the narrow Road to Heaven, and persons may travel more than seven abreast in it: . . . . .And though their Names may be crossed out of the Records of a particular Church on Earth, where Charity fails, yet they will be found written in the Lamb's Book of Life. . . .[56]

Barlow sums up the effect of Isaac Watts's writings in adding, "In his quiet, compromising way, Watts was a great softening influence amongst dissenters and Churchmen alike."[57] The softening influence did not fall on Watts's contemporaries alone, and the mellowing process increased with the passage of time as they read, for example, that it was "perverse fancy" to pronounce a man heretical simply "because all the atoms of his brain are not ranged in the same position as the magistrate's."[58]

Secker's tolerance towards the English Methodists has been noted in his particular restraint of Bishop Green.[59]

Drummond's concerns were directed more against a resurgence of Roman Catholicism than against the activities of Protestant dissenters, so it is unusual to find him apparently irritated with dissenters during a debate in the Lords on 19 May 1772. The details are obscured by the lack of current reports, but there is some evidence that Edmund Burke managed to impute words to Drummond. Eighteen years later, in March 1790, when Burke was speaking in the Commons during the debate on the repeal of the Test and Corporation Acts, he referred verbatim to an exchange in the Lords between Chatham and Drummond in 1772 on which the contemporary accounts of that debate are utterly silent. The evidence from secondary sources is inconclusive, but Drummond was supposed to have called the dissenters "men of close ambition," and Chatham was supposed to have been stung into a reply which has gone down as classic oratory in the dissenters' cause,[60] but which may have been fabricated by Burke to serve his purpose in the debate. Other writers,[61] although content with Burke as the authoritative source for the speech by Chatham, have been puzzled by its uncharacteristic style:

> It was on this occasion [i.e. in 1772] that Dr Drummond, Archbishop of York, attacked the Dissenting ministers as men of close ambition; but they met with an able advocate in the great Earl of Chatham, who made this noble defence: "This is judging uncharitably, and whoever brings such a charge without proof, defames." Here the enlightened statesman paused for a moment, and then proceeded, "The Dissenting ministers are represented as men of close ambition: they are so, my Lords; and their ambition is to keep close to the college of fishermen, not of cardinals; and to the doctrine of inspired apostles, not to the decrees of interested and aspiring bishops. They contend for a scriptural creed and scriptural worship; we have a Calvinistic creed, a Popish liturgy, and an Armenian [sic] clergy. The Reformation has laid open the Scriptures to all; let not the bishops shut them again. Laws in support of ecclesiastical power are pleaded, which it would shock humanity to execute. It is said that religious sects have done great mischief when they were not kept under restraint; but history affords no proof that sects have ever been mischievous when they were not oppressed and persecuted by the ruling church."

The source for this was Burke's speech in 1790. His own private papers imply such a drift of thought.[62] It may be that Burke was using inventive licence to "remind" the Commons what had been "said" in the Lords eighteen years earlier. Whatever the attribution of the phrase "men of close ambition" and the celebrated response from Chatham, there was sufficient reason for Drummond, or any bishop, to have been irritated with Dissent at that time. His own archdeacon of Cleveland, Francis Blackburne, and one of his vicars, Theophilus Lindsey of Catterick, were trying to lower the barriers that still kept the Presbyterians out of the national church that they longed for. Blackburne's theological deviance took him part way towards the Unitarians, and Theophilus Lindsey, vicar of Catterick, started a Unitarian chapel in Essex Road, London. The parliamentary business from February through May that year included four debates in the Commons and the Lords on subscription to the Thirty-nine Articles by Anglicans and dissenters. Blackburne and Lindsey were leading signatories to the Feathers Tavern Petition, which had started these debates. Langford discerns "a strong defensive reaction from the Church" to the wording of their petition which suggested exemption from all religious tests.[63] So the usually amiable Drummond may have been irked.

Part 4: Conclusion

In Drummond's Yorkshire the clergy were accustomed to seeing families on the move and changes in the membership of dissenting churches as enterprise and employment called. Some clergy attempted to keep up with these fluctuations, some had precise answers to give to the archbishop, but others were unaware of what was happening and could not even number their own communicants. Roman Catholic numbers were easier to keep because the practice had become customary. Difficulties in identification presented themselves as the formerly strong Presbyterians declined out of existence in some areas of the diocese and as Independents were not yet embarked on their church-building programs. Baptists were identified as "Anabaptists" still in many parishes, though at the mid century their activities were at a low key. Identifying Quakers was easy, even though they figured in most parishes by as little as one or two families. Identifying the Methodists was harder because they disclaimed dissenter status.

Geographical distribution showed some denominational patterns. Presbyterians were in the largest groups, Quakers in the smallest, and these two sects were often in the same parishes but their memberships were in decline. Roman Catholics and Methodists were increasing in reported numbers and were generally not found in the same parishes. Variations in the fortunes of Dissent were in some cases linked to the level of activity of the Anglican clergy, suggesting that an incumbent's style could either deter or encourage Dissent. The threat to the church from Dissent was strongest where population changes were greatest.

In matters of diocesan control, the church of the 1760s in Yorkshire took a noticeable leap forward over ground that had been left largely untended by Drummond's predecessor, John Gilbert. Drummond had begun this recovery of ground before his own tenure of the archdiocese during his 1758 confirmation tour for Gilbert, when he made lists of notes on the clergy, people, and places (Chapter 3). The message of the visitation returns of 1764, however, was not fully apparent to Drummond. What he noticed was restricted to Roman Catholic growth, and he tried to explain that away. The statistics of loss and gain of ground for the church, that is its membership, compiled from the visitation returns on the interaction of fluctuating dissenter fortunes with population changes, show that, despite the opinion of Ollard and Walker, it was holding its position. But the figures, flattering to deceive, do indicate that its position was precarious, in that the church was safest where change was least.

Drummond did not live long enough to see the growth of problems gathering on the western and southern horizons of his diocese, as the Independents and Baptists were revitalized by the work of the Anglican evangelicals and Methodist revivalists, making it clear that the old parish structure of the church could not cope. That structure, originally one of the strengths of the Anglican church, was beginning to be tested to the limits of that strength in the mid eighteenth century, but boundary reforms and division of parishes were not priorities in the 1760s, and were not seen as such until the Pluralities Act of 1838. As the established church, Anglicanism was, in the view of a Methodist, "truly earthed,"[64] so that the Nonconformists, whether they liked it or not, were part of what the established church saw as its responsibility—its parishioners if not its attenders. This pastorally attractive picture is an ideal somewhat removed from the reality of the eighteenth-century experience which, though it could work well in rural areas with small parishes and landowners' support, could not reach the parts that Nonconformists reached in sprawling parishes with several villages. Pluralism and nonresidence in the mid eighteenth century in Yorkshire were largely contained within their own normality (Chapter 5), though there was ample complacency about their prevalence. The parish system, begun at the very conversion of England, was equipped with its church buildings and with the legal authority to found chapels of ease if numbers and finances were appropriate. So in the large towns of Leeds, Sheffield, Hull, and Halifax, there were chapels of ease, and more were founded elsewhere in the later eighteenth century (sometimes built by evangelical lay patrons). These, however, were without separate pastoral responsibilities and were dependent chapels of the parish church. Although there were some state-financed chapels after 1818, it was not until the legislation of the 1830s, 1840s, and 1850s that more parishes were created with their own churches. The parishes had become an accepted part of society as well as the ground for the operation of the church's ministry, but easy acceptance excluded self-criticism, and where large parishes were experiencing population and other changes, the signs were ominous that the church would soon be unable to cope. It was mainly through their own more flexible systems—of the classes, societies, "Rounds" and unions—that the Methodists and other Nonconformists scored during the later eighteenth and early nineteenth century.

7
Government by Correspondence

Introduction

A study of Archbishop Drummond's correspondence confirms that he tackled the administration of his diocese with the efficiency applauded by S. H. Cassan.[1] Sykes emphasized how difficult it was for bishops to perform the duties of ordination, visitation, and confirmation because of their London residential commitments. He considered that the bishops of Hanoverian England "strove with diligence and not without due measure of success to discharge the spiritual administration attached to their office." His appraisal did not specifically include what one might call desk work,[2] which did, however, use up a great deal of Drummond's time. Peter Virgin argues that administrative skills were never the reason for promoting a bishop within the church of the eighteenth century,[3] but Drummond's correspondence shows that he managed the spiritual role of his calling and dealt capably with the paper work. The early nineteenth century assessment needs to be restated.

Drummond's incoming mail increased during the first three years of his term of office in proportion as it was recognized that he did not linger over each letter but took decisions to end disputes and move business forward. Whereas visitation was a triennial part of church governance, much had to be done and was done by correspondence in 1764 and all other years. The letters studied for this chapter uncover the daily business of a competent archbishop in a large and populous archdiocese. It presents a picture of a man who was welcomed in that office not only with perfunctory or superficial greetings but as one who was known and already respected for his capability and the even manner of his work.

That welcome and those greetings may have been tinged with relief at the prospect of a change from the infirmities of Drummond's predecessor, John Gilbert. Contemporary dislike of Gilbert was blunt and impertinent. He was seen as a glutton,[4] a preacher of leaden sermons,[5] and a man of few administrative capabilities.[6]

Writing to the new archbishop was the only way of drawing his attention to situations which he could not have known about unless one visited personally. The delivery of letters by mail or messenger in the 1760s was sufficiently swift for this to be a useful way of conducting business. The time gap between sending and receiving letters was normally only a matter of days if the distance was within the county of Yorkshire. Letters sent within a town or city could be delivered by personal messenger on the same day.

Archbishop Drummond's correspondence, although bulky, does not compare in substance with that of the duke of Newcastle, the "noble drudge,"[7] who seemed to write letters as he breathed. Drummond's correspondence does not reflect his every turn of thought to each of his close associates, but many of the incoming letters have a note on the reverse, summarizing the contents, with sometimes a directive note for the reply. Those notes are truly notes, with dashes for punctuation and in brief such as "Mr X about a living—it is in the Crown." Most of the outgoing letters are in his own hand and what we see was what the secretary used to write a fairer copy. Eighteenth-century letter writing between clergymen was a genre in which some excelled. Their style and their handwriting become recognizable after a short time. George Legh of Halifax had mastered brevity together with gracious sincerity. The dean of York, John Fountayne, wrote in a large hand and usually remembered to include greetings from his wife to Mrs. Drummond. Scrope Berdmore, the archdeaconry official in Nottinghamshire, usually offered a spare room for hospitality should it ever be necessary. Archdeacon Francis Blackburne wrote factually and without added opinion. Newcastle's own hand, as opposed to the copper plate of his secretary, was a readable scrawl quite similar to Drummond's. They had been at the same school, though separated by a generation; perhaps the same writing master had taught them.

The extant correspondence from 1761 to the 1770s is enough to visualize Archbishop Drummond as comfortable at his desks at Bishopthorpe and Brodsworth as on his feet in the House of Lords. His style was efficient and regular rather than neat. It is possible to follow a series of letters through a matter of weeks. Of course, some issues dragged on for months, and some for years, but that was in the nature of the contents rather than in the speeds available by post.

Administering the Diocese

The diocesan correspondence from 1761 to 1776 in the Borthwick Institute includes inherited and sometimes formal disputes, some going back to the establishment of monastic foundations. There are petitions and reports, gracious exchanges between the dean of York and the archbishop, friendly accounts from former colleagues in Wales, formal letters for restructuring churches, requests for making enclosures and granting benefices. Social and political matters and offers of provisions and services remind us that diocesan administration was not a narrow enterprise. There are also unique letters such as that from a critic who deplored the loading and unloading of waggons on Sundays and the barber outraged that his customers wanted to be shaved on Sundays.[8]

Preliminary Sifting: Correspondence 1761–1763

The letters received during Drummond's first two years as archbishop tested his ability. They enabled him to sort out who was offering sincere congratulations and who wanted a job. The enquiry into this area of his work shows that Drummond knew exactly what he was doing. The archbishop was a newcomer, but he was experienced enough to tackle the large workload.

One of the earliest letters of congratulation was dated 30 September and came from J. Johnson of Chester[9] who wittily combined his good wishes with a sardonic hope for preferment: "though I am now chained down in obscurity, Yet I hope soon to rise by the benevolent influence of your Grace's favour and protection."

Chester was midway between Wales, where Drummond had held his first bishopric, and York, where he was then so much more grandly enthroned as archbishop. Johnson was very quick to appreciate the possible opportunity that this might represent for him. He showed an independent cheerfulness in combining his congratulations with a purposeful hope. His approach was one of the ways open in the eighteenth century to clergymen who hoped to improve their situation. A direct, witty, and personal letter such as his, sent to the man at the top, written at the outset of the archbishop's time in office, might put his name and place in the archbishop's mind just when benevolent feelings might abound. The archbishop might still be full of gratitude to those who had helped him and might be ready, so Johnson of Chester thought, to help another. More than one letter would usually be required to secure preferment, however, and clergymen were accustomed to obtain support from others who had a close connection with a patron. Johnson of Chester was making a bold attempt to write on his own behalf. There is no evidence that he was successful, and there is evidence that the archbishop disliked another early approach for his patronage. This was from a Mr. Hewett, who wrote on behalf of a Mr. Hurst. Hewett made procedural mistakes in his request. He wrote to the duke of Newcastle rather than addressing Drummond first. He asked for a particular living, which was not then vacant. He underestimated the value of the living. His particular request came too early (in October 1761, before Drummond's enthronement). These mistakes put Drummond at a disadvantage with his own patron, because he was unable to oblige the duke on what must have seemed to him a small matter. Hewett received a stinging rebuke from Drummond, who passed on his feeling of being "a little nettled."[10]

John Dealtary, vicar of Bishopthorpe and son of the local physician, wrote on 3 October. His letter is a curious mixture of deference to the great prelate about to arrive (he was thanking Drummond for continuing to employ him) and social ease in welcoming him to his parish; he also included the thanks of the gardener and housemaid who were grateful at being "kept on." The same concern for services rendered was shown by the bishop of Peterborough. He wrote from Twickenham on 7 October 1761 with an early recommendation for a wine merchant:[11]

> Mrs Terrick has a brother and a nephew at York who would be proud to be honour'd with your commands, as your wine merchant. They furnished the late Archbishop and Archbishop Herring with port wine, which always met with their approbation. They are very well known to Mr Baley. If you have no particular engagement I shall take it as a favour if you will employ them.

These two letters remind us that this was a society in which the ability to dispense patronage, even at second hand, was as important as the good fortune to receive it.

The dean of York wrote frequently to Drummond in the autumn of 1761, combining social and official matters. He knew that Mrs. Drummond would soon have her first look at Bishopthorpe and that the first ordinations and confirmations would take place before Christmas.

Because the enthronement was by proxy, Dean Fountayne organized the social side of the occasion and wrote to "settle ye cake affair"[12] for "the whole town without restraint (for they will not be restrained) [to] eat sweet meats and drink wine at your Grace's expense."[13] Planning for the ordination dinners also fell to the dean, who advised against holding them at Bishopthorpe because "ye roads are bad and ye days short"; his suggestion instead was either that some could come to him at the deanery, and some could dine with Mr. Berdmore (the archdeaconry official), or "should your Grace think proper to have a dinner at ye George for ye gentlemen who are ordained, he [Berdmore] would attend there to take care of them."[14]

So began a good working partnership. The patronage to prebends was in the archbishop's gift; he reduced the residence requirement from twenty-four weeks to twelve weeks for the five residentiaries, and confirmed the power of the dean to nominate these dignitaries.[15] Twelve years later they were still on good terms. Drummond's name headed the subscription list for the repair of the roof of the minster in 1773, with a donation of two hundred guineas.

Scrope Berdmore wrote on 5 November 1761[16] to introduce himself as the Nottinghamshire archdeaconry official during the permanent absence of Dr. Hugh Thomas[17] and then reported that there had been no confirmations there since 1753, and that he was

> sorry I am obliged to inform your Grace that there have been no parochial visitations since 1736 because the Dean of Ely's necessary engagements elsewhere will not permit him to attend this part of his duty in person, but I shall be very ready.[18]

This was one of the effects of the large-scale pluralism of Hugh Thomas whose work was not being done entirely effectively by his appointee, Scrope Berdmore. But it drew action rather than criticism from Drummond. He dealt with Hugh Thomas's neglect by putting his own visitation in motion and maintained friendly relations throughout with Scrope Berdmore. (His own predecessor's neglect in confirmations was due to bad health, not to pluralism.) The friendly relations with Scrope Berdmore were marked two years later by Drummond sending him a a hamper of old hock, which was so good that it was "saved for best" as Berdmore wrote with his thanks:[19] "[I] . . . am extremely obliged to your Grace for this very kind and agreeable present, which I shall preserve with the greatest care until good Old Hock becomes really necessary for me." The letters of congratulation continued to arrive throughout the autumn of 1761, so that Drummond was well prepared for the customary "civilities of meeting on ye Road, . . . when ye tradesmen may conduct your Grace to y^{r} Palace as usual on ye

Archbishop's first coming to reside there."[20] Some tradesmen also wrote direct.

Drummond may well have been pleased to hear from Dr. Francis Topham[21] because he was the first to mention a visitation. Topham was an ecclesiastical notary, a lawyer in the church courts. He held multiple offices in the archdeaconries of York, the East Riding, and Cleveland as well as working for several of the residentiary canons. He wrote from a knowledge of the clergy going back twenty years, and referred to his wish for improvements in Cleveland and the East Riding, and further hoped that the archbishop would conduct a visitation because it would "carry greater weight and influence and meet with a higher degree of attention," presumably, than those conducted by the archdeacon. He had a good reason for getting off to a good start with the archbishop. He had been the unfortunate subject of the satirical paper from Laurence Sterne (see last paragraph of Chapter 1), printed and immediately suppressed just two years before Drummond's appointment as archbishop.[22]

These early correspondents, with the exception of the tradesmen, were all clergy or (in Topham's case) those connected with church life. But the parishes of the diocese are not much represented. It was not appropriate for a lowly parish priest to write a letter of congratulations to a mighty prelate. Those in parish situations who did write to Drummond had either known him in Wales or were his personal friends (or both, such as William Herring from Bolton Percy), or the educated and charming George Legh of Halifax. Most clergy would not have "troubled" the archbishop—a term they used when they *did* have to write—with a simple letter of welcome. Only the masters of correspondence or those seeking preferment would have thought of writing a letter of congratulations. It was not that Drummond was unapproachable, but an archbishop was a prince of the church and Drummond was a thorough aristocrat. His work as a bishop in Wales had nevertheless enabled his clergy to make their requests plainly. One of these, Robert Conway, wrote because he had been promised preferment in the diocese of St. Asaph, and he sensibly asked Drummond to recommend him to the new Bishop of St. Asaph so that the promise would be honored. His postscript,[23] "I flatter myself y^{t} y^{r} L^{p} will favour me with an answer," suggests a boldness in style that would not have been used if Drummond were too august to be "troubled."

Settling a Long-Standing Dispute: The Silsden Curacy

The correspondence relating to the Silsden curacy[24] provides an early example of the archbishop settling a pathetically etiolated dispute. The curate at Silsden in 1762 was Jonathan Jackson, appointed in 1721, and the chapel was a recent foundation, having been consecrated in 1712 after a deed of gift in 1711. Within three years of Jackson's appointment, there had been difficulties about his terms of work. Drummond received a letter in April 1762 from the neighboring rector of Addingham who attempted to explain[25] that "poor Jackson was so often sunk in debt that his distressed circumstances forc'd him to withdraw." The situation centered on a longstanding dispute between the curate and the earl of Thanet, the benefactor, who had not been paying the curate's stipend because the latter had not been teaching the school at Silsden, as the earl thought he should. The Silsden parishioners had turned for ministry to William Thompson the neighboring clergyman in the adjacent parish of Addingham, and the arrival of a new archbishop, recognized for his efficiency, prompted Thompson to ask that the situation be put to rights. His move was accurate.

The archbishop's notary made a couple of recommendations in May. The curate of Silsden broke his silence and provided the archbishop with his side of the case in his reply by June 1762, and Drummond was prepared to tackle the earl's auditor that autumn. A satisfactory ending was a long way off, even though a solution was forming while Drummond made his notes. A personality clash is always tricky. Where patronage and benefaction and clerical rights and duties intertwined, and where the neighboring rector was tempted to think that he might be able to muscle in on a pluralist acquisition, it required a bold swathe to cut through.

Archbishop Drummond systematically proposed a deal for the absent and debt-ridden unpaid curate, brought the noble earl to task through the offices of his auditor, warded off the predatory William Thompson, alerted the two patronage authorities at Christ Church, Oxford, and the vicarage of Kildwick, and reaffirmed the annual payment for the Silsden curacy. Last, he made a recommendation for a new curate. All these actions bear the mark of one who knew that his authority had massive weight. William Thompson of Addingham had estimated correctly that he could interest Drummond sufficiently to use that authority.

The key points in this controversy are the ones that highlight the way the archbishop cut through the customary blather. An inquiry into the extent of Jackson's possible debts was made via the neighboring rector, who cited claims of a very modest nature from the grocer, mercer, and butcher. The archbishop decided to settle the affair. He compiled an estimate of the arrears of salary due to the unpaid curate, and showed a lawyer's touch in not raking over the matter of teaching at the Silsden school. But the letter from Jonathan Jackson gave the archbishop the impression that there was something exceptionable about the curate as well as the need to put right a wrong.[26] So he decided that Jackson must go. John Dehane, the vicar of Kildwick, was treated very summarily and obliged to bow to the authority of the archbishop's seal. It was done by the power politics of getting the dean of Christ Church to agree first and to confirm next that the instrument relating to the curacy of Silsden had been sealed. Drummond's last move was to line up Joshua Newby, a young fellow of Brasenose College, to accept twenty pounds a year as the new curate of Silsden. The 1764 visitation return is from Joshua Newby as curate, though it still names Jackson as the assistant curate.

It took Drummond just two years to achieve that resolution at Silsden. After almost forty years of dispute, this ranks as a success. It is a testimony to Drummond's clear dislike of irregularity, and also to his authority and persistence. The case illustrates how the Georgian church, in a small Yorkshire parish, had to pit the weight of the archbishop against the influence of a powerful local aristocrat. The earl had been making life miserable for a poor clergyman by keeping back a stipend of twenty pounds a year, had deprived the chapelry of its minister, and had so demoralized the clergyman that he had left Yorkshire for Berkshire. It was only by the direct approach of a letter from the neighboring parson, who esteemed the archbishop's competence, that the problem was tackled. But the episode also shows how the aristocratic prelate was not prepared to accept insubordination from a mere curate, however badly treated by his aristocratic patron.

Solving a Recent Problem: The Haworth Chapelry

Power politics with the dean of Christ Church would not have been possible in the Silsden case if the archbishop had not been sure of his legal ground. It was a good opening case for establishing confidence in his command. Two parish boundaries away from Silsden was the Haworth chapelry. Haworth was in the parish of Bradford, and the vicar of Bradford, James Sykes, may have heard of the firm line that Drummond was prepared to offer to those who asked for his assistance. If he had not heard, and if he was making his request on its own merits and his own needs, he was providing yet another early opportunity for the archbishop to demonstrate his determination to deal straightly. James Sykes wrote to him from Bradford in April 1763, about the curacy of Haworth. The archbishop's firmness throughout this case is all the more remarkable as Haworth is and was known to have been a powerhouse for the activities of the celebrated evangelical clergyman, William Grimshaw. Grimshaw had just died, leaving the curacy vacant.

James Sykes, the vicar of Bradford, was himself an orderly minded clergyman. Haworth was the westernmost chapelry in his parish. Knowing that the archbishop was due to come to Bradford for a confirmation service in a month's time, the vicar wrote to the archbishop and set out for him all the details to be considered about the vacancy at Haworth. The complex history of the previous nomination to the chapelry, going back before the time of Grimshaw, worried the vicar on two counts. One was the alleged right of the Trustees to nominate their own man at the vacancy. The other was that if that alleged right were witheld, and a candidate not of their choosing were licensed, then the chapel rents might be disbursed differently. These two worries were linked, in the vicar's anxiety, because of Grimshaw's particularly evangelical style of ministry, with the likely wish of the Trustees to continue the evangelical slant of the chapelry by nominating a successor whose ideas were similar to those of Grimshaw. At the time when the vicar of Bradford explained all this in his letter[27] to the archbishop, an evangelical style of ministry was far more of an issue—in a national sense as well as a local sense—than it had been when Grimshaw had arrived. Indeed, Grimshaw's conversion occurred some time after he had been licensed, and led to a unique ministry of pastoral encouragement at a time when the Wesleys were still young.

By 1763, however, when Sykes wrote to Drummond, enthusiasm, whether Methodist or Anglican, was more widespread, more divisive, more feared by some and more disliked by the Church generally. It was also growing more noticeably in Yorkshire, as noted in chapter 4, so the vicar of Bradford was aware that the new archbishop would be alert to the problem of the vacancy at the Haworth chapelry.

The reverse of the letter has notes in the archbishop's hand.[28] The notes show the structure of the archbishop's firm dealings with the diocese, and illustrate the immense support available to the parish clergy, who applied to him for assistance. He itemized the main points of immediate procedure. He would accept the vicar's invitation to breakfast with him when he was going to be there in a month's time for the confirmation. A face-to-face morning meeting of this kind must have been heartwarmingly encouraging to the vicar, in the thick of the evangelical activity not only on the western edges of his own parish, but also in the neighboring areas of Leeds and with only the mildness at Calverley and Idle to reassure him. Before that archiepiscopal breakfast occasion, however, the vicar of Bradford was instructed to warn the Trustees, using the legal formula of a caveat, that they were going to have to produce the deeds, because the archbishop said so, for inspection.

The interested parties in this tangle were as follows: the parishioners—who wanted to preserve the evangelical style of Grimshaw's ministry; the vicar—who wanted to preserve the ancient rights of presentation to the vacancy; the archbishop—who wanted to see Canon Law operating properly as well as peace in Christian worship.

After he had made notes on the reverse of the letter, Drummond took another piece of paper and made a list[29] of the legal questions involved in sorting out the action required.

He was not put off by the parishioners' wish to continue the style of Grimshaw's evangelical ministry. But he was suspicious that money might have been used earlier on to get Grimshaw's nomination, and he wanted to know how the money for the afternoon sermon was currently being used. The visitation return, written by Richardson, the clergyman who won the chapelry, shows that there was an afternoon sermon every Sunday at Haworth, provided for by ten pounds a year. All this is clear evidence of the archbishop's straight dealings. His aim was obviously the worship of God by a contented congregation in accordance with the traditions of the Church of England. His action was that of one who understood how to apply Canon Law and how to deal with clergy and people. The visitation returns show that the evangelical party retained its strength in the immediate aftermath of Grimshaw's ministry: eighty Methodists were meeting every other Thursday evening in an unlicensed house. In the longer term, though, by 1791, the year of Richardson's death, it was the Baptists who had grown in strength, taking numbers over from the evangelical church of England and also from the Methodists, according to Walsh.[30]

Drummond showed good sense in solving the case of the Haworth vacancy, where Richardson, though known as an evangelical, did not quite match up to the example set by Grimshaw. Drummond had been able to keep the good will of the people of Haworth without courting Enthusiasm. He clearly saw that Grimshaw had been a unique parson and that Richardson was not a carbon copy and could safely fill the vacancy.

The Routine Correspondence during the Year of Visitation

The visitation incurred correspondence on the hoof. Sykes saw the extent of the diocese as "sufficient to prevent close oversight,"[31] in ordinary circumstances, but Drummond absorbed the extra workload. In addition to the excuses for not attending the visitation (see Chapter 3), there are 136 items in one part of the Bishopthorpe papers[32] and other boxes of papers relating to specific topics.

The Saga of Thomas Hudson—"a squib in ye papers"

Thomas Hudson, a young curate, had invited a Methodist itinerant preacher into the Stokesley pulpit one Sunday in 1763. The episode drew criticism and the trouble fanned a dispute between the parishioners and their rector, Dr. Francis Wanley, an absentee whom they disliked for his "wearying catechisms" and aloof manner.[33] In thickening intrigue, the parishioners advised Hudson to get a testimonial and take it to the archbishop, hoping to make trouble for the rector, but Hudson's nerve failed, and he went to the rector instead. Aware that the parishioners wanted to bypass their rector, Hudson went back to them with a story he invented of a visit to the archbishop and a personal interview at Brodsworth, with a bit of boasting thrown in about getting a bargain with another curacy. Nobody believed him for long, and as the lies came out he fell foul of them all, and the archbishop placed him under a ban. The arcbishop received about fifteen separate pieces of correspondence in this case.

Hudson became a pathetic figure. He could not understand why he was being punished and spent years of misery, trying to reinstate himself by producing another testimonial. He lacked all knowledge of procedures, writing tear-stained, impassioned letters, pleading with the archbishop to grant the personal meeting that he had originally invented and dressing it up into a drama by marking the letter "Secret," and, back in the parish, further inventing a reply from the archbishop's secretary.

The Hudson saga was a very troublesome undercurrent for the archbishop during 1764, consuming his time and patience during the busiest months of the visitation itself. Hudson's pleas[34] were melodramatic:

> My Lord, give me leave to look up with supplicating tears to your Lordship and crave your compassion. . . . I hope this kind of language

> will not appear too free when I assure your Grace 'tis such as the most bitter distress dictates.

He asked to be rescued from "the greatest calamity that can possibly come upon me—for upon this single throw depends my life, my happiness, my all."[35]

Drummond's disciplinary manner was resolute. He described Hudson's conduct as "extraordinary," ("I really was amazed at the heap of fiction") and declined to answer him by letter. Not answering was harsh ("I do not care to write to Mr Hudson") and only temporarily effective, for Hudson's insistence—there had been about eight letters by then—wore him down. So Drummond granted Hudson's plea for an interview, with others present. The correspondence relating to Hudson shows how the church exercised its authority outside the official area of courts on this unusual issue where those concerned acted according to initiative and personal dignity. Hudson came off badly. He did not see himself as a culprit until the moment when he was brought in to meet the archbishop. Drummond's account of it[36] shows Hudson speechless and overawed. Drummond showed no indulgence, not lifting his ban, requiring Hudson to search for fresh testimonials without any counsel, and reminding him that misery follows misdemeanours. It took Hudson a year to get the testimonials, but he spoiled his case by "not doubting that they would be satisfactory." Meanwhile, he had persuaded Cornelius Rickaby, the curate at Bridlington, to employ him as assistant curate *and* schoolmaster while he was still under the archbishop's ban and without a schoolmaster's licence. He had the gall to write to the archbishop for permission to start officially "next Sunday, to signifiy your Grace's pleasure." When there was no such reply he wrote again, "If the testimonials I sent be lost, I beg to know what farther satisfaction your Grace requires"—another gauche stab in his own back, imputing loss or disorder in the archbishop's filing system. He really was in the depths of depair by then because the congregation at Bridlington had heard about his disgrace, and were guessing at the reasons for it, causing Hudson more misery.

Drummond was angry at being represented as favoring Enthusiastic preachers and affronted at the innuendo of dealing in money for ecclesiastical favors. The whole matter was an irritation especially as the rector of Stokesley, Francis Wanley, was a personal friend whose absenteeism he defended. We glimpse his utter weariness with the matter when we read his advice to the parishioners. There was naught to oblige the rector to residence, that a curate had been sought for carefully to my knowledge . . . to take priest's orders on Trinity Sunday, and that [even if] he put a squib in ye papers . . . it would do neither him nor the parish good.[37]

Perhaps weariness lifted to amusement while he was sitting for his portrait by the artist (see chapter 2), whose name was also Thomas Hudson, and perhaps the dinner table guests at Brodsworth were entertained by the coincidence.

Minor Matters of Business

The correspondence which flowed to the archbishop's desk had its share of tedious content. In Drummond's receiving and reading about minor matters of business and often deciding to do nothing about them, we get an insight into the ordinary and humdrum side of the correspondence of an eighteenth-century archbishop. Drummond emerges as one who would not be diverted from keeping to his visitation schedules by what he regarded as trivia.

Joseph Dowthwaite wrote from Feliskirk[38] asking permission to pull down a cottage. His timing was unfortunate, as Drummond was making all the final arrangements in early April for the visitation. Drummond refused. John Radcliffe (possibly a churchwarden) of Adwick le Street[39] wrote that,

our servants are so ungovernable that neither me nor other masters can get them to ye church . . . which your Lordship please to give me some strict order to put them in ye stocks or any other punishment.

There were no notes for reply about this. Joseph Dowthwaite wrote again in May,[40] referring to the existence of "a powerful envious and malicious party . . . against me . . . take away church profits . . . by artful ways and means," but his cause appears to have been ignored, as the archbishop made no notes on the reverse for any reply. It is possible that such correspondence was dealt with by the secretaries, reporting to Drummond and knowing from experience how to deal with such minor matters of business. It is also possible, however, that Drummond read the letters himself, but found it wearying, and turned away from the effort of replying.

Even an issue such as clergy pay was a trivial matter in the year of the archbishop's primary visitation. In May, Michael Lythe wrote from Pocklington to ask for financial help for the sixty-year-old curate with a wife and six children, but the archbishop took "no notice taken of this. He is the person that the Dean desired . . . [MS is unclear] be postponed to be licensed." The reference to the dean suggests that the correspondent's record was tainted, but there are other cases in which poverty pleading met with a negative response from Drummond. Here he seems almost to have pounced in his refusal to help. Another piece of paper was sent with Lythe's request, and has the statement "We are of the opinion that the Vicar does not allow his Curate a competent salary in proportion to the value of his living," signed by Charles Crosse and John Balderson, churchwardens. No details on the return are given about the curate's pay, but Pocklington was valued in the diocesan lists at sixty pounds a year. Thomas Lovett, the vicar, was also elderly, having been ordained deacon in 1718 and priest in 1719, and inducted to Pocklington in 1722. Drummond's apparent disregard of the lowly churchwardens was in character with his unwillingness to recognize lay opinion, and in this case his unwillingnesss to support the curate against the vicar was assisted by the dean's censure of Lythe.

From Worksop came a complaint that the schoolmaster, Mr. Peacock, had stolen a copy of the Worksop registers.[41] Information came about payments to a dissenting minister, profligate colliers at Mexbrough, a new chapel, a school falling into disuse, enclosures, scrutiny of investments, and road widenings. The details of rebuilding works at Scrooby Sutton were set down for the archbishop to study.[42]

Some of this practical business was very detailed and probably irritating, and the archbishop was obliged to enter into it where he was the patron of the living. Otherwise, such routine business was not the sort to interest Drummond, especially when he was preparing for a visitation, so his notes on the reverse of such items were usually very brief indeed.

Initiatives for Reform, Clergy Pipe Dreams

Robert Fisher wrote from Bolton upon Dearne,[43] thinking that it was appropriate to have "a judicious review of our Liturgy, Canons, Articles and Homilies and a more accurate Translation of ye Scriptures." Neither the timing nor the idea would appeal to Drummond, but the correspondent was not alone in his thoughts. At the end of the year Richard Hardy wrote from Langan,[44] beginning lightly with a plan for "a few Alterations to the Book of Common prayer," and going on to,

> a more literal, pure and elegant Translation of the Holy Scriptures . . . because the protestant Dissenters are very much reconciled to Episcopacy and Forms of Prayer; the deists are sick of the late large and nauseous Doses of Infidelity and profaneness; and many of our Enthusiasts are really at a stand in their search after Divine Truths . . .

He stressed what an appropriate time it was because "We are now at Peace; we have a gracious and religious King." He knew who could do it:

> If our several Colleges would first undertake this Labour, . . . and invite all Mankind to send their remarks to them, . . . the work in a few years might be brought to such . . . perfection . . . as to be fit to lay before the Heads of the Church for their last correction and Approbation.

As a display of optimism, this must be the best example of the year. As a directive on how to make a translation of the Bible, inviting all mankind to send in their remarks, it is quaint. As the view of a loyal royalist it must have pleased the archbishop. As a summary of the whole Church of England it was optimistically positive, referring to *our* Enthusiasts as part of the established church. The note in the archbishop's hand overleaf has merely, "Sent with Answers to my Queries," so we are left wondering what Drummond thought but are reminded that the eighteenth-century church consisted of idealists as well as activists. Some of the laity also had new ideas. John Mulso of Thornhill[45] had parishioners with musical ambitions. He wrote in May,

> The younger part of my parishioners were very sollicitous [sic] for a Gallery, to assemble there together in, as a musical Band, to sing Psalms. . . . [They have the] consent of most . . . [and] at last mine . . . [but I prefer] plain parochial Psalmody. But they are growing impatient of this Restraint, and are now and then introducing Anthems, and I . . . [have difficulty in] restraining them. . . . They promise Obedience but with Reluctance.

In Drummond's hand is the note: "I sent an answer by Mr Greenwood, C[urate], that I was totally against anything but the common Psalm singing." His reply was characteristic of one who appeared to show no interest in the taste of the age for more elaborate sacred and secular music such as *Messiah, Royal Fireworks,* and *Water Music,* which G. F. Handel had left to his sovereign and fellow citizens as perpetual pleasures.

The strangest letter of all was the request for preferment written in terms so veiled as to obscure its meaning. It is a unique piece of servility and came from George Hutton of Gate Burton:[46]

> The manner in which your favourable intentions were at first declared, was so truely honourable, as to excite in me peculiar sensations, of gratitude mingled with much esteem. My observation being now directed to your Grace, it was no wonder if, very soon, I became sincerely ambitious of such a patronage. Perhaps it is impossible to keep a distinguished character long in view, without wishing to partake of its reputation: which, in some degree, must necessarily happen to those who are known to receive favour from your Grace. I have the honour to recommend myself to your Grace's protection and to be, with the utmost perfect esteem and attachment, . . . your . . . servant.

It would be difficult for anyone to reply to such a letter.[47] The modern age has invented "newspeak" and "franglais" to describe jargon and genre. What could this be—"grovelish" or "patronask"?

Fishing

The fishing season led Richard Becher to send a charming note[48] with his gift to Drummond:

> I am just now returned from fishing and not a little tired, and perhaps may soon take a knap [sic] as usual; your Grace will receive the fruits of my labour, four brace of trout and three pairs of tench taken in your Grace's fisherys. . . . I flatter myself that they will be eaten with pleasure.

Foreign Affairs: George Marriott

Foreign correspondence came much more to the archbishop of Canterbury than to the archbishop of York. The matter of a chaplain for a factory in Gottenburg was an exception and took five months of intricate correspondence[49] to negotiate, from the end of June, when Drummond was just starting the second stage of his visitation, until the end of October 1764. The initiative was taken by Joseph Sykes of Hull, who wrote to Drummond asking him to nominate a clergyman for a salary of seventy pounds or eighty pounds a year plus lodging, who could teach English to factory workers' children. George Marriott, a curate for Dr. Lloyd at Puddletown in Dorset accepted the offer at the beginning of August but was delayed because he had not yet been ordained priest. The timing became critical. The choice of a successor for Marriott at Puddletown was a bother, and Marriott pleaded that poverty prevented him from taking a journey to Bristol for ordination. He asked whether he might be ordained in London, before the ship was ready to sail on 7 or 8 October. Drummond was not planning to be in London before then. Clearly the journey to Yorkshire would have been more expensive and time consuming than the journey to Bristol, so the idea was that the bishop of London be asked to ordain. That was not possible either because the bishop of London (like Bishop Green earlier in the year in the case of John Newton) had not arranged for an ordination service until December and was unwilling to do it privately. If the matter were left any longer, there would be no more sailings that winter. Marriott wrote:

> The gentlemen of the factory are extremely pressing to have me at Gottenburg before the winter, and as I cannot obtain Priest's orders I must do myself the pleasure of waiting on your Grace at Brodsworth.

The bishops' regard for a minor clergyman's career was distant and static. It cost them little, Drummond included, to write letters about the matter, but to alter their own schedule of movements and services was not seen as necessary. They knew that such commercial placings as the chaplaincy at Gottenburg were backed with sufficient cash to be able to fund traveling expenses incurred.[50] This was not unreasonable and would be the same in a modern context, where employers, not referees, pay candidates' expenses. Marriott himself clearly understood the hierarchy of social as well as ecclesiastical business, for in his ensuing career in Sweden he helped his employer, Joseph Sykes of Hull, by interviewing men who were thought to be upsetting the balance of labor by sending money from their earnings in Gottenburg back to their Scottish homes.[51]

Laurence Sterne: Miles Emeritus

The archbishop received an opening paragraph from Laurence Sterne that may have reminded him of his own earlier ways of reporting to the duke of Newcastle: "Though there is little in this part of the world worth giving you an account of . . . yet . . . it is my duty to say something." He described some of his health problems, and those of his daughter, and referred to his plans:

I shall encamp like a patriarch with my whole household upon the side of the Pyreneans, this summer and winter at Nice; from whence in Spring I shall return home, never, I fear, to be of much service, at least as a preacher. I have preached too much, my Lord, already; and was my age to be computed either by the number of sermons I have preached, or the infirmities they have brought upon me, I might truly be said to have the claim of a *Miles emeritus,* and was there a Hotel des Invalides for the reception of such established upon any salutary plain betwixt here and Arabia Felix, I would beg your Grace's interest to help me into it—as it is, I rest fully assured . . . of your Grace's indulgence to me in my endeavours to add a few quiet years to this fragment of my life—and with my wishes for a long and happy one to your Grace.

The archbishop would not fail to be charmed by reading this. The letter[52] came at a time when Sterne had become accustomed to the favors that went with his literary fame. It put him at an advantage with the archbishop. He knew all the ways to use his talents on his superior. The letter shows the Georgian church allowing one of its most famous Yorkshire parsons to take advantage of his worldly success and leave his parishes to the care of curates. Archbishop Drummond could accept such blatant and unconcerned absenteeism, the product of the permissive pluralism that put Sterne in charge of three parishes of the York diocese, Sutton on the Forest, Stillington, and Coxwold.

Two Different Archdeacons

Francis Blackburne of Cleveland was a theological scholar of fluid persuasion and a pernickety critic of the clergy of his archdeaconry. Scrope Berdmore of Nottinghamshire was a plainer person who gave more thought to smoothing over difficulties than in winkling them out. Their relationships with the archbishop in the exercise of their responsibility extend our understanding of diocesan governance.

Francis Blackburne wrote systematically about the numbers of Roman Catholics in his archdeaconry and about the clergy who employed curates, keeping lists of unlicensed curates. He charted Sunday services (see Chapter 4), and he included complaints against James Deason, the carousing parson of Danby and concise reports about Laurence Sterne:

> Laurence Sterne, Vicar of Sutton on the Forest, Curate of Coxwold, Vicar of Stillington, Prebendary of York, has his residence abroad and has Marmaduke Callis and James Kilner as Curates.

This type of factual detail arrived throughout the time that his private concerns were growing into *The Confessional,* which reached its third edition in 1770. In the same year as the archbishop's visitation, Blackburne began the series of newspaper articles published in 1774 as *A Collection of Essays in Favour of Public Liberty.* His particular withdrawing approach to the Thirty-nine Articles had been unfolding since 1753. He explained,

> Be pleased then to know, that besides these festivals concerning which you have heard so much of my opinion, there are many other things in the doctrine, discipline, and worship of the Church of England which are very exceptionable, not to say grievous to me, and other clergymen with whom I have conversed.[53]

How far was Blackburne an undermining influence in the Georgian church of Yorkshire? There is no suggestion in the correspondence that Blackburne was deliberately and consciously subverting the archbishop's work. He separated the direction of his theology from his practical supervision as archdeacon, but he made no attempt to hide the impact of his thoughts. Unlike the press in the present age, there was no whipping up of provocation for public concern or news items with partial quotation. Clergymen in the age of Enlightenment were free to write and discuss and publish unorthodox theological matters without fear of being dispossessed. Blackburne's discussions spread widely both geographically and theologically until the participants brought their case before Parliament in 1772 and failed. Only two hundred clerics and forty or fifty lawyers and doctors had signed.[54]

Scrope Berdmore wrote from Nottinghamshire mainly in reply to requests from the archbishop, whereas Francis Blackburne wrote more on initiative. Drummond had asked Berdmore for information about synods and heard[55] that there was not much to report,

> The Chapter . . . are in no way concerned in the Synod; nor is the least notice taken of the Synod in our Chapter Books. . . . [There has been] no business of any sort . . . done in the synod since the Restoration (probably not since the Reformation) except appointing a Preacher for the ensuing synod.

It was characteristic of Drummond to enquire about the importance of the synod as a feature of church administrative life. Although he was busy, he was ready to regard this as one of his duties as archbishop. When he heard that nothing was happening in that area, and Berdmore said that it was Archbishop Sharp who had "put an end to them" in the York diocese, he reacted in conservative and traditional manner by not reintroducing synods.

In the matter of appointing a preacher for the Nottinghamshire part of the visitation, Berdmore was able to smooth over a difficulty, writing with a dry style of remedy on 9 March 1762[56] against a clash of personalities: "I dare say I can procure some neighbour to be ready to preach in case the proper person does not attend, and perhaps that may be the best way of avoiding a troublesome dispute." The relationship between Drummond and Berdmore was a gladder, easier, more friendly one than that between Blackburne and Drummond. These two very different archdeacons served a broad, comfortable church in the mid eighteenth century. Its breadth enabled it to withstand the formal challenges of the Feathers Tavern Petition and the Bill for the Relief of Protestant Dissenters and then to develop in depth when reform and renewal came in the early nineteenth century.

The Two Archbishops

The Traditions of the Archbishops' Authority

The two archbishops of the Church of England in the mid eighteenth century were in theory equal partners but with a tradition of superiority for Canterbury. The archbishop of York was primate of England and the archbishop of Canterbury was primate of all England. Translation from York to Canterbury was an upward career move.

Autonomous authority belonged to each primate within his metropolitan area, each separately responsible and equally powerful in controlling church affairs, but both were jointly in charge of the Church of England in its collective ministry. Besides attending spiritually to their lay and clerical members, they were also politically important as leaders of the Lords Spiritual in Parliament. While Secker and Drummond were archbishops of Canterbury and York (1758–1768 and 1761–1776), their seven-year working partnership from 1761 to 1768 was marked by a regular and detailed correspondence. It reveals them as conscientious and responsible at a time of political and industrial change, and its absorbingly readable quality rewards attention.

Thomas Secker had been archbishop of Canterbury for three years before Drummond was translated to York. Unlike several of his predecessors, Secker had not moved to Canterbury from York.[57] The strength of their partnership by the 1760s was in their complementary attributes. Secker's death in 1768 ended a working team of two talented archbishops whose control of the church brought it special benefits. The tradition of the two interrelated provinces demonstrated the church's unity in which priests and people worked and lived in both north and south and in England and Wales. For example, the duke of Newcastle, one of the outstanding laymen of the eighteenth-century church, owned lands in north Nottinghamshire about twenty-five miles from Drummond's family estates at Brodsworth while his domestic residence was in Esher in Surrey, and controlled the parliamentary privilege in boroughs both in the north and south. For example also, but on a much less exalted scale, two clergymen of Drummond's time held parishes in Yorkshire and resided in Kent and Sussex;[58] another lived on the Isle of Wight.

The exchanges of letters between Secker and Drummond reveal that they shared the same aims for the Church of England in the mid eighteenth century. Their correspondence during 1763 has been consecutively studied and shows what they regarded as important and how they tackled the main issues. Secker wrote mainly from Lambeth, Drummond mainly from Brodsworth and rarely from Bishopthorpe. Secker's handwriting has an open and fair appearance and its content is never obscure. The style is direct in matters of fact and thoughtfully expansive on matters of sadness or speculation. It is possible to follow Secker's gift for making a friendship with his brother in the north entirely by letter. Their meetings must have been restricted to attendances at the House of Lords. There are no social notes, no invitations or acceptances to dinner in the extant papers, though they were often in London at the same times. The social difference in their origins may have distanced them in this way, but their letters confirm that they were very close in matters of intellectual understanding and church governance. Personal meetings or their "waiting on" one another were kept for financial business, such as with the SPG. Secker had the ability to cut the distance between London and York, conveying in his letters a warmth and a trust in Drummond's work, setting out in longhand exactly what he thought. For example, in August 1762 he reported a meeting he had had with a Dr. Smith of Philadelphia, who had persisted in asking him to send recommendatory letters throughout the diocese for a particular cause: "I read him your Grace's Opinion which I told him was also mine. He hoped he could change yours. I said that would be the way to change mine. And I fancy he will write to your Grace." It is a matter of regret that so few of the replies from Drummond have survived.

The Aims and Scope of Archiepiscopal Control

Governing the church by correspondence kept the two archbishops in regular contact during the years studied to an extent that might appear to be in inverse proportion to the importance of the matters they considered. The ensuing examples of insufficiently qualified ordinands and priests with criminous or doubtful records troubled the archbishops beyond what seems now to have been worthwhile. This inverse ratio of effort to results reminds us that Secker and Drummond governed a church in which no one could tell anyone else what to do within his own jurisdiction. Against that background the two archbishops devoted much energy and time in their correspondence to preventing undesirable ordinations and renewal of licenses. This is what makes the correspondence so significant, for it shows, within the system, that these two archbishops were providing a body of clergy as good as they could make it. Together they worked at this aim, each one acting throughout his own province, keeping an eye on what was going on beyond his own diocese, knowing that there was little he could do afterwards if an unsuitable man got his priest's orders. The correspondence also illustrates that the archbishops had very little control if a brother bishop granted priest's orders contrary to their directive or, more usually, in ignorance of such directives. Ignorance of directives in an age of slow communications could even be a cover for a more lax approach to the high standard set by the archbishops, where bishops might be either in their dioceses or in London, or en route between the two or at another residence altogether if they belonged to a landed family.

Training men for holy orders, in so far as it was done at all, took place at the universities, where the archbishops used their influence in such integral parts of the established church. Maintaining appropriate standards for clergymen was a time-consuming task, though it might be one of the quirks of the extant evidence that the two archbishops put so much effort into keeping unsuitable candidates out of the church. Seeing this negative side of their work may have assisted the reformers' view of the Georgian church as a cautious and unspiritual club. Getting into the church in the eighteenth century was attractive to several different levels in society, from grammar school boys to sons of the aristocracy, as the experience of these two archbishops proved. Having themselves (by different routes) been selected to reach the top, they were conscientious enough to want to regulate the standards of their clergy and this warrants commendation instead of criticism.

Correspondence was for much of the time the only method of work. The usual means for alerting episcopal colleagues about unsuitable candidates was for Secker to write to all the bishops in his province, and to Drummond, asking him to do the same for all the York colleagues. Secker initially would have heard from the bishop in whose diocese the offender began his undesirable activities or from another bishop who was quick enough to notice an irregularity. An undesirable applicant for the priesthood might get as far as deacon's orders before suspicion was aroused, but problems began once fully ordained priests committed crimes such as theft and bigamy. Difficulties also presented themselves in terms of Nonconformist clergy seeking to work within the established church and attempting to have their Nonconformist ordinations recognized.

Ordinands

During the 1763 correspondence between the two archbishops, Drummond wrote to Secker in critical terms about the applicants for orders at his recent ordinations. He described nine as a low number of deacons and priests. He was not satisfied that there was an increase in schoolmasters seeking ordination, and noted that the number of curates from the universities was decreasing. In his letter of 6 June 1763 he reported that he had postponed one of the nine candidates, as he was "far from being qualified." Walter Edwards, of St. John's College, Cambridge, who had stolen college silver, went some way to acquire holy orders before he was halted. Not surprisingly, he had failed to get a testimonial from the college when he applied for deacon's orders. The matter came to the notice of Lord James Beauclerk, bishop of Hereford, to whom Edwards was applying for ordination. Suspicion arose, and the bishop decided to consult his colleagues. At their discussion, other business took more time, and the matter of Edwards was left. Edwards had meanwhile slipped to the diocese of St. David's and had been ordained deacon. When the bishop of Hereford remembered to mention it to Secker, the alert was sent out to prevent Edwards from proceeding to priest's orders. There is no hint in the letter about this to Drummond that Secker laid any blame on the bishop of St. David's for ordaining Edwards as a deacon. He was concerned mainly to prevent further wrong. The case was a double one of suspected false credentials for an unsuitable applicant as a minister of the church. The bishop of St. David's may have had a connection of some sort with the thief; he may have acted without reading the papers sufficiently closely; he may have been a more forgiving man than the bishop of Hereford; he may have been more gullible.[59] The nose for finding out the irregularity was initially with the bishop of Hereford. It was Secker and Drummond together who acted quickly to stop the matter going further. They were similarly in agreement about deterring an underage applicant, John Crowe, who applied to the bishop of Llandaff for deacon's orders when he was only twenty years old, saying that he was twenty-three. Secker was incensed by the forgery of Crowe's papers, referring to it as "this Fraud."[60]

The Right Qualifications

At the university level of seeing that the clergy had the right qualifications, the two archbishops exercised vigilance over the Boyle lectureship.[61] Their harmony was just as close in their determination to prevent inroads by the Nonconformists, as shown in the case of Francis Okely. Okely had been ordained deacon by Johannes de Watteville, a Moravian bishop, and had worked ten years in Germany with the Moravians. He returned to England and applied to the bishop of Lincoln for priest's orders while he was working among the Moravians in Bedford. Secker was unswervingly authoritative in his refusal to admit Francis Okely to the order of priest in the Church of England, and wrote to Drummond with all the prejudice of a pre-ecumenical age, keeping Okely out.[62] He was well aware of the undesirability of setting a precedent, but his main purpose was to ensure that only appropriately qualified men joined the ranks of the ordained ministry of the Church of England. Secker and Drummond were at one in this purpose. Their agreement illustrates that the Church of England affirmed its distinctive identity since the Act of Toleration. Secker, the man at the very top of the system, had once been a Presbyterian but was now united with Drummond as an inveterate opponent of Dissent.

Henry Perfect and Other Miscreant Clergymen

The rigmarole of Henry Perfect, trickster and polygamist, occupied several exchanges of letters between the two archbishops during 1763. Perfect had been known to Secker as a regimental chaplain and reappeared through his application to the bishop of St. David's for renewal of orders that he claimed had been lost. The loss was initially as he was "stepping into or out of a post chaise on his landing from I know not what place," and subsequently involved pawning the orders at a public house near Blackheath for the sum of 3/6d. This slippery chaplain generated a great deal of effort to exclude him from parochial office within the church. But Samuel Squire, the bishop of St. David's, was less than vigilant. The son of a Warminster druggist who won a Somerset scholarship to St. John's College, Cambridge, Squire became chaplain to the duke of Newcastle in 1748, retaining the valuable livings of St. Anne's, Soho, and the parish church of Greenwich after his consecration as bishop of St. David's in 1761.[63] He dealt strangely with curates and Methodists in his diocese in 1763[64] and was preoccupied with the publication of a memoir of Thomas Herring, his old friend and patron. Henry Perfect applied to Samuel Squire after he lost his orders in Blackheath because he had known him there as the vicar of Greenwich enough to form a shrewd opinion of him. Other criminous clergymen, according to Secker's information, included the vicar of Bapchild, Sir Samuel Bickley, who was accused of sodomitical practices, was pilloried and then imprisoned;[65] and another who preached a sermon at St. Paul's and made off with the collection, leaving his wife and family, and was "lately running about the diocese of Norwich with a woman."[66] Another drew Secker's ire because he was "master at this time of a slaughter house, and other temporal business."[67]

Dispensations

A dispensation to hold more than one living could be obtained by writing direct to the Archbishop of Canterbury and submitting a piece of Latin prose on a biblical or theological topic. This is an illustration of how Canterbury exercised some jurisdiction over York, in that the examples found were pluralists wholly within the jurisdiction of York and were not applying to Canterbury simply because the second or third living was in the southern province. The Secker Papers contain several such applications, including some from Yorkshire clergy who appeared in the 1764 visitation as pluralists, showing that the procedure was effective at the time when they applied.[68] Thomas Secker showed characteristic eighteenth-century attitudes towards pluralism and absenteeism in a detailed letter to Drummond.[69] Those who applied for dispensations by their Latin proses should have been rich enough to provide adequate curate cover in their parishes or chapelries, but this was not always so. The letter to Drummond is especially interesting because Secker referred to the clergy not knowing widely of this method of obtaining a dispensation. He said he was pleased that the clergy did not make much use of this type of application because he had misgivings about its procedure. The applicant had to state the distance of the livings from each other. Secker complained that he had no means in law of finding out from other bishops how far one living was from another when he was considering granting a dispensation. It is surprising that he should spend so much time on what seems a detail, when he had all sorts of other business to cover: political and parliamentary and court affairs, overseas mail, the application of Queen Anne's Bounty, a fund for the relief of clergy orphans and widows. The answer may lie in the season of the year: in August many people were out of town, and there were no sittings of the House of Lords. The archbishop probably had more time than usual.

There is another shaft of light on the matter of the jurisdiction of the two courts of Canterbury and York, but it came after Secker's death and in the latter years of Drummond's archiepiscopate, when the legality of probates was challenged in some substantial cases where property was held in the north as well as in the south. The Prerogative Court of Canterbury had overreached itself in issuing probate comprehensively. This not only diminished the jurisdiction of York but was held to be illegal. The mistake had arisen even among attorneys because of the comprehensive wording of probates and presumably also because of the need to complete the business, but the situation was being addressed in the closing years of Drummond's archiepiscopate because "the archbishop's testamentary jurisdiction was of great consequence and probably one of the most valuable things in his patronage."[70] The York Exchequer Court was doing more business as some of the townspeople of the north were becoming wealthier.

The hard attitudes shown by the archbishops towards possible recruits as ministers of religion in the mid-eighteenth century do not accord with what is still thought of as an age of negligence. The right to hold livings in plurality because the applicant could write a piece of Latin prose to be filed in Lambeth Palace was not widely exercised. Secker's conscience was disturbed not because that right was part of a faulty system but because it was difficult to check. His attitude to dispensations contrasts with the many Lambeth directives against candidates who were, for example, too young to apply for holy orders, but who were the right age by the time the warnings had been written and circulated. The archiepiscopal attitudes were in keeping with the greater value ascribed to incumbency rather than to people in the parishes, to the respect for property rather than for ministry. There was strictness about the men appointed and laxity about the man-made rules they could not keep.

Upholding the Settlements of 1688 and 1689

The Glorious Revolution and Act of Settlement initially caused the Church of England many "uneasy consciences"[71] among those who were persuaded to swear allegiance to King William, but this did not lessen the need to maintain vigilance against the threat from Rome, which had driven so many members of the church to their uncharacteristic act of disloyalty in 1688. The Toleration Act of 1689 was chiefly for the benefit of Protestant dissenters, and it remained necessary for bishops and archbishops to keep themselves well informed about anything that might concern the strength of the Roman Catholic church abroad as well as at home. Secker had a fortunate and unique source of information about one aspect of the Roman church in that Drummond's brother, Lord Kinnoull,[72] was in Portugal at the time of their correspondence during 1763. Drummond had earlier reported events to Secker and made some plain forecasts about the relations between church and state in Portugal.[73] International politics required a thorough understanding of the Roman Catholic church. The rebellions of 1715 and 1745 were not so distant as to be unrepeatable. The strength of the Roman Catholics in Yorkshire was a continuing piece of information supplied to Drummond by his archdeacons. The year of more sustained correspondence with Secker (1763) was the year of the Peace after the Seven Years' War. It was essential for the Georgian church hierarchy to monitor the relations with Roman Catholic countries.

Maintaining the Freedom and Authority of the Episcopate

The Anglican church of the 1760s relied on the strength of its bishops both for organization of loyal worship and for the declaration of the church's voice in the House of Lords. These ideas are implicit though unmistakable in the correspondence between the two archbishops. Frances Knight has challenged Peter Virgin's criticisms of the bishops' competence,[74] but there is still reason to regard the Bishop of St. David's as a possible weak link in detecting unsuitable candidates for the ministry and granting unwarranted orders. Nevertheless, his actions were not criticized in Secker's letters to Drummond because the freedom to exercise episcopal authority was recognized. Another example of the freedom of the bishops to conduct their business as they pleased—and to leave it alone for much of the time—is in a letter of 13 August in which Secker informed Drummond, as a matter of interest, about the intentions of the new bishop of Exeter, the Honorable Frederick Keppel, who was planning to go into his diocese in October, "if all be quiet there." He was referring to the riots during the debates about the cider tax. According to Sykes,[75] it would have been more usual for a bishop to be traveling from his diocese at this time of year, but this was probably Keppel's first opportunity to visit his new diocese.[76] Bishops were more likely to be constrained by their social and political obligations in London than by anything the archbishops might wish to say concerning their whereabouts at any particular time of year, even if they had thought it were any of their business.

Two other examples of archiepiscopal collaboration over the extension of the church of England abroad show that Drummond's work in his partnership with Secker did reach a higher level of content and consisted of top priority national politics.

Ambitions for the Church in the New World

Secker and Drummond shared a plan for bishops in America that put them out of line with the government's course of action. Their thinking in this matter was in marked contrast with their attitude to every other issue of church governance. In dealing with the church at home in terms of staffing, training, ordination, presentation and patronage, absenteeism and pluralism, discipline and toleration, as has been shown, they were traditional and unadventurous. They were guardians of the status quo, unaware of the potential for change and ill-prepared for reform. America presented them with different opportunities. Their vision was to establish an episcopal system in America, a plan that was neither daring nor innovative. The SPG had set out a scheme for bishops in America in 1712, but the death of Queen Anne had shelved it.[77] Such a scheme must have seemed common sense to the two archbishops. The idea of the bishop of London working through a commissary to deal with the vast and potentially populous area of the North American colonies was so restricting as to impoverish the growth of the Anglican church. Both Secker and Drummond were prepared to argue for the need for change in this matter, but their ideas were quashed by Lord Shelburne. That was as far as they were prepared to go, for they accepted his overruling, seeing that the Church of England took a "minor role in a politically conceived greater scheme of things."[78]

As partners in governing the Church of England in the mid eighteenth century, they were loyal guardians of the work of the SPCK, founded in 1698, and the SPG, founded in 1701. These two societies worked alongside the commission for the American colonies overseen by the Bishop of London. It was no doubt their work for the societies that convinced them of the need for bishops in America. They busied themselves in committee work, dealing with the spiritual and material fortunes of the two societies. They put their energies to fund raising by preaching sermons, writing treatises about Anglican relationships with other denominations in the thirteen colonies and the West Indies, attending board meetings, and negotiating the societies' finances. At the same time they had been preparing their case about bishops for America, biding their time, and awaiting the appropriate occasion.

The arguments in favor of bishops for America were prepared by Drummond and probably requested by Secker. The work is dated June 1764 and forms part of the Secker papers at Lambeth.[79] It is entitled *Thoughts upon the Present State of the Church of England in America by Archbishop Drummond.* It is Drummond's work, handwritten by a copyist. It is a reasoned summary of the need for episcopal control in America, setting out the historical development of the colonies and the connection throughout their growth with denominational issues. It examines the customary usage of the jurisdiction by commissary of the bishop of London and outlines the deficiencies of that system. Drummond described a four-point geographical plan, suggesting Burlington in New Jersey, William and Mary College in Virginia, Charlestown in South Carolina, and Codrington College in Barbados as the episcopal residences of four suffragan bishops. If created, these would have been the first suffragans since the Reformation. As it was, the church had to wait until 1870. For the bishops' salaries, Drummond proposed a minimum of £1,000 and an optimum of £1,500 as "sufficient to secure a proper Respect." He added that "the people of the Colonies must not be burthened with the maintenance of the bishops; but the Income may be raised by many ways, some more eligible than others." This matter was not left to imagination or speculation, and he went on to explain ways in which investments could be made of various benefactions; a reference was also made to the quitrents of Virginia.

Before these ideas had a chance to surface, an opportunity for the SPG to buy an estate in Barbados, belonging formerly to a Mrs. Whitaker, provoked correspondence between the two archbishops. Secker knew that Drummond's expertise in business negotiations was authoritative within the SPG board and that he was able to sort out difficulties of title and ownership. Drummond's opinion was that the matter had to be dealt with by attorneys in the West Indies and that if a full committee of the SPG could not be gathered in London (it was September, when some people might still be away), then it warranted an extraordinary board meeting to do the business as quickly as possible. Purchasing the title to Mrs. Whitaker's estate would be a coup for the society. But the affair ground slowly forwards. The time taken for mail to cross the Atlantic meant that in December 1763 they were still not much closer to acquiring the estate. Drummond was writing in the pre-Wilberforce[80] climate of seeing the plantations in purely economic terms. At the end of the year, Drummond was unwell and could not attend the society's meeting to transact business but he wrote from Dartmouth Street with his apology and some essential advice.[81] His style was uncharacteristically terse, his usual amiability being in short supply because of his indisposition.

One and a half years later, the two archbishops were still corresponding about the purchase of Mrs. Whitaker's estate, but the same letter[82] has information about their hopes for establishing bishops in America. It shows how Drummond's geniality and hospitality were put to some good use in turning to matters of such seriousness. He wrote to Secker,

> I am just out of the hurry of the week of York races, which brings a great deal of company. I had a good deal of conversation with Lord Rockingham: and, among many other matters, I mentioned the ecclesiastical state of Canada and also of all our Colonies, and I shall at his desire, send him a copy of the two papers relating to them. I fear that the very uncertain and disturbed state of the Colonies, which has increased considerably in this last year, will be made a reason to postpone what relates to the Bishops in America.

This illustrates that Drummond was alert to the political process. Rockingham began his term of office as prime minister as recently as 13 July, and Drummond had managed to lobby him when offering hospitality at York only a month afterwards. Bishopthorpe Palace is within a mile of the racecourse at York, so it is little surprise that the local aristocracy found Drummond's hospitality both welcome and convenient. The letter also illustrates that Drummond considered an episcopal settlement for North America as a realistic possibility and that the disturbed state of the Colonies represented only a temporary setback. Rockingham, for his part, was keen to accept hospitality from Drummond because he was one of the "cordial acquaintances" on whom he built and sustained his party and organized his "sensible system," as Steven Watson has explained.[83]

Drummond's part in the attempt to provide bishops for America was genuine and understated. He is not as widely recognized as Secker for being actively in favor of such a spread of Anglican governance and deserves more credit for working alongside Secker in an unpublicized way, seeing people such as Rockingham and putting the arguments together quietly.[84] Ever since the translation of Secker to the primacy, those in the church who wanted bishops for America were optimistic, while the colonists and "most of the dissenters" were fearful.[85] Drummond's partnership with Secker continued firmly on the path towards episcopal government for America until Secker's death. In the spring of 1767 Archbishop Drummond and Archbishop Secker waited on Lord Shelburne, the secretary of state, with the particular aim of speaking to him about the ecclesiastical affairs of Canada and about the appointment of bishops for America. Secker recorded the meeting in his autobiography: "We had a long conversation with him. The Archbishop [of York] dwelt chiefly on the former point, in which he seemed well disposed. I dwelt chiefly on the latter, but could make no impression on him."[86] This was not a failure of the partnership between the two archbishops nor was it because they timed their plan poorly. It was because they had a vision for the church which was denied to the politicians of their day and because those politicians misread the temper of the colonists. Shelburne, though, was hardly likely to be a patron of episcopacy. In 1774 his dissenting interests led him to become Joseph Priestley's patron. It was the misfortune of Secker and Drummond that Shelburne happened to be the southern division secretary of state at the time they sought him. To give Shelburne some credit, however, his own plan of land organization had involved a decentralizing control of the hinterland and a greater freedom for the colonists to expand wherever they could, but "he had been forced by his colleagues to modify the scheme and to admit more supervision by English agents."[87] But he was also forced out of office, and the planning passed to the hands of Townshend and to the system of import duties, which led to the Boston Tea Party of 1773. Lord North's government was too concerned with retribution ever to look again at any scheme for bishops for America. The efforts of Secker and Drummond were twenty years ahead of their time, as it was not until February 1787 that the first bishops were consecrated to the sees of Pennsylvania and New York after an act of Parliament had made that legal. A similar structure for Canada was begun soon afterwards.[88]

There is no record of Drummond's involvement in the sensation created by the knowledge that Secker left two thousand pounds in his will to the SPG, half of which was to help to establish a colonial bishop.[89] By the 1770s it became less and less likely that such a plan could be implemented. Drummond's disappointed realism would have prevailed. The beneficiaries of his own will were strictly within his family.[90]

Defending the Church at Home: Sensitivities to Queen Anne's Bounty

Whereas the death of Queen Anne had blunted the point of the SPG's probe for bishops for America, the ecclesiastical settlements of her reign gave some financial relief to poorer clergy during the rest of the eighteenth century and beyond. An outline of the operation of Queen Anne's Bounty has been given in Chapter 4. A brief reference has also been made to Secker's alarm about the governors of the fund being open to criticism for having too much in hand and being slow in making their allocations. Not only did Secker prepare explanations for the newspapers on that topic, he also wrote to Drummond. In the early part of 1767 the two archbishops joined in intricate but quickly exchanged letters across the Thames to sort out the situation. Not surprisingly, Secker was alarmed when he found that eighty-eight thousand pounds was unappropriated: "How can we answer for this Neglect, to the Publick, to the Clergy, to ourselves? Ought we not to take immediately the speediest methods of reducing this enormous sum to a moderate one?" It was indeed an enormous sum, and Secker's conscience was always acute: "For what if the House of Commons should get to the start of us and and call us to account for our supineness?"

Drummond was equally surprised and concerned but readier with the positive suggestion that the date of the next board meeting should be on 20 or 22 January. After that board meeting, Drummond sent Secker a statement of the fund as it stood at the end of 1766, "as perhaps it may save you a little trouble." Secker took the trouble to copy it all out in his own hand, and he recorded what he did about it in his autobiography:[91]

> And having found, what no one else of the Governors suspected that a very large sum of their money in the Funds was unappropriated, I laid the matter before them at their meeting in January this year, and with the assistance of the Archbishop of York, procured about 200 livings to be immediately augmented by lot with £200 each; which hath reduced the unappropriated money to so moderate a sum, that it can give no ground for complaint.

The interference of the weather in their plans to deal in person instead of by correspondence did not delay the business unduly; the messengers were probably more sprightly people. Crossing the Thames was easier than posting from London to York, and is an instance for good in Sykes's comment about bishops residing mainly in London during the winter.[92]

The Success of their Partnership in Ordering the Georgian Church

The good relations that prevailed between the two primates spills out of the correspondence, and the greater volume extant in the direction of Canterbury to York shows how easy it must have been for the amiable Drummond to work closely with his senior colleague. Secker's letters to Drummond show kindness and care to a colleague too far away in summer time to be able to hear London news firsthand. His written style has an attractive quality. Both cared for the opinion of others regarding the church and its image. Each used his skills to promote the well-being of the church especially when threats arose. Other people viewed them differently. Horace Walpole was one such. He disliked Secker to the point of acidity but had praise for Drummond.[93] Secker, who knew of this dislike, ordered that his *Letter to H. Walpole,* written as early as 1750-51 concerning bishops in America should wait until after his death for publication.

They were secure in the knowledge that they had the support of the monarchy for the bond between church and state. The House of Lords was not affected by the changes that altered economics and society in their time; this meeting point highlighted their official partnership as the two guardians of the Georgian church.

Mutual esteem, grace, and true regard connected the two primates of the Georgian church in the mid eighteenth century. Their correspondence reveals the strengths and weaknesses of the Church of England and, in its lack of focus on issues that were to become of crucial importance for the Church of England, accords with the spirit of their age.

8
Conclusion

The Career of Robert Drummond: A Summary

Robert Drummond made his mark as a diocesan bishop in Wales, Salisbury, and York during the twenty-eight years from 1748 to 1776, a span which should be sufficient for the historian to evaluate his contribution to the wider scene of the Georgian church as well as to the diocese of York. Drummond's nature, however, was untypical of his age—a time when people sought renown or derived dishonor for their discourses and treatises, alignments and associations. Drummond remained reticent towards publishers and developed a disregard for posterity. So his contribution to the Georgian church has been scarcely acknowledged and unwarrantedly obscure. Investigation of the records shows that he conducted visitations, ordinations, and confirmations more regularly than most, and that he was frequent in attendance at and regular in participation of the business of the House of Lords. He ordered a province and administered an extensive diocese with efficiency and traditional confidence in an age of altering circumstances.

Two of Drummond's archdeacons were below par: Scrope Berdmore of Nottinghamshire was a stand-in whose level was friendly inactivity glossed by experienced advice; Francis Blackburne was a tangential activist whose contribution to Anglican church life was potentially damaging and on a completely different plane from that of his archbishop. In this uneasy situation the diocese was commanded by a well-traveled aristocratic intellectual, a straightforward family man, an administrator who had consistently put canonical duty high on his list of priorities, but a prince of the eighteenth-century church who had no wish to alter that church's framework. Drummond's one venture in a cause of national importance, that of promoting bishops for America, was blocked by political opposition on both sides of the Atlantic on a scale that doomed the attempt from its outset. A Newcastle protege, he protested successfully when necessary against being at his patron's beck and call, and he had already been selected by royal favor as chaplain to George II before the Newcastle patronage assisted his ascent. His correspondence with Newcastle while he was in Hanover with the king on campaign was the indicator of his worth as an unofficial foreign correspondent. Drummond gave his patron good measure, faithfully reporting the king's health and temper, the moods of the army and of its commanders, allies and enemies, with a discernment that added to the powerful duke's network of official information. The correspondence is a valuable historical source in its own right. Throughout the years of dependence on Newcastle's patronage, Drummond successfully kept his loyalties within the network (including those from Westminster School), showing courageous fidelity to Andrew Stone and Lord Mansfield. But it was in the exercise of his own proper and ordinary duties that Drummond made his greatest contribution to Hanoverian society as an eighteenth-century prelate, in the regular and repeated visitations of the diocese of St. Asaph and York. Both areas may be reckoned as "difficult," Wales because of the language barrier and cultural distance and York because of its extent and rugged terrain. Robert Drummond's visitations were carefully planned, with clearly structured routes, appropriately designed questions, and efficiently ordered timetables incorporating agreed preachers of sermons for the occasions.

Drummond lacked the raw ambition that drove some of the other Newcastle proteges to push for advancement (chapter 2, section 6), though the family connection with Newcastle gave him further advantage in the patronage scales. The patronage system of preferment, so abhorrent to late nineteenth century writers such as Mary Bateson, is even described by one current writer, studying the Lyall connection, as "compatible with merit."[1] In Drummond's case, the desire to obtain the archbishopric of York found voice only when the possibility seemed realistic. His interest in a church career was based on his respect for authority in church law, and he was content to fulfill its obligations during a thirteen-year period in a Welsh see without the sort of protests made by other bishops on similar career paths. He originally thought of a military career but chose the church. His Scottish family inheritance gave him a comfortable financial and social position, but he was not too aristocratic to marry a woman from the family of a rich London merchant. Impressed by what he saw on the Grand Tour and devoted to a full family life, he eventually found scope for building on a palatial scale by commissioning a redesigned west front and main approach to Bishopthorpe Palace, to which he invited guests and entertained them appropriately. Throughout all this he was tutor to his own large brood of children. His was a time when the higher clergy were the foremost pluralists, but he gave up his one parochial cure at the time of his translation to Salisbury. Drummond's career occupied the very middle of the eighteenth century, and he was typical of that age, comfortable up to the point of complacency, reassuring himself, as did his brother at Canterbury, of *omnia bene*.[2] They passed on this complacency to their successors, who were still of the eighteenth-century church "that had not yet adjusted to the past, when it began to suspect that it was not remotely in touch with its present."[3] With Drummond's attested manly behavior, his contribution across the span of his mid-century career was of duty faithfully and capably done, not as a visionary or a prophet, but confident in the day-to-day, year-by-year diocesan business. It is as easy to relate what he was not, as it is to enumerate his capabilities. Although he was the father of a large family, he was not a nepotist, only the youngest of his sons taking holy orders and going on to serve a parish not in England but in Scotland. Although his politics were Whiggish, his political activities were not faction-ridden and he owed loyalty to the crown before party. He was not like Bishop Green of Lincoln—indolent, though kindly and dignified, but much absent from his diocese.[4] He was not imperious or haughty, as some thought archbishop Gilbert, his predecessor.[5] He was not ambitious for recognition as a preacher. He was not a scholarly recluse but used his legal and administrative talents in parliamentary committee as well as debate. He was certainly not a reformer. He seems to have had no ear for music. His amiability is the characteristic that was most often mentioned in his favor.

The evidence of Drummond's work from one year out of the twenty-eight, that of the 1764 visitation, encapsulates his constant endeavor and reveals his capacity for extra workloads. Equipped with experience from the Welsh see of St. Asaph, where his regular residences and visitations enabled the life of the parishes to run smoothly, he conducted the York visitation with controlled efficiency, preferring to be out and about than to toil over his desk. He elicited from his parish clergy a unique corpus of evidence for the life of a very substantial section of the Georgian church. He paid careful attention to the recusancy figures, and he asked his own clergy some new questions about their accommodation and told them to set out their answers in readable and elegant style. A study of some of his correspondence during that year of visitation allows the historian to appreciate his qualities. He was a Georgian bishop who was not ponderous, not elderly and distant, not reclusive or lame, not theologically controversial, not an archpluralist, not negligent, keeping his amiability through all the encounters of the visitation, with the exception of the untruthful Thomas Hudson whose impassioned letters and fantasy-driven excuses eventually brought him to a boiling point.

The Lingering Ill Repute of the Eighteenth-century Church: Some Perspectives

The bad name of the eighteenth-century church, awarded by its own contemporary enemies and perpetuated by several writers through the nineteenth and twentieth centuries,[6] has contributed to the scant attention paid to Robert Drummond as bishop of St. Asaph and archbishop of York. The current trend of regional historical studies has begun to recognize the relatively competent character of some eighteenth-century bishops and archbishops.[7] Such enquiries depend chiefly on visitation material and are open to the several limitations of this material in establishing exactly what level of ministry the church was achieving during the Hanoverian decades. Much of this work points to a longer period of satisfactory church life and clerical duty than was previously thought, for example by Ollard and Walker, who saw decline after 1743. This longer period of satisfactory church life has been seen to extend in some instances up to as late as 1780,[8] before the problems of pluralism, absenteeism, church poverty, and curtailment of services added up to a failure of ministry. But opinion among historians remains divided, so that an aristocratic prelate such as Drummond, who had no interest in reform or innovation, who showed no strong theological insight, and whose prevailing concerns were with the satisfied maintenance of the steady status quo, has attracted little interest beyond brief tributes to his straightforward competence. Of the two groups of caution identified among the historians of the eighteenth-century church (the cautious optimists and the cautious pessimists)[9] the former could include Drummond in their theme on the basis of his energy, good health, and vigorous discharge of duty. The cautious pessimists, however, would have scope in a survey of the imperfections of the late eighteenth-century church following directly from Drummond's time and in uncovering his own easy, untroubled, and comfortable attitudes. A concluding summary of the 1764 visitation returns is appropriate, however, before a fuller assessment of Drummond's leadership in the mid eighteenth century may be made and his legacy to the Georgian church fathomed.

THE DIFFERENCE MADE BY THE 1764 VISITATION RETURNS: SOME QUANTIFIABLE AND UNQUANTIFIABLE EVIDENCE

The history of the eighteenth-century church in Yorkshire has received somewhat less attention from scholars[10] than the history of the growth and strength of the Nonconformists, especially the Methodists. This is not surprising, in that the history of Methodism was new and was undertaken in a way that mirrored its regional or "circuit" style of organization: new Methodist societies throughout the kingdom bred their own chroniclers, and when the divisions arose subsequently between Wesleyans, Primitives, and Bible Christians, each group had a new story to relate that overshadowed the sameness of the parish church. Such historians could turn to the very detailed information in Wesley's *Journal,* letters, sermons, the minutes of the Methodist conference and all the societies' records of class lists, leaders' names, preachments, and itineraries. Such a wealth of detail, with other Methodist journals, anecdotes and biographies of Yorkshire worthies, and later the evidence of chapel building, has been of great importance, but it has left in its wake the idea that the Church of England itself was somnolent the while. That idea appealed to the reformers of the church so that the Yorkshire of the parishes, with its catechisms and charities, its schools and hospitals, penances even, and church courts became submerged into unattractive emptiness.

Interest revived in the fortunes of the Church of England only when the Evangelicals, the Tractarians and the Oxford Movement crowded the stage, though John Walsh's pioneering study of the Yorkshire Evangelicals of the late eighteenth century remains a lonely reminder of a still neglected area of study. Bearing in mind all the checks and balances essential for the historian's use of Anglican diocesan visitation material as set out in the Introduction, the returns of 1764 have a unique contribution to make to the history of that period before new movements were stirring within the Church in Yorkshire. Impressions of the life of the eighteenth-century Church in Yorkshire, which previously depended chiefly on the work of Ollard and Walker in their editing study of the 1743 visitation returns, can be corrected.

These conclusions, derived from the visitation returns of the

York diocese in 1764, can then be added to other regional studies of the southwest of England,[11] the capital,[12] and East Anglia,[13] along with selective studies[14] over some quite extended periods of visitation evidence in several dioceses. The results on the one hand in part sustain the image of negligence through detailed consideration of clergy incomes and a very elderly hierarchy, and on the other hand replace the image of negligence with one of duty competently undertaken at the parochial level. The weight of data from 621 parishes of the York diocese relating to the one visitation year of 1764 is a strong injection of corroborating evidence for both aspects: the continuation of much clerical poverty as well as the ongoing efforts of much conscientious ministry on the other. The very fact of these visitations, however, is a starting point for crediting the hierarchy, in the person of Robert Drummond in this case, for doing so much diocesan duty and accounting for so many parish clergy complying with so much quantifiable information. In the case of Yorkshire, the visitation returns make it possible to look with comparative analysis at two separate points of the eighteenth-century church—1743 and 1764—a sufficient time distance to allow for the discernment of trends and movements of population, and to conclude that—whatever may have happened later—in 1764 the diocese was in reasonably good health.

If one factor alone were to be selected as the fundamental test for the health of church life out of the 1764 visitation returns, it would be the evidence of catechism. The overwhelmingly positive response on this topic, its lively variety, and its great sensitivity to individual needs is unmistakable for its dedication. Catechism—more than Sunday services and their attendance, more than sermons, more than frequency or rarity of Holy Communion—reveals the clergy and the laity engaged closely and face to face with the teachings of the church. Sermons could go unheard or unheeded, though the evidence is that they were afterwards printed and read; services were the showground of the celebrant and the social forum for the parishioners, but catechism, in its question and answer mode whether formally in church or less formally in parsonages, meant that the learners progressed in understanding or recognition and that the teachers expended effort in instructing, explaining, and examining. The very high number of those involved in catechizing at some time or other during the year (94.5 percent) is a plain fact about church life in the northern province and a reliable guide to the health of the wider Georgian church at mid century. This evidence is sufficient to place the Georgian church a very long way from the descriptions used by the critical writers cited in the Introduction.

The Yorkshire visitation returns of 1764 also contain a subtext of unquantifiable but significant features which add to the picture of the Georgian church. They disclose the church as different from the "spiritual inertness,"[15] "sham,"[16] "spiritual apathy and decadence,"[17] and "indolence . . . factiousness and bigotry,"[18] reported by its denigrators. The tone of the replies to the archbishop's queries—an unquantifiable concept—consists of a variety of attitudes, as noted in chapter 4, the majority of which show conscientious respect for their archbishop and their parishioners, and a minority whose brevity, obsequiousness, or evasiveness stand out in contrast. Those in busy urban situations such as Legh of Halifax and Kirshaw of Leeds are historical vignettes by virtue of the enormous amount of detail crammed nevertheless legibly into a small space. The unquantifiable features of examples such as these have attracted the interest of recent writers in their efforts to dispel the "reform perspective" as a guide to the health of the eighteenth-century church.[19] The unquantifiable features in the returns consist, in the cases of Halifax and Leeds, in the obvious desire of the incumbents to tell every detail fully. In the wider context of the Georgian church, such entries could not have been made by clergy who had "dead consciences" or to whom the rubrics were a "dead letter," or who presided over "a sham."[20] The conscientious records of rural clergy whose total cure of souls was typically about 150 people across two or three parishes have also been noted for their full and apparently truthful answers (chapters 4, 5, and 6). These were clergy who, without *éclat* or renown, served their parishioners with a wholehearted application to the church's calendar and a traditional regard for its festivals, fasts, its penitential seasons, and its thanksgivings. Historically significant, though for opposite reasons, are the entries in one-word answers, written with thick-nibbed pens and giving the least possible information, reinforcing the perception of dissatisfaction among impoverished clergy. So the two parallel interpretations continue among current writers: the cautious optimists and the cautious pessimists.[21] The cautious optimists (Walsh, Barrie-Curien, Gregory and Clark, for example) have used material more consistently from the middle years of the eighteenth century, allotting the "pastoral crisis" to the last two decades of the eighteenth century and "the overwhelming of the Church's parochial system" to 1809. By that reckoning, Drummond's Yorkshire and the Georgian church as a whole acquire a fresher appraisal.[22] On the other hand, the cautious pessimists (Virgin and Brose, for example) have referred in more detail to the last quarter of the eighteenth century and the first quarter of the nineteenth century in arriving at their conclusions. By that reckoning, Drummond's Yorkshire (1761–1776) and the Georgian church stood a little way still from the brink of collapse, and the picture given by the returns of 1764 are significantly valuable for the period of broad and comfortable calm.

Drummond's Church: His Leadership and Legacy

The period of broad and comfortable calm of the Drummond years was neither enduring nor all-pervasive, and might be characterized as superficial. Some writers agree that by 1780—four years after the death of Robert Drummond—the imperfections in the Georgian church were so noticeable as to be serious deficiencies. In the light of the undeniable deterioration of the church's ministry by the later part of the eighteenth century, it may be concluded that Drummond's leadership was to some extent amiss. It maintained the appearance of efficiency but failed to anticipate the problems to come. The visitation returns of 1764 disclose a church able to provide most of the traditional aspects of church life, but in a way that had no forward policy, no thought for the needs of the changing present or the transformation of the future. That level of ministry proved insufficient. Already in 1764 the features that were to become problems were present just below the surface, but went unnoticed by those whose positions required them to look: the church hierarchy. The archbishops and bishops had no plan to relieve the poverty of curates beyond the annual lottery of Queen Anne's Bounty; the bishops and archdeacons did not consider how to prevent the damaging effects of increasingly widespread pluralism and nonresidence; they had no idea of altering the "neighbouring incumbent syndrome" with its easy tendency to settle for one service per Sunday per two parishes. Moreover, they appeared to be uninterested in the paucity of demand for and provision of weekday services and the decreasing frequency of Holy Communion as stated in and implied by the Book of Common Prayer. More significantly, the hierarchy was powerless to prevent the alternative ministries available from the other denominations.

Drummond had the opportunity to discern all the features of this situation—the pluralism and absenteeism, the neighboring incumbent syndrome, the small numbers who held weekday services, the poverty of curates—from his visitation returns of 1764.

His abbreviated written response to the returns (chapter 3, section 7) may have been the prelude to an active "on the hoof" discovery during his successive confirmation tours, or may have been the result of minimal effort. It almost certainly lacked insight into a deteriorating level of ministry in a diocese where people were increasing in number and where the spiritual needs of many were being met by agencies other than the Church of England, for Drummond ignored Methodism and its implications. Within his own diocese he also brushed aside any serious notice of revivalism and its implications.

Drummond's capabilities have been appreciated and his generous and benevolent disposition well attested, but although he occupied the position of superior importance in the northern province of the church, his efficiency was limited by some obvious faults.

In disputes which he was called to settle, such as the aggrieved Jonathan Jackson of Silsden, he chose to assume that a curate was a lesser being. Similarly in the case of Darrington, where the incumbent, John Jones, was an absentee and whose curate, Dade, failed to present himself at the visitation, Drummond favored the incumbent rather than the curate simply on grounds that Jones had had the good manners (or the precaution) to send his apologies in writing. In the case of Thomas Hudson of Stokesley, Drummond imposed his disciplinary ban on the erring curate and added severe comment. These were hardly cases which could have been indications to Drummond that the church was falling short in its ministry at Silsden, Darrington, and wherever Thomas Hudson set his unfortunate foot, as they were the sort of incidents which occur in any age and in other walks of life. They nevertheless indicate the aristocratic attitudes of an archbishop who upheld the class rules of precedence in ecclesiastical as well as social issues. At this time the best and the last features of the old church were still in evidence. His nature was such that he was willingly deceived into thinking that the situation did not require any propping, any deep probing, and warranted no disquiet. His was the easy comfort of the respected archbishop of York, partner to a gracious archbishop of Canterbury who corresponded with him about little flaws in their revered ecclesiastical system, while being unable to see that their satisfaction had not much farther to run. Although Drummond had helped Secker in the attempt to bring episcopal government to the church in America, he was blind to the social and ecclesiastical opportunities that waited for attention in Yorkshire and more widely in England. This weakness was shared by most others of his age and class and calling, and the historian should accord to Drummond the regard due for his efficiency and good order within the limits of his times.

The last years of Drummond's archiepiscopate heralded the expansion of Nonconformity. The founding of new chapels—Baptist, Independent, and Methodist—gathered pace in the last two decades of the eighteenth century. For that to have happened, the founders had to have been confidently active in the immediately preceding years, possibly raising funds, finding suitable sites, and engaging builders, all the while strengthening their own membership. During these years Drummond handed out information regarding Nonconformist activities week by week in various parts of the parishes of his diocese. He had been given information about the numbers who attended those meetings, how frequently they were held, and in some cases the names of people who led them. This data had been collated in response to his own particular questions, and yet it lay untapped, seemingly of less concern to him than the similar answers about the Roman Catholic activities. He held the evidence in his palace at Bishopthorpe but was unaware that it pointed to the precipice which the church was approaching. His years as archbishop marked the end of the old national church before the Methodists separated from it, before the revivalists divided it, before the Americans declared their independence from the Hanoverian monarchy, before the irrevocable divisions in the era of reform.

Few individuals within the eighteenth-century church wished to alter the system. Wesley, Whitefield, Ingham, Blackburne, Lindsey and, later, Wilberforce, all had an interest in Yorkshire, and some of these felt obliged eventually to work outside the Church of England. Clergy initiatives for a new translation of the Bible or a revision of the Book of Common Prayer met with no support from Archbishop Drummond, but a personal request to him for help in providing catechetical instruction booklets was favored. Apparently many churchmen were satisfied with their church and thought that it could withstand turbulence. Those in Yorkshire who suffered at the hands of an overbearing lay patron had an archbishop in Robert Drummond, whose sense and knowledge could rescue them if their cause was justifiable. Those who committed misdemeanours of drunkenness, immorality, and fraud could expect discipline as soon as the archbishop had dealt with letters of parishioners' complaints. But throughout the vast extent of the diocese those who abused the pluralist norms could continue their abuse, risking a presentment only at times of visitation, and even then being able to dodge censure if they wrote their excuses with sufficient charm, grace, or daring.

The visitation returns and other evidence in the time of Archbishop Drummond portray the church in Yorkshire and in the wider national scene as a superficially sound cover over a ground in which deeply damaging cracks were forming. The quality and the depth of the cover varied throughout the aspects of church life, being noticeably strong in catechisms, strong in sermons, quite strong in charities and schools, but at only half strength in offering two services on Sundays in less than half the parishes across the diocese. In observing weekday prayers, the clergy's commitment was generally weak, though the places where Wednesday and Friday prayers and daily prayers were held were the most densely populated. In attracting its members to attend Holy Communion, the Yorkshire church was also generally weak but redeemed by a few areas of noticeable and growing strength.

So the diocese was a patchy affair. The emerging cracks were made worse by the low pay of curates serving large populations and by the slowly gathering power of the Nonconformist denominations. In 1764 these flaws were not easily discernible to those who had no interest in reform and no desire for change, and the damage being caused awaited the reforming drive of a later age. Those who did sense the possibility of problems reacted variously. Henry Venn decided, before he left Yorkshire for Huntingdon, to assist the Independents by providing for their worship in a new chapel. George Burnett relied on his meetings with the other members of the Elland Society. Archbishop Drummond preferred traditional instruction as a counter to Enthusiasm. Wesley doggedly resisted separation from the Church of England. Francis Blackburne failed in his parliamentary attempt to make the Church of England open to a wider membership so that his son-in-law cut adrift from Anglicanism.

In sum, the church in Yorkshire in the mid-eighteenth century consisted of clergy and laity linked in the continuing seasonal activities of worshipping and educating, almsgiving and receiving, in an age of fluctuating Nonconformist fortunes and population changes. Together with the archbishop's correspondence, of which only a selection has been used for this study, the visitation returns warrant systematic scrutiny to contribute to the current picture of the eighteenth-century church as broadly conscientious and successful by its own standards if not by those of a later and more critical age.

Appendix: Archbishop Drummond's Paper of Queries

To the Reverend ....

Good Brother,

Purposing, if it please God, to visit my diocese this summer, I now transmit to you the following paper of Queries, desiring you to write under each question a distinct and full answer, and send it to me at my house in London before the Visitation, or deliver it to me at my Visitation, signed with your proper name: To the end that, by your assistance, I may be better acquainted with the present state of my diocese, and be enabled to discharge more faithfully the great duty incumbent upon me.

To the favour and blessing of the Almighty I heartily commend you and your labours in his church, and am, Reverend Sir,

Your very affectionate
Friend and Brother
R Ebor

Dartmouth St Westminster
February 2 1764

1. What number of Families have you in your Parish? Of these, how many are Dissenters? And of what sort or Denomination are they?

2. Is there any licenced or other Meeting House in your Parish? How many? Of what sort? How often do they assemble? In what number? Who teaches them?

3. Is there any Public or Charity School, endowed or otherwise maintained in your Parish? When and by whom was the school founded? How is it now supported? Who is Master or Mistress? What number of children, Boys or Girls, are in it? In what Language? Are they cloathed, maintained or lodged? What are they taught? Are they then employed in working, and afterwards put

out to husbandry, trades or services? More particularly, is there care taken to instruct the children in the principles of the Christian Religion, according to the Church of England, and to bring them duly to Church, as the canon requires?

4. Is there . . . any Almshouse, Hospital or other Charitable Endowment? Have any lands or tenements been left for the repair of your church or for any other pious use? Who has the direction of such benefactions? How are they managed? Do you know, or have you heard of any abuses or frauds committed in the management of them? Has there been any Augmentation to your church by Benefaction or Lot from Queen Anne's Bounty, and when? Has there been any purchase of lands in consequence of that Augmentation? And what does that purchase consist in, and amount to yearly?

5. Do you reside personally upon your cure, and in your Parsonage House? If not, where do you reside? And what is the reason of your non-residence?

6. Have you a residing Curate? What is his name? How long has he been Curate? Is he duly qualified according to the canon in that behalf? Doth he live in your Parsonage House?
If not, where doth he live? What allowance do you make him?

7. Do you perform Divine Service in any church beside your own? On what days & at what times is Divine Service performed in your church? If not twice every Lord's Day, with a sermon in the morning, for what reason?

8. Do you know any, who come to church in your parish, that are not Baptised? Or that being baptised, and of a competent age, are not confirmed? have you baptised any adults since my coming to be your bishop? If you have, I desire you to exhibit a schedule of their names and ages.

9. How often, and at what times, do you catechise in your church? Do your parishioners duly send their children and servants to be instructed and catechised? Do they learn any, and what, Exposition for the better under-standing of the church catechism?

10. How often is the Sacrament of the Lord's Supper administred in your church? Do you give open & timely notice . . . ? What

number of communicants are there in your parish? How many of them usually receive? Particularly how many of them did communicate at Easter last? Have you refused the Sacrament to anyone? For what reason? And how has the Person so refused behaved himself since that time?

11. Have you any chapels within your parish? What are the names of them? How far are they distant from the parish church? How are they endowed? By whom, & at what times are they served? Is the Curate duly qualified? By whom, & when was he nominated? Have you any chapel in ruins in which no Divine Service is performed?

12. Have any public penances been performed in your church since I became your bishop? Do you know of any commutations of penance made by any of your parish within the same time? By whom was it done? For what money? And to what use was that money applied?

If you have met with any particular difficulties in the discharge of your duty;—If you have discovered any abuses or corruptions in any ecclesiastical officers;—general, if you have any advice to give, or proposal to make, by which the Glory of God and the Honour and Interest of our established church may be promoted, or the government of this diocese be better ordered, I desire you freely to communicate your thoughts to me: And be assured, that no other use shall be made of your answers or suggestions, but to attain these ends. It would be at this time a further satisfaction to me, if you would write down for me, upon this paper, the dates of your Collation or Institution, of your Deacon's and Priest's orders, and your direction after the manner of the following specimen

Middleton V. John King BA inst Sept 19 1763
D Sept 12 1762 R Ebor
P Sept 18 1763 R Ebor At Middleton, nr Malton, Yorks.

Notes

Introduction

1. J. Gregory, "A Just and Sufficient Maintenance: Some Defences of the Clerical Establishment in the Eighteenth Century,'" *Studies in Church History*, vol. 24 (Oxford, 1987).

2. J. Wickham Legg, *English Church Life from the Restoration to the Tractarian Movement, 1660–1833*, (London, 1914), 105.

3. D. R. Thomas, *A History of the Diocese of St Asaph*, (London, 1870), D. R. Thomas, *Diocesan Histories, St Asaph*, (London, 1888), W. Camidge, *History of Methodism in Bishopthorpe, Fulford, York*, etc., (York, 1908), J. Lyth, *Glimpses of Early Methodism in York*, (York, 1885).

4. In an introductory chapter to essays on nineteenth-century churchmen, the author cites Montesquieu in 1730, "There is no religion in England," as the serious basis for the reform program that the essays examine, "for absenteeism was the rule rather than the exception," Elisabeth Jay (ed.), *The Evangelical and Oxford Movements*, (Cambridge, 1983).

5. Olive J. Brose, *Church and Parliament, The Reshaping of the Church of England 1828–1860*, (London, 1959), 8–9.

6. Sir W. Scott, *Speech . . . relative to the Non-Residence of the Clergy*, (London, 1802), 49.

7. Ibid., 55, though he was proved wrong in the case of the resilient Sydney Smith, who obediently resided at Foston and Londesbrough in Yorkshire, adding greatly out of his moderate resources to the wellbeing of the parishioners and building his own parsonage, *DNB*.

8. An Old Observer (Sir R. Hill), *Spiritual Characteristics . . . in consequence of the Clergy Residence Act*, (London, 1803).

9. Ibid., 36–37.

10. James Bean, *Address to Young Clergymen*, (London, 1809), 1.

11. W. J. Conybeare, *Essays Ecclesiastical and Social*, (London, 1855).

12. W. E. Gladstone, *Gleanings of Past Years*, vol. v, (London, 1879), 7–8.

13. Sydney Smith, at the age of 64, advised Gladstone, "Whenever you meet a clergyman of my age, you may be quite sure he is a bad clergyman." Gladstone added, ". . . he could afford this good-humoured self condemnation . . . as the pastor of a parish he appears to have shown a manly earnestness . . . which, if it did not rise alarmingly high, yet was in advance of the times," *Gleanings of Past Years* vol. vii, (London, 1879), 220.

14. C. J. Abbey and J. H. Overton, *The English Church in the Eighteenth Century*, 2 vols., (London, 1887).

15. M. Bateson, "Clerical Preferment Under the Duke of Newcastle," *English Historical Review*, vol. VII, No XXV, (January, 1892).

16. J. H. Overton and F. Relton, *The English Church 1714–1800*, (London, 1906).

17. S. L. Ollard and P. C. Walker, *Archbishop Herring's Visitation Returns 1743*, 5 vols. (Yorkshire Archaeological Society, 1928–1931).
18. N. Sykes, *Church and State in England in the Eighteenth Century,* (Connecticut, 1934).
19. A. Tindal Hart, Ebor: *A History of the Archbishops of York from Paulinus to McLagan, 627–1908,* (York, 1986).
20. L. Elliott Binns, *The Early Evangelicals,* (London, 1953).
21. R. H. Tawney, *Religion and the Rise of Capitalism,* (London, 1948).
22. Ibid., 193.
23. Rowland Hill, *Spiritual Characteristics,* 2.
24. J. D. Walsh, "The Yorkshire Evangelicals of the Eighteenth Century, with especial reference to Methodism," unpublished Ph.D. Thesis, (University of Cambridge, 1956).
25. A. Warne, *Church and Society in Eighteenth Century Devon,* (David and Charles, 1969).
26. W. M. Jacob, "Church and Society in Norfolk 1707–1806," unpublished Ph.D. Thesis, (University of Exeter, 1982).
27. V. Barrie-Curien, *Clerge et Pastorale en Angleterre au XVIIIe siecel. Le diocese de Londres,* (Paris, 1992).
28. L. Sterne, *A. Political Romance,* (York, 1759), *The Life and Opinions of Tristram Shandy,* (York, 1759); and Ian Jack, ed., *A Sentimental Journey,* (Oxford, 1984).
29. J. Woodforde, *The Diary of a Country Parson,* J. Beresford, ed., 5 vols., (Oxford, 1968).
30. James Downey, *The Eighteenth Century Pulpit,* (Oxford, 1969).
31. Rupert Davies and Gordon Rupp, eds., *A. History of the Methodist Church in Great Britain,* vol. 1, (Epworth, 1965).
32. Henry D. Rack, *Reasonable Enthusiast, John Wesley and the Rise of Methodism,* (Epworth, 1989).
33. F. C. Mather, "Georgian Churchmanship Reconsidered: Some Variations in Anglican Public Worship 1714–1830," *Journal of Ecclesiastical History,* vol. 36, No. 2, (April 1985); *High Church Prophet. Bishop Samuel Horsley (1733–1806) and the Caroline Tradition in the Later Georgian Church,* (Oxford, 1992).
34. Mather, "Georgian Churchmanship," 275–78.
35. Ibid.
36. Ibid., *High Church Prophet,* 10–18.
37. J. C. D. Clark, *English Society 1688–1832,* (Cambridge, 1985).
38. Clark, *English Society,* 217.
39. P. Virgin, *The Church in an Age of Negligence: Ecclesiastical Structure and Problems of Church reform 1700–1840,* (Cambridge, 1989).
40. Frances Knight, "The Hanoverian Church in Transition: Some recent Perspectives," *The Historical Journal,* 36, 3 (Cambridge, 1993).
41. J. Gregory, "The eighteenth-century Reformation: the pastoral task of the Anglican clergy after 1689," in J. Walsh, C. Haydon, S. Taylor (ed.), *The Church of England ca. 1689–ca. 1833 From Toleration to Tractarianism,* (Cambridge, 1993).
42. J. Gregory, "The Speculum of Archbishop Thomas Secker: The Diocese of Canterbury 1758–1768," read to the Church of England Records Society, (Lambeth, 1993, for publication by Boydell and Brewer).
43. Walsh, Haydon, and Taylor, *The Church of England 1689–1833, From Toleration to Tractarianism* (Cambridge, 1993), 4.
44. Ibid., 9.

45. Ibid., 3.
46. Ibid., 13.
47. J. S. Macauley and R. W. Greaves, ed., *The Autobiography of Archbishop Thomas Secker, Archbishop of Canterbury,* (Kansas, 1988).
48. Dr. Hugh Thomas (see chapter 5) and Laurence Sterne, to name two in Yorkshire.
49. Mather, *High Church Prophet,* 37–38.
50. Sykes, *Church and State,* 124.

Chapter 1. Yorkshire and Its Archbishop in the Mid–Eighteenth Century

1. F. O'Gorman, *Voters, Patrons and Parties,* (Oxford, 1989), 289.
2. N. Sykes, *Church and State,* 53–55.
3. Newcastle to Devonshire, 16 November 1762, Add MSS 32945, f 53, British Library, and Sykes, *Church and State,* 53.
4. Drummond to Newcastle, 16 November 1763. Add MSS 32952, f370, British Library.
5. Paul Langford, *Modern British Foreign Policy, The Eighteenth Century 1688–1815,* (London, 1976), 153.
6. O'Gorman, *Voters, Patrons and Parties,* 16, 17.
7. Wilkes laid out £11,000 for Berwick-on-Tweed, which he lost, and Aylesbury, which he won, *Dictionary of National Biography,* (Oxford, 1975), vol. 2, micrographically reproduced text, 243, and F. C. Price, "The Parliamentary Elections in York City 1754–1790," (unpublished M.A. Thesis, Victoria University of Manchester, 1958), 113–16).
8. E. A. Wrigley and R. S. Schofield, *The Population History of England 1541–1871* (Arnold, 1981), 403 and 408.
9. Bp Rec. Ret. H 2. 9 (72), Borthwick Institute of Historical Research (BIHR).
10. W. Riding Treasurer's Accounts, R Bp ex 20 A/B, 174, BIHR.
11. Rack, *Reasonable Enthusiast,* 214.
12. Ernest Payne, "Toleration and Establishment: 1," in Nuttall and Chadwick (ed.), *From Uniformity to Unity,* (SPCK, 1962), 267.
13. Rack, *Reasonable Enthusiast,* 304.
14. Y V/CB 14, BIHR. Christopher Smith was presented for common swearing and John Edmondson was presented in 1759 for swilling ale and keeping disorderly company in his house at Carlton during Divine Service. In 1760 William Shires of Aberford was presented for rude and disorderly behavior during Divine Service. Those presented had to have lawyers to write for them, and the courts often had to convene a second time to claim the payment of these small sums and to hear that other miscreants would behave better in future.
15. Joseph Hunter, *South Yorkshire,* 2 vols., second edition, (Sheffield, 1974), vol. 1, "He presided over this large province with singular propriety and dignity . . . (he) was wont to draw around him a circle of friends distinguished by their attainments and their genius. He much improved the mansion-house and the surrounding grounds and he saw the plantations of his father rise into the character of almost native forests," 315. Brodsworth had been the family home since 1713.

16. Old age and illness are two targets for the criticism of P. Virgin, *The Church in An Age of Negligence,* (Cambridge, 1989).

17. John Ingamells, *Catalogue of Portraits at Bishopthorpe Palace,* (Borthwick Institute of Historical Research, St Anthony's Hall, University of York, 1972), 10. The decision to be painted in that manner must have been a deliberate act of retrospect, as the date of the sittings is given as 1764–1765, well after the consecration as Archbishop of York. Drummond held the see of Salisbury for a matter of months only in the summer of 1761. A version at Salisbury was destroyed in 1963.

18. Ingamells, *Catalogue,* v.

19. Gilbert to Drummond 2 August 1758, R Bp 23/1, and 19 August 1758, R Bp 23/6, BIHR, and E. Venables, "he languished rather than lived through a pontificate of four years, when he sank under a complication of infirmities," *DNB*.

20. Paul Langford, *A Polite and Commercial People, England 1727–1783,* (Oxford, 1989).

21. Drummond to Holdernesse, 6 February 1760, Eg.MSS 3439 f 118, Br Lib. This was about a house in Privy Gardens, a location that Drummond knew well, it being where his friend Andrew Stone lived.

22. R Bp 1A/3, Borthwick Institute of Historical Research. "A Schedule of the Household furniture at Bishopthorpe . . . October 21 1761." The inventory consists of eleven pages of entries, bound in wallpaper, arranged by rooms such as "the next garret upon the left, . . . the iron chest room, the next room."

23. R Bp 1A/2, BIHR.

24. R Bp G 2.20, BIHR.

25. Clapham to Drummond, 17 October 1764, R Bp 20 d 123, BIHR.

Clapham paid tribute to the attention to his sick child shown by Drummond's wife and daughter, "[I have] great hopes that under Mrs Drummond's and Miss Auriol's kind directions he will still do well . . . [he had] Mrs Drummond's powders, which seem to have taken effect. . . . [He was] quiet for six hours and no more than three motions in that time . . ."

26. Nikolaus Pevsner, *Yorkshire, The West Riding,* second edition, (Penguin Books, 1967), 108.

27. Ibid., 109.

28. Drummond to Secker, 26 August 1765, Secker Papers, vol. 4, f 275, Lambeth Palace Library.

Chapter 2. The Making of an Archbishop

1. George Henry Hay, seventh Earl of Kinnoull (son of Thomas Hay, Viscount Dupplin), was created a British peer by the title of Baron Hay, 31 December 1711, being one of the twelve created that day to secure a majority in the House of Lords. S. H. Cassan, *Lives and Memoirs of the Bishops of Sherborne and Salisbury,* 309.

2. G. H. Drummond, *Memoirs of the Life of R. H. Drummond,* (Edinburgh, 1803).

3. Bishopthorpe Papers, Borthwick Institute of Historical Research (BIHR), R Bp or Bp C & P, according to the process of recataloging during this research.

4. Drummond to the Duke of Leeds, 23 November 1745, "Mr Wade's march [is] a great alarm, for it is now in their power to come to York. . . . I quitted Northumberland mostly with a view to be of some relief to the Family here, I

think it my duty to stay with them till there is more reason for their being quieter than at present . . ." Add. MSS 28051 f 347, Br Library. He asked the Duke of Leeds to explain to the Duke of Newcastle why he was not back at his cure at Bothall.

5. Drummond to Newcastle, 10 July 1750, "I cannot flatter myself that she will live another winter . . ." Add. MSS 32721 f 299, Br. Library.

6. Drummond to Newcastle, 6 August 1750, "It is your happiness to have softened the distress of a family who have lost the best of parents. . . . My heart is too full of different passions to write." Add. MSS 32722 f 61, Br Lib.

7. Drummond to Newcastle, 15 November 1766, "Mrs. Drummond tells me that Thursday is a day yt I cannot be away from home. Indeed I did not think of it myself, that it is my Birthday and we are all to be together. You'll allow me then to wait upon you on Friday morning." Add. MSS 33071 f 45, Br. Lib. By 1766 he could afford to be direct with Newcastle.

8. Brodsworth parish register:

Henrietta Auriol buried 9 June 1765
Abigail buried 9 August 1766
Charlotte Frances buried 23 March 1769

9. G. H. Drummond, *Memoirs,* xx.

10. Ibid., xxvi.

11. Ibid., xxvii.

12. The institution books in the Public Record Office show that Robert Hay received his Northumberland living from Edward, Earl of Oxford and Mortimer [his uncle] and the Earl's wife as patrons. Although this lady's dowry of £500,000 from the Newcastle fortunes was spent by the Earl on poetry, the main part of the Newcastle estates went to Thomas Pelham Holles who continued the support given to the young Rector of Bothall.

13. John Walton, clerk, continued as curate in the parish until 1740, and was succeeded by Charles Ward, MA. The clergy call books have Charles Ward again in 1746, and by 1758 Thomas Murray, clerk, was Curate of Bothall; Charles Ward was listed for Hebburn, the dependent Chapelry, from 1747.

14. Information about Drummond's living of Bothall has been received gratefully from Miss M. S. McCollom, Assistant Keeper in the Department of Palaeography and Diplomatic at the University of Durham.

15. She noticed him in a school play. "He was performing the part of Brutus in *Julius Caesar* when . . . the plume of ostrich feathers, which he wore, caught fire, and was instantly in a blaze; . . . he calmly, putting his hand to his forehead, pushed the cap off and went on with his speech without any other emotion than what belonged to the part. The Queen, charmed with his intrepidity, sent him a handsome present, and marked him as a lad, in whose future success in life she should feel herself interested," G. H. Drummond, *Memoirs,* xii.

16. Sykes, *Church and State,* 154.

17. Sykes describes the clergymen who were royal chaplains as "a class apart in the contest for promotion." Ibid, 151.

18. Drummond to Newcastle, 20 August 1743, Add. MSS 32701 f 3, Br Lib.

19. Ibid., ". . . I'm very happy that you put it in my power to obey your commands."

20. Drummond to Newcastle, 22 August 1743, "[the king] continues out of order, but does not yet own it; he has a great deal of inflammation in his eyes; his feet are very wetted. He has frequent headaches and his purging continues.

This I know to be so, but it is a secret to most people here." Add. MSS 32701, ff 9, 17, Br Lib.

21. Drummmond to the Duke of Leeds, ". . . we most shamefully left our wounded on the Field, not having waggons to bring ym away. The French took ym up ye next day with yr own and sent ym to us." Add MSS 28051 ff 341–48, Br Lib.

22. Ibid., "Fatigue agrees with me. I lay upon straw two nights and had not my boots off for 48 hours. I was glad to eat a piece of bread as black as my hat and a drop of water and yet I never was in better health."

23. Improper behavior at confirmations in Norfolk provoked a critical letter to the "Right Revd Father in God, Lewis Lord Bishop of Norwich," by "A Friend in Genuine Christianity," 1784. The bishop was berated because the mob broke into the church and tore the gowns of several of the clergy, W. M. Jacob, "Church and Society in Norfolk 1717–1806," unpublished Ph.D. Thesis, (University of Exeter, 1982). Such ripping scenes are pale compared with Drummond's experience in 1743 of taking cover by Lord Carteret's coach during a close bombardment by the French.

24. Drummond to the Duke of Leeds, 25 June 1743, Add. MSS 28051 f 337, Br Lib.

25. Sykes, *Church and State,* 130.

26. Drummond to the Duke of Leeds, 10 July 1743, "those of the Household . . . were taken little care of but we were left to shift for ourselves." Add. MSS 28051 ff 341,342, Br Lib.

27. Sykes, *Church and State,* 124.

28. He was unlike Zachary Pearce, who wrote to the duke in January 1746/7, "Instead of . . . Bangor . . . I may be appointed to such English bishopric as shall become vacant . . . as your Grace was pleased to tell me that Bangor is a fortunate see, and I shall think it so if I can be happy as to avoid such a long journey," quoted from Add. MSS 32714 f 111 by M. Bateson, "Clerical Preferment under the Duke of Newcastle," *The English Historical Review,* (1892), 688.

29. "Newcastle . . . did not achieve his results merely by a watchful eye and a cautionary reprimand. He could enforce discipline because of the wide disparity between the incomes of the various sees. . . . Initially [men were appointed] to the poorer sees; then, on proof of good behaviour, the bishop might begin the slow climb towards the rewards of unwavering loyalty." G. R. Cragg, "The Churchman," J. L. Clifford ed., *Man versus Society in Eighteenth Century Britain,* (C U P, 1968), 57.

30. D. R. Hirschberg, *Episcopal Incomes & Expenses 1660–1760,* in R. O'Day and F. Heal, ed., *Princes and Paupers in the English Church 1500–1800,* (Leicester, 1981), 226.

31. Clwyd Record Office, Hawarden, D/P 145,146; D/DM 764, 136, 137, 143. The terms of the different agreements for the subsequent lessees, Thomas Roberts, gent, and Watkin Williams, gent, accord with the trend of renewing leases in times of agricultural prosperity, C. Clay, "The greed of whig bishops? Church landlords and their lessees 1660–1760," *Past and Present,* Number 87, (May 1980), 128–57.

32. D. R. Thomas, *Diocesan Histories, St Asaph,* (SPCK, 1888), includes Drummond in the eighteenth-century bishops who were nonresident, but does so in a broad sweep of criticism that covers the second half of the eighteenth century indiscriminately,

For from 1750 to 1795, a half century of momentous importance for the welfare of the Welsh church, not one of the bishops of St Asaph resided in his diocese for more than a month or two in the summer of each year, 101.

33. Ibid., 98.
34. Edward Edwards, *Continuation of Browne Willis, Survey of St. Asaph, revised (1801),* 2 vols., (Wrexham, 1801), vol. 1, 156.
35. D. R. Thomas, *The History of the Diocese of St. Asaph,* 3 vols., (Oswestry, 1908 edition) vol. 1, 301.
36. Drummond to a rural dean, 17 Jan 1748/9, Westminster Abbey Muniment MS 64828, 6 leaves, stitched to be 12 pages, "from time to time to acquaint me, especially, . . . Of the language in wch ye publick Ministerial offices are performed in every Church and Chapel, whether in Welch or in English: If in both, how often, and what part in one, and how often and what part in ye other. I must intreat you to inform me, as particularly as you can, what in this respect wd be most for ye edification of ye generality of ye hearers."
37. E. G. Rupp, *Religion in England, 1688–1791,* (OUP, 1986), 500.
38. S. L. Ollard, G. Crosse and M. F. Bond, *A Dictionary of English Church History,* (Mowbray, London, 1912), 550. The one archdeaconry was "held in commendam by the Bishop from 1573 to 1844, when it was released and divided into . . . two."
39. R. H. Drummond, *Directions to Clergy, 1749,* St. Deiniol's Library, Hawarden.
40. G. Rupp, *Religion in England,* 500.
41. Walsh, "Yorkshire Evangelicals, 10, quoting J. Milner, *Essays on Several Religious Subjects,* 3.
42. Deposition before the Cabinet Council, Eg MSS, 3440 f 52, Br Lib.
43. Charles J. Abbey, *The English Church and its Bishops 1700–1800,* 2 vols., (London, 1887), vol. 2, 209.
44. H. Walpole, Earl of Orford, *Memoirs of the Last Ten Years of the Reign of George the Second,* 2 vols., (London, 1822), 312,

"Drummond of St Asaph, sensibly and in a manly style, urged that the bishops could not have opposed the bill without indulging a spirit of persecution, abhorrent from the spirit of the Gospel."

45. Ibid., vol. 1, 261.
46. Sermon by Bishop Drummond 15 February 1754 at the parish church of St. Mary le Bow for the Anniversary meeting of the SPG. Text in York Minster Library YM/c 62.12 [1761], and Lambeth Palace Library H5 133 56.
47. T. Secker, *A Very Particular Account of the Coronation of King George III,* MS 1130, Lambeth Palace Library.
48. Clark, *English Society,* 217.
49. Ibid.
50. Bateson, Clerical Preferment. "He liked receiving and writing letters, and no application was treated as waste paper."
51. N. Sykes, "The Duke of Newcastle as Ecclesiastical Minister," *English Historical Review,* vol. lvii, January (1942), 60. "He shared all the information with his political and family confidants before deciding, desiring to escape the responsibility of decision."
52. Stand or fall, make or break.
53. Ibid., 74.

54. Ibid., 74. Lord Bute had complained, "Must not the king make one bishop? By this your Grace will have a friend or creature of your own at London," Newcastle to Devonshire 5 August 1761, Add MSS 32926 f 187. Bute's complaint was also relayed to Hardwicke, "first I would have a bishop of London, then I would make an archbishop of York, and my Lord Hardwicke would recommend the new bishop. That this had offended the King, and that though he [the king] loved and esteemed the Bishop of Salisbury more than any one bishop upon the bench, he did not knoe what the King would do. His majesty was so offended with the Duke of Newcastle for recommending to *everything* . . ." Newcastle to Hardwicke, 17 August 1761, Add MSS 32927 f 68, Br Lib.

55. Overton and Relton, *The English Church,* 160.

56. Add. MSS 32714 f 111, Br Lib.

57. Add. MSS 32954 f 182, Br Lib.

58. Walpole, *Memoirs,* 298.

59. Add. MSS 32988 f 380, Br Lib.

60. Add. MSS 32988 f 411, Br Lib.

61. Drummond to Newcastle, June 1761, Add MSS 32954 f 182, Br Lib.

62. my underlining

63. Kay A. Kelch, *Newcastle, A Duke without Money: Thomas Pelham-Holles, 1693–1768,* (London, 1974), 185. Newcastle informed Drummond that he had begun to read Addison and was at that time reading Tillotson's sermons. He also regularly read the Lesson of the Day, Add. MSS 33071, f 71, Br Lib.

Chapter 3. The Making of a Visitation

1. SA/QA/4–5 and SA/QA/5, National Library of Wales, Aberystwyth.

2. R. Burn, *Ecclesiastical Law,* (London, 1809), vol. 4, 15.

3. Ibid., ". . . visitations . . . usually about Easter and Michaelmas evidently sprung from the two yearly synods of the clergy."

4. Ibid., 15.

5. Bp V Misc. [alternatively Bp G2.13 during the process of recataloging. Most of the separate items are unmarked with a catalog number.]

6. V. E. Neuburg, *Popular Education in Eighteenth Century England,* (London, 1971), chapters 4 and 6.

7. Westminster Abbey Muniment 64828, and R Bp 23/8, BIHR, and please see chapter 2, footnote 36.

8. Sykes, *Church and State,* 103.

9. Jacob, "Church and Society in Norfolk," 200.

10. R Bp 23/ 1, BIHR. ". . . I send you a list of the parishes, with the names of their respective ministers, who are ordered to attend at the places where your Lordship is so good as to undertake the Fatigue of Confirming. . . . With feet and ankles which will hardly carry me over a plain floor I tremble for your Lordship."

11. R Bp 23/3, 4 & 5, BIHR.

12. R Bp 23/28, BIHR.

13. R Bp 23/29 & 30, BIHR.

14. R Bp 23/6, BIHR.

15. Sykes, *Church and State,* 135.

16. A crudely printed playing card, the 9 of spades, measuring 9×6.25cm, has on its reverse,

"Confirmed in the York peculiars 238
Archdeaconry of Durham 13
Archdeaconry of Northumberland 251
502, and is kept between the confirmation lists of 1764 and 1768, R Bp 23/51A, BIHR.

17. R Bp 23/12–26, BIHR.

18. S. L. Ollard, "Laurence Sterne as a parish priest," *Times Literary Supplement,* (1926), 217. It was already outgrown in 1743 in Sterne's parish, where he was cited not as avoiding this duty but as exemplary in catechizing for three hours on Lent Sundays at his home.

19. Downey, *Eighteenth Century Pulpit,* 16, 17.

20. The one change he made about confirmation arrangements was in his draft for the visitation of 1758 in St. Asaph, where he decided that the minimum age for catechumens should be increased from fourteen to sixteen. This would perhaps have had the effect of reducing the number of candidates, but was surely designed to attract more mature candidates.

21. A lecturer had to have more qualifications than a schoolmaster, but had a less demanding commitment. Lectures could be weekly but were sometimes annual or biennial. Schoolteaching was daily. But the lecturer was a preacher; the schoolmaster was not, unless he were also a curate.

22. R. S. Tompson, *Classics or Charity,* (Manchester, 1971). Tompson lists types of schools—dame, petty, subscription, charity at pleasure, charity unendowed—where unlicensed teaching may have been taking place. His portrayal of the changes is convincing, but his reference to Robert Hammond (68) instead of Drummond as Archbishop of York is an uncharacteristic error.

23. It was after that point that Drummond thought of making an alteration to Gilbert's draft. Archbishop Gilbert had included questions about observing holy days and fast days, and about marrying people on Sundays or without a license or privately. The section is crossed out in ink, but in the margin is "Stet."

24. G. V. Bennett, *To The Church of England* (Churchman, 1988), 115.

25. V. S., *Gentleman's Magazine* (February, 1764).

26. Mather, "Georgian Churchmanship," 261, n 34.

27. Exhibit Book V 1759–60, BIHR.

28. Inst AB 14, 252, BIHR.

29. See Chapter 5, section 2, "Becoming a Curate."

30. J. Wesley, *Journal,* 20 February 1760.

31. Bernard Martin, *John Newton* (London, 1950), 200.

32. In the course of that day, Newton had walked and run from his lodgings to Drummond's London home (because the information about the ordination had reached him when it was almost too late), then to the earl of Dartmouth's residence, and then back again to Drummond—a distance of about ten miles. By the afternoon he had not had time for dinner or tea, but yet "was the most cheerful person," in the company at his friend's house that evening because the earl wrote immediately to the bishop of Lincoln. Martin, *John Newton,* 200.

33. Ibid.

34. Bp V 1764 Papers, BIHR.

35. Bp V 1764/CB, BIHR.

36. Bp V Misc (Bp G2. 13), BIHR.

37. R Bp 20D 110–13, BIHR.

38. R Bp 20D 109, BIHR.

39. A New England farmer, at a moment's notice, ran and rode with his wife

twelve miles to be in Middletown by ten o'clock to hear George Whitefield preach on 23 October 1740. They found a huge concourse gathered to hear the preacher. J. Pollock, *George Whitefield and the Great Awakening* (Lion publishing, 1986 edition), 164–66.

40. M. Bateson, "Clerical Preferment."

41. Gladstone, *Gleanings,* vols. v & vii; see Introduction.

42. J. D. Gay, *The Geography of Religion in England* (London, Duckworth 1971), 69–71; Virgin, *Age of Negligence,* 152–62.

43. V Misc, or Bp G2.13, BIHR.

44. P. M. Tillott, "The Parish Churches," in P. M. Tillott, ed., *A. History of the County of York, the City of York, [Victoria County History]* (London, 1961), 367, showing a Table of the Unions of Benefices.

45. Ibid.

46. Ibid., 371.

47. Ibid.

48. It may be more than coincidence that the next parochial unions, during Archbishop Thompson's reforms of 1885, were St. Crux with All Saints Pavement, and St. Trinity, Kings Court with St. Sampson's. St. Crux's church was actually demolished, *VCH,* 367, 378.

49. See chapter 3, last paragraph of section 3 for the statistics on the playing card.

50. G. H. Drummond, *Memoirs,* xx.

51. Drummond was not the first eighteenth-century bishop to grieve bitterly at the death of a grown daughter. Francis Atterbury, an earlier alumnus of Westminster and Christ Church, Oxford, and bishop of Rochester 1713–1723, was devastated in 1729 when his daughter's horrific journey to visit him in exile at Montpellier ended with her death in his arms. G. V. Bennett, *The Tory Crisis in Church and State* (Oxford, 1975), 300–301.

Chapter 4. The State of the Diocese

1. The increase of "squarsons" is put at one in every five clergymen towards the end of the Georgian era. Virgin, *Age of Negligence,* 110.

2. E. G. Rupp, *Religion in England 1688–1791,* (Oxford, 1986), 508.

3. C. E. Shipley, *The Baptists of Yorkshire* (Bradford, 1912), 234–246. Salendine Nook had sixty-one members in 1743. A Mr. James Cartledge was developing the coal mines in the neighborhood, and built a chapel at Blackley in 1789.

4. Venn's intensive pastoral care centered on meetings in the church and invitations to call at his vicarage (Walsh, "Yorkshire Evangelicals," chapter V). His wider travels, outside his parish, were to other revival centers—campaigns organized by the Countess of Huntingdon and preachments in London. His curates conducted the parish visiting, including touring catechizing and Sunday patrols. Venn ventured up the Colne Valley at Easter to collect his Dues from that part of the township of Marsden that lay in his parish, but the road lay up the other side of the valley and away from the Baptist chapel.

5. Bp C & P VII ex. 3–6/ R Bp 5 293, BIHR.

6. He wrote a key to explain the grading scheme:

"* denotes where there is a default
= denotes where there is an improvement
*= denotes where the default hath been amended."

7. F. Blackburne, *A sermon preached on Friday 5 January 1753* (London, 1753).

8. F. Blackburne, *Remarks following the Reverend Dr Powell's sermon in defence of subscription, preached before the University of Cambridge on the Commencement Sunday 1757,* (1758).

9. See chapter 6, Part 3, section 4.

10. F. Blackburne ed., *A. Collection of Letters and Essays in favour of Public Liberty,* first published in newspapers annually from 1764–1770, then in 3 vols. (London, 1770), vol. 1, 26, 27.

11. Ibid., "I deny that episcopacy has anything to do with our church, any further than it is connected with the State. . . . [I] beg leave to recommend it to our prelates to regulate church affairs in this country, and to put them on a more respectable footing, before they think of sending Bishops across the Atlantic. . . . It seems that sending Bishops among these poor savage idolaters is judged to be the most helpful method. . . . ," 22 April 1765, vol. 3 70, 71, 77.

12. R. A. Hall and J. T. Lang, "St. Mary's Church, Levisham, North Yorkshire," *Yorkshire Archaeological Society,* vol. 58 (1986), 57–83.

13. Frances Knight supports this view in her "Review Article, The Hanoverian Church in Transition: Some Recent Perspectives," *The Historical Journal,* 36, 3, (1993), particularly in relation to Virgin's specific criticism of the Georgian Church for its number of elderly clergy.

14. Pevsner, *Yorkshire: East Riding,* 164, 227, and 355. The restoration at Thornton was at the end of the nineteenth century. At Fangfoss the rebuilding was done in 1849–50, and used the Norman masonry.

15. See next chapter, under "The Conscientious Efforts of Curates."

16. This was not the right answer. This question required an assessment of the total number of communicants in the parish or chapelry, not an estimate of the number usually present.

17. Mather, "Georgian Churchmanship."

18. Walsh, "Yorkshire Evangelicals," Chapter 3.

19. Rack, *Reasonable Enthusiast,* 20.

20. The letter was written a month before he incurred blame from the archbishop for the visitation sermon, preached at Malton on 25 June, for which, please see below in the section on preaching. Conyers was likely to have been preparing that sermon at the time when he wrote his supporting letter.

21. Rupp, *Religion in England 1688–1791,* 517.

22. G. H. Drummond, *Memoirs,* footnote, xxviii: "The Archbishop left many excellent Sermons and Charges in manuscript, but expressed an unwillingness that they should be prepared for the press." My search for the sermons and charges in manuscript produced only those printed for publication.

23. Dickenson Rastall, *History of the Collegiate Church of Southwell,* cited by G. H. Drummond, *Memoirs,* xvii.

24. The exception is Laurence Sterne. Racked as he was by asthma in a hostile climate in three parishes whose scenery was among the most dramatic of Yorkshire, his sermons drove his congregations through some of the obscure passages of the Bible. He was at the height of his literary fame in 1764, and could have acquired his mannerism of extended asides from his pulpit custom. His own definition of preaching was "a theological flap upon the heart." Downey, *Eighteenth Century Pulpit,* 106. The saga of Sterne's *Political Romance* depended on the ambitious grasp of Trim to get the warm watch-coat; his close association

with the bitterness of the Yorkshire winter season had assisted the theme for his character.

25. See under *Itineraries of the Visitation* in chapter 3.

26. Bp V 1764/CB, BIHR.

27. Walsh, "Yorkshire Evangelicals," Chapter 4, quoting *The Christian's Magazine* (1792).

28. A. C. H. Seymour, ed., *The Life and Times of Selina, Countess of Huntingdon* (London, 1840), vol. 2, 280.

29. Walsh, "Yorkshire Evangelicals," Chapter 4.

30. Ibid., chapter 5.

31. My underlining

32. H. Venn, *An Earnest and pressing call to keep holy the Lord's Day Addressed equally to the rich and poor of his flock* (Leeds, 1760), Cambridge University Library, syn.7.76.41/7.

33. Stokesley correspondence, R Bp 20d 16–20, BIHR.

34. Jacob, "Church and Society in Norfolk 1707–1806," 203, and quoting from de la Rochefoucauld (Marchand's edition).

35. Sykes, *Church and State,* 124, quoting figures collected by Canon Ollard in S. L. Ollard, *Confirmation in the Anglican Communion* (SPCK, 1926), 199–201.

36. The figure of 15,000 at one tour in 1758 for Gilbert (see chapter 3, section 3, "Early experience at York") would have to be multiplied only by 3—in other words only three other confirmation tours would be necessary—to top Sykes's estimate, and we know that Drummond undertook many more than three confirmations during the period 1761–1776, let alone the three known occasions at St. Asaph.

37. W. Wake, *The principles of the Christian religion explained in a brief commentary upon the church catechism* (London, 1699), Br Lib 1018.1.33.

38. W. Beveridge, *The Church Catechism explained for the use of the diocese of St Asaph,* 6th edition (1704), Br Lib, 3504.c.29.

39. J. Lewis, *The Church Catechism Explained* (1732), Br Lib 682.1.1.

40. J. Williams, *A. Brief Exposition of the Catechism* (1691), Br Lib C.130.bb.3(1).

41. H. Stebbing, *The Young Christian Instructed,* 9th edition (London, 1756), Br Lib 3503.d.15.

42. S. Clarke, *An Exposition of the Church Catechism* (1729), Br Lib 845.c.12.

43. T. Bray, *The whole course of catechetical instruction, through the classes of catechumens, consisting of . . .* (five sections) (London, 1704), Br Lib 3505.c.26.

44. J. Gregory, "Eighteenth-Century Reformation," 71.

45. Walsh, "Yorkshire Evangelicals," 57. Walsh adds that they became a closely knit fraternity by correspondence and personal contact.

46. Overton & Relton, *English Church,* 294.

47. Gregory, "Speculum of Thomas Secker."

48. Sons of the Clergy Papers, Misc MSS 1121, ff 193–204, Lambeth Palace Library.

49. See below, in reference to Samuel Brook of Flockton chapel.

50. He added, "Within these few weeks there is come another Master to teach in the School but of him I can give no manner of account." The difference in evidence from Brook and Rishton shows exactly how confusions arise.

51. An account of his schoolmastering is given by D. F. E. Sykes, *The History of the Colne Valley* (Slaithwaite, 1896). Murgatroyd, unlike Brook, was active in

his school, employing his knowledge of the Humanities, a resident of Lingards and a well known "venerable looking" figure in his "powdered wig and long cloak." Sykes, *Colne Valley,* 146.

52. William Smith, ed., *Old Yorkshire,* New series (London, 1889), 148–63.

53. J. Lawson, "Endowed Grammar Schools of East Yorkshire," *East Yorkshire Local History Society,* Local History Series, No. 14 (York, 1962).

54. Arthur Francis Leach, "Early Yorkshire Schools," 2 vols., Record Series, *Yorkshire Archaeological Society,* 1903 (York, 1903), vol. 2, lxxxv.

55. R. S. Tompson, *Classics or Charity* (Manchester, 1971). M. Sanderson, *Education, Economic Change and Society in England, 1780–1870* (Macmillan, 1983), chapter 2.

56. Ibid., 46.

57. Drummond to Governors of Heath grammar school, 16 and 28 Dec. 1769, R Bp G2.3/39 and 3/43, quoted by Tompson, *Classics or Charity,* 39.

58. N. Pevsner, *Yorkshire: York and the East Riding, The Buildings of England* (Penguin, 1972), 329 and 357.

59. Robert Drummond's charge concerning terriers to the clergy of the diocese, St. Deiniol's Library, I 85.9 SA/7, 31 Jan. 1748/9.

60. See below under "Evidence . . . about Absenteeism . . ."

Chapter 5. Drummond's Yorkshire—Some Problems and Opportunities

1. A. D. Yonge, *Church Acts and Measures, Halsbury's Statutes of England,* 3rd edition (London, 1969), 458.

2. W. L. Mathieson, *English Church Reform 1815–1840* (London, 1923), 148.

3. It was the nonresident Bishop Richard Watson of Llandaff (1782–1816), "a veritable monument to clerical abuse (sixteen livings) . . . who urged a fairer distribution of ecclesiastical revenue to improve parochial religion," in a letter to the archbishop of Canterbury in 1783, R. A. Soloway, *Prelates, and People. Ecclesiastical & Social Thought in England 1783–1852* (London, 1969), 3.

4. B. M. Scott, "Benjamin Ingham," *Wesley Historical Society,* No. 40, August 1982 (York 1982).

5. V. Barrie-Curien, "The clergy in the diocese of London in the eighteenth century," in Walsh, Haydon, Taylor, ed., *The Church of England c1688-c1833 From Toleration to Tractarianism* (Cambridge, 1993), 97.

6. Overton & Relton, *English Church,* 293.

7. Ibid., 90–92.

8. See chapter 3, section 5, The Process of the Visitation, "Preliminaries."

9. "An odd, unclerical man with a big nose," is the description used by David Cecil, *The Stricken Deer* (London, 1929), 109.

10. Bernard Martin, *John Newton* (London, 1950), 184.

11. *York Courant,* 11 September and 18 September 1764 for ordinations on 4 November at Brodsworth.

12. G. G. Perry, *DNB,* 488, 489.

13. Mather, *High Church Prophet,* 151.

14. *York Courant,* 24 April 1764: Curate wanted by end of May.

15. See chapter 7, section 2.

16. See above, n. 13.

17. 9 and 11 June 1764, R Bp 20d 16–20, BIHR. It may be a little unfair to

quote Stokesley as an example of a curate better known than the rector to his parishioners, in that this was where the notorious Thomas Hudson [see chapter 7] had been curate until the previous year, but this particular piece of correspondence was related to the search for a new curate there.

18. Charles Augustus Hulbert, *Annals of the Church in Slaithwaite, (near Huddersfield), West Riding of Yorkshire, from 1593 to 1864* (London, 1864).

19. J. Mallinson, *Methodism in Huddersfield* (London, 1898), 17-21.

20. Rishton to Drummond, 17 November 1764, R Bp 8.24, BIHR.

21. See chapter 4, "The Yorkshire Evangelicals and Holy Communion."

22. Walsh & Taylor, *Toleration to Tractarianism,* 50.

23. Walsh, "Yorkshire Evangelicals," chapter IV.

24. G. G. Cragg, *Grimshaw of Haworth* (London, 1947), 56 & 72, F. Baker, *William Grimshaw 1708–1763* (Epworth, 1963), 132, R. Spence Hardy, *William Grimshaw, Incumbent of Haworth 1742–1763* (London, 1860), 232–34, and A. Strachan, *Life of George Lowe* (London, 1848), 35–37.

25. Alan Savidge, *The Foundation and Early Years of Queen Anne's Bounty* (SPCK, 1955), 1.

26. See below for extracts from Secker's draft letter to the *Evening Post* in 1760 and 1762, Secker Papers, MS 1120, f 45/ 82,83, Lambeth Palace Library.

27. G. F. A. Best, *Temporal Pillars* (Cambridge, 1964), 25.

28. Virgin, *Age of Negligence,* 64–74.

29. *Lloyd's Evening Post and British Chronicle,* No. 412, Wed. 5 March to Friday 7 March 1760, Lambeth Palace Library in MISC 1120.

30. The values of the livings are those given in the Diocesan Book that Drummond inherited in 1761.

31. Thomas Secker, MS 1120 f 45, Lambeth Palace Library.

32. Best, *Temporal Pillars,* 539. Elwes was Treasurer 1724–1776.

33. Ollard and Crosse, *Dictionary of English Church History,* 486, 487.

Chapter 6. Population, Dissent, and the Church

1. Bennett, *Tory Crisis,* 22.

2. Walsh, *Toleration to Tractarianism,* 17.

3. See Part 4: Conclusion.

4. A check through the dissenting meeting houses licenses would suggest that many of these were not purpose built places—and certainly not chapels as such—but meetings in rooms in private houses that would not be obvious even to a resident incumbent.

5. J. Bossy, *The English Catholic Community 1570–1850* (London, 1975), 189.

6. Robert Harrison, *DNB,* vol. 1, 710–11.

7. Ibid.

8. Ollard and Walker, *The Herring Returns,* Introduction, x.

9. Bp Rec Ret. H 2. 8, 1–75, and Bp Rec. Ret. H 2. 9 70–79, BIHR.

10. Bp Rec Ret H 2 9 (72), BIHR.

11. J. S. Rowntree, *Quakerism, Past and Present* (London, 1859), 65, 74, 153, 169, and John Punshon, *Portrait in Grey, A Short History of the Quakers* (London, 1984), 135–50.

12. W. A. Speck, *Stability and Strife, England 1714–1760* (Arnold, 1977), 101.

13. C. Gordon Bolam, Jeremy Goring, H. L. Short, Roger Thomas, *The English Presbyterians* (London, 1968), 223.

14. The population growth in Hull was in parallel with its success in trade, business, and industries of all kinds. The merchants grew rich and powerful, and the city corporation held the patronage to Holy Trinity Church. The evangelical tradition flourished also, particularly with the work of Joseph Milner. J. E. Williams and J. A. Woods, "Hull 1700–1835," *VCH, York East Riding*, vol. 1 (Oxford, 1969), 174–214.

15. J. G. Miall, *Congregationalism in Yorkshire* (London, 1868), 295. At Idle, the Rev. J. Huthwaite (1729–65) "left the congregation in a state of great declension."

16. Ibid, 230. The source suggests a congregation of 250 early in the eighteenth century.

17. Bolam, *English Presbyterians*, 177.

18. Bolam, *English Presbyterians*, 177, and G. M. Ditchfield, "Anti-Trinitarianism and Toleration in Late Eighteenth Century British Politics: the Unitarian Petition of 1792," *Journal of Ecclesiastical History*, vol. 42, no. 1 (January, 1991).

19. R. Tudor Jones, *Congregationalism in England, 1662–1962* (Independent Press, London, 1962), 151.

20. E. G. Rupp, *Religion in England*, 128.

21. Payne, *Baptist Union*, 36.

22. Ollard and Walker, *Herring Returns*, vol. 1, 1.

23. G. G. Perry, *DNB*, vol. 1, 489, when Secker advised Bishop John Green not to publish another harsh tirade against the Methodists.

24. F. Braudel, *Civilisation and Capitalism 15th–18th Century*, 2 vols., (London, 1981), vol. 1, *The Structures of Everyday Life*, 33 and 47, where the increase is put at 4 per thousand per annum during 1750 and 1800.

25. Wrigley & Schofield, *Population History*. The growth rate of Nonconformity is insubstantial until after 1780, 89; they decide that although the population doubled between 1731 and 1811, the rise rate in 1743–1764 was gentle, 403.

26. Rupp, *Religion in England*, 115, and Tudor Jones, *Congregationalism in England*, 145.

27. Miall, *Congregationalism in Yorkshire*, 336.

28. Ibid., for the Presbyterian chapel at Attercliffe, which existed until 1758, and the Presbyterian chapel at Cleckheaton, with 150 as the number of members.

29. Licenses FAC. Bk 1 and DMH/1 & /6, BIHR.

30. W. E. Blomfield, *The Baptists of Yorkshire* (Baptist Association, 1912), 53–112.

31. Ibid., 102.

32. Tudor Jones, *Congregationalism in England*, 153.

33. J. D. Walsh, "Methodism at the end of the Eighteenth Century," in Davies and Rupp ed., *Methodist Church in Great Britain*, vol. 1, 294.

34. Langford, *A Polite and Commercial People*, 253: "The poor were suitable cases for treatment primarily because they lacked the diversity of opportunity for sin available to the rich."

35. J. D. Walsh, "Wesley and the Poor," (seminar, University of York, 1989), and subsequently in "John Wesley and the Community of Goods in Protestant Evangelism: Britain, Ireland, Germany and America c 1750–c1950," Keith Robbins ed., *Studies in Church History, Subsidia 7* (Blackwell, Oxford, 1990).

36. Virgin, *Age of Negligence*, 159.

37. Best, *Temporal Pillars*, Appendix VI, 545, quoting net income of see at 1851.

38. Stephen Hyde Cassan, *Lives and Memoirs of the Bishops of Salisbury,* (Salisbury, 1824), "On his promotion to York, he found the greatest confusion among the papers belonging to the see. These he methodized with the most scrupulous exactness, and made to them a very considerable addition in his own handwriting—a work too laborious and unentertaining to have been dictated by any motive but . . . conscientiousness," 291.

39. Ollard and Walker, *The Herring Returns,* vol. 1, viii, n. 5.

40. Rupp, *Religion in England,* 493. The Church also married the population, though this was a legal requirement.

41. Ibid., 499.

42. Virgin, *Age of Negligence,* 5. Bishop Butler's visitation returns of 1789 contrasted so unfavorably with the situation there in 1747 that he was "unwilling to recite the numbers" of communicants at the great festivals.

43. Barrie-Curien, "Clergy in the London Diocese," Walsh, Haydon and Taylor, *Toleration to Tractarianism,* 86.

44. Frances Knight, "The Hanoverian Church in Transition: Some recent Perspectives," *The Historical Journal,* 36, vol. 3, (Cambridge, 1993).

45. Virgin, *Age of Negligence,* 5.

46. Walsh, "Yorkshire Evangelicals," 233, 234.

47. Kenneth Hylson Smith, *The Evangelicals in the Church of England 1734–1984* (Edinburgh, 1988), 34, 35.

48. See above in final section of "Statistical Survey."

49. ER V/CB.18, BIHR.

50. D. Napthine and W. A. Speck refer to a list made in 1753 of thousands of "jeremiads" since 1660, "Clergymen and Conflict 1660–1763," *Studies in Church History,* Vol. 20, *The Church and War* (Oxford, 1983), 231, and R. Hole, *Pulpits, Politics and Public Order 1760–1832* (Cambridge, 1989), 137.

51. Virgin, *Age of Negligence,* 115.

52. Clark, *English Society,* 277.

53. See also chapter 1, n 14.

54. J. C. D. Clark, *English Society,* 316.

55. R. B. Barlow, *Citizenship and Conscience* (Philadelphia, 1963).

56. Isaac Watts, *An Essay Against Uncharitableness* (1707), 17, 18.

57. Barlow, *Citizenship & Conscience,* 102.

58. Ibid., 102, quoting from I. Watts' *Essay.*

59. See above, n 23.

60. Seymour, *Life and Times of the Countess of Huntingdon,* vol. 1, 288–89; Miall, *Congregationalism in Yorkshire,* 154, 155; and Basil Williams, *Life of William Pitt, Earl of Chatham,* 2 vols., (London, 1913), 294–95.

61. Lord Mahon, *History of England,* 7 vols., (London, 1858), vol. 3, 16 and 17, and vol. 5, 303–4 concluded that Chatham was giving vent to "waywardness of temper that overmastered his judgment," and cited Gladstone, *Church Principles Considered in their Results* (London, 1840), who described the triple phrase beginning "Calvinistic creed," as a "shallow witticism, little worthy of so illustrious a man, in which grains of truth are mingled and lost in masses of delusion." Lord Mahon's perceptive footnote was, "This saying of Lord Chatham is not to be found in the meagre Parliamentary records of the day."

62. E. Burke, *The Speeches of the Rt Hon Edmund Burke in the House of Commons and in Westminster Hall* (London, 1816), 101–3 and 472–83. In the text of a speech, probably undelivered, discovered among his papers at his decease, there is, "Dissent, not satisfied with toleration, is not conscience, but ambition."

63. P. Langford, ed., *Party, Parliament, and the American Crisis* in *The Writings and Speeches of Edmund Burke,* vol. 2 (Oxford, 1981), 359, 368, 465.
64. Rupp, *Religion in England,* 493.

Chapter 7. Government by Correspondence

1. See chapter 6, 38.
2. Sykes, *Church and State,* 145.
3. Virgin, *Age of Negligence,* 159.
4. "He feeds more like a pig of Epicurus than the head of a Christian Church," Elizabeth Montagu, quoted by J. Wickham Legg, *English Church Life,* 8. Wickham Legg added his own subjective censure, that Gilbert did not have "the excuse of teetotallism for gluttony, since teetotallers are commonly gross feeders."
5. Even the gods yawned at his preaching:

> Churches and Chapels instantly it reach'd;
> St James's first, for leaden Gilbert preach'd.

A. Pope, *Dunciad,* 4, 608. But Pope's editor defends Gilbert: "the word "leaden" may be intended by Pope to characterise Gilbert's matter; it does not do justice to his manner, for he is said to have wept in the pulpit while preaching a funeral sermon on Queen Caroline, 25 December, 1737," Egmont, ii, 458, J. Sutherland (ed.), *Dunciad* (London, 1963), 403–4.
6. E. Venables, *DNB,* 1209–10.
7. Speck, *Stability and Strife,* 258.
8. R Bp 16; 17: 44–48; 20a: 117–55, 20c: 1–155, 20d: 1–136; 4a ex 3–6; 23: 1–85, and ex 28, BIHR.
9. R Bp 20 A/89, BIHR.
10. Add MSS 32930, ff 308–10, Br Lib.
11. Bp C & P VII ex 28, BIHR.
12. Dean Fountayne to Drummond, 4 October 1761, R Bp 20A 95, BIHR.
13. William Herring (a personal friend and former colleague in Wales) to Drummond, 7 October 1761, R Bp 20A 96, BIHR.
14. Dean Fountayne to Drummond, 22 November 1761, R Bp 20A 123, BIHR.
15. Tindal Hart, *Ebor,* 151.
16. Scrope Berdmore to Drummond, Bp 20A 115, BIHR.
17. See chapter 5, "Pluralism: the flaws."
18. Ibid., 27 November 1761, R Bp 20A 124, BIHR.
19. Ibid., 26 May 1764, R Bp 20D 57, BIHR.
20. Dean Fountayne to Drummond, 19 November 1761, R Bp 20A 121, BIHR.
21. Topham to Drummond, R Bp 20 A 98, BIHR.
22. Sterne came out as the winner of this incident although his *Political Romance* was suppressed, in that he had stumbled on the theme for his great work, *Tristram Shandy,* as well as obtaining in 1760, perhaps as compensation, the £100 per annum living of Coxwold. Sterne also won from the Dean the Commissaryship of the Peculiar Court of Pickering and Pocklington, one of the two offices denied to Topham.
23. Conway to Drummond, R Bp 20A 121, BIHR.
24. R Bp 16 1–36, BIHR.
25. Thompson to Drummond, R Bp 16 6, BIHR.

26. Jackson to Drummond, from Berkshire, June 1762, R Bp 16, 11, BIHR. Jackson outlined the progress of his treatment at the hands of the Earl of Thanet, ". . . I comply'd, resign'd my school and return'd to Silsden where I taught and constantly preached seven years till finding ye Earl inexorable & still unwilling to pay me my Arrears . . . [he has] driven me like a banished man. . . . But good my Lord, please to consider, when strip't of wt I was ordained to . . . I was forced near 20 years to seek my Bread elsewhere & hope yr Grace will take ye Blame off me . . ."

27. Sykes to Drummond, R Bp 8 78, BIHR.

28. Ibid.

"He should enter a caveat—The Trustees sh'd show ye writings
I shall breakfast with him—
NB to write to Mackley abt ye deeds NB a Curate licensed on the
Nomination of the Vr of Bradford
Mr Richardson who put in Mr Bliss but he displeases Mr Richardson in going there
NB The Trustees sh'd have ye deeds at Bradford
Apr 12 temp Eliz . . . . .ye power of alienating ye people if they had not the choice of Curate."

29. Questions from Mr. Sykes:

If the Trustees of the Lands belonging to the Chapel of Haworth sh'd exhibit their writings, please to inquire,
1 Whether they exhibit the original purchase deeds?
2 Whether they purchased the lands belonging to the Chapel with monies collected by themselves or formerly left to the Chapel by several benefactors?
3 Whether there is not a rasure or interlineation, where the Uses are mentioned in the Purchase Deeds?
4 Why these Deeds were not made use of in the time of the late Mr Smith, Curate of Haworth?
5 Whether the late Mr Kennett was not induced by a Present of 50 or 60 pounds to him, or Mr Sunderland, to agree to the joint Nomination of the late Mr Grimshaw?
6 In what manner they have disposed of a sum of money left to the Chapel of Haworth for a sermon in the afternoon?

R Bp 8 80, BIHR.

30. Walsh, "Yorkshire Evangelicals," 240–42.

31. Sykes, *Church and State,* 96.

32. R Bp 20D, BIHR.

33. See chapter 4, n 34.

34. Hudson to Drummond, 11 August 1764, R Bp 20d 100, BIHR.

35. Hudson to Drummond, 21 August 1764, R Bp 20d 101, BIHR.

36. On the reverse of Hudson's letter to him, R Bp 20d 100, BIHR.

37. Drummond to Matthews (a parishioner), 11 June 1764, R Bp 20D 16–20.

38. Dowthwaite to Drummond, 4 April 1764, R Bp 20D 25, BIHR.

39. Radcliffe to Drummond, 7 May 1764, R Bp 20D 43, BIHR.

40. Dowthwaite to Drummond, 9 May 1764, R Bp 20D 45, BIHR.

41. Ward to Drummond, R Bp 20D 26, BIHR.

42. Various correspondents to Drummond, R Bp 20D, BIHR.

43. Fisher to Drummond, 13 April 1764, R Bp 20D 27, BIHR.

44. Hardy to Drummond, R Bp 20D 134, BIHR.

45. Mulso to Drummond, 11 May 1764, R Bp 20D 46, BIHR.

46. Hutton to Drummond, 16 July 1764, R Bp 20D 94, BIHR.

47. There is no note by the archbishop on the reverse, but we know that Hutton had already asked for Epworth rectory, from a letter to Wm. Leving Esq., 3 July 1762, R Bp 4A 28, 29, BIHR. Epworth went within Drummond's own family, at the request of the Duke of Leeds, so Hutton tried later for a prebend at Southwell, Hutton to Drummond, 17 October 1767, R Bp 20E 123, BIHR, but he declined a prebend at Southwell because it was not the one he had wanted. Drummond's notes have: I gave Chaple's [sic] prebend to Marsden [one of his chaplains] and Hutton declined taking that vacated by Marsden.

48. Becher to Drummond, 16 June 1764, R Bp 20D 81, BIHR.

49. R Bp 20D 83–89, BIHR.

50. See chapter 6, n 14.

51. Thomas Southcliffe Ashton, *Iron and Steel in the Industrial Revolution* (Manchester, 1963), 200–204, and *Calendar of Home Office Papers 1760–1765,* Nos. 1339 and 1347.

52. D. Grant, ed., *Laurence Sterne* (London, 1950), 728.

53. Blackburne, *Sermon, 5 January 1753,* 26.

54. Barlow, *Citizenship and Conscience,* 149, 150.

55. Berdmore to Drummond, 24 September 1761, R Bp 17 44, BIHR.

56. Ibid., 9 March 1762, R Bp 17 45, BIHR.

57. See chapter 2, last section.

58. Pierrepoint Cromp and John Jones, see chapter 3.

59. see below, under "Henry Perfect and other miscreant clergymen."

60. Secker to Drummond, 27 September 1763, R Bp 20 c 134, BIHR.

61. Secker Papers, Vol. 4 f272, & f274, Lambeth Palace.

62. "Let the Moravian Bishops, if they are Bishops, ordain for their own congregations. We have no proper method of knowing any of them, or of their Acts. . . . If we admit their deacons, we must admit their priests too. If the Moravian Bishops in Germany may send us clergymen, Bishop Gambold, and for aught I know other Moravian Bishops, in England, and in America, may furnish us likewise; and a fine set they will be." Secker to Drummond, 28 July 1763, R Bp 20 C 108, BIHR.

63. William Prideaux Courtney, *DNB,* vol. 2, 847, 848. "The Duke of Newcastle is said to have expressed dissatisfaction at Squire's promotion and wished 'the world to know that he had no part in it.'"

64. W. L. Bevan, *Diocesan Histories, St David's,* (SPCK, 1888), 218–21, and F. W. B. Bullock, *Evangelical Conversions in Great Britain 1696–1845* (St. Leonards, 1959), 57–59.

65. Secker to Drummond, 28 July 1763, R Bp 20 c 108, BIHR.

66. Ibid., 10 March 1763, R Bp 20 c 49, BIHR.

67. Ibid., 21 May 1763, R Bp 20 c 68, BIHR.

68. Samuel Kirshaw, vicar of Leeds, wrote two sides of foolscap setting out seven points to answer the title, Probitur ex sacra scriptura Christum esse Deum, writing also in Greek in paragraph three. Robert Cotes of Hornsea, Rise, and Riston (all 1759) in Holderness, Thomas Mosley of Wigginton (1754) and Strensall (1761), and Samuel Phipps of Denby (1753) Silkstone (1757) and Penistone (1761) also obtained plural holdings by sending their Latin prose to Archbishop Secker.

69. Secker to Drummond, 25 August 1762, R Bp 20 c 117, BIHR.

70. B. D. Till, "The Administrative System of the Ecclesiastical Courts in the Diocese and Province of York, Part III: 1660–1883, A Study in Decline," unpublished typescript, BIHR (York, 1963), 253.

71. Bennett, *Tory Crisis,* 10–11.

72. Robert Drummond's elder brother was Thomas Hay, Viscount Dupplin, 9th Earl of Kinnoull, and Chancellor of the Duchy of Lancaster from 1754–1762.

73. There had been a plot by Jesuits for the assassination of the King of Portugal. The plot was detected and the Jesuits were vilified also in France. Drummond to Secker, 24 September 1760, "The Court of Portugal has printed all the papers. . . . They probably will try to imitate the liberties of the Gallican Church: but do not mean anything further, tho' their enemies and ours . . . give out that they mean a Reformation. They are at present all quiet there." Secker Papers, MS 1123 Part 2, f 199, Lambeth Palace Library.

74. Knight, "Hanoverian Church," *Historical Journal,* 36, 3, 745–52.

75. Sykes, *Church and State,* 94.

76. Keppel's problems continued to occupy Secker's gossip with fellow bishops, for he was writing to Sodor and Man in early November that, "the bishop of Exeter dares not yet venture into his diocese, having voted for the cyder bill." Weeden Butler (ed.), *Memoirs of Mark Hildesley, Bishop of Sodor and Man* (London, 1799), 447–48.

77. N. Sykes, *From Sheldon to Secker* (Cambridge, 1959), 210.

78. A. Smith, *The Established Church and Popular Religion 1750–1850, Seminar Studies in History* (Longman, 1971), 4.

79. MS 2589, ff 83–91.

80. a) Wilberforce was only four years old at the time of this letter, and did not begin his studies at St. John's College, Cambridge, until a few months before Archbishop Drummond's death in 1776. When Mrs. Whitaker's estate was up for sale, Drummond had no compunction about negro slavery. "The negroes seem from their price to be fine ones. . . . Deducting the old and infirm and the very young, the Men are about £64 each, the Women at £55; the boys at £37; the girls at £28. There seem to be 125 good men and women and children." Drummond to Secker, 15 September 1763, MS 1123 f 321, Lambeth Palace Library.

b) Drummond changed with the times, so that he was known as "a warm advocate for the cause of freedom [for slaves]," in a letter from Granville Sharp of 30 July 1772, York Minster Library, COLL 1896/1.

81. "The time of selling out of the stocks may be unlucky, but we shall want to sell only 3,500 of the S(outh) Sea Old Ann[uitie]s by 19 January [the year would then be 1764]. The Board should *direct the Treasurer to sell such a quantity of stock and to pay with that and other money in that Act the first payment for the purchase of Mrs. Whitaker's plantation,* according to the directions of the Barbadoes Committee on January 19. And also to sell out such other stock. . . . This order of the Board may be put in better form but I only mean that such order is necessary." Drummond to Secker 16 Dec 1763, MS 1123, ff 333,335, Lambeth Palace Library.

82. Drummond to Secker, 26 August 1765, Secker Papers, Vol. 4, f 275, Lambeth Palace Library.

83. J. Steven Watson, *The Reign of George III 1760–1815,* (OUP, 1960), 113, 114.

84. Carl Bridenbaugh, *Mitre and Sceptre: Transatlantic Faiths, Ideas, Personalities & Politics 1689–1775* (New York, 1962), 269.

85. Ibid., 109.

86. Macauley and Greaves, *Autobiography of T. Secker,* f 74.

87. Steven Watson, *Reign of George III,* 190.

88. C. Sydney Carter, *The English Church in the Eighteenth Century,* (London, 1948), 109.

89. Bridenbaugh, *Mitre and Sceptre,* 270.
90. Drummond's will, D & C. Vacancy, Dec. 1776, BIHR.
91. Macauley and Greaves, ed., *Autobiography of T. Secker,* xiii, "Secker wrote his autobiography in a fairly small book of good paper, written throughout in [his] characteristically careful hand: regular, rounded, neat, fairly small, legible, and rarely ambiguous." The editors also quote Montagu Burrows, *Worthies of All Souls* (London, 1874), 392, in saying that "in point of handwriting the Primates bear away the palm."
92. Sykes, *Church & State,* 93.
93. Walpole, *Memoirs,* vol. 1, 56, 57, and 312; vol. 2, 290.

Chapter 8. Conclusion

1. Clive Dewey, *The Passing of Barchester* (London, 1991), 4.
2. Gregory, "Speculum of Thomas Secker."
3. R. A. Soloway, *Prelates and People. Ecclesiastical Social Thought in England 1783–1852* (London, 1969), 5.
4. W. Hunt, in Ollard, Crosse & Bond, ed., *Dictionary,* 332, and G. G. Perry, *DNB,* Bishop Green was "not remarkable as a theologian, nor as an active administrator of his diocese . . . [and] enjoyed a high position in society," vol. 1, 488, 489.
5. E. Venables, *DNB,* 1209, 1210, refusing to allow the civic mace to be carried before him in the cathedral precincts at Salisbury.
6. See Introduction, 4–9.
7. Mather, *High Church Prophet;* Macauley & Greaves, *Thomas Secker;* Gregory, "Speculum of Secker"; Walsh, Haydon & Taylor, *Toleration to Tractarianism;* Barrie Curien, *Diocese de Londres.*
8. Virgin, *Age of Negligence,* 264, Walsh & Taylor, *Toleration to Tractarianism,* 20, Barrie Curien, "Diocese de Londres," 97, Gregory, "Eighteenth-Century Reformation," 71.
9. Walsh, Haydon & Taylor, *Toleration to Tractarianism,* 12–13.
10. The honorable exception was Norman Sykes.
11. Warne, *Eighteenth Century Devon.*
12. Barrie-Curien, "Diocese de Londres."
13. Jacob, "Church and Society in Norfolk."
14. Virgin, *Age of Negligence;* Clark, *English Society;* Mather, "Georgian Churchmanship," and *High Church Prophet;* Gregory, "Eighteenth Century Reformation."
15. Abbey & Overton, *English Church,* 40.
16. Gladstone, *Gleanings,* vol. v, 8.
17. Thomas, *Diocesan Histories, St Asaph,* 105.
18. Abbey, *English Church,* vol. 1, 316.
19. J. Walsh, C. Haydon and S. Taylor, *The Church of England c1689-c1833 From Toleration to Tractarianism* (Cambridge, 1993), 12–13.
20. See Introduction, "The bad name of the Georgian Church."
21. Walsh and Taylor, "The Church and Anglicanism in the 'long' eighteenth century," Introduction to Walsh, Haydon and Taylor, ed., *From Toleration to Tractarianism,* 3.
22. Ibid., 18.

Bibliography

Archive Material

Borthwick Institute of Historical Research

The Returns to Archbishop Drummond's Primary Visitation of the Diocese of York, 1764, Bishopthorpe Papers, V 1764.

Drummond's Correspondence, Bishopthorpe Papers, Bp C & P VII, 3–28.

The Archiepiscopal Book of the Livings &c Augmented in the Diocese of York, Bp Dio 7.

The Court Book.

Dissenters' Certificates: DMH 1755–1761/1, 1766–1776.

Dissenters' Licences: FAC.Bk 1, 1736–1768.

Parish Terriers for

Acklam	Ter K
Ackworth	Ter E
Almondbury	Ter E
Barton in the Street	Ter L
Beswick	Ter I
Birstall	Ter E
Bishopthorpe	Ter B
Bolton Percy	Ter B
Bossall	Ter N
Bracewell	Ter D
Coxwold	Ter N
Halifax	Ter E
Helperthorpe	Ter K
Helmsley	Ter L
Hornsea	Ter H
Huddersfield	Ter E
Ledsham	Ter B
Leeds	Ter C
Otteringham	Ter H
Settrington	Ter K
St Helens, Stonegate	Ter A
St Saviour	Ter A
Stillington	Ter N

Sutton on the Forest	Ter N
Swine	Ter K
Tadcaster	Ter B
Tickhill	Ter F
Todwick	Ter F
Ulrome	Ter H
Wakefield	Ter E
Warmfield	Ter E
Weaverthrope	Ter K
Wharram le Street	Ter J
Whitby	Ter M

Archdeacon Francis Blackburne's Visitation material, Bp C & P VII, ex 3–6, R Bp 5, 293.

W Riding Treasurer's Accounts, R Bp ex 20 A/B 174.

Clwyd County Record Office, Hawarden

Leases and Releases of lands and mills, D/P 145, 146; D/DM/764/136, 137, 143, 149. 150, 151.

St. Deiniol's Library, Hawarden

Bishop Robert Drummond's Charge Concerning Terriers to the Clergy of the Diocese, I 85.9 SA/7.

York Minster Library

Chapter Acts of York Minster, 11 November 1756–23 October 1771.

Letter Book of Granville Sharp 1768–1773, COLL 1896/1.

Sermon SPG Anniversary 15 February 1754, YM/C 62 12 [1761].

Lambeth Palace Library

The Secker Papers, M 1119–1124, M 1130, M 2589.

Bishop Drummond's House of Commons Sermon 30 January 1747–48, H5 133 49.

Bishop Drummond's SPG Anniversary Sermon, 15 February 1754, H5 133 56.

Bishop Drummond's House of Lords Sermon 16 February 1759, H5 133 57.

Archbishop Drummond's Coronation Sermon, 1761, MS 1083(b).

The British Library

Correspondence between Drummond and the Duke of Newcastle,

Add MSS 32700, 32701, 32703, 32707, 32720, 32721, 32722, 32726, 32730, 32732, 32736, 32861, 32890, 32902, 32905, 32907, 32918, 32922, 32924, 32926, 32927, 32929, 32930, 32932, 32938, 32943, 32945, 32952, 32953, 32954, 32956, 32961, 32965–32968, 32974, 32977–32987, 32990, 32991, 33070–33072

Drummond's letters to Archbishop Secker, Add MSS 39311 ff 127, 135.

Secker's letter to Lord Bute, 5726.D.f205.

Drummond's Deposition to Cabinet Council, Eg.3440 f 52.

Westminster Abbey Library

Drummond's Letter to a Rural Dean, 17 January 1748, Westminster Abbey Muniment 64828.

Published Material

Abbey, Charles J. *The English Church and its Bishops 1700–1800*. 2 vols. London, 1887.

Abbey, C. J. and Overton, J. H. *The English Church in the Eighteenth Century*. 2 vols. London, 1878.

Addy, John. *The Archdeacon and Ecclesiastical Discipline in Yorkshire, 1598–1714, Clergy and the Churchwardens,* BIHR, St. Anthony's Hall Publications, No. 24 York, 1963.

Anderson, C. A. and Schnaper, M. *School & Society in England: Social Backgrounds of Oxford and Cambridge students*. Washington, 1952.

Armitage, W. H. G. *400 Years of English Education*. Cambridge, 1964.

Armstrong, Anthony. *The Church of England, the Methodists and Society 1700–1850*. University of London, 1973.

Ashton, T. S. *Iron and Steel in the Industrial Revolution*. Manchester, 1963.

Baker, Frank. *John Wesley & the Church of England*. Epworth, 1970.

———. *William Grimshaw 1708–1763*. Epworth Press, 1962, 3.

Baker, P. S. and others. *The Private Papers of James Boswell,* Research Edition. vol. 4. *The Correspondence of James Boswell with David Garrick, Edmund Burke, & Edmond Malone*. London, 1986.

Barlow, Richard Burgess. *Citizenship and Conscience*. Philadelphia, 1963.

Barrie-Curien, Viviane. *Clerge et Pastorale en Angleterre au XVIIIe siecle. Le diocese de Londres*. Paris, 1992.

Bateson, M. "Clerical Preferment under the Duke of Newcastle." *English Historical Review,* vol. VII, No. 25 (January) London, 1892.

Bean, J. *Zeal Without Innovation, Address to Young Clergymen*. London, 1809.

Beckett, J. V. The Aristocracy in England 1660–1914. Oxford, 1986.

Bennett, Gareth V. *The Tory Crisis in Church and State 1688–1730*. Oxford, 1975.

———. *To The Church of England,* (Churchman Publishing, Worthing, 1988).

Best, G. F. A. *Temporal Pillars*. Cambridge, 1964.

Bevan, W. L. *Diocesan Histories, St David's,* (SPCK, 1888).

Blackburne, F. *A sermon preached on Friday 5 January 1753*. London, 1753.

———. *Remarks following the Reverend Dr Powell's sermon in defence of subscription, preached before the University of Cambridge on the Commencement Sunday 1757*. London, 1758.

———. *A Short Discourse on the Study of the Scriptures*. London, 1763.

———. *The Confessional,* 3rd edition. London, 1770.

———. *A Collection of Letters and Essays in favour of Public Liberty,* first published in newspapers annually 1764–1770, then 3 vols. London, 1774.

Blomfield, W. E. and Shipley, Cecil E. *The Baptists of Yorkshire.* Bradford, 1912.

Bolam, C. G., Goring, J., Short, H. L., and Thomas, R. *The English Presbyterians.* London, 1968.

Bossy, J. *The English Catholic Community 1570–1850.* London, 1975.

Braudel, F. *Civilisation and Capitalism 15th–18th Century.* 2 vols. London, 1981.

Brewer, J. *Party Ideology and Popular Politics at the Accession of George III.* Cambridge, 1976.

Bridenbaugh, Carl. *Sceptre and Mitre: Transatlantic Faiths, Ideas, Personalities and Politics.* New York, 1962.

Brooke, J. *King George III.* London, 1972.

Brose, O. J. *Church and Parliament, The Re-Shaping of the Church of England 1828–1860.* London, 1959.

Bull, J. *John Newton.* London, 1868.

Bullard, J. V. *Constitutions and Canons Ecclesiastical 1604.* London, 1934.

Bullock, F. W. B. *Evangelical Conversion in Great Britain 1696–1845.* St. Leonards, 1959.

Burke, E. *The Speeches of the Rt Hon Edmund Burke in the House of Commons and in Westminster Hall.* 4 vols. London, 1816.

———. *Works.* vol 3. London, 1896.

Burn, R. *Ecclesiastical Law.* London, 1809.

Butler, Weeden ed. *Memoirs of Mark Hildesley, Bishop of Sodor and Man.* London, 1799.

Camidge, William. *The Bedern & its Chapel.* York, 1906.

———. *Methodism in Bishopthorpe.* Coultas & Volans, York, 1908.

———. *Methodism in Fulford.* Coultas & Volans, York, 1908.

———. *Methodism in Huntington.* Coultas & Volans, York, 1908.

———. *Methodism in Nun Monkton.* Coultas & Volans, York, 1908.

———. *Methodism in York.* Coultas & Volans, York, 1908.

Cannon, John. *Aristocratic Century.* Cambridge, 1984.

Carter, C. Sydney. *The English Church in the Eighteenth Century.* London, 1948.

Cassan, Stephen Hyde. *Lives and Memoirs of the Bishops of Sherborne and Salisbury.* Salisbury, 1824.

Cecil, David. *The Stricken Deer.* London, 1929.

Chadwick, O. *The Victorian Church.* 2 vols. London, 1966.

Clark, J. C. D. *English Society 1688–1832.* Cambridge, 1985.

———. "On Hitting the Buffers: The Historiography of England's Ancien Regime. A Response." *Past and Present,* No 117 (November 1987).

Clay, C. "The greed of whig bishops? Church landlords and their lessees 1660–1760." *Past and Present,* No. 87. May, 1980.

Cobbett, W. *The Parliamentary History of England.* 36 vols. vol. XVII. London, 1812–20.

Collinson, Patrick. "Lectures in Combination": *Bulletin of the Institute of Historical Research.* London, 1975.

Colman, F. S. "A History of Barwick in Elmet." *Thoresby Society,* vol. xvii. Leeds, 1908.

Conybeare, W. J. *Essays Ecclesiastical and Social.* London, 1855.

Cragg, G. G. *Grimshaw of Haworth.* London, 1947.

Cragg, G. R. "The Churchman" in J. L. Clifford (ed.). *Man versus Society in Eighteenth Century Britain.* Cambridge, 1968.

Crump, W. B. *Huddersfield Highways Down the Ages.* Huddersfield, 1949. Reprinted Kirklees Leisure Services, 1988.

Curnock, N. ed. *Journal of John Wesley.* 8 vols. London, 1909–16.

Currie, R., Gilbert, A., and Horsley, L. *Churches & Churchgoers, Patterns of Church Growth in the British Isles since 1700.* Oxford, 1977.

Currie, R. "A micro-theory of Methodist growth." *Proceedings of the Wesley Historical Society,* XXXVI. 65–73. Epworth, 1967.

Davies, R. and Rupp, G. *A History of the Methodist Church in Great Britain.* vol. 1. Epworth, 1965.

Debrett, J. *Parliamentary Debates.* 7 vols, vol vi. London, 1792.

———. *The Parliamentary Register.* Second series, vol. 27. London, 1775–1813.

Dewey, Clive. *The Passing of Barchester.* London, 1991.

Dictionary of National Biography. Micrographically reproduced text. 2 vols. Oxford, 1975.

Ditchfield, G. M. "The parliamentary struggle over the repeal of the Test & Corporation Acts, 1787–1790." *English Historical Review,* vol. LXXXIX, no. 352 (July 1974).

Ditchfield, G. M. "Anti-trinitarianism and toleration in late eighteenth-century British politics: the Unitarian Petition of 1792." *Journal of Economic History.* vol. 42, no. 1 (January 1991).

Downey, James. *The Eighteenth Century Pulpit.* Oxford, 1969.

Drummond, G. H. Prebend of York, *Memoirs of the Life of R H Drummond.* Edinburgh, 1803.

———. *Sermons on Public Occasions.* London, 1760.

———. *Sermon, Christ Church, London 26 April 1753.* London, 1760.

———. *A Letter on Theological Study.* Edinburgh, 1803.

Edwards, Edward. *Continuation of Browne Willis, Survey of St Asaph.* 2 vols. Wrexham, 1801.

Elliott-Binns, L. E. *The Early Evangelicals.* London, 1953.

Emden, G. *Alumni Oxonienses 1501–1540.* Oxford, 1974.

Evans, Eric J. "Some reasons for the growth of English rural anti-clericalism c1750-c1830." *Past and Present.* No. 60 (1975).

Fountayne, J. *A letter . . . in relation to a promise made . . . by Dr Topham.* York, 1758.

Foster, J. *Alumni Oxonienses 1715–1886.* Oxford, 1888.

Fryde, E. B., Greenway, D. E., Porter, S., and Roy, I. ed. *Handbook of British Chronology.* 3rd edition. London, 1986.

Garbett, H. *The History of Harthill with Woodhall & its hamlet Kiverton Park.* Stockwell, 1950.

Gay, J. D. *The Geography of Religion in England.* London, 1971.

Gee, Eric. *Bishopthorpe Palace.* York, 1983.

Gentleman's Magazine, The. Various numbers.

Gilbert, A. D. *Religion & Society in Industrial England. Church, Chapel, & Social Change 1740–1914.* Longman, 1976.

Gladstone, W. E. *Gleanings of Past Years.* Vols. v & vii. London, 1879.

Grant, D. ed. *Laurence Sterne.* London, 1950.

Gray, Mrs. Edwin. *Papers and Diaries of a York Family 1764–1839.* London, 1927.

Greaves, B. "An analysis of the spread of Methodism in Yorkshire during the Eighteenth Century." Unpublished M.A. Thesis. University of Leeds, 1961.

Green, R. *Anti-Methodist Publications issued during the Eighteenth Century. A Bibliography.* London, 1902.

Gregory, J. "A Just and Sufficient Maintenance: Some Defences of the Clerical Establishment in the Eighteenth Century." *Studies in Church History.* Vol. 24. Oxford, 1987.

———. "The Eighteenth Century Reformation: the pastoral task of the Anglican clergy after 1689." Walsh, Haydon & Taylor (ed.). *The Church of England c1689-c1833 From Toleration to Tractarianism.* Cambridge, 1993.

———. "The Speculum of Archbishop Thomas Secker: The diocese of Canterbury 1758–1768." Read to the Church of England Records Society. Lambeth, 1993.

Gunn, J. A. W. *Beyond Liberty & Property.* Ontario, 1983.

Habgood, K. "The Hidden Hamlets." *Yorkshire Life* Y052 (October 1971) York, 1971.

Hans, Nicholas. *New Trends in Education in the Eighteenth Century.* London, 1951.

Hempton, David. *Methodism & Politics in British Society 1750–1850.* Hutchinson, 1984.

Hill, C. *A Turbulent, Seditious, and Factious People: John Bunyan and his Church.* Oxford, 1988.

Hill, Rowland. *Spiritual Characteristics . . . in consequence of the Clergy Residence Act.* London, 1803.

Hinchcliffe, G. *A History of King James's Grammar School.* Huddersfield, 1963.

Hirschberg, D. R. "Episcopal Incomes & Expenses 1660–1760." In Rosemary O'Day & Felicity Heal (ed.). *Princes and Paupers in the English Church 1500–1800.* Leicester, 1981.

Hodgson, Christopher. *An Account of the Augmentation of Small Livings by the Governors of Queen Anne's Bounty.* London, 1826 and 1845.

Hole, R. *Pulpits, Politics and Public Order 1760–1832.* Cambridge, 1989.

Holmes, G. "The Achievement of Stability: the social context of Politics from the 1680s to the age of Walpole." In J. A. Cannon (ed.). *The Whig Ascendancy: Colloquies on Hanoverian England.* London, 1981.

Holtby, R. T. *Daniel Waterland 1683–1740, A Study in Eighteenth Century Orthodoxy.* Carlisle, 1966.

Home Office Papers 1760–1765, Calendar of.

Horn, D. B. and Ransome, Mary ed. *English Historical Documents 1714–1783*. London, 1957.

Hughes, Edward. *North Country Life in the Eighteenth Century: the North East, 1700–1750*. London, 1952.

Hulbert, C. A. *Annals of the Church in Slaithwaite*. London, 1864.

Hunter, Joseph. *South Yorkshire*. Sheffield 1828–1831. Reprinted in 2 vols. 1974.

Hylson-Smith, Kenneth. *Evangelicals in the Church of England 1734–1984*. Edinburgh, 1989.

Ingamells, John. *Catalogue of Portraits at Bishopthorpe Palace*. York, 1972.

Jacob, M. and J. J. *The Origins of Anglo-American Radicalism*. London, 1984.

Jacob, W. M. "Church and Society in Norfolk 1707–1806." Unpublished Ph.D. Thesis. University of Exeter, 1982.

Jay, Elizabeth ed. *The Evangelical and Oxford Movements*. Cambridge, 1983.

Jenkins, D. T. *The West Riding Wool Textile Industry, 1770–1835*. Edington, Wilts, 1975.

Jenkins, Hester and Caradog, Jones D. "The Social Class of Cambridge University Alumni of the Eighteenth and Nineteenth Centuries." *British Journal of Sociology*. Vol. 1 (1950).

Jervis, W. G. *The Poor Condition of the Clergy and the Causes Considered, with suggestions for remedying the same*. London, 1856.

Jones, Tudor R. *Congregationalism in England 1662–1962*. London, 1962.

Journal of the House of Lords, 1747–1765.

Kelch, Kay A. *Newcastle, A Duke Without Money: Thomas Pelham Holles, 1693–1768*. London, 1974.

Kemp, E. W. *An Introduction to Canon Law in the Church of England*. London, 1957.

Knight, Frances. "The Hanoverian Church in Transition: Some Recent Perspectives." *The Historical Journal* 36, 3. Cambridge, 1993.

Langford, P. *Modern British Foreign Policy. The Eighteenth Century 1688–1815*. London, 1976.

———. *A Polite and Commercial People, England 1727–1783*. [Chapter 6]. Oxford, 1989.

———. *Public Life and the Propertied Englishman, 1689–1798*. Oxford, 1991.

———. ed. *The Writings and Speeches of Edmund Burke*. vol. 2. *Party, Parliament and the American Crisis*. Oxford, 1981.

Lawson, A. B. "John Wesley & some Anglican Evangelicals of the Eighteenth Century." Unpublished Ph.D. Thesis. Sheffield, 1973.

Lawson, J. "Endowed Grammar Schools of East Yorkshire." *East Yorkshire Local History Society*. Local History Series, No. 14 (1962). York, 1962.

Lawson-Tancred, T. *Records of a Yorkshire manor*. Aldborough, 1937.

Lawton, G. *Collectio Rerum Ecclesiasticarum de diocesi Eboracensis*. London, 1842.

Leach, Arthur Francis. "Early Yorkshire Schools." Record Series. *Yorkshire Archaeological Society*. Vol. 2, 1903, York, 1903.

Lecky, W. E. H. *The History of England in the Eighteenth Century*. 8 vols., Vol. 3. London, 1882.

Legg, J. Wickham. *English Church Life From the Restoration to the Tractarian Movement 1660–1833*. London, 1914.

Lessenich, R. P. *Elements of Pulpit Oratory in England 1600–1800*. Cologne, 1972.

Leys, M. R. D. *Catholics in England 1559–1829, A Social History*. Longmans, 1961.

Lloyds Evening Post and British Chronicle No. 412 (5–7 March, 1760).

Lyth, J. *Glimpses of Early Methodism in York*. York, 1885.

Macauley, J. S. and Greaves, R. W. ed. *The Autobiography of Thomas Secker, Archbishop of Canterbury*. Kansas, 1988.

Mahon, Lord. *The History of England 1713–1783*. 7 vols., vol. 5. London, 1858.

Mallinson, Joel. *Methodism in Huddersfield*. London, 1898.

Marchant, Ronald A. *The Church Under the Law: Justice, Administration and Discipline in the Diocese of York 1560–1640*. Cambridge, 1969.

Marshall, D. *The English Poor in the Eighteenth Century*. London, 1926.

Marsland, J. "Methodism in Baytown." *The Dalesman*. Vol. 41, No. 3 (June, 1979) York, 1979.

Martin, Bernard. *John Newton*. London, 1950.

Mather, F. C. "Georgian Churchmanship Reconsidered: Some Variations in Anglican Public Worship 1714–1830." *Journal of Ecclesiastical History*. Vol. 36, No. 2 (April, 1985).

Mather, F. C. *High Church Prophet–Bishop Samuel Horsley (1733–1806), and the Caroline Tradition in the Later Georgian Church*. Oxford, 1992.

Mathieson, W. L. *English Church Reform 1815–1840*. London, 1923.

Miall, J. G. *Congregationalism in Yorkshire*. London, 1868.

Middleton, Erasmus. *Biographica Evangelica*. London, 1786.

Mingay, G. E. *English Landed Society in the Eighteenth Century*. London, 1963.

Minutes of the Methodist Conference, 1765 & 1766.

Moore, E. Garth. *An Introduction to English Canon Law*. Oxford, 1967.

Nelson, J. *Journal*. York, 1767.

Napthine, D. and Speck, W. A. "Clergymen and Conflict 1660–1763." *Studies in Church History*. Vol. 20, *The Church and War*. Oxford, 1983.

Neuburg, V. E. *Popular Education in Eighteenth Century England*. London, 1971.

le Neve, J. *Fasti Ecclesiae Anglicanae 1541–1857, IV, York Diocese*. London, 1975.

Newton, John. *Works*. 9 vols. London, 1822.

Newton, Thomas. *The Life of Dr Thomas Newton, written by himself* in *The Lives of Edward Pocock, Dr Zachary Pearce, Dr Thomas Newton, and the Reverend Philip Skelton*. 2 vols. London, 1816.

Nuttall, G. and Chadwick, O. ed. *From Uniformity to Unity*. SPCK, 1962.

O'Gorman, F. "Party in the later Eighteenth Century." As Chapter 4 in Cannon ed. *The Whig Ascendancy*. Arnold, 1981.

———. "The Recent Historiography of the Hanoverian Regime." *The Historical Journal*. Vol. 29, No. 4. (1986).

———. *Voters, Patrons and Parties*. Oxford, 1989.

Ollard, S. L., Crosse, G., and Bond, M. F. *A Dictionary of English Church History.* Mowbray, London, 1912, 1919, 1948.

———. "Laurence Sterne as a parish priest." *Times Literary Supplement.* (1926).

Ollard, S. L. and Walker, P. C. *Archbishop Herring's Visitation Returns, 1743.* 5 vols. Yorkshire Archaeological Society, 1928–1931.

Overton, J. H. and Relton, F. *The English Church 1714–1800.* London, 1906.

Owen, Dorothy M. "From the Restoration until 1822." In G. E. Aylmer and R. Cant ed. *A History of York Minster.* Oxford, 1977.

Parish Registers

Payne, E. *The Baptist Union–A Short History.* London, 1958.

———. "Toleration and Establishment: 1." Nuttall and Chadwick ed. *From Uniformity to Unity.* SPCK, 1962.

Pevsner, Nikolaus. *Yorkshire: The West Riding.* Penguin, 1967.

———. *The Buildings of England, Yorkshire: York and the East Riding.* Penguin, 1972, 1985.

Price, F. C. "Parliamentary Elections in York City, 1754–1790." Unpublished M.A. Thesis. University of Manchester, 1958.

Phillimore, Sir R. *The Ecclesiastical Law of the Church of England.* 2 vols. London, 1873.

Pollock, J. *George Whitefield and the Great Awakening.* Lion, 1986.

Punshon, J. *Portrait in Grey, A Short History of the Quakers.* London, 1984.

Purvis, J. *The Condition of the Yorkshire Church Fabrics.* St. Anthony's Press, BII31. London and York, 1958.

Rack, Henry D. "Religious Societies & the Origins of Methodism." *Journal of Ecclesiastical History.* Vol. 38, No. 4. (October 1987).

———. *Reasonable Enthusiast, John Wesley and the Rise of Methodism.* Epworth, 1989.

Rastall, Dickenson. *History of the Collegiate Church of Southwell.*

Rose, E. A. "Early Methodism in the Upper Calder Valley." *Proceedings of the Wesley Historical Society,* Yorkshire Branch (September 1978).

Rouse, R. and Neill, S. R. ed. *A History of the Ecumenical Movement 1517–1948.* SPCK, 1967.

Rowntree, J. S. *Quakerism, Past and Present.* London, 1859.

Royle, E. *Modern Britain: A Social History 1750–1985.* Arnold, 1987.

Rupp, G. *Religion in England 1688–1791.* Oxford, 1986.

Russell, A. *The Clerical Profession.* London, SPCK, 1980.

Sanderson, M. *Education, Economic Change and Society in England 1780–1870.* Macmillan, 1983.

———. "Grammar Schools." *British Journal of Educational Studies.* (1962).

Savidge, Alan. *The Foundation and Early Years of Queen Anne's Bounty.* SPCK, 1955.

Scott, Beatrice M. "The Reverend Benjamin Ingham 1712–1772." *Proceedings of the Wesley Historical Society,* Yorkshire Branch. No. 40 (August 1982): 2–14. York, 1982.

Scott, Sir Wm. *Speech . . . relative to the Non-Residence of the Clergy.* London, 1802.

Seymour, Aaron C. H. *The Life and Times of Selina, Countess of Huntingdon.* 2 vols. London, 1840.

Shipley, C. E. *The Baptists of Yorkshire.* Bradford, 1912.

Sheils, W. J. *Sources for the History of Dissent and Catholicism at the Borthwick Institute.* BIHR Bulletin, Vol. 3, no. 1 (1983).

Smith, Alan. *The Established Church and Popular Religion 1750–1850, Seminar Studies in History.* Longman, 1971.

Smith, William. *Old Yorkshire.* New Series. London, 1889.

Soloway, R. A. *Prelates and People, Ecclesiastical Social Thought in England 1783–1852.* London, 1969.

Sosin, J. M. "The Proposal in the Pre-Revolutionary Decade for Establishing Anglican Bishops in the Colonies." *Journal of Ecclesiastical History,* 13. (1962).

Speck, W. A. *Stability and Strife, England 1714–1760.* Arnold, 1977.

Spence, Hardy, R. *William Grimshaw, Incumbent of Haworth 1742–1763.* London, 1860.

Sterne, L. *The Life and Opinions of Tristram Shandy.* York, 1759.

———. *A Political Romance.* York, 1759.

———. *A Sentimental Journey.* Ian Jack (ed.). Oxford, 1984.

Steven, Watson J. *The Reign of George III 1760–1815.* Oxford, 1960.

Strachan, A. *Life of George Lowe.* London, 1848.

Sutherland, Lucy S. ed. *The Correspondence of Edmund Burke.* 2 vols. Cambridge, 1960.

Sykes, D. F. E. *The History of the Colne Valley.* Slaithwaite, 1896.

Sykes, Norman. *Church and State in England in the Eighteenth Century.* Connecticut, 1934.

———. *From Sheldon to Secker.* Cambridge 1959.

———. "The Duke of Newcastle as Ecclesiastical Minister." *English Historical Review.* vol. lvii (January 1942).

Tawney, R. H. *Religion and the Rise of Capitalism.* London, 1948.

Taylor, W. S. and Pringle, J. H. ed. *The Correspondence of William Earl of Chatham.* 4 vols. London, 1840.

Thomas, D. R. *Diocesan Histories, St Asaph.* SPCK, 1888.

Thomas, P. D. G. "Sir Roger Newdigate's Essay on Party, c1760." *English Historical Review.* (1987).

Till, B. D. "The Administrative System of the Ecclesiastical Courts in the Diocese and Province of York, Part III: 1660–1883, A Study in Decline." Unpublished typescript, BIHR. York, 1963.

Tillott, P. M. "The Parish Churches." *A History of Yorkshire, The City of York.* Victoria County History, London, 1961.

Tillyard, Frank. "The Distribution of the Free Churches in England." *The Sociological Review.* Vol. xxvii, No. 1 (January 1935).

Tindal, Hart A. *Ebor: A History of the Archbishops of York from Paulinus to McLagan, 627–1908.* York, 1986.

Tompson, R. S. *Classics or Charity.* Manchester University, 1971.

———. "The English grammar school curriculum in the eighteenth century: a reappraisal." *British Journal of Educational Studies.* Vol. 19: 32–39 (1971).

Torbet, Robert G. *A History of the Baptists.* London, 1963.

Tudor, Jones R. *Congregationalism in England 1662–1962.* Independent Press, London, 1962.

Venn, Henry. *An Earnest and Pressing Call to Keep Holy the Lord's Day Addressed equally to the Rich and Poor of his Flock.* Leeds, 1760.

———. *Christ the joy of the Christian's life, and death his gain.* Leeds, 1763.

Venn, John. *Alumni Cantabrigienses,* parts 1 & 2. Cambridge, 1922 and 1947.

Virgin, Peter. *The Church in an Age of Negligence, Ecclesiastical Problems of Church Reform 1700–1840.* Cambridge, 1989.

Wallace, Charles Isaac Jr. *Religion and Society in C18 England: Geographic, Demographic, and Occupational Patterns of Dissent in West Riding of Yorkshire, 1715–1801.* Ph.D. Thesis. Duke University, 1975.

Wallis, P. J. and Tate, W. E. "A Register of Old Yorkshire Grammar Schools." *Leeds University Researches and Studies.* No. 13: 64-104 (1956).

Walpole, H., Earl of Orford. *Memoires of the Last Ten years of the Reign of George the Second.* 2 vols. London, 1822.

Walsh, J. D. "The Yorkshire Evangelicals of the Eighteenth Century, with especial reference to Methodism." Unpublished Ph.D. Thesis. University of Cambridge, 1956.

———. "Origins of the Evangelical Revival." in G. V. Bennett and J. D. Walsh (ed.). *Essays in Modern English Church History.* Black, London, 1966.

———. "Methodism and the Mob in the Eighteenth Century." *Studies in Church History.* Vol. 8. (1972).

———. "Religious Societies: Methodist and Evangelical 1730–1800." *Studies in Church History.* Vol. 23 (1986).

———. "John Wesley and the Community of Goods in Protestant Evangelicalism: Britain, Ireland, Germany and America, c1750–c1950." *Studies in Church History, Subsidia 7.* Blackwell, Oxford, 1990.

———, Haydon, C., Taylor, S. *The Church of England 1689–1833, From Toleration to Tractarianism.* Cambridge, 1993.

Ward, W. R. "Power and Piety: the origins of religious revival in the early eighteenth century." *Bulletin of the John Rylands Library* 63, No. 1. University of Manchester, 1980.

Warne, A. *Church and Society in Eighteenth Century Devon.* David and Charles, 1969.

Watson, J. *The History and Antiquities of the parish of Halifax.* T. Lowndes, 1775, republished Manchester, 1973.

Watts, Michael Robert. *The Dissenters: From the Reformation to the French Revolution.* Oxford, 1978.

Welsby, P. A. ed. *Sermons and Society.* Penguin, 1970.

Whitaker, T. D. *The History & Antiquities of the Deanery of Craven.* London, 1805.

Whiteley, J. H. "Wesley's Anglican Contemporaries, Their Trials and Triumphs." *Wesley Historical Society Lecture.* No. 5. Epworth, 1939.

Williams, Basil. *The Life of William Pitt, Earl of Chatham.* 2 vols. London, 1913.

Williams, J. E. and Woods, J. A. "Hull 1700–1835." *The Victoria History of the*

Counties of England, York East Riding. Vol. 1, *The City of Kingston upon Hull.* Oxford, 1969.

Woodforde, J. *The Diary of a Country Parson*. Edited by J. Beresford. 5 vols. Oxford, 1968.

Wrigley, E. A. and Schofield, R. S. *The Population History of England, 1540–1871*. Edward Arnold, 1966.

Yonge, A. D. ed. *Church Acts and Measures, Halsbury's Statutes of England.* 3rd edition. London, 1969.

York Courant, The. (1762–1764).

Index